Social Media for Communication and Instruction in Academic Libraries

Jennifer Joe
University of Toledo, USA

Elisabeth Knight
Western Kentucky University, USA

A volume in the Advances in Library and Information Science (ALIS) Book Series

Published in the United States of America by
IGI Global
Information Science Reference (an imprint of IGI Global)
701 E. Chocolate Avenue
Hershey PA, USA 17033
Tel: 717-533-8845
Fax: 717-533-8661
E-mail: cust@igi-global.com
Web site: http://www.igi-global.com

Library of Congress Cataloging-in-Publication Data

Names: Joe, Jennifer, 1985- editor. | Knight, Elisabeth, 1961- editor.
Title: Social media for communication and instruction in academic libraries / Jennifer Joe and Elisabeth Knight, editors.
Description: Hershey, PA : Information Science Reference, [2019] | Includes bibliographical references.
Identifiers: LCCN 2018046995| ISBN 9781522580973 (hardcover) | ISBN 9781522580980 (ebook)
Subjects: LCSH: Online social networks--Library applications. | Social media in education. | Academic libraries--Marketing. | Web applications in libraries. | Libraries and the Internet.
Classification: LCC Z674.75.S63 S633 2019 | DDC 025.5/2777--dc23 LC record available at https://lccn.loc.gov/2018046995

This book is published in the IGI Global book series Advances in Library and Information Science (ALIS) (ISSN: 2326-4136; eISSN: 2326-4144)

British Cataloguing in Publication Data
A Cataloguing in Publication record for this book is available from the British Library.

All work contributed to this book is new, previously-unpublished material. The views expressed in this book are those of the authors, but not necessarily of the publisher.

For electronic access to this publication, please contact: eresources@igi-global.com.

Advances in Library and Information Science (ALIS) Book Series

Alfonso Ippolito
Sapienza University-Rome, Italy
Carlo Inglese
Sapienza University-Rome, Italy

ISSN:2326-4136
EISSN:2326-4144

Mission

The **Advances in Library and Information Science (ALIS) Book Series** is comprised of high quality, research-oriented publications on the continuing developments and trends affecting the public, school, and academic fields, as well as specialized libraries and librarians globally. These discussions on professional and organizational considerations in library and information resource development and management assist in showcasing the latest methodologies and tools in the field.

The **ALIS Book Series** aims to expand the body of library science literature by covering a wide range of topics affecting the profession and field at large. The series also seeks to provide readers with an essential resource for uncovering the latest research in library and information science management, development, and technologies.

Coverage

- Electronic Resources
- Return on Investment (ROI) in Libraries
- Digital Literacy
- Community Outreach
- Digital Library Economics
- Collection Development
- Databases
- Paraprofessionals in Libraries
- Recruitment of Library Professionals
- Partnerships in Library Communities

IGI Global is currently accepting manuscripts for publication within this series. To submit a proposal for a volume in this series, please contact our Acquisition Editors at Acquisitions@igi-global.com or visit: http://www.igi-global.com/publish/.

The Advances in Library and Information Science (ALIS) Book Series (ISSN 2326-4136) is published by IGI Global, 701 E. Chocolate Avenue, Hershey, PA 17033-1240, USA, www.igi-global.com. This series is composed of titles available for purchase individually; each title is edited to be contextually exclusive from any other title within the series. For pricing and ordering information please visit http://www.igi-global.com/book-series/advances-library-information-science/73002. Postmaster: Send all address changes to above address.

Titles in this Series

For a list of additional titles in this series, please visit: www.igi-global.com/book-series

Enhancing the Role of ICT in Doctoral Research Processes
Kwong Nui Sim (Victoria University of Wellington, New Zealand)
Information Science Reference • copyright 2019 • 278pp • H/C (ISBN: 9781522570653) • US $185.00 (our price)

Social Research Methodology and New Techniques in Analysis, Interpretation, and Writing
M. Rezaul Islam (University of Dhaka, Bangladesh & University of Malaya, Malaysia)
Information Science Reference • copyright 2019 • 320pp • H/C (ISBN: 9781522578970) • US $195.00 (our price)

Ethics in Research Practice and Innovation
Antonio Sandu (Stefan cel Mare University of Suceava, Romania) Ana Frunza (LUMEN Research Center in Social and Humanistic Sciences, Romania) and Elena Unguru (University of Oradea, Romania)
Information Science Reference • copyright 2019 • 373pp • H/C (ISBN: 9781522563105) • US $195.00 (our price)

Marginalia in Modern Learning Contexts
Alan J. Reid (Coastal Carolina University, USA)
Information Science Reference • copyright 2019 • 250pp • H/C (ISBN: 9781522571834) • US $175.00 (our price)

Scholarly Publishing and Research Methods Across Disciplines
Victor C.X. Wang (Grand Canyon University, USA)
Information Science Reference • copyright 2019 • 372pp • H/C (ISBN: 9781522577300) • US $195.00 (our price)

Advanced Methodologies and Technologies in Library Science, Information Management, and Scholarly Inquiry
Mehdi Khosrow-Pour, D.B.A. (Information Resources Management Association, USA)
Information Science Reference • copyright 2019 • 684pp • H/C (ISBN: 9781522576594) • US $275.00 (our price)

Exploring the Relationship Between Media, Libraries, and Archives
Collence Takaingenhamo Chisita (Harare Polytechnic, Zimbabwe & University of South Africa, South Africa) and Alexander M. Rusero (Harare Polytechnic, Zimbabwe)
Information Science Reference • copyright 2019 • 263pp • H/C (ISBN: 9781522558408) • US $175.00 (our price)

Literacy Skill Development for Library Science Professionals
S. Thanuskodi (Alagappa University, India)
Information Science Reference • copyright 2019 • 410pp • H/C (ISBN: 9781522571254) • US $175.00 (our price)

IGI Global
DISSEMINATOR OF KNOWLEDGE

701 East Chocolate Avenue, Hershey, PA 17033, USA
Tel: 717-533-8845 x100 • Fax: 717-533-8661
E-Mail: cust@igi-global.com • www.igi-global.com

Editorial Advisory Board

Table of Contents

Detailed Table of Contents

This chapter will explore how social media assessment is used for library marketing. It will build upon existing literature on how other libraries quantify social media impact in promoting their services. This includes methods on how libraries can gather native application statistics from popular platforms such as Facebook, Twitter, YouTube, and Instagram. An exploration into web analytics will also be explored as evidence of social media impact. The chapter will use case-studies of the Ursula C. Schwerin Library of the New York City College of Technology (City Tech), CUNY, and how social media platforms are used to advertise library events and disseminate news.

The academic library profession has discussed the importance of diversity and inclusion, but has yet to explore their intersection with social media marketing. Given changing demographics and an increase in activism on college campuses, libraries must produce social media content that resonates with underrepresented groups. This chapter introduces strategies for effectively incorporating diversity and inclusion into social media and advice on avoiding mistakes. The author examines social media use at her library and lessons learned from a campaign that received criticism. The chapter concludes with challenges to practicing diversity in social media, including recruiting diverse staff and discrimination that emerges from new social media technologies.

The chapter serves as a primer for academic librarians on helping patrons with disabilities receive, protect, and understand disseminated content on a multitude of popular social media networking platforms. The content of the chapter provides introductory material on the Americans with Disabilities Act (ADA) and the Family Educational Rights and Privacy Act. The first part of the chapter discusses the inclusion of best practices and web accessibility applications for structuring written incorporation to help all patrons understand the expressed material within social media networking pages. The second part of the chapter discusses the importance of respecting patron privacy within FERPA guidelines. This section discusses social networking pages and best practices for helping safeguard the patron's identity concerning inadvertent HIPAA violations.

serve their unique populations more effectively, promote engagement within the local community, and establish a presence for the branch within the institution. The authors provide strategies and suggestions for managing Twitter based upon their own experiences while managing the Southampton Campus Library of Stony Brook University Twitter account.

Preface

Social media are the virtual networks used to communicate ideas between individuals. These social media networks can take many forms, from Facebook, to Pinterest, and beyond the big names to more niche websites and applications. In today's society, it seems like everyone has an account on at least one network, and often times, multiple networks, as they attempt to reach different people. An individual may have a Facebook account, to keep up with family and friends, a LinkedIn to keep track of their colleagues, and an Instagram account to follow the trends. The examples could continue, but the point is that a staggeringly large part of the population are using these networks, and they are gaining information from them, whether they know it or not. A Pew Internet Research (2018a) survey found that 69% of the adult American public uses some type of social media site, and further research into eight popular social media platforms found that 73% of social media users use more than one social media site (p. 7). In addition, these networks have all but replaced many more traditional means of communication – newsletters, bulletin boards, and the like – and the reason is simple and unsurprising. Social media networks allow users to engage in a way that they could not before. Unfortunately, as noted in the literature time and again, academic librarians have been slow to embrace social media (Charnigo & Barnett-Howard, 2007; OCLC, 2007; Huber, Carter, & Moore, 2018), though the numbers have increased dramatically in the last five years (Harrison, Burress, Velasquez, & Schreiner, 2017). Virtually the only mode of non-internet mass communication still in substantial use is television, with about 49% of Americans reporting that they receive their news from TV (Pew Research Center, 2018b). This is to say nothing of how people gather non-news information, which is harder to track.

This rise in social media use combined with reticence to use those same networks, has created challenges in academic libraries in particular, because their users fit in the demographic most likely to use social media and other non-traditional modes of communication. These challenges are changing the way that academic libraries approach their entire patron population, but most notably their students, who are typically 18-24 years old. The demographic range into which they are typically categorized, 18-29-year-olds, has the highest percentage use of social media of all demographic ranges, with 88% of those surveyed reporting some type of social media use (Pew Research Center, 2018a, p. 4). 18-24-year-olds are also leading users of newer social media sites, such as Snapchat and Instagram (Pew Research Center, 2018a). This has forced libraries to consider social media as a way of reaching out to and engaging their users in meaningful ways that will help them stay connected to the library and aware of the resources that are available to them, and to broaden their use of social media networks. The awareness of the usage trends in social media, and the idea that all other libraries are using social media have resulted in an increase in social media presence by academic libraries (Harrison, Burress, Velasquez, & Schreiner, 2017). This "normative influence" as described by Harrison, et al, has motivated libraries onto the social media scene, but there still challenges to navigating social media use.

THE CHALLENGES

Academic libraries need to have a presence in social media in order to reach and engage their users, because those traditional means of communication will not work. Many students are using the library's resources remotely, whether it is from the comfort of their dorm room, or from a place halfway around the world. Some institutions are even hiring remote instructors. In order to reach these patrons, the information that the library wants to present must be available online. Moreover, the information, and the means of acquiring it, should be interactive, because patrons expect it, having engaged with other accounts throughout the last decade, as social media has increased in use.

There are three types of social media initiatives:

1. Broadcasting, in which the institution simply pushes a message about services and events.
2. Communication, in which the institution uses social media not only to push a message, but to also answer questions, and
3. Engagement, in which the institution actively tries to get users to interact on social media in a meaningful way – though meaningful can mean different things to different people.

A study of these types of initiatives shows an evolution and sophistication of social media use in academic libraries over the last decade, even as some libraries lag behind the curve.

Unfortunately, it is not enough for libraries to simply create a message and then send it out into the world, especially if the institution is trying to reach a higher level of social media use. Social media use by institutions, who have a goal and a reputation to maintain, must have a plan. One common pitfall among academic libraries, for a variety of reasons, is to push the same exact message, often word-for-word and scheduled well in advance to all of the social media platforms that the library subscribes to. Despite being a time-saving practice, this is not the most effective way to promote the library's message, because different networks are used for different things by different people. Other common pitfalls include not having a regular schedule of content, such that posts become hidden from users' feeds, or not having content that is clearly aligned with the institutional goals. Swanson (2012) identifies a fear of content creation as one of the largest obstacles to social media use in libraries (academic or otherwise), but it does not have to be scary if the institution has clear goals in their social media use, because these goals can guide content creation, and better content creation will make it easier to reach the institutional goals. Beyond these common problems, though, there are more issues that the academic library must contend with. Social media managers or committees must concern themselves with legal issues, such as FERPA, social issues, such as diversity and inclusion, and economic issues of budget and staff time. Because of this, the use of social media and the selection of networks to participate in are decisions that should not be entered into lightly.

However, the problem set before academic libraries is two-fold. Yes, academic libraries need to use social media to interact with the student patron population, but they also need to consider social media as a tool for student learning and information gathering. Students are gaining information from their social media accounts indiscriminately and at an ever-increasing pace. This can lead to poor vetting practices and information overload. Previously, it has been the academic library's job to help students learn how to evaluate sources and fact-check information, and social media should not be any different. As centers for information and instructors in the methods and modes of gathering information, it is part of the academic library's charge to address the information issues surrounding social media. Furthermore, by incorporating different types of social media platforms into the classroom, librarians are giving students a chance to learn about new platforms that they may not have heard of and might be useful for other classes, and can teach the students about best practices for social media use; after all, social media networks are a two-way exchange of information, something that students may not have thought about.

Because social media use looks different for every institution, and has such a wide application, the target audience of this book is all academic library personnel who engage with patrons, plan programming for patrons, market to patrons, or are interested in understanding how social media networks fit into the workflows and complement the mission statements of the modern academic library. It also may be useful to librarians in special or research libraries who have an interest in educating their patrons through social media. It will be most useful for librarians and library staff who have ideas, plans, and active implementations of social networking initiatives. It exists to inspire and guide these activities. Administrative personnel, too, would be interested to see how social media plans can support important institutional goals, such as diversity, assessment, and engagement.

POTENTIAL SOLUTIONS

First, it is up to each institution to decide the stage in which their social media use falls, and start gathering ideas to evolve their interactions with patrons if they so choose. The evolution of social media use at an institution halts for a variety of reasons, including staffing, funding, legality, and sheer burnout, among others. It can be time consuming and complex on an emotional and intellectual level to maintain a robust social media program.

The urgency with which a library needs to develop a social media plan can also be impacted by the type of library it is. Digital libraries, for example, are likely to need a strong social media presence. Whereas modern traditional academic libraries will have an opportunity to interact physically with a large portion of their patrons, and can promote information that way, digital libraries have no opportunity to meet their patrons face to face. They rely entirely on making their information available to their patrons through virtual means, and consequently, may rely on social media networks more than physical libraries. This is an important concern for academic institutions, both non-profit and for profit, which consider themselves to be primarily or entirely online, because that forces the library to be online as well. Library outreach in this context can be difficult without using social media networks. It is important then, that the digital library not only have a social media presence, but evolve that social media presence quickly, in order to reach the engagement stage.

Once an organization has evaluated their current social media use, they can decide how much they want to change it and set goals. Their goals might be voiced in terms of some staff-side concerns, like consistency of posting schedules, or branding and messaging, or they may be voiced in terms of user-side concerns, like level of interaction and engagement with posts and events. An ideal plan, though, would take both of the aspects into consideration. Once these goals have been developed though, the hard part begins, because representatives of the institution – whether it is a social media manager or a committee – must begin to think about how to best achieve these goals, and also, what problems may lay ahead in reaching them. They may also need to consult the literature or even the social media feeds of other institutions to develop ideas about what kind of content they want to provide, what they are able to provide, and what will best align with their goals.

Even with the best planning though, problems will arise. It may be a complaint about content from a patron or an administrator. It may be the loss of staff. In these cases, it is important to refocus the institutional goals to address the problem with the least possible disruption to the message, so as not to lose any momentum gained. Social media is, to large extent, a medium of consistency of use, and on some platforms, most notably Facebook, consistency is imperative; the type of post, as well as how many people engage with the post, both affect where a post is seen in a users' feed (Facebook, 2019). Many of these issues and how deal with them are addressed in this book.

The engagement level is where it is easiest to marry the ideas of social media as a communication tool and social media as an instruction tool. This can be done in the classroom, addressing the topic head on in information literacy sessions and workshops, or it could be done on the social media networks themselves, with communication campaigns and interaction that rise to an instructional level. A study conducted by Purdue University found that their students most wanted to see their library on Facebook, Twitter, Snapchat and YouTube (Howard, et. Al, 2018), and though there are a few differences, this aligns closely with the popularity of the networks in general (Pew Research Center, 2018). The most notable differences in the two lists are Pinterest (which many libraries have tried with varying degrees of success) and LinkedIn, which would be better used by the institution as a whole, rather than just the library. All of these networks can be used to help strengthen library instruction, though some are better than others; see the chapter on Virginia Commonwealth University's Twitter campaign, #VetYourSources, in the book for an example.

ORGANIZATION OF THE BOOK

The book is organized into three sections with a total of 15 chapters. The 15 chapters are as follows:

Chapter 1 is a literature review of existing information available about social media networks in academic libraries, covering the use of social media from the identification of the Web 2.0 phenomenon in 2005, to the present day. This overview gives the reader an idea of where libraries have been and where they are going with regards to social media.

Chapter 2 focuses on the use of social media in digital libraries specifically. While digital libraries may be academic or non-academic in nature, they are different from libraries that have physical components, and their social media use will reflect this.

Chapter 3 delves into the first of many issues with social media use: finding a strategy for creating and maintain content on various networks that is achievable by the institution. It presents the steps toward achieving that goal and provides a case study of the steps in practice.

Chapter 4 expounds on strategizing by focusing on diversifying content to create campaigns best suited for the network on which they will be communicated. It presents content strategies and the real-world results of using those strategies.

Chapter 5 covers assessing social media use, both in instruction and marketing, laying out a project plan to guide institutions through the process. Through this project plan, libraries can ensure that not only are they are developing the best plan for their situation, but that the plan continues to serve them well, by emphasizing assessment.

Chapter 6 covers using application statistics and web analytics to assess the institution's reach and ultimately assess the social media plan, including information on gathering statistics from within many popular social media platforms.

Chapter 7 is about biases and other social media blunders that could distort the institution's message, and how to best avoid them, with examples taken from the author's institution. It also includes a discussion on recruiting a diverse staff.

Chapter 8 is about legal problems that might arise from the use of social media at the institution. Two major pieces of legislation, the Americans with Disabilities Act (ADA) and the Family Educational Rights & Privacy Act are discussed with regards to social media.

Chapter 9 is about one institution's experience with peer-to-peer marketing and allowing students to create content for social media, and how it can help with the problems of understanding student preferences and maximizing the library's social media exposure.

Chapter 10 is about engaging with distance learners through social media, focusing on social media's capability to livestream events and engage learners at a distance in real-time, with an example from the Open University (UK) Library.

Chapter 11 is about one institution's experience with using Twitter to enhance information literacy skills. The aforementioned Virginia Commonwealth University's Twitter campaign, using the hashtag #VetYourSources is detailed in this chapter.

Chapter 12 is about creating a social media plan for special collections and archives, and how to best approach creating an adaptable and usable plan for social media use in the context of special collections and their unique audiences.

Chapter 13 is a case study about the Library of Congress's social media program, focusing on the four area studies divisions which have come together to create a collaborative social media program that benefits all of the participants.

Chapter 14 expands the topic of social media use internationally by discussing the opportunities and challenges of implementing a social media program in a developing country, and offers solutions to meet these challenges where possible, using social media use in Nigeria as its example.

Chapter 15 is about using social media, and specifically Twitter, at branch campus libraries and other institutions where the budget may be minimal. These strategies were developed at the Southampton Campus Library of Stony Brook University, but are applicable to any campus of similar size and resources.

As outlined, this book contains information on the short but important history of social media use in the academic library, common issues that might arise from the implementation and use of social media networks, and case studies of social network use that might inspire and energize the reader. So much of the literature readily available to the profession about social media is about public libraries; geared solely to academic and research libraries, it addresses issues that are unique to these types of libraries. This book is also updates the available literature, collating case studies and information about recent implementations and concerns that have arose as the use of social media has increased.

Jennifer Joe
University of Toledo, USA

Elisabeth Knight
Western Kentucky University, USA

REFERENCES

Charnigo, L., & Barnett-Ellis, P. (2007). Checking Out Facebook.com: The Impact of a Digital Trend on Academic Libraries. *Information Technology and Libraries*, *26*(1), 23–34. doi:10.6017/ital.v26i1.3286

Facebook. (2019). *How News Feed Works*. Retrieved January 12, 2019, from https://www.facebook.com/help/1155510281178725

Harrison, A., Burress, R., Velasquez, S., & Schreiner, L. (2017). Social Media Use in Academic Libraries: A Phenomenological Study. *Journal of Academic Librarianship*, *43*(3), 248–256. doi:10.1016/j.acalib.2017.02.014

Howard, H., Huber, S., Carter, L., & Moore, E. (2018). Academic Libraries on Social Media: Finding the Students and the Information They Want. *Information Technology and Libraries*, *37*(1), 8–18. doi:10.6017/ital.v37i1.10160

Pew Research Center. (2018a). *Social Media in 2018* [Complete Report]. Retrieved from www.pewinternet.org/wp-content/uploads/sites/9/2018/02/PI_2018.03.01_Social-Media_FINAL.pdf

Pew Research Center. (2018b). *Social media outpaces print newspapers in the U.S. as a news source*. Retrieved from http://www.pewresearch.org/fact-tank/2018/12/10/social-media-outpaces-print-newspapers-in-the-u-s-as-a-news-source/

Swanson, T. A. (2012). *Managing social media in libraries: finding collaboration, coordination and focus*. Oxford, UK: Chandos Pub. doi:10.1533/9781780633770

Acknowledgment

The editors would like to acknowledge the help of all the people involved in this project and, more specifically, to the authors and reviewers that took part in the review process. Without their support, this book would not have become a reality.

First, the editors would like to thank each one of the authors for their contributions. Our sincere gratitude goes to the chapter's authors who contributed their time and expertise to this book. We know that each contribution to this body of work took a great deal of time and effort, and your efforts are appreciated.

Second, the editors wish to acknowledge the valuable contributions of the reviewers regarding the improvement of quality, coherence, and content presentation of chapters. Most of the authors also served as referees; we highly appreciate their double task. Furthermore, we would like to thank our Editorial Advisory Board, without whom, this book would not have been completed on schedule.

We would also like to thank IGI-Global, for recognizing the importance of this topic at this time, and allowing us the opportunity to publish with them. We especially express our thanks to Maria Rohde, Assistant Development Editor, and the entire Book Development team, who answered our questions promptly and professionally.

Finally, thank you to our colleagues and administration at Western Kentucky University and the University of Toledo, for supporting us this past year. The process was more complicated than we thought it would be when we set out, but their encouragement and guidance saw us through.

Jennifer Joe
University of Toledo, USA

Elisabeth Knight
Western Kentucky University, USA

Section 1

The History of Social Media in Academic Libraries

Chapter 1
Making Social Media More Social:
A Literature Review of Academic Libraries' Engagement and Connections Through Social Media Platforms

Elia Trucks
University of Denver, USA

ABSTRACT

This chapter explores how academic libraries have used social media for broadcasting information, responsive communication, and engagement. Many libraries focus on the marketing aspect of social media, since it is a successful method of promoting events, services, and resources. However, exclusively using social media as a marketing tool ignores the best part of social media: the connections it fosters between people. The online community is just an extension of the in-person community that the academic library serves. This chapter examines the state of the literature on libraries' use of social media through the lens of increasing engagement and connections with the community as the key to successful social media.

INTRODUCTION

Social media is ubiquitous and pervasive on the digital landscape today, including in higher education and academic libraries. One only has to turn on the television to see any commercial promoting the company's Facebook presence or website for details. Despite the differences among the multitude of social media platforms, the main commonality they share is that they are used to connect people with other people. Facebook, Twitter, Instagram, and YouTube are among the many tools people use to reach out to old friends, make new friends over a shared interest, and learn more about hot topics and current events.

The massive scale of the Internet has made it necessary for academic libraries to have an online social media presence to meet users where they are. The biggest social media platform in use at the time of this writing is Facebook, with 2.196 billion active users monthly. Other major platforms include You-

DOI: 10.4018/978-1-5225-8097-3.ch001

Tube with 1.9 billion users, Instagram with 1 billion users, and Twitter with 336 million users (We Are Social, n.d.). This chapter will focus on Facebook and Twitter as the primary networks that libraries are using or can use to reach their communities, but the rising popularity of Instagram and YouTube will also be discussed. There are many different networks currently in use by public, academic, and special libraries. Gonzalez, Marks, and Westgate (2018) launched a Social Media Directory of Academic Libraries that lists accounts associated with various academic libraries across the globe, along with contact information for the librarian or representative responsible for the accounts. At the time of this writing, the directory includes 173 libraries on Facebook, 157 libraries on Twitter, 128 libraries on Instagram, and 101 libraries on YouTube.

The boundaries between online and offline have blurred significantly since the Internet has become a pervasive influence in society. A library's community exists in both online and offline spaces simultaneously, and it is necessary to bridge the gap between these spaces to create a holistic experience for the community. Young and Rossmann (2015) emphasize the need to integrate the offline presence of the library into the online world. Social media is "a tool that enables users to join together and share in the commonalities of research, learning, and the university community" (p. 22). Social media can bring together individuals in a community, and libraries must learn to use these tools more effectively to bridge the gaps.

This crossover between the digital and physical worlds has become even more enmeshed with the rise of mobile technology. The Pew Research Center (2018, February 5) reports that 95% of Americans own a cellphone, and 77% own smartphones. This instant connection to social media, news, businesses, and information has changed behaviors. New Media Consortium's (2017) Horizon Report indicates that mobile learning is a major trend for higher education. Convenience and communication drive this trend, and ease of access can improve learning outcomes for students all over the world (Adams Becker, et al, 2017).

This chapter's objectives are to determine how academic libraries have used social media in less than effective ways, how they are using social media for communication or engagement with their communities, and how to incorporate best practices for readers to improve user engagement on social media. This narrative literature review examines the state of academic libraries' social media presence and their use for engagement with students. A search of the Library Information Science and Technology Abstracts database (LISTA) with the keywords "social media" and "libraries" brings back over 2,800 results. A search adding the keyword "engagement" to the previous search string returns only 141 results. A further limitation using the search string "social media AND academic libraries AND engagement," reflecting the focus of this review, returned only 31 articles. Focusing on these articles and examining their references for relevant materials became the basis for this chapter. The search was limited to articles published between 2011 and 2018, but relevant references cited by more than one paper were also examined and included for context. College and Research Libraries News offers additional resources of interest, since many of these are not "scholarly" peer review articles but focus on trends in the field that are important for working professionals. A similar search of "social media" on the College and Research Libraries News archive returned 262 items, comprising many "how-to" articles, strategy tips, and descriptions of successful campaigns or promotions.

In order to share a common vocabulary, the following are some definitions of popular terms used at length in this chapter:

- **Content**: Material created for and shared through social media networks including but not limited to images, text, and videos;
- **Platform**: The website or technology upon which a social network is built;
- **Social Media**: Social networking websites that allow users to follow, "friend," or interact with chosen people. This chapter primarily discusses Facebook and Twitter;
- **Users**: People in the community of a specific library, often the target audience of a marketing strategy, including students, faculty, staff, and community members;
- **User Engagement**: "The emotional, cognitive, and behavioural connection that exists, at any point in time and possibly over time, between a user and a resource" (Attfield, Kazai, Lalmas, & Piwowarski, 2011).

BACKGROUND

Since its inception, the Internet has continuously grown and developed. The concept of Web 2.0 has influenced how libraries utilize the Internet and social media for many years. O'Reilly (2005) coined the term Web 2.0 as a new, interconnected version of Internet technologies focusing on community-driven participation that, while not quite idealized in its utopian form, influenced the way social media networks were built and utilized. O'Reilly emphasizes interactivity between companies and users, including "trusting users as co-developers [and] harnessing collective intelligence" (p. 5) as core competencies for these websites. Academic libraries led the adoption and use of Web 2.0 applications like blogs, RSS feeds, instant messaging, social networking services, wikis, and social tagging (Chua & Goh, 2010).

Early goals of using these networks were to forge connections and share information between users and librarians (Chua & Goh, 2010). These goals have remained relatively static through the years, even as the tools have changed. An examination of social media policies at academic libraries found that most libraries' goal for using social media is to "engage the community in conversations and to share information" (p. 403).

While the goals have not changed, opinions about the usage of social media have. In the mid-2000s, many librarians did not see the value of having libraries participate with social media. An Online Computer Library Center (OCLC) study by De Rosa, Cantrell, Havens, Hawk and Jenkins (2007) explored librarians' viewpoints on aspects of the networked world including sharing information, privacy concerns, and future involvement. The study revealed that librarians did not see a place for the library on social media. Twitter, Facebook, and YouTube were still in their infancy, the possibilities still unseen. Librarians reported using social bookmarking sites like Delicious, sharing videos on YouTube, and maintaining individual blogs for themselves or their libraries. The librarians were not necessarily wrong. Koerwer (2007), a 19-year-old college sophomore, wrote a column about his experiences and described how seeing librarians on Facebook "seemed like another instance of adults arriving too late to a fad, like a soccer mom wearing a Pikachu T-shirt" (p. 40). He goes on to say there may be opportunities for librarians to ingratiate themselves gracefully, but with strict limitations.

Attitudes have changed since 2007, and many articles have explored librarians' social media preferences, usage, and presence. More recently, Chu and Du (2013) surveyed librarians on their perceptions of various social networking tools. The majority of their 38 respondents currently use or plan to use social networking. Librarians value the promotion and marketing features, the convenient dissemination of news, and the possibility of engagement with users. These benefits outweigh the costs, which they describe as little to none; however, they face challenges of inadequate time and training, and a relatively unengaged user base. Social media platforms had saturated the market by this point in 2013, and many more librarians have become more familiar with how these networks work.

LIBRARIES' USE OF SOCIAL MEDIA

Broadcasting

As opinions about social media in academic libraries changed, its goals and uses remained static. Librarians feel most comfortable using social media platforms for promotion and advertising, or broadcasting. Broadcasting most accurately describes the practice of posting on social media to share information and raise awareness, but without engaging in conversation or deeper online responses. This one-way communication can be effective for just-in-time messages, but without user interactions it can feel like shouting into the void. Broadcasting is the current status quo for libraries who use social media, and it can be an ineffective method for communicating, engaging, and bridging the gap between the online and offline worlds. The literature explores in great detail the history of how librarians use social media for broadcasting, and the benefits and challenges of the practice.

One of the earliest studies of libraries' social media posting habits examined Twitter use in libraries. Aharony (2010) collected tweets from 30 public and academic libraries in the United States between August and October 2009. These tweets revealed similarities in the content that each created. Aharony labeled tweets in five major categories: "library, information about, miscellaneous, technology, and general information" (p. 345). Seven years later, Harrison, Burress, Velasquez, and Schreiner (2017) analyzed the social media habits of six Midwestern academic libraries and found very similar themes in the types of postings, falling into the categories "Make community connections, create an inviting environment, and provide content." Considering the time that elapsed between the two previous studies, the content that libraries are publishing has not changed much. Providing basic information about the library itself and promoting resources and events are basic elements of social media.

The most popular use for social media is to promote services or resources at the library. Surveys of librarians in the U.S. and internationally show that librarians recognize the utility of social media as a marketing tool, the most important aspect of their usage (Ayu & Abrizah, 2011; Hendrix, Chiarella, Hasman, Murphy, & Zafron, 2009; Omeluzor, Oyovwe-Tinuoye, & Abayomi, 2016). The Mansfield Library Archives and Special Collections developed a program to feed into Instagram's Application Program Interface to create a dynamic embedded feed of images from their collection (Wilkinson, 2018). Their content promoted rare, interesting, and light-hearted materials, selected to create "user delight."

In addition to the surveys of librarians, studies of the social media postings themselves confirm that librarians use social media for promotion purposes. Since social media platforms have a wide reach and little monetary cost except for time, it is a cost-effective method of marketing. Many librarians explore the uses and effectiveness of social media as a marketing tool in libraries, as well as in other businesses (Sachs, Eckel, & Langan, 2011; Sriram, 2016; Thomsett-Scott, 2014).

Understandably, there is little literature from librarians describing why this is an ineffective method of social media use. Young and Rossman (2015) at Montana State University Library struggled with their social media presence prior to their engagement strategy. An analysis of their tweets determined that the majority of their postings about workshops, library spaces, and event promotion yielded very low interaction rates. This prompted a new approach, which is discussed later in this chapter.

Responsive Communication

Some librarians have determined that broadcasting their messages does not help them reach their users. They have begun to ask their users exactly what they want and to build strategies around their particular preferences. This strategy can be considered "responsive communication," the practice of determining what kinds of messages, platforms, and methods users prefer, and strategizing to take account of those preferences.

Users have a variety of information-retrieval methods, and it is necessary to understand the preference of the library's audience before making general assumptions about the best way to reach them. The librarians who have written about their experiences with responsive communication emphasize the importance of each individual library looking at its specific population, since results vary so much.

A survey undertaken by Booker and Bandyopadhyay (2017) asked library users about their social media habits and preferences. The majority of respondents use social media platforms and think it is important for the library to have a social media presence. However, they do not prefer to get their information about the library from social media, but rather the email and flyers in the library. Users under age 35 prefer to get information from the library webpage or the newsletter before social networking sites. They still feel that the library should be present on social media platforms, but not mainly for promotion. Similarly, Gustafson, Sharrow, and Short (2017) created and disseminated a survey to gauge how the campus community preferred to receive information. This informed a marketing strategy used by the authors to promote events and services. Social media was found to be less useful than email or posters, but useful for "instant gratification and just-in-time communication" (p. 429).

Stvilia and Gibradze (2017) created a survey to determine the perceived value of different types of library tweets. They asked 120 undergraduate students to rate which library services they valued most and how important different categories of social media postings were to them. Students stated overwhelmingly that they value the library as a place to study (90%), and the next highest ranked service was access to information and resources (58%). The social media postings they most valued were operations updates, study support, and event information.

Some libraries include reference assistance as a goal of for their social media presence, assuming that a reference interview requires conversation and engagement between a librarian and a user. Sachs, Eckel, and Langan (2011) at Western Michigan University created a social media policy with this as one of their goals. However, a survey of their users revealed that users were not seeking to interact with the library on social media and would likely not use that service. Their social media management team took this preference into consideration and dropped the goal from their social media policy.

The major takeaway from the literature is that each library's users have different preferences, and every author emphasizes the importance of learning about your own users before creating a social media presence. Responding to users' preference is important, but is it engagement? As Attfield et al. (2011) describe, user engagement is the connection between a user and a resource. Crafting a social media approach to cater to the library's population can lead to user engagement, but it requires strategic tactics that move beyond responsive communication.

Moving Beyond Responsiveness: Engagement or Active Communication

Libraries that use social media platforms to engage with their users participate in active communication, in which libraries initiate conversations that can move from the online world into the offline world by affecting policy, bringing people into the library space, or providing assistance. Historically, libraries have not been very successful in this endeavor. A study of academic-library Twitter accounts found that few accounts were using social media for conversation or engagement: "Most of the libraries were not being mentioned by their followers; in fact, only four library Twitter accounts had more than ten mentions" (Del Bosque, Leif, & Skarl, 2012, p. 209). However, some librarians have successfully developed their social media presence to build connections with their users.

As mentioned earlier in this chapter, Young and Rossmann (2015) created a social media group that analyzed the Twitter activity and usage at Montana State University Library and developed methods to focus on building community rather than one-way broadcasting and promotion. Their target audience was students at their university, and their goal was to increase interaction rates as measured by favorites, retweets, and mentions. Their most popular topics before beginning their new strategy included workshops, library spaces, and events, common themes found frequently on many library social media accounts. The community-focused approach included more personality in the tone of tweets, focusing on topics their community wanted to hear about such as student life or local community, and quick responses:

We prioritized responsiveness, availability and scholarship with the goal of connecting with students and building a sense of community. . . . By creating personality-rich content that invites two-way interaction, our strategic social media program has helped form a holistic community of users around our Twitter activity. (Young & Rossmann, 2015, p. 30)

Their plan worked, and their Twitter account saw a 366% increase in student followers.

Stewart, Atilano, and Arnold (2017) developed a "Social Listening" strategy. The Thomas G. Carpenter Library at the University of North Florida used a customer relationship management concept to connect with students, gauge their interest, and make their social media presence more engaging. Social listening, a process more prominent in private businesses than in libraries, focuses on listening and responding to users' input rather than broadcasting and marketing. The social media team prioritized social listening on their social media platforms rather than creating original content. They observed any "mention" of the library, "check in" at their location, and popular hashtags related to the university, and responded to every comment. Regardless of the sentiment of the comment, whether it was complaining about noise or gratitude for study rooms, librarians responded. Librarians note that this method has worked. User engagement has increased, their Twitter impressions rose to 15,000 per month, and they receive feedback from their users. By building reciprocity and trust between their students and the library, they in turn receive more feedback from their students and provide more help.

Another practice to improve engagement is to work with students directly to create resources and marketing strategies. Luo, Wang, and Han (2013) created a video series called "Falling in Love with the Library" that they developed, created, and executed in partnership with students. They looked at specific social media sites that their students were using, to determine where they could best reach their target audience and make the most impact. Youku, the Chinese version of YouTube, seemed a likely candidate. Librarians worked together with students to create and promote the video series, which was a smash hit. The authors identify four factors contributing to their success: content, style, venue, and partnership with students. The authors note that this last factor, partnership with students, is the most important, as it ensured that the previous three would be relevant and engaging for other students on campus.

In an attempt to create engagement with their campuses, some libraries interact heavily with other departments or units at the same school. This can be useful, as many student life or official university accounts have more activity, followers, and interactions than library accounts. By interacting with other institutional accounts, library postings and presence can find a wider audience of users still connected to the university or college. Stewart and Walker (2018) examined 16 Historically Black Colleges and Universities (HBCU) library social media accounts to see if patrons are engaging with them, by focusing on hashtags, retweets, and sentiment analysis. Retweets showed only 11% of followers engaged with library content. A majority of interaction came from other institutional accounts or non-followers engaging with posts related to institutional boosterism, the practice of creating content that focuses on the school's culture or events in a positive manner. These tweets focused on sports, campus activities, and popular culture, and usually contain slogans, mascots, or other university events. The authors found an over-representation of campus culture on library twitter feeds rather than original content, promotion of library events or services, or focus on the library as a place. They found that "library-centric content, at its best, appears rather generic in tone and did not evoke transcendent and enthusiastic engagement with followers" (p. 123). The Twitter accounts they studied did not encourage two-way communication; rather those accounts used the platform as a broadcasting service focusing on the campus culture. The HBCUs they examined made attempts at engagement but fell short.

One major challenge to improving engagement with social media is that many people use social media passively. Passive social media use is when a person observes, rather than interacting with others using the platform (Zhu & Bao, 2018). Students reported privacy concerns, the desire to control and manage their impression on other users, and social network fatigue as contributing factors to passively using social media networks. These factors are not addressed in library literature, but can explain why engagement, which requires active participation, can be a challenge. Prior to the rise of social media, passive use of message boards and other online communities was a recognized issue. Jakob Nielsen (2006) examined internet communities and coined the 90-9-1 rule: 90% of users are "lurkers" who read or observe without contributing to the discussion, 9% of users contribute occasionally, and 1% of users participate greatly and account for the majority of the content. Reference services on social media may be depressed for this reason. Sachs, Eckel, and Langan (2011) found this to be the case when trying to add reference assistance to their social media.

Despite this challenge, other fields within higher education successfully use social media to create connections and further engagement. Academic libraries can look to models created by colleagues in classroom instruction and student life for inspiration in their social media usage. Chugh and Ruhi (2018) examine how Facebook has functioned as a powerful tool, used to engage in after-class discussion groups, seek assistance outside the formal classroom setting, and foster learning communities among students and instructors. Junco, Heiberger, and Loken (2011) used Twitter in their freshman seminar for in-class discussions and coursework and found that student and faculty engagement increased. Discussions that could not have achieved depth in a one-hour seminar found rich answers and connections between students, study groups formed for other classes, and students who discovered mutual interests that formed the basis of new relationships. Harris (2016) describes ways in which other campus departments and entities can use social media to support Student Life initiatives. Athletics, student affairs, community relations, and campus safety all have unique relationships with students, and social media can enhance interactions. The examples given by each of these authors can provide guidelines or ideas for academic librarians, and even if we may not have the exact same goals, there are correlations that can be implemented.

SOLUTIONS AND RECOMMENDATIONS

Best Practices for Engagement

Developing a strategy is key for a cohesive and effective social media experience. There are many articles and books about how to develop marketing strategies or marketing plans for libraries. Even if advertising is not high on the priority list for the library's social media presence, these strategies can be used to reach the target audience, plan content, and develop better relationships. Creating a strategic marketing plan can focus and streamline social media efforts. Deploying an unfocused series of social media posts or platforms can feel unorganized and chaotic to the user, so having a strategy is important (Chua & Goh, 2010).

Libraries can take a cue from business and marketing professionals when considering their strategy. Potter's (2012) *The Library Marketing Toolkit* lays out the marketing cycle and provides methods to design a plan based on these stages. Libraries can use this step-by-step plan for their social media approach to improve their engagement. The marketing cycle is as follows:

1. Decide on your goals;
2. Market research;
3. Segmentation;
4. Set objectives;
5. Promotional activities;
6. Measurement;
7. Evaluation; and
8. Modification.

Set Goals

The first step in creating a social media presence is to determine a purpose and set goals. One might frame one's goals by answering the question, "Why are we doing this, and what do we hope to gain from it?" (Burkhardt, 2010). The answers to these questions will help to inform the kind of platforms to use, the messages to put out, the content to produce, and the target audience.

Social media policies can help to set goals and create a strategic presence. Policies can be instrumental in making sure all stakeholders understand the priorities, mission, and limits of using social media. Johnson and Burclaff (2013) examined academic library policies regarding social media, and found that very few academic libraries have such policies. Many share the general social media policy created by the larger university without adapting it to fit the library's specific needs. The authors recommend considering the library's mission and goals and crafting a policy that aligns with those priorities. "The library mission should drive the library's activities and should therefore be present in these guiding policies" (p. 404).

Creating goals for a library's social media account can vary. Popular goals include raising awareness about the library, reaching a certain number of people in a time frame, or creating original content. Strategies that support engagement often move beyond these goals. Young and Rossman (2015) developed goals to "connect with students and build community" with the activity focus of "information sharing [and] social interaction," with specifics for "tone and tenor, posting frequency, posting categories, and posting personnel" (p. 26). Each component contributed to the overall goal, and created a cohesive strategy for their team to follow.

Market Research and Segmentation

Market research is the process of analyzing the market and where one sits in it (Potter, 2012). This can involve looking at similar institutions and studying the demographics of a community. There is no one-size-fits-all approach to all users that will work for every library. Focusing on meeting the library's users where they are will eliminate costly diversions to platforms that do not work for them. Look at the age group of the community's user base. If the library's social media target audience is freshmen, part of the Gen Z cohort, they may be using different platforms than most librarians have ever used. The 18-to-24-year-olds embrace a wide variety of platforms, including Snapchat, Instagram, and YouTube, and they are leaving Facebook at a rapid pace (Pew Research Center, 2018, March 1). Other populations have different preferences as well, so consider adult learners, international students, transfer students, and other user groups that may be overlooked. Consider different strategies for reaching those populations and develop specific goals for them.

The first step is to identify the target audience for a social media platform, and find out if they are responsive to social media connections with the library. Many of the surveys looking at student preferences examine how students want to receive marketing or advertising from the library (Gustafson, Sharrow, & Short, 2017; Booker & Bandyopadhyay, 2017). Look back at the goals for one's social media presence and determine if one's audience will be receptive.

Set Objectives

Based on the goals determined at the beginning of this process, objectives are measurable and attainable benchmarks that can determine if one is progressing toward meeting those goals.

Objectives can be a simple measure of analytics, such as "obtaining 60 followers within the first four months of using the service and using multiple likes per image" (Ramsey & Vecchione, 2014). Other objectives can include posting a certain number of unique items within a time frame, creating an amount of original content, or sharing a certain number of links back to library resources. For engagement, different goals are needed. Stewart, Atilano, and Arnold (2018) established goals focusing on content creation and awareness of the library in their first iterations of their social media policy, but as they developed their Social Listening strategy, their goal shifted to "seeking out opportunities to reply to, connect with, and encourage library customers to reach out to the library" (p. 54). Their objectives focused on responding to every mention and check-in at the library, which led them to achieve their overall goal.

Libraries should create a team to manage their social media presence. This will alleviate the pressure on a librarian or staff member and has multiple benefits. A team can create a calendar and update more regularly, make sure that each department or subject is represented fairly, and set bigger goals that align with other marketing objectives (Jansen, 2017). Librarians who use a variety of social media platforms can get bogged down or overwhelmed by producing content for each channel. Having a team, a strategy, and a plan can help to avoid this.

Time is a major concern for librarians using social media, especially for those interested in building relationships with their users. Posting several times per day can be daunting and takes a great deal of time. Librarians must set aside time to learn the platforms; update their knowledge of constant changes on the platforms in the face of user requests and technical fixes; respond to users' queries or comments quickly; and create content that is interesting and engaging. One major concern for librarians using these platforms is the cost of their time (Chu & Du, 2013; Dickson & Holley, 2010).

Promotional Activities

Creating unique content that fits user preferences is an integral and sometimes difficult part of maintaining a social media presence. Graphics, pictures, and visual media are the most popular posts on many of these platforms. A survey of the target population will help guide decisions about the kind of content of most interest or use to them, and those preferences should guide the goals, strategy, and content. From their survey results, Stvilia and Gibradze (2017) learned that students prefer operations updates, study support, and event information. Content that caters to these themes may better engage them than faculty and staff profiles or collections updates.

In addition to creating content for each platform, it is also important to respond to users who interact with an account. Stewart, Atilano, and Arnold (2017) used "social listening" to improve engagement. Students felt heard by the library and that built trust between them. This responsiveness, in addition to content that appeals to them, can generate goodwill and develop relationships.

Looking at other libraries' postings and modifying them to fit the library's vision can be easy and inspirational; however, this can lead to homogeneity in its overall social media presence. Harrison, Burress, Velasquez, and Schreiner (2017) found overwhelmingly similar postings in their analysis of six Midwestern universities, despite differences in sizes, populations, and strategies. Adherence to mimicking other successful posts might overshadow analyzing the effectiveness of posting.

Measurement, Evaluation, and Modification

Assessment of social media can be a challenge for librarians. Clearly defined and measurable goals can improve the experience for managers. In the early days of social media, quantitative data about the effectiveness and success of these platforms was not readily available (Dickson & Holley, 2010). However, in recent years a plethora of tools and methods has become available to librarians.

One easy way to measure engagement is to look at followers, retweets, and replies. Counting mentions, retweets, shares, likes, or comments on various platforms can be a quick tool for measurement. Kim, Abels, and Yang (2012) examined 10 academic libraries' tweets to find out who was sharing their content, and found that university organizations and students are the two largest groups who retweet library accounts. Stvilia and Gibradze (2014) analyzed tweets from six major university libraries to measure the most popular topics and effectiveness of those themes. The most popular categories of tweets include event, resource, and community building. Retweets and favorites determined which content was most effective, and study support was the most popular category by far, followed by community building and resources. Some of the most frequently used words in the "community building" category included "learning, hope, great, student, luck, best, follow, awesome" (p. 139). Based on their description of the category and these kinds of words, this would relate to engagement and building connections with users.

Native tools on each platform can be powerful. Facebook has a sophisticated suite of tools called Page Insights that can provide information about who is engaging with posts, the volume of people, and common traits that may help provide better understanding of the audience. The key terms for these metrics include "impressions," the number of times a post is shown; "reach," the number of unique users who have seen a post; and "frequency," the average number of times a user sees an ad (Nonprofits on Facebook, n.d). Using these tools can help align the target audience with the people actually interacting with posts, determine what days and times are most successful for increasing engagement, and develop new methods and strategies (Ramsey & Vecchione, 2014; Vucovich, Gordon, Mitchell, & Ennis, 2013). Twitter, Instagram, and YouTube also have their own programs that measure algorithms and audiences to provide similar sophisticated information (Twitter for Business, n.d.; Instagram, n.d.; Youtube Creator Academy, n.d.). Many of the tools provided by these companies focus on advertising revenue, which may not be relevant for libraries who do not purchase ad space from them. Third-party tools also provide assessment capabilities if the native tools or individual measurements do not provide enough information. Klout, SumAll, and StatCounter are three alternatives with similar functions.

The marketing cycle requires continuous adaptation and updating. Once the assessment data has been analyzed, determine if the goals made at the outset have been met or if they need to be tweaked in order to reach a desirable outcome. This can lead to improving strategies and developing new goals based on the information one has obtained, which begins the cycle anew.

CONCLUSION

One major issue in the literature about academic libraries' social media use is the privacy of users. Privacy has been discussed in terms of what information universities and colleges collect about students, what corporations collect, and what private information is freely available, but this topic has not been studied in terms of what academic libraries collect from social media. When a library follows or friends a user, any manager on the account can usually see a great deal of information about that user unless they have strict privacy settings. This can give the library much more information than the amount with which the user may feel comfortable. Assessment tools such as Page Insights and Twitter Analytics can provide even more information in the aggregate about the user base. Librarians must consider the implications of collecting that much data about students or the community. Dickson and Holley (2010) considered privacy in their research, but few others have recently looked at social media use through this lens.

Even with all of the analytics tools available to librarians today, these may not be sufficient for measuring engagement. Assessment and evaluation are an important aspect of the marketing cycle, and libraries currently can't determine outcomes that may be more complicated than reach or impressions. Engagement is about connection with individuals, and a gap exists for measuring engagement in social media.

Another issue that carries with it an opportunity is the concept of using social media to incorporate participatory culture for collective knowledge creation. One promise of Web 2.0 was that users could communally build knowledge together. A participatory culture is one that breaks down the hegemonic imposition of cultural and structural barriers on knowledge. Deodato (2014) discusses how libraries are considered the organizers of knowledge, but through collection development, classification, and restriction of access, they are actually creators of knowledge that support, or choose to subvert, the cultural hegemony. The proliferation of Web 2.0 was thought to subvert the top-down hierarchical creation of knowledge by letting users become involved in that creation. For example, websites like Yahoo Answers allow for the creation of collective knowledge where users can post questions, answer others' questions, and rate answers. This could be possible in social media, allowing for more participation from users in the communal creation of knowledge, growing beyond engagement into something more inclusive.

The rapid growth of social media over the past decade has created new opportunities for academic libraries to bridge the gap between the online and offline realms. At the moment, libraries that incorporate engagement into their social media strategies are one-off success stories rather than trends that are taking off. This is an opportunity for libraries to move beyond broadcasting our promotional messages into the social media void, while considering the questions surrounding privacy, assessment, and participatory culture. Building connections and having conversations with students, faculty, and the community to develop relationships, improve real-world services and resources, affect policy, and meet target goals can improve the social media experience for librarians, patrons, and the community.

REFERENCES

Adams Becker, S., Cummins, M., Davis, A., Freeman, A., Hall Giesinger, C., & Ananthanarayanan, V. (2017). *NMC Horizon Report: 2017 Higher Education Edition*. Austin, TX: The New Media Consortium.

Aharony, N. (2010). Twitter use in libraries: An exploratory analysis. *Journal of Web Librarianship*, *4*(4), 333–350. doi:10.1080/19322909.2010.487766

Attfield, S., Kazai, G., Lalmas, M., & Piwowarski, B. (2011, February). Towards a science of user engagement (position paper). *WSDM workshop on user modelling for Web applications*. Retrieved from: http://www.dcs.gla.ac.uk/~mounia/Papers/engagement.pdf

Ayu, A. R., & Abrizah, A. (2011). Do you Facebook? Usage and applications of Facebook page among academic libraries in Malaysia. *The International Information & Library Review*, *43*(4), 239–249. doi:10.1080/10572317.2011.10762906

Booker, L., & Bandyopadhyay, S. (2017). How academic libraries can leverage social networking to popularize their services: An empirical study. *Journal of the Indiana Academy of the Social Sciences*, *16*(2), 129–146. Retrieved from https://digitalcommons.butler.edu/jiass/vol16/iss2/12/

Burkhardt, A. (2010, January). Social media: A guide for college and university libraries. *College & Research Libraries News*. Retrieved from https://crln.acrl.org/index.php/crlnews/article/view/8302/8391

Chu, S. K. W., & Du, H. S. (2013). Social networking tools for academic libraries. *Journal of Librarianship and Information Science*, *45*(1), 64–75. doi:10.1177/0961000611434361

Chua, A. Y., & Goh, D. H. (2010). A study of Web 2.0 applications in library websites. *Library & Information Science Research*, *32*(3), 203–211. doi:10.1016/j.lisr.2010.01.002

Chugh, R., & Ruhi, U. (2018). Social media in higher education: A literature review of Facebook. *Education and Information Technologies*, *23*(2), 605–616. doi:10.100710639-017-9621-2

De Rosa, C., Cantrell, J., Havens, A., Hawk, J., & Jenkins, L. (2007). *Sharing, privacy, and trust in our networked world: A report to the OCLC membership.* Dublin, OH: OCLC Online Computer Library Center. Retrieved from https://www.oclc.org/content/dam/oclc/reports/pdfs/sharing.pdf

Del Bosque, D., Leif, S. A., & Skarl, S. (2012). Libraries atwitter: Trends in academic library tweeting. *RSR. Reference Services Review, 40*(2), 199–213. doi:10.1108/00907321211228246

Deodato, J. (2014). The patron as producer: Libraries, Web 2.0, and participatory culture. *The Journal of Documentation, 70*(5), 734–758. doi:10.1108/JD-10-2012-0127

Dickson, A., & Holley, R. P. (2010). Social networking in academic libraries: The possibilities and the concerns. *New Library World, 111*(11), 468–479. doi:10.1108/03074801011094840

Gonzalez, C., Marks, G. J., & Westgate, H. (2018). *Social media directory of academic libraries.* Retrieved from: https://sites.google.com/wpunj.edu/nj-social-media-directory/home

Gustafson, J. C., Sharrow, Z., & Short, G. (2017). Library marketing on a small liberal arts campus: Assessing communication preferences. *Journal of Library Administration, 57*(4), 420–435. doi:10.1080/01930826.2017.1300459

Harris, P. (2016). Drinking from the fire hose: Social media on campus. *Security Technology Executive*, 32-34. Retrieved from: https://search-proquest-com.du.idm.oclc.org/docview/1777246161?accountid=14608

Harrison, A., Burress, R., Velasquez, S., & Schreiner, L. (2017). Social media use in academic libraries: A phenomenological study. *Journal of Academic Librarianship, 43*(3), 248–256. doi:10.1016/j.acalib.2017.02.014

Hendrix, D., Chiarella, D., Hasman, L., Murphy, S., & Zafron, M. L. (2009). Use of Facebook in academic health sciences libraries. *Journal of the Medical Library Association: JMLA, 97*(1), 44–47. doi:10.3163/1536-5050.97.1.008 PMID:19159005

Instagram. (n.d.). *What are Instagram Insights*? Retrieved from: https://help.instagram.com/788388387972460

Jansen, A. (2017). Likes, shares and follows: Launching a Facebook page for your academic library. *JLAMS, 13*(1), 1-12. Retrieved from: https://scholarsarchive.library.albany.edu/jlams/vol13/iss1/6/

Johnson, C., & Burclaff, N. (2013, April). Making social media meaningful: Connecting missions and policies. In *Imagine, innovate, inspire: Proceedings of the ACRL 2013* (pp. 10–13). Conference. Retrieved from http://www.ala.org/acrl/sites/ala.org.acrl/files/content/conferences/confsandpreconfs/2013/papers/JohnsonBurclaff_Making.pdf

Junco, R., Heiberger, G., & Loken, E. (2011). The effect of Twitter on college student engagement and grades. *Journal of Computer Assisted Learning, 27*(2), 119–132. doi:10.1111/j.1365-2729.2010.00387.x

Kim, H. M., Abels, E. G., & Yang, C. C. (2012). Who disseminates academic library information on Twitter? *Proceedings of the American Society for Information Science and Technology, 49*(1), 1–4. doi:10.1002/meet.14504901317

Koerwer, S. (2007). Commentary—One teenager's advice to adults on how to avoid being creepy on Facebook. *Computers in Libraries*, *27*(8), 40. Retrieved from https://search-proquest-com.du.idm.oclc.org/docview/231113980?accountid=14608

Luo, L., Wang, Y., & Han, L. (2013). Marketing via social media: A case study. *Library Hi Tech*, *31*(3), 455–466. doi:10.1108/LHT-12-2012-0141

Nielsen, J. (2006). *The 90-9-1 rule for participation inequality in social media and online communities.* Retrieved from: https://www. nngroup. com/articles/participation-inequality

Nonprofits on Facebook. (n.d.). *Page insights*. Retrieved from: https://nonprofits.fb.com/topic/page-insights/

O'Reilly, T. (2005). *What is Web 2.0: design patterns and business models for the next generation of software*. Retrieved from: https://www.oreilly.com/pub/a/web2/archive/what-is-web-20.html

Omeluzor, S. U., Oyovwe-Tinuoye, G. O., & Abayomi, I. (2016). Social networking tools in library service delivery: The case of academic libraries in South-East Zone of Nigeria. *DESIDOC Journal of Library and Information Technology*, *36*(5), 269–277. doi:10.14429/djlit.36.5.10174

Pew Research Center. (2018, February 5). *Mobile fact sheet*. Retrieved from: http://www.pewinternet.org/fact-sheet/mobile/

Pew Research Center. (2018, March 1). *Social media use in 2018*. Retrieved from: http://www.pewinternet.org/2018/03/01/social-media-use-in-2018/

Potter, N. (2012). *The library marketing toolkit*. London: Facet Publishing. doi:10.29085/9781856048897

Ramsey, E., & Vecchione, A. (2014). Engaging library users through a social media strategy. *Journal of Library Innovation*, *5*(2), 71–82. Retrieved from http://citeseerx.ist.psu.edu/viewdoc/download?doi=10.1.1.679.6263&rep=rep1&type=pdf

Sachs, D. E., Eckel, E. J., & Langan, K. A. (2011). Striking a balance: Effective use of Facebook in an academic library. *Internet Reference Services Quarterly*, *16*(1-2), 35–54. doi:10.1080/10875301.2011.572457

Sriram, V. (2016). Social media and library marketing: Experiences of KN Raj Library. *DESIDOC Journal of Library and Information Technology*, *36*(3), 153–157. doi:10.14429/djlit.36.3.9810

Stewart, B., & Walker, J. (2018). Build it and they will come? Patron engagement via Twitter at historically black college and university libraries. *Journal of Academic Librarianship*, *44*(1), 118–124. doi:10.1016/j.acalib.2017.09.016

Stewart, M. C., Atilano, M., & Arnold, C. L. (2017). Improving customer relations with social listening: A case study of an American academic library. *International Journal of Customer Relationship Marketing and Management*, *8*(1), 49–63. doi:10.4018/IJCRMM.2017010104

Stvilia, B., & Gibradze, L. (2014). What do academic libraries tweet about, and what makes a library tweet useful? *Library & Information Science Research*, *36*(3-4), 136–141. doi:10.1016/j.lisr.2014.07.001

Stvilia, B., & Gibradze, L. (2017). Examining undergraduate students' priorities for academic library services and social media communication. *Journal of Academic Librarianship*, *43*(3), 257–262. doi:10.1016/j.acalib.2017.02.013

Thomsett-Scott, B. C. (Ed.). (2013). *Marketing with social media: A LITA guide*. Chicago: American Library Association.

Twitter for Business. (n.d.). *How to use Twitter Analytics*. Retrieved from: https://business.twitter.com/en/analytics.html

Vucovich, L. A., Gordon, V. S., Mitchell, N., & Ennis, L. A. (2013). Is the time and effort worth it? One library's evaluation of using social networking tools for outreach. *Medical Reference Services Quarterly*, *32*(1), 12–25. doi:10.1080/02763869.2013.749107 PMID:23394417

We Are Social. (n.d.). Most popular social networks worldwide as of July 2018, ranked by number of active users (in millions). *Statista—The Statistics Portal*. Retrieved from https://www.statista.com/statistics/272014/global-social-networks-ranked-by-number-of-users/

Wilkinson, J. (2018). Accessible, dynamic web content using Instagram. *Information Technology and Libraries*, *37*(1), 19–26. doi:10.6017/ital.v37i1.10230

Young, S. W. H., & Rossmann, D. (2015). Building library community through social media. *Information Technology and Libraries*, *34*(1), 20–37. doi:10.6017/ital.v34i1.5625

Youtube Creator Academy. (n.d.). *Get insights with Youtube Analytics*. Retrieved from: https://creatoracademy.youtube.com/page/course/analytics-series?hl=en

Zhu, X., & Bao, Z. (2018). Why people use social networking sites passively: An empirical study integrating impression management concern, privacy concern, and SNS fatigue. *Aslib Journal of Information Management*, *70*(2), 158–175. doi:10.1108/AJIM-12-2017-0270

ADDITIONAL READING

Bess, M., Wu, S. K., & Price, B. (2015). 49er alerts: Utilizing mobile marketing technology for library outreach. *Public Services Quarterly*, *11*(4), 291–299. doi:10.1080/15228959.2015.1088816

Brookbank, E. (2015). So much social media, so little time: Using student feedback to guide academic library social media strategy. *Journal of Electronic Resources Librarianship*, *27*(4), 232–247. doi:10.1080/1941126X.2015.1092344

Collins, G., & Quan-Haase, A. (2014). Are social media ubiquitous in academic libraries? A longitudinal study of adoption and usage patterns. *Journal of Web Librarianship*, *8*(1), 48–68. doi:10.1080/19322909.2014.873663

Cuddy, C., Graham, J., & Morton-Owens, E. G. (2010). Implementing Twitter in a health sciences library. *Medical Reference Services Quarterly*, *29*(4), 320–330. doi:10.1080/02763869.2010.518915 PMID:21058176

Gardois, P., Colombi, N., Grillo, G., & Villanacci, M. C. (2012). Implementation of Web 2.0 services in academic, medical and research libraries: A scoping review. *Health Information and Libraries Journal, 29*(2), 90–109. doi:10.1111/j.1471-1842.2012.00984.x PMID:22630358

Garofalo, D. (2013). *Building communities: Social networking for academic libraries.* Cambridge, UK: Chandos Publishing. doi:10.1533/9781780634012

Grieve, R., Indian, M., Witteveen, K., Tolan, G. A., & Marrington, J. (2013). Face-to-face or Facebook: Can social connectedness be derived online? *Computers in Human Behavior, 29*(3), 604–609. doi:10.1016/j.chb.2012.11.017

Palmer, S. (2014). Characterizing university library use of social media: A case study of Twitter and Facebook from Australia. *Journal of Academic Librarianship, 40*(6), 611–619. doi:10.1016/j.acalib.2014.08.007

Phillips, N. K. (2011). Academic library use of Facebook: Building relationships with students. *Journal of Academic Librarianship, 37*(6), 512–522. doi:10.1016/j.acalib.2011.07.008

Swanson, T. (2012). *Managing social media in libraries: Finding collaboration, coordination, and focus.* Cambridge, UK: Chandos Publishing. doi:10.1533/9781780633770

Tarantino, K., McDonough, J., & Hua, M. (2013). Effects of student engagement with social media on student learning: A review of literature. *The Journal of Technology in Student Affairs, 1*(8), 1–8. Retrieved from http://studentaffairs.com/ejournal/Summer_2013/EffectsOfStudentEngagementWithSocialMedia.html

Tomcik, L. (2015). Tying it all together: Utilizing market research to inform a marketing plan and further library branding. *Public Services Quarterly, 11*(1), 59–65. doi:10.1080/15228959.2014.995856

Wan, G. (2011). How academic libraries reach users on Facebook. *College & Undergraduate Libraries, 18*(4), 307–318. doi:10.1080/10691316.2011.624944

Wright, J. (2015). Assessment of social media in the library: Guidelines for administrators. *Journal of Library Administration, 55*(8), 667–680. doi:10.1080/01930826.2015.1085251

Chapter 2
Social Media and Social Networking in Digital Libraries

Elisha Ondieki Makori
https://orcid.org/0000-0003-1966-3253
University of Nairobi, Kenya

ABSTRACT

The modern knowledge economy has transformed library and information organizations to adopt and embrace digital social media platforms. Proliferation and growth of social media and social networking technologies continue to play pivotal roles in establishment and operation of digital library and information systems in organizations. The purpose of the chapter is to examine the extent to which information professionals and practitioners understand the impact of social media and social networking technologies on digital library and information systems. The author also analyzes how information professionals manage and promote the adherence to copyright and intellectual property laws in digital library contexts. This chapter specifically discusses the rationale for social media and social networking in digital library and information systems; emerging social media platforms and their applications; legal aspects of social media, copyright and intellectual property protection, and risk management; as well as professional ethics and guidance on social media.

INTRODUCTION

Evolution and revolution of digital information systems has influenced modern information organizations and professionals. New Internet platforms such as social media and social networking sites have become fundamental tools that enhance interpersonal communication. Social media and social networking technologies are powerful business tools used to provide, manage and support information and knowledge in digital libraries. An analysis of the modern technological trends in digital libraries reveal a greater adoption and use of different types of social media and social networking systems that also need copyright and intellectual property protection. Digital libraries provide different types of social media and social networking technologies that manage data, information and knowledge in organizations. Information and knowledge management in digital libraries depend upon social media synergies that connect staff,

DOI: 10.4018/978-1-5225-8097-3.ch002

clients and supplies. The predominant goal of digital library systems is to develop and facilitate access to new information and knowledge. Information professionals and practitioners need to understand and appreciate the fundamental benefits of social media and social networking technologies in digital libraries.

Social media and social networking technologies are widely applied in the political, social and economic aspects of human life. Business, industrial and information organizations in equal measure utilize social media platforms for regular operations and the delivery of services. Fundamental aspects of analysis and discussion include modern social media and social networking technologies plus management of copyright and intellectual property protection in digital libraries. This chapter examines modern social media technologies and copyright protection laws applied in digital libraries. Objectives of the chapter are to:

- Understand the significance of social media and social networking technologies in digital libraries;
- Examine emerging social media technologies and their applications in digital libraries;
- Examine social media platform optimization strategies in relation to digital library and information systems;
- Explore legal requirements governing use of social media technologies in digital libraries;
- Evaluate copyright and intellectual property protection practices and strategies in digital libraries.

BACKGROUND

Historically, the development of digital libraries began in the first decade of the 21st Century with many varied names and concepts used to describe the entities such as virtual library, electronic library and library without walls. The digital library is the collection, organization, preservation and management of information services and objects (Mishra, 2016). Similarly, a digital library may be considered as a potentially virtual organization that comprehensively collects, manages and preserves for the long length of time rich digital content, and offers it to its targeted user communities (Candela et al., 2011). Digital library encompasses professionals from different fields such as data science, information sciences, information systems, human computer interaction and digital curation. Digital libraries are organizations that provide and manage electronic information and knowledge. Simply means modern digital libraries or computerization of traditional libraries.

Digital libraries provide endless access and unlimited opportunities to information and knowledge. In the digital library environment, social computing and technological systems are used to manage and support information resources such as electronic books and journals (e-books and e-journals), bibliographic databases, websites, reference and citation management tools as well as digital theses and dissertations. The digital library is a geopolitical organization (borderless and boundary-less) with highly advanced technologies, hyper-connectivity and Internet-based platforms that provide diverse information services and resources. This is the library that applies technological systems and solutions to provide electronic information products and services beyond the physical borders and boundaries of the institution and organization. The digital library (also known as electronic or virtual library) is the multifunctional enterprise information system that provides and manages information products and services.

The digital repository is the process of developing, acquiring, processing, preserving, utilizing, disseminating and managing of internally produced intellectual content for lifelong purposes in organizations. The primary core function of digital repositories is to preserve for lifelong purposes while that of digital libraries is to provide access to electronic information.

Development of the Internet of Things has redefined the context of the digital library. Internet of Things environment provides digital platforms that share and disseminate information and knowledge through discussion, participation and content creation although professionals and researchers normally use common phrases of social media, social networking, social media sites, social networks and media, and social media technology synonymously to refer to the same. For this purpose, social media technology is used as the general concept for all the terms. Social media is the use of web-based and mobile technologies to turn communication into interactive dialogue (Gallardo, 2013); or technology platforms that allow people all over the world to connect and communicate in new ways (Determann, 2012). Similarly, social media technology (SMT) refers to web-based and mobile applications that enable individuals and organizations to create, engage, and share new user-generated or existing content, in digital environments through multi-way communication (Davis et al., 2012).

Social media technology is the application and use of digital platforms to enable content creation, online collaboration and participation, broadcasting and sharing of information and knowledge by individuals and organizations. Internet communities communicate and share information and content in the virtual world. Social networking technology is built on strong Internet-based platforms and capabilities of web of things that enables sharing of content to the general public through Facebook, Twitter, WhatsApp, Wikis, Blogs and LinkedIn. Learning content management systems and content management systems such as Blackboard, LearnDash, Desire2Learn and Dashboard are mainly accessible and used in educational and academic institutions. Web of things is the integration of Internet and virtual things into the World Wide Web through social computing, telecommunication systems and hyper-connectivity technologies to host and provide social networking sites (SNSs).

SOCIAL MEDIA TECHNOLOGIES AND DIGITAL LIBRARIES

Social media technologies are fundamental and powerful tools for transacting electronic information products and services in digital libraries. With the revolution of the Internet, digital methods and communication tools for creation and sharing of information and knowledge have become popular and literally accessible through social computing and mobile devices. In digital library and information systems, avalanche of classical or traditional social media interfaces are used by clients to communicate and create, edit, publish and share content beyond the physical four walls, boundaries and geopolitics of the organization - Facebook, Myspace, Twitter, LinkedIn, YouTube and Blogs. Due to technological innovations, strategic new social media platforms are exerting huge influence in digital libraries. Information professionals should be aware of these strategic technologies in order to ensure effective adoptions and integrations. The top two trending new social media technologies widely used to facilitate information and communication in digital libraries include Snapchat and Pinterest. Snapchat is one of the most rapid and unprecedented in the history of instant messaging services and social networking sites (Piwek & Joinson, 2016) while Pinterest is among the latest popular (Elaine, 2012). Pinterest and Snapchat appeal most to digital nomad clients of Generation Z and Millennials, the technology-savvy.

In digital libraries, fundamental aspects of online communication and information and knowledge seeking by the digital natives and texting generation are mainly done via social media technologies. In this way, the boundaries between online and "real-world" communities are rapidly stretching if not completely deteriorating (Davis et al., 2012). Digital information professionals (librarians, content managers and information systems) normally use social media applications to interact and communicate with clients.

Information organizations use the digital platforms to perform many functions. Snapchat is the fastest growing method of ephemeral communication (Anderson, 2015) that is popular among young people for back and forth multimedia messages. This social media app provides innovative and creative ways of engaging and commuting with librarians. Pinterest provides unique features and functionalities that allow users to collect, organize, categorize and share images from the Internet (Elaine, 2012). In addition, Pinterest works cooperatively with Facebook, Twitter or Flickr to broaden social networking webs. Digital library and information systems in educational and academic institutions connect teaching and non-teaching staff with students and associated clients through social networking influence.

Social Media Technologies

Development of the social media is a force and idea that has proved to be unstoppable in the modern digital with many software applications being produced and applied in many sectors of the economy – information, commerce, agriculture, education, health, banking, entertainment and transport. There are numerous social media technologies widely used in information organizations although there is no universally accepted classification scheme. In principle, the wide range of technologies and tools are classified into two levels of interaction and intensity of interaction. Social media platforms can be classified either as modern or traditional and weakest or strongest tools. Modern social media platforms are new and emerging tools that are very popular among young people (Snapchat and Pinterest). Traditional tools are old and common versions (Facebook and Twitter). Media platforms that allow for sharing of photos and videos to the public are referred to as weakest while those ones used for direct interaction, participation and sharing are the strongest.

Fundamental features and characteristics of social media technologies include online interaction and collaboration, sharing of information (public, private or peer-to-peer), ability to provide information and messages freely without any specific request from the client, provides information and knowledge on numerous areas and topics, and designed with simple and friendly interfaces. Popular social media technologies widely applied in digital library and information systems include social networking sites, media sharing sites, push technologies, social bookmarking or tagging sites, virtual or online communities, and virtual worlds (Gamboa & Gonçalves, 2014, Deng & Tavares, 2013, Heap & Minocha, 2012, Makori, 2012, Sranamkam, 2012, Bonsón & Flores, 2011, Lee & Kim, 2011).

Social Networking Sites

Social networking sites are powerful business tools that allow people and organizations to create and build online communities of relationships and friendships. The most widely used platforms to promote communication opportunities and information sharing among individuals, professional associations and organizations include video sharing sites (YouTube), community sites (Facebook, Twitter and Google Plus+ and user tagging sites (Digg and LinkedIn). The platforms focus on particular clients that have common interests to share social interactions and acquaintances through online or virtual communities. Digital libraries and information professionals connect with clients regularly through SNSs for online interaction, personal communication, knowledge sharing, marketing and promotion, customer relationship management as well as education and training. With the mobile of things and mobile application the use of social networking sites especially Snapchat has increased tremendously although the other platforms are equally important in digital libraries.

Media Sharing Sites

Media sharing sites are platforms that allow people and selected communities to upload, organize and share multimedia information including videos, audio and photos. The primary focus is sharing of images and videos through YouTube, Instagram and Flickr. The sites were initially used for sharing of personal information and materials with friends and other people but due to development and innovation the tools have become sophisticated communication channels for companies to promote products and corporate image using conveyance of organization messages to stakeholder groups or communities, and educational and academic organizations to support student learning by distributing digital information resources.

Push Technologies

Blogs and Microblogs are push technologies that allow authors to post writings, messages and information while hopping for someone to read. Personal postings with features that allow comments or suggestions usually published personally or institutionally or a webpage that is created and used as a diary or news journal - Blogs. In general, Blogs are used to post and share messages, information, opinions, ideas, interests and daily activities with other people whether known or unknown like the blogger.com. Microblogs are short lived postings where messages and information are quickly created, replaced and updated like Twitter. Technology advancement has increased and made micro-blogging sites easily available and accessible with handheld devices. From the digital library perspective, Blogs offer opportunities for sharing knowledge as well as online discussion and participation usually with comments that provide instant information feedback. Blogging promotes critical thinking and development of writing skills. As with much digital information on the Internet, discriminating between good-value sites and the background noise can be challenging, but links to some of the best thematic Blogs continue to be informative and popular. Push technologies provide digital libraries with excellent opportunities for informal communication and information feedback, news and updates, referencing, newsletter publishing, posting comments, education and training, marketing and promotion, and customer relationship management.

Social Bookmarking Sites

Internet platforms that provide services and facilities to store, organize, search, share and manage web information and contents such as Pinterest and Digg. The tagging system creates online community where like-minded clients, professionals or people with similar ideas and interests share information and knowledge. The social tagging sites allow digital libraries and information professionals to annotate and share interesting content and information in the websites. Marketers also use social bookmarking sites for promotion such as creating viral campaign and conducting collaborative activities.

Online Communities

Digital and media landscape provide software communication technologies and tools that facilitate online or virtual interaction and collaboration among people and organizations. Virtual or online communities are social networks of individuals or people sharing similar or common interests, personal and professional opinions and specific information communicating through interactive tools such as e-mails, instant messaging, chat rooms, forums and discussion boards, dashboards, for example, Lonely Planet and Yahoo Answers. Participants involved are not necessarily friends and acquaintances but may end up creating influential online communities for collaboration, discussion and knowledge sharing. Instant messaging is the Internet communication media and application interface that allows interaction, discussion and sharing of knowledge between two or more people. The application extensively applied in digital libraries has evolved from the text messages format to sharing of multimedia information resources such as photos and videos. Digital libraries and information professionals widely use instant messaging to offer quick online reference services and instant and automatic alerts. Web of things provides unlimited opportunities beyond geographical or political boundaries hence making online communities influential in sharing of information and knowledge among the participants. Information professionals should learn from the ideas, opinions and knowledge that is normally shared through online communities for the betterment of the organization.

Virtual Worlds

The power of the Internet has led to human-computer simulation and interaction of online virtual environments or second lives, which allows online communities to interact with virtual representations of the site participants. Interactions are usually private rather than public. Virtual worlds are platforms for business transactions and product introductions. The virtual worlds represent a big business opportunity that attracts interest from many researchers in marketing, knowledge sharing, collaborative activities and other areas.

Emerging Social Media Technologies

Digital libraries are defined and influenced by the dynamics of new and emerging social media technologies. Rapid applications of social media technologies are extensively applied in digital information organizations with new innovations being developed. The social media platforms and applications provide different functions and services in digital library libraries. Emerging and trending technologies featured include Snapchat and Pinterest. Snapchat is a mobile social media application or app that allows users to capture pictures and videos (Sousa, 2017). The content and messages, commonly called "snaps" has the characteristic of self-destruction after a determined period of time. Snapchat only runs as mobile application using either IOS or Android, which is downloaded from Apple App Store or Google Play (Anderson, 2015). Installation process requires a phone number and standard profile information such as username, email, password, notifications and privacy settings, adds the author. Snapchats platforms connect online communities where multimedia messages and information are exchanged and communicated. Libraries and librarians use the platform for outreach and marketing purposes where promotional events and programs are communicated in addition to sharing of information and news. Platform also has excellent features that allow for creation of content and graphic designs for identification and location of place.

Pinterest is a social curation site that combines features of gathering, creating and sharing with the information management characteristics of successful data curation (Danielle & Abby, 2013), or a pin board-style social photo-sharing website and popular site for many individuals collecting images for planning, organizing, and exploring any topic of interest (Hansen et al., 2012). Libraries are known for being sources of reliable information and librarians are relied upon to help users locate information quickly and efficiently (Danielle & Abby, 2013). Detailed opportunities of Pinterest in digital libraries as exemplified by the authors include:

- Creates social values that connect families, friends and associates, and also promotes online presence of organizations to the audiences.
- Creates interests through running contests that involve participation of audiences.
- Provides features that help to discover, create and share content with the audiences.
- Offers interactive online forums that allow open and public discussion on creation, utilization and sharing of resources.
- Creates online collaboration and participation that allow conversation and sharing of information.
- Promotes information literacy learning and teaching opportunities through visual curation approach.
- Provides visual power that displays book covers linked to catalogues and indicates new acquisitions and reading lists.

APPLICATION OF SOCIAL MEDIA IN DIGITAL LIBRARIES: SOLUTIONS AND RECOMMENDATIONS

Organizations and people use social media technologies for multiple purposes although digital libraries and information professionals embrace the platforms for diverse reasons such as collaboration and communication, scholarly communication, online education and training, digital marketing and promotion and building customer relationships.

Collaboration and Communication

Historically, social media technologies and tools developed primarily as applications for communication although with innovation new aspects of collaboration have been integrated. Social media platforms provide online environments where friends, individuals, people, communities and organizations engage in collaboration and communication in Pinterest, Snapchat and Blogs. The power of popular media sites allow digital libraries, information professionals and online communities to follow one another while sharing the messages and comments generated from the threads. From the digital library perspective, social media technologies have created very intimate sense of online collaboration and communication similar to face-to-face format. In online communication and discussion the participants usually engage with one another in various activities and tasks. Fundamental value of social media is to facilitate collaboration and communication of online communities through participation, interactions and conversations. Online communities are normally motivated by the manner in which updated messages and information are broadcast. In a sense social media platform provides the potential means of internal and external communication with online communities in digital libraries.

Scholarly Communication

In the context of digital libraries, scholarly communication is the process of writing, publishing and sharing information and knowledge with online communities - individuals, friends, acquaintances, followers and organizations. Digital libraries and information professionals have the potential to advance and expand knowledge through curation, integration and inclusion of social media applications. Many media technologies are used in creation and sharing of digital collections with online communities in information organizations. Researchers have a variety of information practices, and that librarians need to incorporate social media in ways to further scholarly communication (Gu & Widen-Wulff, 2011). Perhaps one of the ways that librarians could potentially strengthen information practices is through the incorporation of social media in digital library collections. Social media platforms provide digital libraries with excellent opportunities to create and advance scholarly information and communication through online interaction and participation. Tellingly, the tools contribute and facilitate sharing of information and knowledge through Pinterest, Blogs and mobile applications. Digital libraries provide electronic information collections including repositories and multimedia applications that are shared through the social platforms. Websites and home pages of digital libraries are prime sources of electronic information collections – e-books and e-journals.

Online Education and Training

Modern education and training environment in which the responsibility of teaching and learning takes place through digital and online platforms is increasingly gaining favor in academic institutions. Online education and training programs integrate the principle of knowledge and learning without any limit to physical boundaries whether global or local level through innovative social media applications. Social media platforms were initially designed to provide online interaction and communication although the interfaces are increasingly being incorporated to facilitate and support research, teaching and learning in academic and educational institutions including digital libraries and information systems. Digital natives in higher education prefer the application of social media in aspects of collaboration, communication and learning. Globally, the principle of online learning takes place through creative initiatives where information and knowledge are provided through academic blogs, Pinterest and mobile application as opposed to traditional or conventional classrooms. In the virtual learning environment, the platforms provide updated information and knowledge that the digital natives share via videos, audio clips and podcasts.

Many social media interfaces are blended into e-learning, e-information and virtual education platforms through live videoconferencing, interactive and responsive websites, mobile phones and Moodle learning management system. Online discussions is influenced by a set of factors concerning the technical tools, subjective perceptions, goals within a community, rules for participation, and roles of the participants (Deng & Tavares, 2013). Social media also supports development of educational instructions and facilities and creation of web-based environment necessary for research, teaching and learning in academic institutions. Sranamkam (2012) developed web-based instruction model using social media applications to enhance knowledge management skills of teachers on computer tablets. Digital natives usually engage and communicate on aspects of online education and learning through social networks. Twitter facilitates sharing of ideas and instantaneous peer-to-peer communication in the knowledge creation of group learners, although the character limit constrained students' critical thinking and self-reflection (Kassens-Noor, 2012). With social media platforms and mobile devices digital natives engage and communicate online where information, knowledge and learning materials are posted, received and shared as well as questions asked and answered instantly. Digital libraries and information professionals also engage in creation of knowledge through provision of information literacy education and training programs and instruction learning methods using social media tools and technologies (Pinterest and Snapchat).

Digital Marketing and Promotion

Social media is the trendiest marketing tool and technology that promotes products and services anywhere anytime provided one is connected even with mobile devices. Digital marketing has received considerable attention in academic institutions and digital libraries though not as much as in business organizations and industries. The increasing attention however is a pointer to the crucial role of social media platforms in marketing and promotion of information products and services. In particular, numerous social media networking sites market and promote information services in digital libraries. Facebook enhances the relations that increase loyalty through trust, customer satisfaction, perceived value and commitment, which are stronger for fans of the brand than for non-fans, and that customer satisfaction is the strongest determinant of loyalty (Gamboa & Gonçalves, 2014). Blogs are fundamental marketing and promotion tools that provide information and knowledge applied in webometrics ranking of higher education and learning institutions. Digital marketing provides online interaction and communication environment where digital natives engage through instant messages and information.

Customer Relationship Management

Customer relationship management (CRM) strategy supports organizational interactions with customers that involves the process of finding, attracting, nurturing, retaining, enticing and reducing the costs of marketing the service (Piyawan et al., 2011). Purpose and application of the strategy is to improve and add value to organizations including information based agencies. Digital libraries and information professionals normally engage in customer relations where queries are raised and instantly communicated with answers and information feedback using social media applications such as Pinterest and Snapchat. In particular, this creates positive results of mutual and trust with the clients leading to long term relationships of regular engagement. Online communities engage and share views and opinions regarding information products and services. Pinterest, Blogs and WhatsApp platforms when applied appropriately create positive relationship where messages and information are broadcast to the massive audience of online communities across the globe. In effect, social media technology has not only led the direction of how conversations between institutions and people alike occur but also provided the tools to maximize the social connectivity of the broader world (Davis et al., 2012).

Potential Benefits of Social Media Platforms

Social media interfaces provide numerous benefits and opportunities in digital libraries that information professionals use to promote and upscale delivery of services and resources to the clients. Digital libraries use media technologies and tools to provide access to information and communication. Social media platforms provide excellent opportunities for connecting with digital natives while marketing information services and resources in academic institutions. Academic libraries use social media platforms to promote services and highlight resources to patrons (Collins & Haase 2012). Advancing digital inclusion through access to information and communications technologies supports sustainable development goals and practices and improves people's lives, and libraries provide the infrastructure, help people develop the capacity to use information effectively, and preserve information to ensure ongoing access for future generations (IFLA, 2015).

Enhances Interaction and Communication

Social media technologies enhance online interaction and communication through the Internet and network forums that normally develop and maintain relationships and friendships among the participants (individuals, people or organizations). These provide instant and effective means of two-way communication where concerns and issues involving clients are discussed and amicably answered. The platforms offer unlimited opportunities to online interaction and communication even through handheld devices (mobile phones and tablets). Online communities of information professionals and digital natives engage on discussion and collaboration where comments, messages and information are created and shared on media platforms such as Pinterest and Snapchat. In addition, the online medium provides excellent opportunities for question answer forum where issues are conveniently discussed and addressed. Social media platforms create instant interaction and communication forums that provide for information feedback to the online communities. Digital libraries have benefited from social media platforms where online interactions and communications with instant feedback and direct information equivalent to face-to-face exchange are made possible.

Promotes Information and Knowledge Sharing

Internet media platforms promote sharing of electronic information resources in digital libraries. With social networking and media sharing sites information professionals create profile accounts for sharing and exchanging electronic resources, messages and opinions with clients. Media sites provide data analytics from digital knowledge hubs that help to identify and locate relevant electronic information resources and services. Social media applications provide powerful tools and technologies for real time information and knowledge sharing, for example, Pinterest and Blogs. In the digital environment, different social media platforms and applications are connected with electronic information resources and associated materials leading to increased knowledge sharing. The platforms provide potential opportunities where digital collections are linked with similar or physical materials.

Branding, Marketing, and Promotion

Digital libraries widely use social media technologies in branding, marketing and promotion of information products and services. Internet branding or online marketing is simply the process of advertising and promoting business products and services to the clients. Digital librarians use media platforms to promote information events and programs to the customers anywhere anytime. Internet branding and marketing facilitate online communication, information discovery and knowledge sharing. Digital librarians use social media tools to create awareness and advocacy to wider audiences of digital natives with minimum costs and expenses. Pinterest is useful in introducing information products and services to new online communities of friends and acquaintances hence widening business opportunities of digital libraries. Social media applications provide potential and appropriate opportunities of branding, marketing and promotion of electronic information products and services.

Promotes Client Brand Loyalty

Social media environment establishes and maintains online communities of relationships and friendships where participants communicate and exchange information openly and freely. Digital libraries build client brand loyalty and long term relationships with online communities who regularly use electronic resources. Interaction and engagement in digital libraries is normally through social media technologies and tools, and in situations where that is not provided then there is no any meaningful attraction for the clients to use information products and services. Libraries have created own personal brands for years just like celebrities and media commentators (Gall, 2010). Academic libraries have well known strategies of building and promoting lasting relationships with different stakeholders – administrators, researchers, academic staff and students. Online relationships of friends and acquaintances increase the virtual image of digital libraries and electronic information products and services. Digital collaboration and participation connect people, places and things with new information products and services. The power of social media through regular postings, notifications and reminders to the online communities and organizations creates very strong client brand loyalty.

Open and Free Intellectual Discourse

Social media applications provide ideal ground with online communities where academic and intellectual discourse, ideas and opinions are solicited and discussed openly and freely. Professionals in particular fields with similar interests normally engage and collaborate in social networks where issues are critically analyzed and solutions suggested. In effect, engaging in online discussions where information and knowledge are shared through Pinterest and Blogs is similar to having physical session on face-to-face interaction. Social media applications provide the ideal environment where individuals and organizations come together to share information and knowledge on aspects of human life (social, economic and political). Online communities and digital natives have benefited from social media tools and initiatives that usually connect to global base of information and knowledge. Formation of professional social networks, sharing of electronic information resources, promoting critical thinking and writing skills, and presentation of academic and educational activities are some of the ways in which online communities engage in intellectual discourse.

Economics and Affordability

Many of the social media technologies and systems require absolutely zero or minimum cost provided there is adequate information infrastructure and Internet connectivity. Many organizations advertise and promote business products and services on social media platforms with very low costs. Social media accounts are normally created freely and used with low financial cost implication. Digital librarians market and promote electronic products and services through social media applications. Online interaction and communication is extremely free of charge. Digital collaboration provides personal preferences of products and services that promote and share the comment threads through "like" or follow. Digital libraries being nonprofit making organizations can economically benefit from social media platforms. Social networking sites provide digital platform for hosting electronic information products and services while building and maintaining online communities. Besides, the overall process of managing and promoting electronic information products and services is economically pocket friendly. Power of social media technologies is easy to embrace, quick to access and use, fast to broadcast, gives regular updates and post, and most important saves time and financial resources.

Professional Ethics and Social Media

With rapid development of social media technologies in various sectors of the economy, focus has also turned into professional applications of the platforms in delivery of services in organizations especially digital libraries. Professional principles and guidelines are very essential insofar social media platforms are concerned. Practices and ethics impart information and knowledge useful in guiding and providing better use of social media interfaces irrespective of the field of study and sector. Strong concern is focusing upon the risks of social media in professional practice, especially in relation to issues of information sharing and client access (Fenwick, 2016). Professionalism of social media means that there must be principle ethics including standards and legal regulations governing and guiding the practices. Disciplinary professionalism or e-professionalism with distinct new paradigm requiring particular training, codes and practices must regulate the platforms (Spector et al., 2010), although policies have emerged in professional associations and schools to guide social media use (Greysen, et al., 2010).

Professional ethics deals with aspects of accountability, morality, honesty and integrity that might compromise the fundamental purpose and use of social media technologies and tools. Online communities irrespective of the profession have to be accountable for the deeds and actions performed through social media platforms and must practice honesty and promote moral values without any hatred or malice. Online interactions and communications of social media applications are first and foremost based on the desirable behavior of the individual person or organization controlled through regulations and legislations whether basic or complex. Digital communities should practice and maintain integrity in all aspects dealing with social media interactions and collaboration. Integrity and honesty are achieved through respect and observation of the rules and regulations of engagement with the online communities. Digital libraries, information professionals and online communities have to be guided by the professional code of conduct for social media technologies. Information associations and stakeholders also play a key role in professional ethics and aspects that promote development, use and management of social media platforms.

Social media information and messages can compromise the professional and client relationship if managed and supported openly without regulations. Overall, there is a general concern that online environments loosen inhibitions and create false sense of intimacy, producing inappropriate postings that can be amplified immediately and internationally (Greysen, et al., 2010). Social media platforms are potential tools for sharing of information and knowledge although maximum professional care must be taken to protect the privacy of the clients. Individual responsibility and culture are also important in developing and understanding professional ethics and self-regulations for online communities and participation in social media platforms. Professionalism and ethical principles and practices stresses must be adhered and followed to the letter. Social media online communities are normally guided by the natural law of respecting one another. Individuals need to note that in open and free intellectual discussion and collaboration the principle rule is agree to disagree or disagree to agree politely while keeping the respect. In addition, it is important to understand the content and the nature of the social media platforms because once messages and information are broadcast to reverse the action is impossible and nothing can change the negative impact and damage done. Online communities and participants must be mindful and attentive while on the social media interfaces. Security control and access to data and information are normally enhanced through standard procedures such as keeping passwords safe and applying social media for the intended task.

SOCIAL MEDIA TECHNOLOGIES AND COPYRIGHT IN DIGITAL LIBRARIES

Digital Copyright and Intellectual Property Protection

Social media technologies are quite widely applied in digital libraries although there are numerous critical challenges and ethical issues associated with the laws of copyright and intellectual property protection. In managing digital libraries and social media technologies, information professionals have no choice but to interpret and apply the principles and practices of the copyright law and other intellectual property rights. Digital copyright law provides protection to owners and authors of online information and content from exploitation and infringement. Copyright and intellectual property protection across the world have become more difficult due to technological advances that make content sharing extremely easy and inexpensive, and due to drastic increase in utilization of Internet-related platforms like social media (Bradley, 2010).

Copyright is the law of literary and artistic property that regulates the ownership and exercise of rights derived from creative works and vests exclusive rights in the creators of works of authorship (Ginsburg, 2016). The legal protection of creative intellectual works provides bundle of exclusive legal rights to the content creator or owner (author, author's employer or someone to whom the author has assigned ownership such as publisher, gallery or estate) for a defined period of time (University of Kansas n.d). This law gives creators protection and exclusive rights to copy, distribute and sell, modify and adapt, convert to other formats, and publicly perform or display the work. Intellectual property consists of two categories or branches - industrial property and copyright. Industrial property includes patents for inventions, trademarks, industrial designs and geographical indications while copyright covers literary works (such as novels, poems and plays), films, music, artistic works (drawings, paintings, photographs and sculptures) and architectural design. The law as outlined in Article 27 of the Universal Declaration of Human Rights provides for the right to benefit from the protection of moral and material interests resulting from authorship of scientific, literary or artistic productions. The rights do not apply to the physical object in which the creation may be embodied but instead to the intellectual creation as such.

Social Media and Copyright Protection Laws

Digital social media technologies allow online communities to communicate and share content and information. Besides, digital libraries, information professionals and online communities have to follow legal, ethical and moral principles to guide use and protection of resources. Social media technologies provide legal parameters, regulations and policies that guide copyright and intellectual property protection. Fundamental copyright and intellectual property issues applied in dealing with social media technologies in digital libraries include defamation, patent, copyright, trademark and trade secrets (Blaine, 2010). Defamation elements through social media interfaces may include making false statement, published to third party without privilege or authorization, with fault amounting to at least negligence, and causing special harm or constituting defamation per se. Internet provides source of information, and therefore online communities involved in social media defamation may resort to delete or remove the content and messages but without much success. Social media platforms must provide all the necessary communication and information guidelines to avoid legal challenges from the affected or aggrieved parties. In patent protection, public disclosure and sharing of the invention through social media shall be done in accordance with the legal parameters. Digital information in any nature and form is first and foremost print publication that needs to be protected. Information professionals as the custodians of digital information must be educated and informed in applying the copyright and intellectual property protection laws.

Copyright protection deals with the twin issues of the content of the creator and the content of others. In copyright terms, the content creator is usually the original owner of the material and information per se. Protection of the content of the creator and the content of others is guided by the legal interpretation of the terms of service and copyright policies of the social media platforms. In social media platforms, the contract is guided by the terms of service (TOS) where every user agrees to abide and follow when joining, and in this case the breadth of rights transferred when agreeing to the conditions can vary substantially in each online platform (Schlackman, 2016). Media platforms provide legal regulations and policies that protect the interests of Internet and online service providers, sites and online communities from legal cases of defamation, public disclosure without authority or permission and plagiarism. In protection of the creator, social media technologies legally indicate that the information and content posted and shared belongs to the online community and not the platform. This legal covenant protects social media technologies while making online communities own the information and content posted and shared, although the platforms have rights to freely use, broadcast, reproduce and redistribute the materials while benefiting more without compensating the creators, owners or holders.

Comprehensive information from the American Library Association (2017) notes that, the Digital Millennium Copyright Act (DMCA) provides the mechanism for digital copyright and intellectual property protection and guidance on online content where the law allows the author to notify the Internet service providers (ISPs) and online service providers (OSPs) the moment one is aware of infringement of any material. This might be followed by the removal of the material or blocking the user who repeatedly infringes the copyright law. The law also protects the service providers or carrier of digital information (including libraries) from copyright liability and makes no change to the "fair use" doctrine or other information user privileges and rights. Digital copyright and intellectual property rights (IPR) depend on the laws of the individual country although the international conventions and treaties work together in harmony. In line with the fair use principle, all libraries are protected against infringement of the copyright laws provided the information is used to benefit the public or citizens and not for commercial purposes.

Intellectual property protection also deals with issues of trademark involving infringement, impersonation, parody and name squatting. In accordance with the law, it is illegal to adopt, embrace or use original or similar trademark already owned by another organization or entity. Impersonation involves the application of possible user names that confuse others about the source or dilute the trademark. Social media interfaces do not allow online communities to engage in username squatting via registering or using a name in bad faith and with intent to profit from goodwill belonging to someone else. Elements of trade secret misappropriation include existence of valid trade secret, secret disclosed or used without consent; defendant knew, or should have known that the trade secret was acquired by improper means; and harm to the owner of the trade secret. In the social media platform, the postings and sharing constitute possible scenarios of trade secret misappropriation.

Managing Digital Copyright and Intellectual Property Rights

Libraries and information organizations require significant expertise in respect to digital literacy in order to meet the requirements for the privacy and security of information without contravening copyright provisions. Information professionals should verify the source of emails before opening attachments, using antivirus software and installing such programs in timely manner (Burkell et al., 2015). Digital libraries should undertake training in information and cyber-security for the employees or staff and users in order to demonstrate awareness leading to better enactment of information security practices, adds the author. In most cases, Internet users demonstrate misunderstanding and lack of knowledge regarding aspects of online privacy including data flows, behavioral tracking, and have difficulty understanding the content of privacy policies that ostensibly disclose data collection and sharing practices. This leads them to believe that anything on the Internet is for free use irrespective of the rights of the creator. This also creates a notion that if the originators posted the information online then they have permission to the use of that contact. If need be, digital libraries can obtain permission to license and distribute content for commercial purpose so as to pay royalty to contributors (Amollo, 2011).

Digital libraries and information professionals need to establish legal parameters to guide and enforce social media policies and regulations. The policies provide the foundation for managing and addressing issues of copyright and intellectual property rights. Information professionals should educate and train fellow employees and digital natives in order to ensure friendly working environment devoid of any confrontation in relation to social media platforms and copyright and intellectual property laws. Organizational and institutional review of policies guiding copyright privileges, principles of fair use, accountability, and academic integrity and plagiarism are essential in protection of intellectual property rights. Information professionals' ethics and code of conduct enshrined in respective associations and educational programs emphasis on the need to uphold integrity and the rule of law and justice at all times no matter what or the consequences. The American Library Association has been in the forefront in developing, enforcing and advocating awareness in respect to social media and copyright laws including digital rights and privileges. Information professionals and associations across the globe have the moral authority to uphold and ensure accountability and integrity in respect to legal application of social media platforms and protection of digital copyright and intellectual property rights.

Intellectual property law provides protection and promotes innovation by balancing the benefits and rewards of the invention of the content creator and the distributor. In the emerging knowledge-based economy, intellectual property rights' awareness promotes technological innovations among the creators of information and knowledge although in the digital environment it is becoming difficult to prove rights violation whenever that occurs (Mir, 2016). Without protection, creators and inventors would derive neither benefit nor gain from new ideas from own work, and the investment made would never be compensated. Intellectual property represents valuable ownership and exclusive right to use, manufacture, reproduce and promote unique creation or idea. In the sense of wealth creation and sustainable development, intellectual property is valuable asset that is owned, sold and exchanged. Digital libraries should follow the intellectual property laws in order to offer incentives to the individual for the new creation, provide recognition to the creators and inventors, offer material rewards, and ensure availability of the genuine and original products (Mir, 2016). Copyright and intellectual property laws protects the knowledge, skills, competencies and labor of the creators and inventors of the original works and ideas in line with national and international legal parameters and treaties - Digital Millennium Copyright Act, Berne Convention and World Intellectual Property Organization. Digital libraries apply information technology and use of the Internet which gives room for reproduction, saving and distribution of culture, arts and sciences. Information professionals, in most cases, face dilemmas on matters concerning copyright and intellectual property laws because of legal issues such as software use, collection, database protection, digitization, archiving and distribution of protected works. The risks of copyright infringement sometimes prevent digital libraries from creating new works while utilizing new technologies.

CONCLUSION

Fundamental application of social media interfaces is normally guided by principles and regulations at individual or personal and institutional level. Principle knowledge and understanding at the individual level entails that the online participant and community must make the right decision using the social media platforms either for private or publication purpose. Individuals including professionals normally fail to observe the simple basic rules of using social media platforms for the intended purpose while also maintaining different accounts. Institutions and organizations must provide the necessary legal regulations and standard policies to guide misuse of social media applications if inappropriate messages and information are broadcast and shared, and the measures to take should such as an embarrassing moment and action happen. Increased emphasis on social media platforms have created tremendous copyright impact that digital libraries and information professionals need to address. Different social media technologies provide potential opportunities and benefits with limited applications depending on the nature of the platform. In addition to massive data and information, lack of formal standard and structure of metadata makes organization and searching of digital materials difficult, for instance, use of shared terms and concepts with common phrases (e-information and e-information). In particular, openness and freeness of the social media applications need special attention and vigilance to provide the necessary security, safety and privacy to online communities. Trendiness and the changing nature of social media platforms are the biggest challenges that face digital libraries and information professionals perhaps than ever before.

REFERENCES

American Library Association (2017). *DMCA: The Digital Millennium Copyright Act.* Author.

Amollo, B. (2011). Digitization for libraries in Kenya. *Second International Conference on African Digital Libraries and Archives (ICADLA-2).*

Blaine, T. B. (2010). *Social Media: Implications for intellectual property law.* Syracuse, NY: PLLC.

Bonsón, E., & Flores, F. (2011). Social media and corporate dialogue: The response of global financial institutions. *Online Information Review, 35*(1), 34–49. doi:10.1108/14684521111113579

Bradley, S. S. (2010). *Copyright protection in the digital age.* Association of Corporate Counsel. Retrieved from http://www.acc.com/legalresources/quickcounsel/icpituscaeu.cfm

Burkell, J. A., Fortier, A., Di Valentino, L. & Roberts, S. T. (2015). *Enhancing key digital literacy skills: Information privacy, information security, and copyright/intellectual property.* Library and Information Science Publications.

Candela, L., Athanasopoulos, G., Castelli, D., El Raheb, K. & Innocenti, P. (2011). *The digital library reference model.* London: DL.org Project Deliverable.

Collins, G., & Haase, A. Q. (2012). Social media and academic libraries: Current trends and future challenges. *Proceedings of the Association for Information Science and Technology*, *49*(1), 1–4. doi:10.1002/meet.14504901272

Davis, C. H., Deil-Amen, R., Rios-Aguilar, C., & Manuel, G. C. (2012). *Social media in higher education: A literature review and research directions.* Center for the Study of Higher Education, University of Arizona and Claremont Graduate University.

Deng, L., & Tavares, N. J. (2013). From Moodle to Facebook: Exploring students' motivation and experiences in online communities. *Computers & Education*, *68*, 167–176. doi:10.1016/j.compedu.2013.04.028

Determann, L. (2012). Social media privacy: A dozen myths and facts. *Stanford Technology Law*, *7*, 1–14.

Fenwick, T. (2016). Social media, professionalism and higher education: A sociomaterial consideration. *Studies in Higher Education*, *41*(4), 664–677. doi:10.1080/03075079.2014.942275

Gall, D. P. (2010). Librarian like a Rockstar: Using your personal Brand to promote your services and reach distance users. *Journal of Library Administration*, *50*(5 & 6).

Gallardo, R. (2013). *Social Media for libraries.* Social Media Use. Retrieved from https://www.webjunction.org/events/webjunction/Library_Social _Media_Use.html

Gamboa, A. M., & Gonçalves, H. M. (2014). Customer loyalty through social networks: Lessons from Zara on Facebook. *Business Horizons*, *57*(6), 709–717. doi:10.1016/j.bushor.2014.07.003

Ginsburg, J. C. (2016). Overview of Copyright Law: Forthcoming, Oxford Handbook of Intellectual Property. Columbia Public Law Research Paper No. 14-518.

Greysen, S. R., Kind, T., & Chretien, K. C. (2010). Online professionalism and the mirror of social media. *Journal of General Internal Medicine*, *25*(11), 1227–1229. doi:10.100711606-010-1447-1 PMID:20632121

Gu, F., & Widen-Wulff, G. (2011). Scholarly communication and possible changes in the context of social media: A Finnish case study. *The Electronic Library*, *29*(6), 762–776. doi:10.1108/02640471111187999

Heap, T., & Minocha, S. (2012). An empirically grounded framework to guide blogging for digital scholarship. *Research in Learning Technology Proceeding of the 2012 Conference.* 10.3402/rlt.v20i0.19195

Iris, X. (2014). Social media application in digital libraries. *Online Information Review*, *38*(4), 502–523. doi:10.1108/OIR-11-2013-0261

Kassens-Noor, E. (2012). Twitter as a teaching practice to enhance active and informal learning in higher education: The case of sustainable tweets. *Active Learning in Higher Education*, *13*(1), 9–21. doi:10.1177/1469787411429190

Lee, J., & Kim, S. (2011). Exploring the role of social networks in affective organizational commitment: Network centrality, strength of ties, and structural holes. *American Review of Public Administration, 41*(2), 205–223. doi:10.1177/0275074010373803

Makori, E. O. (2012). Bridging the information gap with the patrons in university libraries in Africa. *Library Review, 61*(1), 30–40. doi:10.1108/00242531211207406

Mir, F. M. (2016). Intellectual property rights issues and challenges of academic libraries in digital environment. *International Journal of Computer Engineering In Research Trends, 3*(12), 639–644.

Mishra, R. K. (2016). Digital libraries: Definitions, issues, and challenges. *Innovative Journal of Education, 4*(3), 1–3.

Piyawan, S., Kulthida, T., & Cholabhat, V. (2011). Factors affecting customer relationship management practices in Thai academic libraries. *The International Information & Library Review, 43*(4), 221–229. doi:10.1080/10572317.2011.10762904

Schlackman, S. (2016). *Losing copyrights through social media.* Academic Press.

Spector, N. D., Martz, P. S., & Levine, L. J. (2010). E-Professionalism: Challenges in the age of information. *The Journal of Pediatrics, 156*(3), 345–346. doi:10.1016/j.jpeds.2009.12.047 PMID:20176180

Sranamkam, S. (2012). *Losing copyrights through social media.* Art Law Journal.

University of Kansas. (n.d.). *Information paper on copyright law.* Retrieved from http://www2.ku.edu/~counsel/_pdf/Information_Paper_on_Copyright_Law.pdf

Waycott, J., Dalgarno, B., Kennedy, G., & Bishop, A. (2012). Making science real: Photo-sharing in biology and chemistry. *Research in Learning Technology Proceeding of the 2012 Conference.*

ADDITIONAL READING

Cervone, H. F. (2017). Evaluating social media presence. *Digital Library Perspectives, 33*(1), 2–7. doi:10.1108/DLP-10-2016-0040

Henner, T. (2014). From the Literature. *Medical Reference Services Quarterly, 33*(2), 227–234. doi:10.1080/02763869.2014.897526 PMID:25023012

How We Operate the Digital Branch. (2012).. . *Library Technology Reports, 48*(6), 16–18.

Kosztyánné Mátrai, R. (2018). How to make an electronic library accessible. *The Electronic Library, 36*(4), 620–632. doi:10.1108/EL-07-2017-0143

Media, S. (2012).. . *Library Technology Reports, 48*(6), 23–27.

Milone, Hill, N. (2014). How Libraries Are Changing to Accommodate Patron Wants and Needs. *Public Libraries, 53*(3), 14–17.

Schrier, R. A. (2011). Digital Librarianship & Social Media: The Digital Library as Conversation Facilitator. *D-Lib Magazine*, *17*(7/8), 1–7.

Wilson, J. (2013). Ultimate Outreach: Exploring the Outreach Sea within the Engineering, Math and Physical Sciences Libraries at Cornell University. *Science & Technology Libraries*, *32*(1), 68–83. doi: 10.1080/0194262X.2012.758459

Section 2

Areas of Concern in the Use of Social Media

Chapter 3
Finding Your Voice:
Developing a Content Strategy for Social Media That Works!

Karen L. Yacobucci
NYU School of Medicine, USA

Stephen Maher
NYU School of Medicine, USA

ABSTRACT

This chapter aims to provide an indispensable introduction to content marketing based on industry best-practices and help academic libraries navigate this essential but often overlooked marketing practice. The chapter will begin by addressing some of the consistent challenges organizations have starting their social media marketing campaigns and developing a social media strategy. Next, the chapter will focus on defining the tone and voice of their social media messages. Then, it will discuss sustaining the campaign by curating content and avoiding "content fatigue." Finally, the authors share an example of how an academic library but them into practice. They are confident this chapter will give academic librarians the vocabulary and techniques they need to talk and walk their way through meaningful and engaging marketing campaigns for their libraries using social media.

INTRODUCTION

In 1996, Bill Gates wrote and published an essay titled "Content is King" where he declared the Internet was a "marketplace of ideas, experiences, and products-a marketplace of content" (Evans, 2017). Since that time, the predictions Gates made regarding the importance of content on the Internet have largely been accurate. Unlike television or radio, where consumers have advertisements interrupt their entertainment experience, consumers willfully search for content on the Internet. This drive to seek out and consume information by choice has made way for the rise of content marketing.

DOI: 10.4018/978-1-5225-8097-3.ch003

According to the Content Marketing Institute, "Content marketing is the strategic marketing approach of creating and distributing valuable, relevant and consistent content to attract and acquire a clearly defined audience – with the objective of driving profitable customer action" (Content Marketing Institute, 2018).

Simply put, Content Marketing strategically positions content in front of the consumer. But what exactly is content?

Depending upon one's work, content can mean a lot of different things. In the field of marketing and communication, however, content has a very specific meaning and can be described as "the information and experiences that are directed towards an end-user or audience" (Lee, 2013). Other fields see content as an information exchange. It is the tangible information communicated through any point of contact between two or more entities; Business to Consumer (B2C), Business to Business (B2B), and in our case, Library to End-User. Yet it is important to emphasize, the content experience not only comes from the exchange itself, it's also the emotional value that the intended audience derives from that exchange.

With the ever-increasing rise and popularity of various social media platforms, it's no wonder that content marketing and social media seem synonymous. Successful content marketing almost always includes a strong social media component, and for the purpose of this chapter, focus is placed on the creation of a content strategy for social media.

BACKGROUND

One of the challenges in surveying the implementation of content strategy in academic libraries is a matter of terminology. The term "content strategy" has been attributed to web site governance rather than marketing. Rebecca Blakiston has penned a number of articles on web content strategies for academic libraries whereby content is "curated Web content that promotes, explains, and instructs users about various services and resources" (Blakiston, 2013). And Ilka Datig's article envisions "content strategy as a holistic tool that encompasses all library outreach platforms, including websites, social media, and other digital and print materials" (Datig, 2018). Combining web content with marketing is perhaps unavoidable as social media has become more pervasive but, as Darlene Fichter and Jeff Wisniewski assert in their article,

The world of content has changed. Regardless of the specific platforms, tools, or technologies, libraries need to strategically create and deliver content in ways that are efficient, effective, sustainable, and engaging. (Fichter & Wisniewski, 2014)

Although to date literature on academic libraries looking at content strategy strictly in terms of marketing purposes has been scant, librarians have written about marketing and outreach for some time. A recent white paper reported the results from a survey administered by the Association of College and Research Libraries' (ACRL) Marketing and Outreach Information Group. The survey found that many academic libraries do not have dedicated staff for marketing and that when outreach campaigns have launched they have not been analyzed to determine their impact (Park & Dantus, 2018). These results reinforce findings from a study conducted almost 10 years ago wherein although "libraries participate in different types of outreach, they often do so in informal and ad hoc ways without the benefit of systematic and well thought out outreach programs" (Carter & Seaman, 2011). Similar to the term "content strategy", the literature found on the concept of "user persona" is not directly associated with marketing.

The concept is identified in the context of User-centered Design (UCD), a "process focused on optimizing interfaces" typically rather than marketing or outreach (Tempelman-Kluit & Pearce, 2014). Even then it is admitted that the development of user personas based of common needs and patterns among library patrons is rare (Zaugg & Rackham, 2016). These examples support the need to more closely examine the content strategy life cycle in the context of an academic library. The next section will recount a case study where an academic library used the social media platform Twitter to promote scholarly communications among the institution's research faculty.

There are many examples in the literature of academic libraries utilizing Twitter, including the institution in the aforementioned case study (Cuddy, Graham, & Morton-Owens, 2010). Of the web 2.0 social media platforms, Twitter is one of the most widely adopted among academic libraries for marketing purposes (Del Bosque, Leif, & Skarl, 2012; Gunton & Davis, 2012; Milstein, 2009). One of the features of Twitter is the ease in which users can analyze the effectiveness and dissemination of their messages - tweets and retweets. A study of academic libraries at Drexel University examined the account types that retweeted library content - grouping them into categories (e.g. librarians, students, scholars, and university organizations) (Kim, Abels, & Yang, 2012). Another study of Twitter followers from a library at Texas A&M University was found to provide valuable insight into the accounts that receive library information (Sewell, 2013). And libraries have since reported ways to further investigate and understand their Twitter followers and its impact on how it uses its messaging via Twitter (Shulman, Yep, & Tomé, 2015). This would suggest, although not stated in the framework of the content strategy, academic libraries are including Measurement in its use of Twitter.

MAIN FOCUS OF THE CHAPTER

Content Strategy

In order for a Library to successfully translate their message to its intended audience, a comprehensive content strategy will need to be established, specific to the unique, fast paced, and ever-changing needs of social media. There are many different ways to approach content strategy, and this process will undoubtedly go through a series of refinements until an individual library can identify what works best for them. Regardless of whatever strategy is employed, at its core should be four distinct phases which encompass a complete content strategy lifecycle: assessment, creation, promotion, and measurement. Figure 1 illustrates the perpetual flow of a content strategy lifecycle.

Assessment

Before content can be developed for social media channels, completing two initial actions are recommended. The first involves conducting an audit of the current social media landscape and selecting channels that would resonate with the identified target audience. The second action involves evaluating the successes and struggles a library may have already had with social media. Ilka Datig of Nazareth College emphasizes that a library's "first step in applying content strategy is to get the lay of the land by conducting various assessments" which includes a comprehensive content audit (Datig, 2018).

Figure 1. Content strategy lifecycle

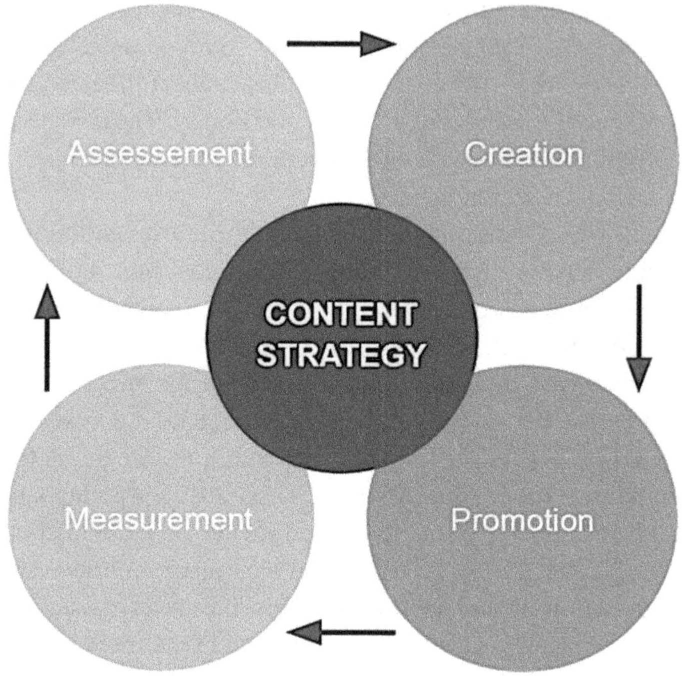

Survey the Landscape

Surveying the current social media landscape can help identify which channels are popular with an intended audience as well as the style of content that they engage with most or has the most use-value for them. Datig writes, "librarians should consider what type of content is most effective at reaching users and creating engagement" (p.66, 2018). For example, if it is determined that users are engaging more with photo or video-sharing platforms, exploring social networks that capitalize on that format, like Instagram or YouTube, could be a better source for sharing as well as a better allocation of a library's time and effort in content creation. In addition, if it is discovered that users seem more interested in sharing music or book recommendations, Spotify and GoodReads would prove to be more meaningful channels for those users.

Libraries that have trouble identifying their audience can learn from organizations similar to theirs. For example, a small academic library looking to jump into social media, but not sure how to begin, can easily start by identifying other academic libraries who already have a strong and successful social media presence and adopt the same platforms and similarly structured content. According to the Pew Research Center, "a majority of Americans use Facebook and YouTube, but young adults are especially heavy users of Snapchat and Instagram" (Pew Research Center, 2018). A survey conducted by the Association of College and Research Libraries (ACRL) discovered similar results. Sabine Dantus and Jennifer Park write, "not surprisingly, this number aligns with the results of this survey, which show Facebook as the most-used social media platform among academic libraries" (Park & Dantus, 2018).

Evaluate Success

The second phase of assessment involves evaluating what a library has already done and identifying the areas with which they have been successful or struggled in regards to social media. Successful social networks are able to consistently engage their users. Although engagement can be a one-off interaction with an audience through social likes and shares it is also the open line of communication developed with an audience over time. In addition to one-off interactions, the way in which an audience engages and communicates through social media should be noted; Are they asking questions? Are they making comments? Which styles of content are receiving more likes and shares? Increased user engagement is a factor which can positively influence a user's perception of brand trust in an online environment (Dessart, Veloutsou, & Morgan-Thomas, 2016).

Fortunately, most social media platforms have some form of performance analytics which makes it easy to identify topic trends, top performing posts, likes, social shares, etcetera. Undoubtedly, content that is consistent, clear, and meaningful will increase the number of followers any network has, as well as increase engagement as is evidenced by performance analytics. When a social network is struggling, performance analytics suffer and less engagement will be seen from users. Social networks that are created and left to languish will fail at drawing the attention of their intended audience.

This two-pronged approach to auditing social media content allows academic libraries to take a closer look and what has and has not worked in their current plan and helps to identify which digital assets or social platforms are best suited for their library's needs.

Creation

After the social media assessment phase, development of content can begin. The creation phase of social media strategy involves identifying the target audience as well as planning and brainstorming content suitable for that audience.

Identify the Target Audience

If a library knows who their target audience is, they can better develop content which is designed to specifically speak to the needs, wants, and desires of that audience. The librarians who manage social media channels successfully have a firm understanding of their audience and are able to craft unique content for them. Their social media strategy has more user engagement, resulting in a a stronger library brand.

One straightforward way to create this level of specified content is to develop a set of user-personas intended to identify the unique drivers of target audiences. User-personas have long been used by web designers and usability experts in order to increase the quality and effectiveness of their work. Now more than ever, social media content managers are using this same practice in order to better identify and communicate with their audience. Essentially, a user-persona is a fictional representation of an ideal user that establishes the who, what, and sometimes the where of any particular group of individuals who make up the target audience or end-user.

For example, a basic user-persona which might be developed for an academic library could be a Research Scientist, who is looking for creative approaches to communicating data. In that simple declaration, the who (the Research Scientist) and the what (looking for creative approaches to communicating data) are established, and specific content which meets that user's needs can be more easily developed. User-personas can be as basic or as detailed as needed. More detailed user-personas might include a picture, demographic information, level of skill with a variety of technology, reading habits, frustrations, and more. An example of a basic user-persona is illustrated in Figure 2.

For some, creating user-personas may seem like an unneeded extra step, or a distraction that merely detracts from getting the job done, but when carefully created and used to their fullest potential, user-personas can be a powerful tool. Librarian Tara J. Brigham from the Winn-Dixie Foundation Medical Library writes, "personas can assist library staff in gaining insight to what users need and want. This can not only help improve the library's services and access to resources but also might create loyal library users" (Brigham, 2013).

Content Planning and Brainstorming

As previously mentioned, during the content strategy assessment phase, social media platforms best suited to meet the needs of the library should be identified. Different platforms allow for communication of different types of information and in different ways. Twitter, for example, is a great way to communicate small bursts of information under 280 characters, while Facebook doesn't have limits on the amount of text that can be published. Spotify caters to music lovers, and Instagram primarily delivers information by way of images. Whichever platform is used, content needs to be created which is suitable for that platform.

The following tools and concepts can be used to streamline the content creation process:

Figure 2. User-persona overview

User-Persona Overview

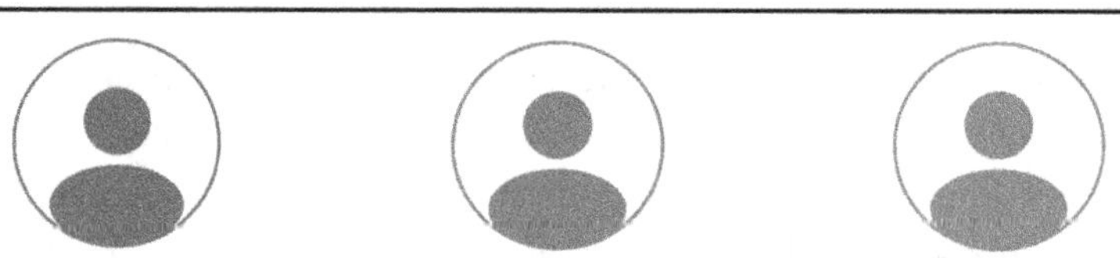

Persona	Research Scientist	Student	Professor
Goals/Objectives	Looking for creative approaches to communicating data.	Wants to be able to access Library subscribed textbooks from off-campus.	Needs to provide access to relevant coursework in an online environment throughout the semester
Challenges	Has some experience with data visualization tools, but wants to explore using more advanced software for data visualization	Does not know where to find textbooks in the Library catalog.	Looking for a streamlined approach to communicating course material needs with the library.

Cross-Channel Marketing and Content Development

Simply put, cross-channel marketing, also known as multi-channel marketing, is all about engaging with users across multiple digital channels and on any device, be it a laptop, smartphone, or tablet. At its core, this type of marketing aims to provide an integrated experience for users. When thinking about cross-channel marketing it's important to remember how this effects content development. As previously mentioned, libraries that have more than one social media platform will want to push the same content across all platforms, but content must be designed to fulfill the technical requirements or limitations of each platform. For example, an ideal size for an Instagram square image will be roughly 1080px x 1080px, whereas the ideal size for an image used in a Twitter post would be around 1024px x 512px (Hootsuite, 2018).

When designing content, libraries need to consider the ways in which their audience will engage with those platforms. Ensuring that content can easily be read and understood via mobile devices, desktop computers, or any conceivable device can bring libraries even closer to their users.

Editorial Calendar

Establishing and adhering to an editorial calendar might seem like extra work, but it's a great way to manage the full content lifecycle and maintain quality control. After content has been generated and approved for publication, it should be scheduled in an editorial calendar. Content can be scheduled to coincide with important dates relevant to the library or its parent institution, as well as national observances. Using and adhering to an editorial calendar can also prevent overlapping content from being published, help maintain a consistent editorial tone, and establish a structured workflow.

Furthermore, if balancing multiple social media platforms, an editorial calendar provides the added benefit of tracking which pieces of content have been posted and which have not, all visible in one location. Much like user-personas, editorial calendars can be as basic or complex as you need them to be. Below is an example of a basic editorial calendar created as an Excel spreadsheet.

Figure 3. Editorial calendar example

Author	Description	Content (cut/paste)	Attachments	Platform/Digital Touchpoints	Posting Date	Observances
Karen	Go Red For Womens Heart Health	NYU Health Sciences Library wears red for women's heart health! #GoRed #GoRedForWomen #WearRedDay	<go red image>	Twitter, Facebook	2/2/18	National Wear Red Day, Groundhog Day
					2/3/18	
					2/4/18	
Stephen	#NYUBragMonday	Spotlight on @nyulangone faculty article in @Nature Translational Psychiatry. Chemistry-based molecular signature underlying the atypia of #clozapine http://bit.ly/2m1eYb0 #NYUBragMonday	<image>	Twitter	2/5/18	
Lita		Make an art button that's yours to keep! Join us in the Farkas Breezeway on 2/8. Educators from The Metropolitan Museum of Art will have a table where you can make an art button from your favorite Met image! 2/8/18: 9:00-11:00AM Come and learn about CIAC's Reflecting Art in Nursing Practice spring series!	<image>		2/6/18	
					2/8/18	
Karen	#WeekendReads	"You cannot separate passion from pathology any more than you can separate a person's spirit from his body." [i]Letters to a Young Doctor[/i] by Richard Selzer. Find this book and more at the Sid and Ruth Lapidus Library! #WeekendReads	<image>	Intranet	2/9/18	
Lita		Nurses, want to increase your advanced searching skills? Come to the workshop Tuesday February 13: 9:00AM - Finding the Best Nursing Evidence Every Time. You'll get hands-on practice to bring your searching skills to the next level! Location is Lapidus Library, Consultation Room. Please sign up in FOCUS for 1 hour of CE. (It's a really good class!)	<image>	Intranet, Twitter, Facebook	2/9/18	

Social Media Management Systems

Libraries working with 3 or more platforms may want to invest in a Social Media Management System in order to streamline their workflow. Social Media Management Systems are designed to support social network integrations from a variety of social networking services (i.e., Facebook, Twitter, Instagram, LinkedIn,) which helps to systematize content creation by making modification, scheduling, and publishing easier. Hootsuite, Sprout Social, and Buffer are all examples of social media management systems designed to perform these essential functions all from the convenience of one dashboard.

Promotion

After content has been created and perfected to reach target audiences, developed for one or multiple social media platforms, and built into an editorial calendar, it's ready to be shared with the world.

Here is another area where early stage assessment comes full circle. During that process, libraries may be able to more clearly identify days and times when their audience was more likely to engage with social media. It should be noted that engagement rates do vary between platforms and industry, which means that the best time for a nonprofit organization to post on Instagram will most likely be different for an academic university who posts on Twitter. Experimentation is encouraged when trying to identify best days and times to post. Combinations of different days and times may yield different results and should be noted. In most cases, engagement rates increase when people have down time. That could be at 5am, when they are just waking up and getting ready to start their day, between 12 and 2pm, when they are sitting down to have their lunch, or 5pm when they are getting ready to leave work or commuting home. There are many guides online which can provide input on when to promote content, but ultimately a library's own analytics and measurement will be the best guide. Sharing the right kind of content at the best times ensures that it can be viewed by a larger number of people. Naturally, the more content is viewed, the more chance for engagement it has. Dalal, O'Hanlon, and Yacobucci write, "the more mentions, shares, reposts, retweets, likes, and reviews your content receives, the stronger your brand becomes and the more likely it is your content will continue to be shared and engaged with" (Dalal, O'Hanlon, & Yacobucci, 2017).

Scheduling posts in advance is a great way to automate the publishing process. A social media management system is designed to scheduled content and publish across multiple platforms all at once.

In addition to posting the right content at the right time, many social media platforms provide an option for paid promotion. Paid promotion allows for organizations to pay a platform to advertise specific content as a means to reach a wider audience. Paid promotion is a great way to get content in front of a wider audience, but as the name implies, it does come with a cost.

Measurement

Understanding analytics is essential for auditing, assessing, and improving the performance of social media platforms. Being able to measure the success of these platforms is just as important as the content itself.

Different organizations care about different types of analytics, which is why defining a success matric is recommended. A success matrix combines all the data that is meaningful for communicating and measuring the perceived success or health of an organizations' social media content. This can include the amount of traffic the platform gains in a particular timeframe, the number of social shares, engagement (audience interaction), mentions, influencers, top content, and more.

Different social media platforms report different analytics, and it can be easy to get caught up in a lot of differing data points. Value may not be found in collecting each and every data point, but Libraries should be looking at more than one at any given time, since no single analytic is enough to understand how an audience perceives a library's brand. For example, if a library is interested in knowing if their audience prefers video content over other types of content, they may focus on analytics for most popular posts and social shares, and identify which of those posts included a video and if they outperformed content which did not include a video.

CASE STUDY: CONTENT STRATEGY IN PRACTICE AT THE NYU HEALTH SCIENCES LIBRARY

The following is a real-world example of content strategy in action at an academic library.

Faculty publication metrics had been a growing service among academic libraries (Vieira et al, 2014). Libraries collect data on their institution's faculty publications as a way to demonstrate institutional memory, support promotion, and tenure discussions. Knowledge of this scholarly activity has more than internal value though. By using social media the library can promote these publications not only as a way to market the institution's research productivity but also the library as the means by which people can access and obtain this research.

Several commercial databases offer customizations for users to be alerted when articles on a specific subject area have been published. Databases like Web of Science and Scopus allow authors to set alerts on their own published articles to know when they have been cited in another publication, informing them about the legacy of their research. Government databases like NIH RePORTER allow institutions to track the research productivity associated with grants they have obtained. These customizations can be powerful tools for libraries to develop greater institutional memory on the publications authored by its faculty and students.

As the authors have explained, content marketing is "the information and experiences that are directed towards an end-user or audience". How does information about recent publications authored by individuals affiliated with the academic institution meet this definition and who is the end-user or audience? The following library's approach to content strategy through it's distinctive four phases: assessment, creation, promotion, and measurement attempts to answer these questions.

Assessment

The NYU Health Sciences Library (NYUHSL) is the medical library for the New York University School of Medicine and NYU Langone Health, a network of hospitals and ambulatory care centers across the five boroughs of New York City, Long Island, and beyond. The medical school was ranked third in the nation according to U.S. News and World Report 2018-2019 'Best Graduate Schools' for research, and has won numerous awards over the past several years (U.S. News & World Report, 2018).

In a major metropolitan area like New York where advertising, marketing, and public relations are well-established industries, NYU Langone Health has launched several high profile advertising campaigns to promote its hospital and medical facilities. They have also undergone a major reorganization of its websites to ensure consistency of font, color, and other design elements that define the current NYU Langone Health and NYU School of Medicine brand.

This rebranding process has extended to social media. There is an NYU Langone Health twitter account and many of the research centers and academic departments have accounts as well. Although a comprehensive count has not been taken, several faculty members have twitter accounts that promote their professional and personal research, conference appearances, and article publications.

For almost two decades scholarly research has been published electronically, transitioning away from the print journal or book. The publishers of those print journals, however, have maintained much of the scholarly communications market by successfully transforming its print journals into online or e-journals while keeping the reputation of the journal's name and associations with quality peer-review and editorial practices.

Perhaps one of the most significant changes with this transition from print to electronic publishing is the ability for publishers and large-scale subscribers (i.e. libraries) to track how frequently a journal is read. Internet metrics such as clicks and page-views tell a publisher which articles are garnering the most attention from its audience. These statistics have informed decisions to launch new publications. For libraries, which subscribe to many journals from a single publisher, the usage statistics it receives indicate which journals are more frequently read, informing its decisions on which titles to renew for the following year.

Building upon these Internet 1.0 metrics, social media – and its new platforms for people to discuss, share and create content – introduced ways to deepen the public's engagement with scholarly communications. The most well-known metrics for tabulating how articles are discussed and shared via social media comes from article-level metrics called as altmetrics and are collected by an organization with the same name. The qualitative data Altmetrics (the company) collects can tell authors and publishers how often their content (journal articles, datasets) are being discussed on the Internet. These altmetrics create an impression of the interest surrounding the content. It does not tell the whole story but it can serve as the starting point for understanding an article's impact on scholars in its discipline and broader scholarly community.

Beyond utilizing altmetrics, many publishers have turned to social media as a means to promote its content; new articles, conference proceedings, and newer nontraditional means of scholarly communications such as podcasts. While almost every major academic scholarly publisher has its own Twitter account, many of their individual journal titles also have accounts as well.

For these reasons, NYUHSL chose Twitter as the primary social media platform for this campaign. As a large-scale academic library, NYUHSL subscribes to thousands of journals in the field of health science and STEM related subjects. Promoting faculty publications reinforced one of the central missions of the Library, to provide access to library subscribed content. The next challenge was to identify the best way to share content which reinforces that message to the NYU Langone Health community. Choosing articles authored by researchers at NYU School of Medicine and NYU Langone Health provided a direct approach for this challenge. What made the articles relevant for the NYUHSL Twitter feed was its focus on who authored it, not necessarily what the article was about or its relative meaning to its disciplines. The campaign, therefore, would have two core messages; celebrate the research authored by NYU faculty and emphasize that the library provides access to that research.

Creation

When NYUHSL first launched this Twitter campaign, tweets were limited to 140 characters. Because of this, the Library needed to be economical with what would be said about a particular article. At the same time, the Library also wanted the tweets to denote a human touch rather than an automated copy and paste of an article title and its URL. The Library also wanted tweets to have visual impact, utilizing any images or figures from an article, in order for it to stand out as an end-user scrolled through their Twitter feed. And lastly, the Library wanted to make these tweets engaging by tagging relevant individuals such as the article author(s), using a distinct hashtag, and linking back to our parent institution by always including their Twitter handle.

Before NYUHSL could promote the articles, they first had to find them. For this, the Library utilized bibliographic databases that track publications across multiple publishers and collect extensive metadata about each article. NYUHSL wanted to track articles based on the author's affiliation. If an article was published by an author affiliated with New York University, the bibliographic databases would make that clear. The two databases used for this project were Elsevier's Scopus and Web of Science by Truven Analytics. Although both yielded similar results, in time, it was decided to use only Scopus because of its user interface and ability to easily set email alerts when new articles were added to the database that matched the Library's search criteria.

At least once per week NYUHSL librarians would receive an email with a list of articles co-authored by someone affiliated with NYU. From here the librarians would review the list looking for notable journal titles (e.g. JAMA, The New England Journal of Medicine, Academic Medicine, etc.). Next, the librarians would identify the articles which had significant NYU contribution. This was mainly accomplished by identifying whether or not an NYU author was listed as a first, second, or last author. Finally, catalog holdings were checked to ensure that the Library had subscribed access to the article. If each of these criteria were met, then the content would be written and the Twitter post would be scheduled in the Library's editorial calendar.

Each tweet began with the text, "Spotlight on @nyulangone faculty" (or research), and would go on to briefly describe the article. Occasionally, an article would be authored by someone affiliated with a department or lab with its own Twitter account. In those cases, we would replace the NYU Langone handle with that department or lab's twitter handle.

If an individual author had their own Twitter account, librarians would include that handle as well. In order to identify whether or not an author had a personal Twitter account, librarians would search for their name using Twitter's internal search function. Occasionally adding an "MD" to the search would help narrow the results. Even if a person's name was found on Twitter, account descriptions would be read in order to ensure the account actually belonged to the author. The same process was applied to journals as well. If an article was published in a journal with a Twitter account, then the post would also include the journal's handle.

When describing the article, usually a variation of the title would be enough, but occasionally the abstract would have to be paraphrased. As the article's description was written, possible trending Twitter themes would also be identified and any relevant hashtags would be included. If some were found, a hashtag would be placed in front of the word. The description beginning with "Spotlight on" would then look like something this:

Figure 4. Spotlight Tweet example

As previously mentioned, not only was it important to highlight the NYU faculty author, it was equally important to highlight the Library provided access to the article. Including a call-to-action encouraging individuals to read the article provided an opportunity to emphasize the content's connection to the Library. This call-to-action came in the form of a link to the article. Because Library subscribed resources are not available to the public, there was a lot to consider with this inclusion. Each NYU faculty publication tweet had to provide a link to the Library subscribed full-text article, but librarians also had to be cognizant that the general public could also view this content. This could be problematic for the general public attempting to access library subscribed content. Most of the content licensed by NYUHSL has its web proxy protocol embedded into the URL. This protocol prompts individuals to authenticate with institutional login credentials in order to gain access to subscribed content. Although this solved the issue of providing access to authorized individuals, it was a concern that it could have the negative effect of alienating or frustrating the general public. For this reason, it was decided rather than direct users to the article they would be directed to the article's PubMed record.

Maintained by the United States' National Library of Medicine (NLM), PubMed is a search engine for references and abstracts to journal articles and other scholarly publications in the health sciences. Given the size and scale of Pubmed, with nearly 28 million records and the addition of over 500,000 new records every year, the Library was confident that all of the selected articles would be found in PubMed. An additional benefit of directing the Twitter audience to an article's PubMed record was that NLM allows libraries to directly link to subscribed full-text from within the PubMed database by way of OpenURL. OpenURL lets libraries connect users to its subscribed journals through its standardized encoding format and its placement in information platforms (i.e. catalogs and databases) on the Internet (Needleman, 2002). Simply put, although PubMed records can be viewed by anyone, OpenURL lets libraries connect users to its subscribed journals.

Once it was identified that the Library would point users to the article's PubMed record, the URL itself needed to be considered. URLs vary from publisher to publisher. This variety could impact the character limit of each tweet. Using a URL shortening service like Bit.ly would not only decrease the

Figure 5. PubMed OpenURL example

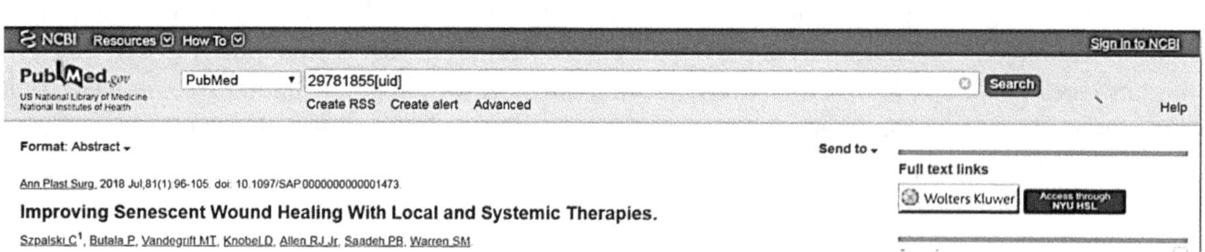

length of the URL, but also provide another measurable analytic for tracking whether or not the URLs were actually being clicked on.

Promotion

The library's Twitter account is used to promote a number of library services, such as classes, newly acquired resources, as well as celebrate the work of librarians and staff in supporting the research and education mission of the institution. Based on the Scopus email alerts, the Library had the potential to send tweets about NYU affiliated authored publications multiple times a day, over multiple days. This practice though would risk overwhelming the purpose of the library's Twitter account and, to be quite candid, despite the workflows set in place to create each tweet, would be too time-consuming for librarians to maintain in conjunction with other responsibilities. It was for these reasons that it was decided to schedule these tweets once per week, each Monday.

After refining and scheduling the tweets, the next step was to put internal content management workflows into practice. NYUHSL had already been using the social media dashboard application, TweetDeck, for managing the Library twitter account, but for the purposes of this campaign the Library took advantage of its scheduled tweets feature. With this feature, tweets about articles authored by NYU faculty and researchers could easily be scheduled in advance. This was especially effective when the alert emails contained more than one article that fit the criteria for promotion.

Figure 6. Full Tweet example

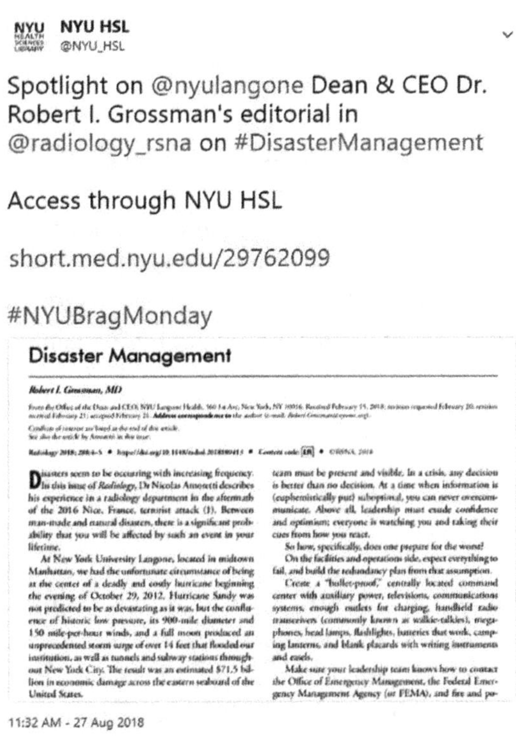

Figure 7. Full Tweet example 2

Another benefit of TweetDeck is its ease for adding images to a tweet. Occasionally an article would contain an interesting graphic, like a chart, figure, x-ray, or MRI scan. Images can positively impact user engagement with social media posts. When an image was found in an article, it would be saved, and later included as an attachment to the post via TweetDeck. If the article did not contain a suitable image, often times an image of the Journal's cover would be included.

Over time as theses tweets were perfected, the Library was easily able to coordinate tweets alongside national observances, like Women's History Month. The Library would also plan tweets to coincide with events happening at NYU Langone Health and NYU School of Medicine.

Measurement

One of Twitter's most exciting advantages is how quickly one can witness the impact of their tweets. Whether a tweet is liked or retweeted, it can quickly be identified that what you wrote or shared has been viewed.

Since the campaign began in December 2015, NYUHSL has posted over 140 tweets as part of the faculty publication campaign. Based on Twitter analytics, on average each of these tweets have been liked 1.04 times and retweeted approximately 0.46 times. These may not seem like large numbers, but since incorporating faculty publications into the NYUHSL social media strategy, followers, profile visits, and mentions have all increased dramatically.

Because a link manager was also used for embedding URLs in each post, the Library has been able to track total clicks by date for each URL. The most clicked URL (http://short.med.nyu.edu/28541383) having been clicked on over 130 times. This same tweet was also liked 6 times and retweeted 4 times.

The purpose of the campaign has been twofold, (1) celebrate the research authored by our NYU faculty and (2) emphasize the library provides access to that research. While this campaign has been successful in meeting these goals, there were other benefits in launching this campaign. Tracking an institution's research publications is important for building and maintaining its reputation. It is also important for the authors whose productivity is measured to some degree by their scholarly activity. Although our library was already active in the process of collecting data on the institution's published research and the authors associated with it, the twitter campaign gave its librarians an opportunity to get more familiar with that research and the individual researchers and faculty involved. This gave its librarians a deeper sense of institutional memory seeing more details in the raw numbers such as total publications and citation count.

Another benefit to the campaign has been how it introduced librarians to how Twitter can work as a social marketing tool. Although none of the tweets went viral by industry standards, the Library gained a better understanding of the reach of Twitter and how by promoting the research of its institution's community of scholars. It also strategically positioned the Library as a knowledge-based organization of value. NYU authors with Twitter accounts were able to see that their library recognized their research and valued their contributions to the field of health sciences. For the publishers and journals with Twitter accounts, they saw that NYUHSL recognized their role in the scholarly communication process. This recognition was also seen by other libraries, authors, and scholars from other institutions.

CONCLUSION

Developing a content strategy for social media at any Library can be a rewarding experience. In addition to leveraging its strengths to support an organization's core mission and values, it opens up possibilities for end-users to engage with Libraries in new and innovative ways.

Figure 8. Tweet activity

Developing and adhering to a specific content strategy for social media allows libraries to communicate their brand to target audiences. For many academic libraries, Twitter, has been a successful platform to disseminate information about its services and relationships to the scholarly communities it supports. Although marketing and outreach plans have historically been ad hoc endeavors, applying the content strategy framework of Assessment, Creation, Promotion, and Measurement can serve as a model for librarians and staff to carry out and follow-through on their campaigns.

REFERENCES

Blakiston, R. (2013). Developing a Content Strategy for an Academic Library Website. *Journal of Electronic Resources Librarianship, 25*(3), 175–191. doi:10.1080/1941126X.2013.813295

Brigham, T. J. (2013). Personas: Stepping Into the Shoes of the Library User. *Medical Reference Services Quarterly, 32*(4), 443–450. doi:10.1080/02763869.2013.837737 PMID:24180652

Carter, T. M., & Seaman, P. (2011). The Management and Support of Outreach in Academic Libraries. *Reference & User Services Quarterly, 51*(2), 163–171.

Content Marketing Institute. (2018). *Getting Started*. Retrieved August 2, 2018, from https://contentmarketinginstitute.com/getting-started/

Cuddy, C., Graham, J., & Morton-Owens, E. G. (2010). Implementing Twitter in a Health Sciences Library. *Medical Reference Services Quarterly, 29*(4), 320–330. doi:10.1080/02763869.2010.518915 PMID:21058176

Dalal, H. A., O'Hanlon, R., & Yacobucci, K. L. (2017). *Video Marketing for Libraries: A Practical Guide for Librarians*. Rowman & Littlefield. Retrieved from https://books.google.com/books?id=3vK_jwEACAAJ

Datig, I. (2018). Revitalizing library websites and social media with content strategy: Tools and recommendations. *Journal of Electronic Resources Librarianship, 30*(2), 63–69. doi:10.1080/1941126X.2018.1465511

Del Bosque, D., Leif, S. A., & Skarl, S. (2012). Libraries atwitter: Trends in academic library tweeting. *RSR. Reference Services Review, 40*(2), 199–213. doi:10.1108/00907321211228246

Dessart, L., Veloutsou, C., & Morgan-Thomas, A. (2016). Capturing consumer engagement: Duality, dimensionality and measurement. *Journal of Marketing Management, 32*(5–6), 399–426. doi:10.1080/0267257X.2015.1130738

Evans, H. (2017, January 29). *"Content is King"—Essay by Bill Gates 1996*. Retrieved August 29, 2018, from https://medium.com/@HeathEvans/content-is-king-essay-by-bill-gates-1996-df74552f80d9

Fichter, D., & Wisniewski, J. (2014). Content Marketing and Strategy for Libraries. *Online Searcher, 38*(6), 74–76.

Gunton, L., & Davis, K. (2012). Beyond broadcasting: Customer service, community and information experience in the Twittersphere. *RSR. Reference Services Review*, *40*(2), 224–227. doi:10.1108/00907321211228282

Hootsuite. (2018, July 18). *Social Media Image Sizes: A Quick Reference Guide for Each Network*. Retrieved November 29, 2018, from https://blog.hootsuite.com/social-media-image-sizes-guide/

Kim, H. M., Abels, E. G., & Yang, C. C. (2012). Who disseminates academic library information on Twitter? *Proceedings of the American Society for Information Science and Technology*, *49*(1), 1–4. doi:10.1002/meet.14504901317

Lee, O. (2013, March). *What is Content? Learn from 40 Definitions*. Retrieved February 20, 2014, from https://www.toprankblog.com/2013/03/what-is-content/

Milstein, S. (2009). Twitter FOR Libraries (and Librarians). *Computers in Libraries, 29*(5), 17–18.

Needleman, M. (2002). The OpenURL: An Emerging Standard for Linking. *Serials Review*, *28*(1), 74–76. doi:10.1080/00987913.2002.10764714

Park, J., & Dantus, S. (2018). *Marketing Academic Library Resources and Services (White Paper)*. ACRL. Retrieved from http:// choice360.org/librarianship/whitepaper

Pew Research Center. (2018). *Social Media Use 2018*. Pew Research Center. Retrieved from http://www.pewinternet.org/2018/03/01/social-media-use-in-2018/

Rouse, M. (2016, June). *What is Content Management System (CMS)*. Retrieved August 2, 2018, from https://searchcontentmanagement.techtarget.com/definition/content-management-system-CMS

Sewell, R. R. (2013). Who is following us? Data mining a library's Twitter followers. *Library Hi Tech*, *31*(1), 160–170. doi:10.1108/07378831311303994

Shulman, J., Yep, J., & Tomé, D. (2015). Leveraging the Power of a Twitter Network for Library Promotion. *Journal of Academic Librarianship*, *41*(2), 178–185. doi:10.1016/j.acalib.2014.12.004

Tempelman-Kluit, N., & Pearce, A. (2014). Invoking the User from Data to Design. *College & Research Libraries*, *75*(5), 616–640. doi:10.5860/crl.75.5.616

U.S. News & World Report L.P. (2018). *New York University (Langone) - Best Medical Schools - US News*. Retrieved August 29, 2018, from https://www.usnews.com/best-graduate-schools/top-medical-schools/new-york-university-04073

Vieira, D., McGowan, R., McCrillis, A., Lamb, I., Larson, C., Bakker, T., & Spore, S. S. (2018). The Faculty Bibliography Project at the NYU School of Medicine. *Journal of Librarianship & Scholarly Communication*, *2*(3), 1–15.

Zaugg, H., & Rackham, S. (2016). Identification and development of patron personas for an academic library. *Performance Measurement and Metrics, 17*(2), 124–133. doi:10.1108/PMM-04-2016-0011

ADDITIONAL READING

Anderson, C. L. (2012). LibraryPalooza: A marketing case study. *New Library World, 113*(1/2), 55–64. doi:10.1108/03074801211199040

Colburn, S., & Haines, L. (2012). Measuring Libraries' Use of YouTube as a Promotional Tool: An Exploratory Study and Proposed Best Practices. *Journal of Web Librarianship*, *6*(1), 5–31. doi:10.1080/19322909.2012.641789

Deodato, J. (2018). Overhyped Fad or Missed Opportunity? A History of Academic Libraries and the Social Web. *Journal of Web Librarianship*, *12*(1), 1–27. doi:10.1080/19322909.2017.1390424

Henner, T. (2014). From the Literature. *Medical Reference Services Quarterly*, *33*(2), 227–234. doi:10.1080/02763869.2014.897526 PMID:25023012

Richardson, H. A. H., & Kennedy, M. R. (2014). How to Market Your Library's Electronic Resources. *The Serials Librarian*, *67*(1), 42–47. doi:10.1080/0361526X.2014.899289

Rossmann, D., & Young, S. W. H. (2015). Using Social Media to Build Community. *Computers in Libraries*, *35*(4), 18–22.

Young, S. W. H., & Rossmann, D. (2015). Building Library Community through Social Media. *Information Technology and Libraries*, *34*(1), 20–37. doi:10.6017/ital.v34i1.5625

Chapter 4
Diversifying Content Across Social Media Platforms

Maggie Clarke
California State University – Dominguez Hills, USA

Jillian Eslami
California State University – Dominguez Hills, USA

ABSTRACT

In this chapter, the authors describe how a committee of librarians' project to revamp the social media presence at a public comprehensive university library has helped foster deeper student engagement. By temporarily restructuring the library social media committee into subcommittees and assigning each one a single social media platform, librarians were able to develop stronger understanding of the content, norms, and audience of each platform and create more diverse and targeted content for each. This change has resulted in increased interaction with students across all platforms leading to higher attendance at library events. Preliminary findings also suggest that increased student engagement has the potential to illuminate opportunities for partnership across campus.

INTRODUCTION

Social media has a huge presence in students' lives. With students increasingly invested in an ever-changing social media landscape, librarians concerned with meeting students at their point of need cannot ignore the importance of social media. This constantly evolving mode of communication is now an essential way for academic libraries to connect with their students, faculty, and the larger academic community. At the same time the need for academic libraries to demonstrate their value, often by quantifying their impact on student success, makes it increasingly important that libraries take measures to maintain their visibility in the campus community and in students' academic lives.

As Clark and Melancon observed, social media has changed marketing into an interactive media which encourages "two-way conversations (Clark & Melancon, 2013, p. 132). Social media allows academic libraries to both tell students about events and resources and invite student response at various levels. This chapter will describe how the University Library at California State University Dominguez Hills

DOI: 10.4018/978-1-5225-8097-3.ch004

(CSUDH) is using social media to more effectively facilitate these interactions in support of the library's Vision. CSUDH University Library defines its Vision as the desire to:

- Be the center of intellectual and creative life at CSUDH, facilitating teaching, learning, research, intellectual inquiry, and curiosity.
- Be an innovative, collaborative, inclusive, and flexible organization that provides responsive, learner-centered services and technologies that meet the evolving information, curricular, and research needs of CSUDH students, faculty, and staff and the surrounding community.
- Provide vibrant, welcoming, and engaging learner-centered physical **and virtual spaces** [emphasis ours] that facilitate innovation, collaboration, and boundary-free access to information. (CSUDH, 2018)

In the spirit of innovation, flexibility, and centering learners embedded in this Vision, the University Library makes it a priority to meet students where they are. Students who cannot come to campus and visit the library in person, who are enrolled in distance education programs, or who suffer from library anxiety, all have the option of accessing help from a librarian online via chat reference, virtual research consultation meetings, or library email. It is the authors' hope that the library's social media presence will function not only as a marketing tool but as an extension of the library's virtual spaces. Social media includes all students who follow-- regardless of if they are on campus students can read a tweet or see a post on Instagram. Students can access the library and its various social platforms at their leisure, and decide whether they want to utilize a resource or attend an event. They can also learn more about the library's resources and services without having to visit in person or consciously choose to seek out that information on our website. Using social media in this way has the potential to bridge the gap between feeling comfortable in the library and avoiding it due to library anxiety. A student may be less inclined to talk to other students in person about a library event, a book, or a resource, but have no qualms about posting or replying to a comment on Twitter or Facebook. The usage of social media goes beyond advertisement and promotion of the library to engage and support the students as well (Mellon, 2015).

In this chapter, the authors will describe how a project to revamp the social media presence by a committee of librarians at a public comprehensive university library beginning in January 2018 has helped increase attendance at library related events and fostered deeper student engagement. By restructuring the library social media committee into smaller groups and assigning each one a single social media platform, the different accounts have evolved unique voices suited to the content, norms, and audience of each platform. The decision to offer different information across each, or the same information in a variety of ways, allows the committee to better tailor the content on each platform to its audience based on students' feedback and engagement.

BACKGROUND

In considering social media as a tool for promoting student engagement, the natural question to begin with is whether students are willing to interact with library social media accounts at all. In 2015, roughly two-thirds of adults reported using social media, up from just 7% in 2005. Though this increase can be seen across all demographics, it is most marked among the demographic associated with the majority of college students: young adults. Participation in social media for this demographic has risen from 12% in 2005 to over 90% in 2015 (Perrin, 2015). Among young adults, surveys indicate that Instagram and Snapchat are the most used social media platforms, followed by Facebook and Twitter (Alhabash & Ma, 2017; Anderson & Smith, 2018). Despite this variance in popularity, 71% of young adults use more than one social media platform suggesting that an effective social media plan will need to keep in mind the needs of multi-modal users (Lenhart, 2017).

As for how and why students (and others) use social media, research suggests that, depending on the platform, what users hope to find on social media (as opposed to what they hope to communicate to others) can be distilled into three primary categories: entertainment, social interaction, and information seeking (Whiting & Williams, 2013; Brookbank, 2015) . Though entertainment and social interaction may fall somewhat out of the scope of an academic librarian's area of expertise, recognizing our social media feeds as an information source for university students, faculty, staff, and outside stakeholders makes developing a strong social media presence integral to meeting students at their point of information need. As early as 2001, the American Library Association was reporting on the perceived benefits of an effective social media presence for libraries (ALA, 2001). Since then research on libraries and social media has illustrated that academic libraries have used their social media feeds as tools to share announcements about library events, photos, and resources (Chen, Chu, & Xu, 2012; Hendrix et al., 2009; Jacobson, 2011; Lihn, 2008), to define their brand and encourage positive perceptions of the library (Harrison, et al., 2017), and as a means to communicate directly with students (Ntaka, 2017).

Of course, just because both students and libraries use social media does not guarantee they are engaging with one another. Huber, et al. (2018) address this question in their study using a recent study from Purdue University in which students were surveyed electronically about their perceptions and preferences related to academic libraries on social media. They found 40% of students responded that they were either "very likely "or "somewhat likely" to follow the library on Instagram and Twitter. The specific information needs students' bring to library social media are addressed by Stivilia and Gibradze (2017) who note that students find "postings related to operations updates, study support services, and events as the most useful." These findings demonstrate general agreement between what students consider to be the most useful content available from library social media platforms and the content being prioritized by libraries themselves. However, it is worth noting that the studies above utilize students' self-reported data to predict the potential for student engagement with library social media accounts. In considering the efficacy of academic library social media analytic data is also an essential component to assessing impact (King, 2015). Furthermore, though the demographic and qualitative data presented above has been foundational for our team in forming a more robust and effective social media plan, it is essential to recognize that social media is defined by its mutability. There can be no doubt that these numbers will change as platforms evolve and new social media networks arise. Frequently revisiting the available literature on both academic libraries in social media, and broader trends in social media use, is recommended to maintain librarians' facility with social media technology and trends, and develop responsive strategies to inevitable changes.

MAIN FOCUS OF THE CHAPTER

Issues, Controversies and Problems

A close examination of the previous social media policy revealed that, though well-intentioned, encouraging ad hoc posting by all members of the social media committee across all platforms resulted in inconsistency in terms of frequency and content of posts as well as excessive repetition- all of which negatively impacted student engagement. While the overall idea was to promote the library by ensuring the same information was presented on all platforms, frequent cross posting does not account for each platform being better suited for certain types of information and promotion. Twitter, though known for its brevity, did increase its character count from 140 characters to 280 characters in late 2017 (Rosen & Ihara, 2017). While having the character count doubled did help in creating longer posts, Twitter remains best suited to short and incisive posts, usually accompanied by hashtags that help circulate the information by making it easier for other users to find. Facebook, on the other hand, has a huge character limit (over 60,000 characters for a text post with no images or video), making it more appropriate for longer, text-heavy information such as events with more details. Additionally, while hashtags can be used on Facebook, our experience suggests that they are not as effective as they are on Twitter for making information accessible. These two platforms are a good example of how cross-posting identical material to both accounts ultimately ignores the affordances and weakness of each platform, as well as users' expectations for the content they will find there. What can be said on Twitter, can be expanded on Facebook. Unfortunately, in the past, the committee would schedule the same content, verbatim, across both, under utilizing both platforms.

Additionally, changes to the sorting and display algorithms of Facebook and Instagram in 2018 (Gollin, 2018a; Gollin, 2018b) seriously impact the number of impressions being generated by our social media content. As a public institution, the University Library welcomes community engagement in our physical and virtual spaces, however much of what appears on our social media platforms is naturally of limited interest to those not affiliated with our university. Even before developing documentation surrounding committee goals and outcomes, general consensus in the group was that communicating with the campus community was our primary mandate rather than merely gathering large numbers of followers. With no budget for proprietary tools to gather rich data on engagement with our social media platforms the committee had never made a consistent practice of documenting changes in our social media account analytics beyond discussion of number of followers for each account. However, after a noticeable drop in engagement with our Facebook page, illustrated in Figure 1, we began monitoring our page's reach.

Facebook defines reach as "the number of people who had any content from your Page or about your Page enter their screen" ("What's the difference between Page views and Page reach on Facebook?", 2018). We discovered that between October 1, 2017 and March 31, 2018 our page Reach had plummeted by 80.5%. In order to adapt to these changes (and changes which will certainly arise in the future), a revitalized social media strategy was necessary.

SOLUTIONS AND RECOMMENDATIONS

The first step towards redeveloping the social media team was to look at the existing committee and how it had been structured in the previous academic year, 2016-17. The committee was relatively new and

Figure 1. Weekly Facebook reaches

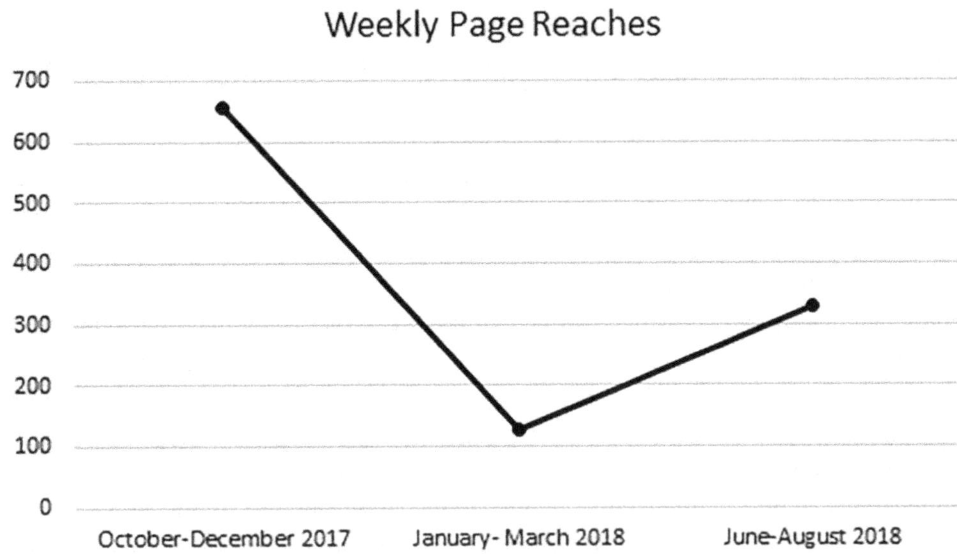

most of the social media platforms for the institution had only been created only in the previous three years. Furthermore, the committee itself had experienced numerous changes in membership with librarian involvement fluctuating from semester to semester. The only criteria to be a part of the committee was the desire to be on it and no specializations or explicit time commitments were required. The social media committee for the 2017-18 academic year was ultimately a team of six librarians, each with full time-appointments in Reference, Outreach, and Instruction Services (RIOS) or Circulation, Acquisitions and Processing Services (CAPS), as well as campus service and scholarship responsibilities.

Once the new team was formed, the next step to revitalizing our social media presence was a thorough review and revision of committee goals including creating schedules for posting and documenting the type of content desirable to create and promote. No previous documentation surrounding outcomes for engaging with students via social media, goals for the social media committee, or responsibilities of its members was available and the lack of clear vision as to the purpose of the library's social media presence was immediately identified as a key issue in need of redress. In order to provide necessary guidance in creating committee policy the following goals were adopted:

- Reach out and engage the students, staff and faculty of CSUDH
- Cultivate an open, professional and responsive dialogue with our users in order to meet them at their point of need
- Promote the value and importance of services offered by the faculty and staff of the CSUDH Library
- Advertise library and campus events to increase student attendance
- Promote research tips and useful tools for scholarship to aid student and faculty research

In light of these clarified goals, a strategic plan of how to enact them while respecting the already full schedules of our committee members was essential. A decision was made to create subcommittees for each of our active social media platforms: Facebook, Twitter, Instagram, and our institutional student engagement network, Torolink. This structure would allow each subcommittee to develop a unique voice for their platform rather than merely cross posting, as well as to assess and respond to student engagement with that specific platform. This policy was documented in a departmental social media style guide created using Springshare's LibGuides, which also outlines the mission, goals, and vision of our social media presence. This social media guide also includes best practices, styles guidelines for creating posts across different platforms, and university-wide social media policies. The social media guide was also a resource for finding successful hashtags and peak times for posting which all committee members' reference when planning their social media posts.

In creating the subcommittees, the hope was that each team would then create the content with the platforms unique features in mind. Some examples of this would be short, brief tweets with eye-catching images and relevant hashtags on Twitter. For Facebook, similar content could be used, but expanded in description and maybe with multiple images or links could be included to highlight and promote the library. Instagram is very image driven, so more emphasis might be placed on creating visual information, with shorter captions to accompany. The committee would get a list of upcoming library events that could be included as posts, compiled by the head of the committee. It would be up to the head to signify which events needed to be included, such as upcoming hour changes/holidays/events, and each team would then create the content as they saw fit.

As noted above, no requirements were imposed for committee members' experience with social media technology in order for them to join. In the midst of creating the smaller teams within the committee, some valuable professional development opportunities arose. Though committee members were enthusiastic about joining subcommittees, experience with using the platforms themselves was varied. As such, it became necessary to train the team in the different platforms. The value of having the small teams was so the content would vary, and that the individuals on the teams would feel most comfortable on the platform they signed up for. This presented the committee with a chance to delve into each platform and discuss not only what content would be best for each, but the most effective ways to employ each platform to maximize engagement. Though Twitter, Facebook, and Instagram are similar in many ways, each has its own nuances when it comes to creating and scheduling content as well as interacting with followers. In order to ensure all committee members were comfortable with the basics of their assigned platform, librarians worked together in informal peer training groups to address gaps in knowledge. This included a range of activities, such as signing up for an individual Instagram account to link to the library's account and the adding of members to the Facebook page administration page so everyone could approve or edit posts. There are opportunities here, depending on your institution and the committee's overall experience with social media, to offer workshops on the various platforms. Our committee also utilized Lynda.com, a proprietary platform for training and skill development videos subscribed to by University Library, as a training resource for more experienced librarians.

In order to remain aware of what content was being shared across platforms and to ease some of the time burden of creating and posting new content frequently, we began using a social media management system, Hootsuite, to schedule posts for each platform, as well as to manage cross posting of content. All committee members can access Hootsuite and schedule content. Using this service has made it easier for more events and programs to be advertised as it gives the members of the social media committee autonomy over posting.

Like many academic librarians, those on our social media committee were keenly aware of the discrepancy between services offered and student awareness of them. Reflected in the revised goals for our committee was the desire to increase student engagement not just online, but in the physical library. These changes to our social media activity coincided with (and were likely influenced by) an expansion of the University Library programming schedule to include multiple new workshops and events during the year and more Stress Relief Weeks programming, an ongoing, two week-long event hosted by the University Library to help students practice self-care during a possibly stressful time leading up to and during final exams. As such, we planned to assess our success not only by analytic changes related to our social media accounts (increased followers and interactions), but through increased student engagement with services and events like Finals Stress Relief Week and Open Access Week, program attendance, and participation in passive programming activities. Passive programming includes aspects of the event/program that does not need to be monitored or led by a librarian/library staff. An example would be a table stocked with coloring pages, markers/crayons/pencils, a table with an in progress puzzle, etc. These are programs where students, faculty and staff can participate in with no start or stop time.

Once committee members felt that they had develop sufficient proficiency with their platforms, the social media committee revised the subcommittee structure to allow more flexibility for members to post across all platforms if they chose. The social media committee for the 2018-19 academic year was also expanded to include full-time staff members who were interested in joining. The committee began blending the content, meeting once a month to create most or all of the content for the month and schedule it all out together. This approach helped the keep the committee accountable for their content and it also allowed them to address their social media commitment in full, for the month. This provided a solution for a lack of consistency of posting as well as enabled more content to be shared more efficiently. In scheduling out content as a team, the group is able to create a month's worth of content in just an hour. Consistency and efficiency, as well as accountability were the overall improvements the committee noticed.

Content

Though a voice which is in line with an individual library's goals, audience, and institutional requirements will of course be highly individual and largely dependent on the creativity of the librarians involved, here we will break down some of the content strategies which have proven useful for us. Due partly to limitations of the available analytics, these strategies were developed out of trial and error as well as our own observations of how users responded to differences in content across platforms.

In considering the library's "voice" across platforms, it is essential to consider the form content takes as this will necessarily affect how users communicate. It should also be noted that, though the content of each platform as a whole is tailored to that platform and audience, there are some instances of cross posting identical or very similar content across platforms. This is both for efficiency and because some content works well for all or most platforms. Figure 2 describes the types of content we have found to be most appropriate for each platform based on the the platforms' features and user engagement.

The library focuses primarily on original content across all platforms (not reposts or retweets), using free, online design applications such as Canva and Piktochart, as well as utilizing Creative Common licensed images whenever possible. The library also makes use of popular "days", such as "National Coffee Day", "International High Five Day", etc., as material for content creation. Promotion of library events, hours, holidays, research tools, or a highlight of the print collection are other examples of content that can be created. The library might make three different posts, all promoting the same service, but in different ways that suit the platform the best. For example, if we are highlighting a new online tutorial,

Figure 2. Types of content posted by platform. Note: AMA stands for Ask Me Anything, an invitation for followers to ask direct questions to an account

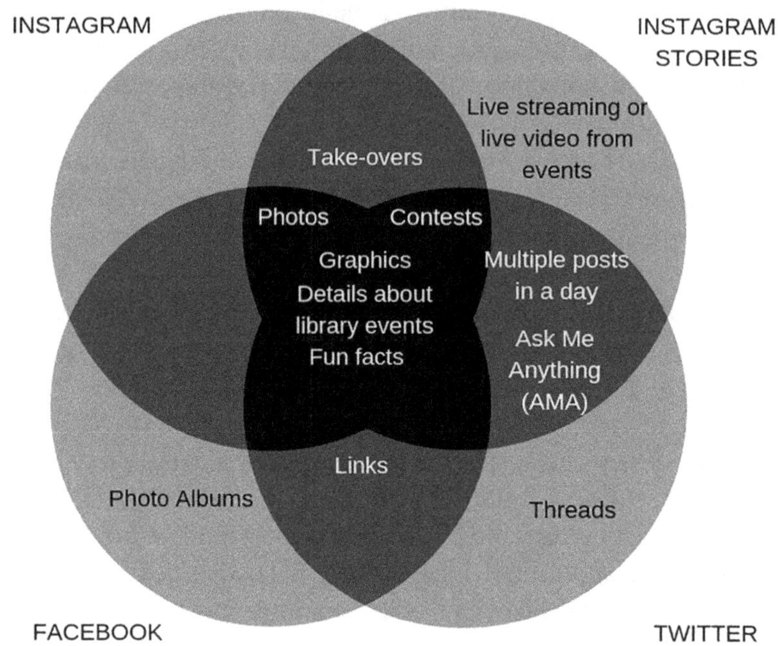

we might make a Facebook post that describes the tutorial and who might find it useful. The post would also include videos as well as provide a direct link. For Twitter, we might include a simpler description and a direct link, along with appropriate hashtags to make the tweet more findable between users. Since Instagram does not allow for links in individual posts it would not be the best platform for this type of post, but if we were to include it we might create a screen grab of the tutorial or create a different image to accompany a caption with information on where students can find the video.

The library also attempts to utilize the unique features of each social media platform. For example, InstaStories allows users to create short-term post(s) that will only be available for 24 hours or stream live video which appears only on this platform. Facebook also has a "Stories" feature that can be used in the same way although we have seen significantly more engagement with InstaStories. This feature is a great tool for "live streaming" an event as it is happening or using it to engage with students directly by asking questions or creating a poll. The stories function can include live, in the moment content, and then filters, stickers, gifs, etc., can be added to them, or previously created content can be added and altered. Stories can also be added to a "highlights" reel, where your followers can view the stories indefinitely.

Below are examples of posts pertaining to passive Stress Relief Week programming from the end of the spring 2018 semester which illustrate how a single event can be represented differently across platforms.

Though each of these posts has the same basic purpose- to inform students of some of the stress relieving activities that will be available to them in the library throughout their finals- the way the content is present on each platform is unique. Figure 3 includes a photograph from right after the table was set up. This static image is a visual representation of what is described in the text-- a table full of coloring sheets, crossword puzzles, and craft supplies. Since Facebook has no limits on the amount of text the description can be longer than on other platforms and the image can serve to illustrate what is found in the text and let students know what to look for if they want to make use of this service.

Figure 3. A Facebook post from May 1, 2018 describing some of the passive programming being offered in the library for Stress Relief Weeks

Figure 4. A screen capture of an InstaStory about puzzles in the library from Stress Relief Weeks

Figure 5. A tweet from May 1, 2018 about passive programming in the library for Stress Relief Weeks

The same space is presented very differently in our InstaStory. As seen in Figure 4 the table is presented as a hub of collaborative activity giving students a sense of the experience of being there with other students. In addition to the screengrab shown here, our InstaStory included videos of students coloring and working on puzzles at the table. Rather than detailing the specific amenities available these images and videos speak for themselves (at times literally) rather than relying on significant amounts of text.

The tweet shown in Figure 5 includes a graphic rather than a photograph as well as briefer text than what is seen in the post from Figure 3. Because of Twitter's text limits some information, in this case, the location of the event, is provided in the image itself. Creating graphics which blend text and images allows more information to be shared without encountering character limits.

The library's voice across all the platforms aims to be professional, friendly and helpful, just as the librarians themselves. We want our students to not only become more aware of the events and resources the library has to offer, but also feel comfortable engaging and responding to the social media accounts.

Results

Since making the above changes to the library's social media strategy, student engagement across platforms has made significant increases in spite of algorithmic changes. As noted, our committee does not have a budget for advanced third-party analytics tools and has been reliant on Facebook and Instagram's "Insights" tools and Twitter's "Analytics" tool to gather data. In analyzing the available data our focus is on metrics which are most reflective of how many users are actually seeing and engaging with our content. However, engagement does not mean the same thing across platforms. For example, while Facebook Reach measures, "The number of people who had any content from your Page or about your Page enter their screen" Twitter Impressions measures the, "Number of times users are served your Tweet in timeline, search results, or from your profile" (emphasis ours) ("What's the difference between Page views and Page reach on Facebook?", 2018; "About account home," 2018). Facebook defines their Engagement metric as the number of post clicks, reactions, comments, and shares while Twitter measures engagement by, "Total number of times a user interacted with a Tweet. Clicks anywhere on the Tweet, including Retweets, replies, follows, likes, links, cards, hashtags, embedded media, username, profile photo, or Tweet expansion," ("Insights," 2018; "About your activity dashboard," 2018). Instagram likes and comments may be more transparent metrics to an average user but do not map easily to the metrics which are freely available from Twitter and Facebook. Because of these variances, as well as the subcommittee structure which encourages the librarians responsible for each platform to monitor and respond to the analytics for that platform, we have chosen to assess each platform's performance separately.

As seen in Figure 6, thus far Facebook has shown the greatest growth in engagement, which subverted the committee's initial belief that Instagram would be the most popular platform among students. Though continued algorithmic changes, evolving audiences, and the vagaries of the academic calendar all impact the reach of the library's social media presence, consistent growth can be seen on all platforms.

As indicated in Figure 7, average likes per Instagram post have increased by over 500% in the past year. Though growth in the average number of comments on Instagram posts has been less robust, Figure 8 also illustrates a clear upward trend.

Though Figure 9 indicates significant fluctuation in average Tweet Impressions despite overall growth, Figure 10 illustrates that the overall percentage of users who see our content and engage with it is rising. This potentially indicates an improvement in the relevance and quality of content to our followers related to more frequent posting and close monitoring direct and indirect user feedback by the Twitter subcommittee.

Figure 6. Average engagements per Facebook post

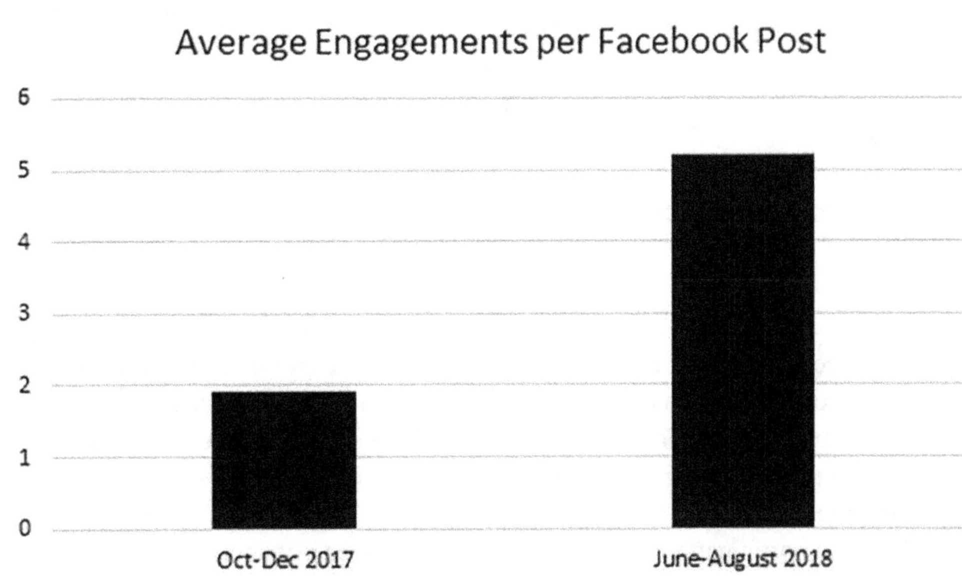

Figure 7. Average likes per Instagram post

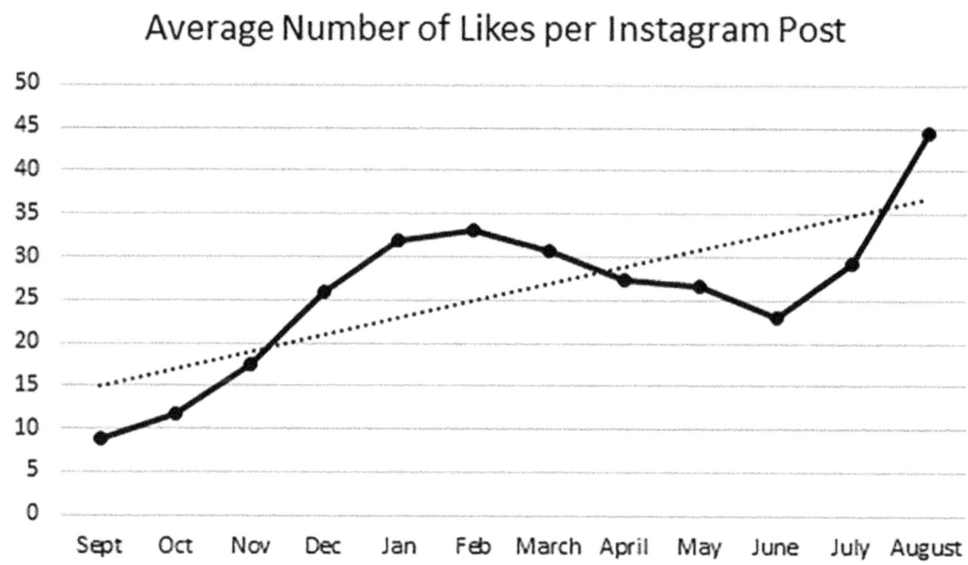

Figure 8. Average number of comments per Instagram post

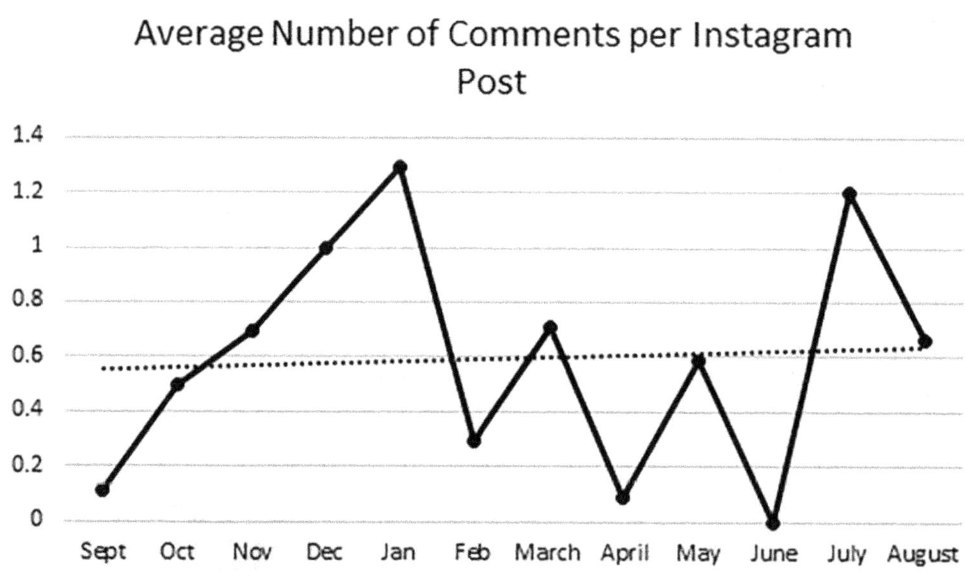

As previously discussed, though a useful tool, analytics are not the primary means by which our committee assesses success. Perhaps the most compelling area of growth affected by adopting a more structured approach to social media has been student participation in library events and programming. As indicated in Figure 11, between the Fall 2017 and Spring 2018 semesters, we have seen a 60% increase in attendance for active programming held within the library for Finals Stress Relief Week. Prior to our social media intervention, the library had minimal promotion of the events surrounding Finals Stress Relief Week, and student participation mirrored those efforts. Once a concerted effort was made towards

Figure 9. Average impressions per Tweet

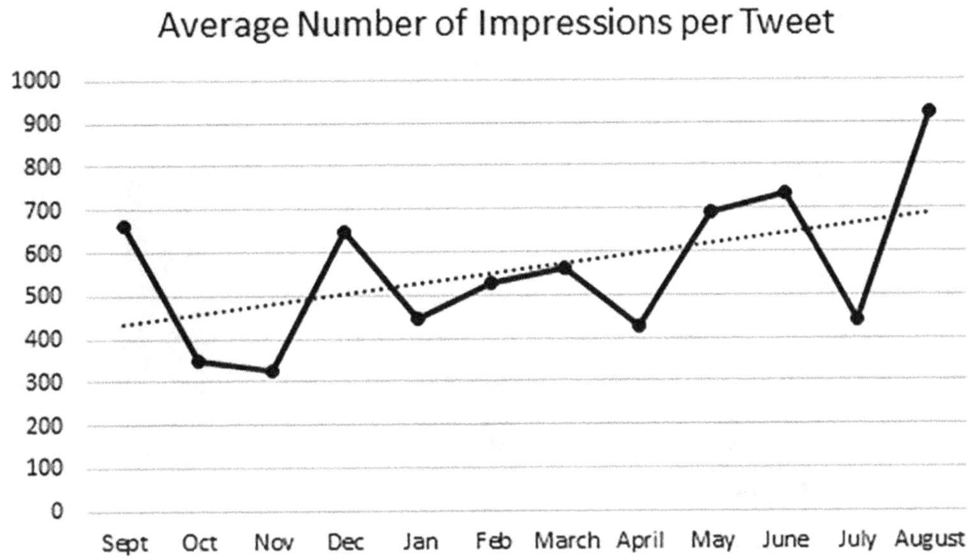

Figure 10. Average % engagement per Tweet

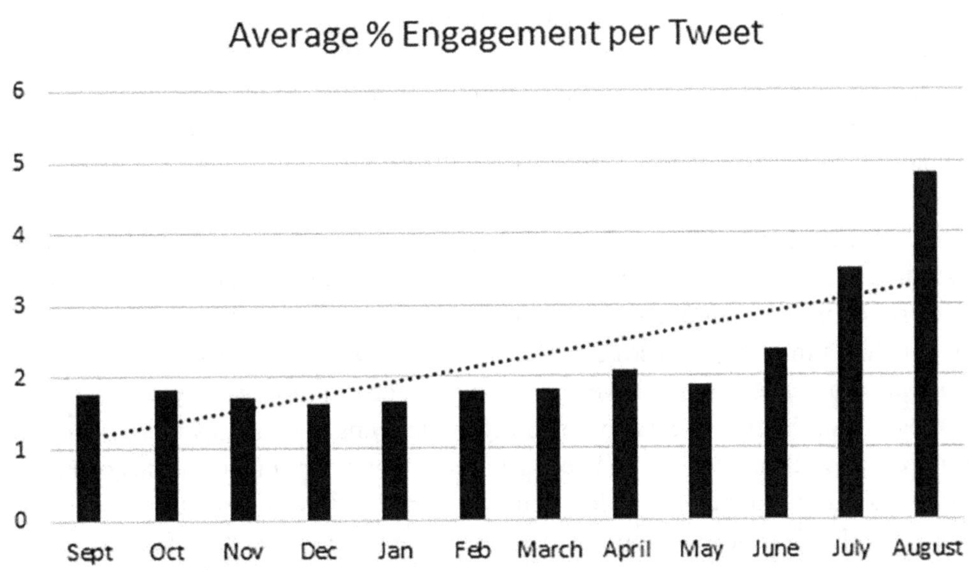

engaging the students across multiple platforms, marketing events sufficiently resulted in a quick return on investment regarding student engagement and involvement. Part of the efforts made in breaking out the social media platforms into teams also involved the planning and scheduling of content, which made the promoting and marketing of events easier to manage. Increase of participation from students in the Fall of 2017 provided useful information as to what types of events students seemed most interested in and as a result, the events for the Spring 2018 semester were more tailored to what the students wanted, including more therapy dog visits and free drinks and snacks. Feedback was collected both in person with anonymous evaluations as well as online via the platforms polling and messaging features.

Figure 11. Participants in active programming during Stress Relief Week: 2017-2018

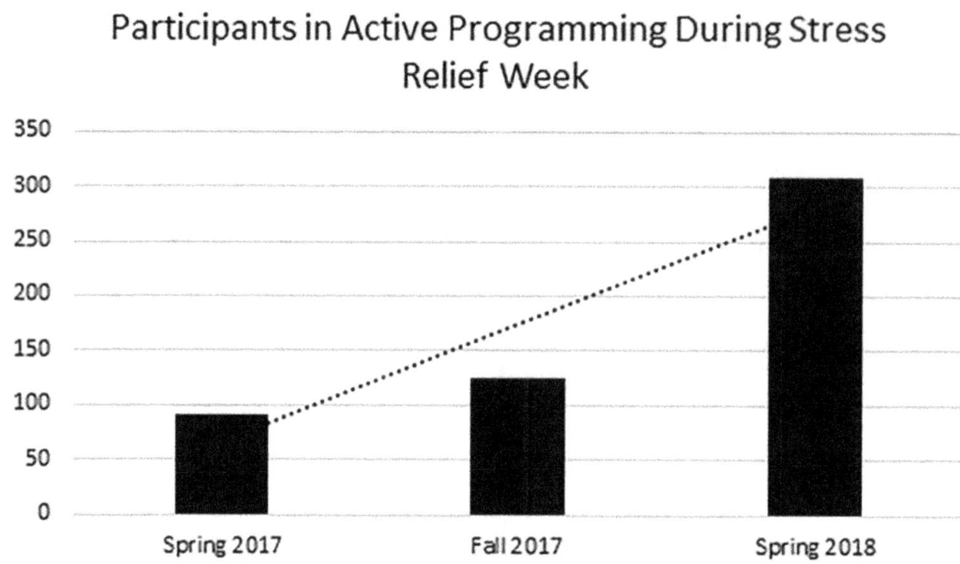

While the committee currently does not have a structured schedule for posting content, studies have shown that because of current algorithms, posting consistently several times per week, rather than posting multiple times per day (sometimes characterized as spamming) to the accounts, not only increases visibility and engagement, but keep the pages relevant. Depending on the type of account you are representing, such as a brand page or a media page, posting once per day seemed to be the ideal number ("How often should you post on your Facebook pages?", 2011).

As much as consistency matters regarding engagement with the campus as a whole, content matters too. According to Harrison et al (2017), there has been little research done on the content that libraries choose to post, and with that the overall impact using social media libraries has in regards to the institution. In our case, the social media committee approaches content by aligning the medium with the purpose, using a design method similar to our instructional material design. The library attempts to create content in a variety of ways so that it can be viewed and comprehended in the variety of ways students learn. Facebook is great for promoting events and eliciting student engagement, as there is no real character limit, and pictures, as well as text, can be used. Twitter is better for smaller pieces of information, accompanied with a picture/infographic in which students can digest the information in a more visual way. Instagram is the similar, in that it is more visually driven, even more so than Twitter, relying more on the graphic than the text. However, both Twitter and Instagram are better vehicles for promotion through hashtags(#), making the content easier to find to users who may not already be following the accounts.

Analysis of Perceived Content Effectiveness

One unanticipated boon to the reach of University Library's social media not reflected in these analytics has been expanded collaboration and engagement with other campus affiliates. These collaborations have included event cross-promotion with our campus student government, resource centers, student groups, and individual faculty to raise awareness about library resources and collections. For example, the library collaborated with the University Veterans' Resource Center to curate a book display, promoting not only the library's military collection, but a student center housed in the library that serves students in an entirely different way. The collaboration resulted in multiple Instagram posts where each departments were tagged, cross promoting the material in very different ways, to two different student audiences. This was only one such example that illustrates how, by collaborating and promoting through the various social media, the library has increased student engagement.

As more collaborations develop, the more the campus at large acknowledges and appreciates the library as more than just a building. As Harrison, et al said, "Social media, which empowers libraries to connect with and engage its diverse stakeholder groups, has a vital role to play in moving academic libraries beyond their traditional borders."(Harrison, et al, 2017, p. 248). Social media has allowed the library to improve not only its resources and services, but also to expand its presence as a main hub on campus for students and faculty alike, with the increased engagement and collaboration across multiple departments. Social media has been a vital addition to the library's marketing strategy which shows growing success when it comes to connecting not only with students, but staff, faculty, and campus stakeholders. In expanding the library to beyond the physical walls, the collaborations that have resulted have helped increase the libraries identity and recognition throughout the campus.

Another unexpected benefit from our subcommittee structure has been facilitating faster responses to questions and concerns shared by users via our social media platforms. While the librarians are accessible through an online reference chat service, some students have taken to messaging the library through Twitter or Facebook and, to a lesser extent, Instagram, particularly during hours when chat reference isn't available. These messages mostly consist of noise complaints or questions about library hours. With fewer platforms for individual librarians to monitor, student messages have been received and answered in a more timely manner, while in the past these messages might have been unanswered for weeks, even months. By having more people involved with a specific platform, faster response times have resulted in more positive student experiences, hopefully encouraging them to continue the use of the social media as a way to reach out to the library.

FUTURE RESEARCH DIRECTIONS

As a new semester starts, the library's social media committee will continue to meet and assess the data that the various social media platforms produce. While the overall transition into smaller teams to represent each account was a step in a new direction, the library realized that there were definite flaws in the original concept. In addressing those flaws, the social media committee was able to improve not only the consistency overall, but the content as well. As the committee works together and make continuous changes, they acknowledge that the library is ready and willing to adapt to new and more progressive forms of social media to meet users' needs for a social media presence from the library. Based on our success in increasing student engagement since moving aways from platform based subcommittees, the social media committee plans to continue with the structure of shared creation and scheduling with a few refinements. Now that we have had a chance to review the results of our strategic changes the committee has a benchmark from which to assess future performance and implement evidence-based practices. To facilitate this assessment we have added the following Outcomes to our committee guide to supplement the committee's Strategic Goals:

- Increase average reach/engagement on Instagram, Facebook, and Twitter by 10% each semester
- Produce 4-6 weekly posts per platform
- Increase overall attendance at/ participation in in-person programs within the library by 10% each semester

Another area for future research is to solicit direct feedback from users. There are a multitude of ways social media can be used to enhance library services outside of student engagement. Since students are using these platforms already, reaching out to them in this way makes sense. All three platforms most used by the library have polling features, which we can use to ask students questions and use those results to implement new ideas or programs based on student-driven feedback. There could even be an opportunity to invite users of the library to share what they look for in an organization's social media, what their likes and dislikes are so the library or organization might have a better understanding of their users, their campus, and the overall drivers of the library, the students.

Furthermore, though our initial changes have focused on increasing student engagement, the social media committee acknowledges the importance of staff, faculty, and other campus stakeholders in our campus community. In the coming year we hope to solicit direct feedback from faculty and staff with the aim to initiate more collaborations and foster opportunities to cross-promote and represent the library and campus through a wider lens.

Beyond developing expertise with the social media platforms themselves, we have also found that members of the social media committee are seeking additional support in managing and creating content through a variety of third party services for example: using a management system like Hootsuite and creating content in using various digital design applications like Canva, Piktochart, or Adobe Photoshop. This presents further opportunities for professional development to support our committee in creating and sharing impactful content. A series of peer lead workshops has been suggested with the potential to include staff and faculty outside the library who may also wish to develop these skills.

CONCLUSION

As communication increasingly takes place in digital spaces, developing a well-curated, impactful social media presence is essential for academic libraries to meet users at their point of need and maintain the library's visibility in their campus community. Creating and maintaining relevant and engaging social media pages requires dedicated time and consideration from the librarians tasked with this responsibility and, as such, should be approached with clear goals and expectations. Our research suggests that dividing social media responsibilities by platform could allow librarians the space to develop their mastery of one platform, rather than splitting their focus. This can improve content quality and, as a result, interest in and engagement with the library's social media posts, while minimizing workload for librarians. However, as was in the case of the University Library, the subcommittee approach did evolve into the more collaborative direction that is now being used. We further recommend that libraries interested in adapting either model for their own use make a practice of frequent assessment in order to effectively align with the needs and expectations of their campus community.

ACKNOWLEDGMENT

The authors thank our colleague, Carolyn Caffrey Gardner, at the California State University Dominguez Hills University Library whose insight and generous comments greatly improved the quality of this research.

This research received no specific grant from any funding agency in the public, commercial, or not-for-profit sectors.

REFERENCES

About account home. (n.d.). Retrieved August 29, 2018, from https://help.twitter.com/en/managing-your-account/twitter-account-home

About your activity dashboard. (n.d.). Retrieved August 29, 2018, from https://help.twitter.com/en/managing-your-account/using-the-tweet-activity-dashboard

ALA. (2001). *Libraries making good use of social media and Web 2.0 applications*. Retrieved August 21, 2018, from http://www.ala.org/news/mediapresscenter/americaslibraries/socialnetworking

Alhabash, S., & Ma, M. (2017). A tale of four platforms: Motivations and uses of Facebook, Twitter, Instagram, and Snapchat among college students? *Social Media Society*, *3*(1). doi:10.1177/2056305117691544

Anderson, M., & Smith, A. (2015) Social Media Use 2018. *Pew Research Center*. Available at: http://www.pewinternet.org/2018/03/01/social-media-use-in-2018/

Brookbank, E. (2015). So much social media, so little time: Using student feedback to guide academic library social media strategy. *Journal of Electronic Resources Librarianship*, *27*(4), 232–247. doi:10.1080/1941126X.2015.1092344

Chen, D. Y., Chu, S. K., & Xu, S. (2012). How do libraries use social networking sites to interact with users. *Proceedings of the American Society for Information Science and Technology*, *49*(1), 1–10. doi:10.1002/meet.14504901286

Clark, M., & Melancon, J. (2013). The influence of social media investment on relational outcomes: A relationship marketing perspective. *International Journal of Marketing Studies*, *5*(4), 132–142. doi:10.5539/ijms.v5n4p132

Gollin, M. (2018a). *The 2018 Instagram algorithm change: what it means for marketers*. Retrieved August 13, 2018, from https://www.falcon.io/insights-hub/topics/social-media-strategy/the-2018-instagram-algorithm-change-what-it-means-for-marketers/#/GEN

Gollin, M. (2018b). *How will the 2018 Facebook algorithm change affect marketers?* Retrieved August 13, 2018, from https://www.falcon.io/insights-hub/industry-updates/social-media-updates/facebook-algorithm-change/#/GEN

Harrison, A., Burress, R., Velasquez, S., & Schreiner, L. (2017). Social media use in academic libraries: A phenomenological study. *Journal of Academic Librarianship*, *43*(3), 248–256. doi:10.1016/j.acalib.2017.02.014

Hendrix, D., Chiarella, D., Hasman, L., Murphy, S., & Zafron, M. L. (2009). Use of Facebook in academic health sciences libraries. *Journal of the Medical Library Association: JMLA*, *97*(1), 43–46. doi:10.3163/1536-5050.97.1.008 PMID:19159005

Howard, H., Huber, S., Carter, L., & Moore, E. (2018, March). Academic libraries on social media: Finding the students and the information they want. *Information Technology and Libraries*, *37*(1), 8–18. doi:10.6017/ital.v37i1.10160

Insights | Facebook Help Center | Facebook. (n.d.). Retrieved August 29, 2018, from https://www.facebook.com/help/794890670645072/?helpref=hc_fnav

Jacobson, T. B. (2011). Facebook as a library tool: Perceived vs. actual use. *College & Research Libraries*, *72*(1), 79–90. doi:10.5860/crl-88r1

King, D. L. (2015). Chapter 5: Analytics, goals, and strategy for social media. *Library Technology Reports*, *51*(1), 26–32.

Lenhart, A. (2015). Teens, social media & technology overview 2015. *Pew Research Center*. Retrieved from http://www.pewinternet.org/2015/04/09/teens-social-media-technology-2015/

Linh, N. C. 2008. A survey of the application of Web 2.0 in Australasian academic libraries. *Library Hi Tech, 26*(4), 630–53.

Mellon, C. (2015). Library anxiety: A grounded theory and its development. *College & Research Libraries*, *76*(3), 276–282. doi:10.5860/crl.76.3.276

Ntaka, A. (2017). *The use of social media sites by university library staff to facilitate undergraduate students* (Dissertation). Retrieved from http://urn.kb.se/resolve?urn=urn:nbn:se:lnu:diva-68483

Perrin, A. (2015) Social networking usage: 2005-2015. *Pew Research Center*. Available at: http://www.pewinternet.org/2015/10/08/2015/Social-Networking-Usage-2005-2015/

Rosen, A., & Ihara, I. (2017, September 26). *Giving you more characters to express yourself.* Retrieved from https://blog.twitter.com/official/en_us/topics/product/2017/Giving-you-more-characters-to-express-yourself.html

Socialbakers. (2011, April 19). *How often should you post on your Facebook pages?* Retrieved from https://www.socialbakers.com/blog/147-how-often-should-you-post-on-your-facebook-pages

Stvilia, B., & Gibradze, L. (2017). Examining undergraduate students priorities for academic library services and social media communication. *Journal of Academic Librarianship*, *43*(3), 257–262. doi:10.1016/j.acalib.2017.02.013

What's the difference between page views and page reach on Facebook? | Facebook Help Center | Facebook. (n.d.). Retrieved August 29, 2018, from https://www.facebook.com/help/274400362581037

Whiting, A., & Williams, D. (2013). Why people use social media: A uses and gratifications approach. *Qualitative Market Research*, *16*(4), 362–369. doi:10.1108/QMR-06-2013-0041

ADDITIONAL READING

Al-Daihani, S. M., & Abrahams, A. (2018). Analysis of academic libraries' facebook posts: Text and data analytics. *Journal of Academic Librarianship*, *44*(2), 216–225. doi:10.1016/j.acalib.2018.02.004

Ballard, T. 2012. Google this!: putting Google and other social media sites to work for your library. Oxford [England]: Chandos Pub, Chandos Publishing.

Collins, G., & Quan-Haase, A. (2012). Social media and academic libraries: Current trends and future challenges. *Proceedings of the American Society for Information Science and Technology*, *49*(1), 1–4. doi:10.1002/meet.14504901272

Dale, P., Beard, J., & Holland, M. (2011). *University libraries and digital learning environments*. Farnham, Surrey, England; Burlington, Vt.: Ashgate.

Ezumah, B. A. (2013). College students' use of social media: Site preferences, uses and gratifications theory revisited. *International Journal of Business and Social Science*, *4*(5).

Garofalo, D. A. (2013). *Building communities: Social networking for academic libraries*. Philadelphia, PA: Chandos Publishing. doi:10.1533/9781780634012

Nicholas, W., Watkinson, A., Rowlands, I., & Jubb, M. (2011). Social media, academic research and the role of university libraries. *Journal of Academic Librarianship*, *37*(5), 373–375. doi:10.1016/j.acalib.2011.06.023

Sahu, M. K. (2016). Best practices of social media in academic libraries: A case study of selected engineering college libraries of Odisha. *DESIDOC Journal of Library and Information Technology*, *36*(5), 302–308. doi:10.14429/djlit.36.5.10445

Valenza, J. K. (2014). *Social media curation*. Chicago, IL: ALA TechSource.

Chapter 5
Assessing Social Media Use in Instruction and Marketing

Jennifer Joe
https://orcid.org/0000-0002-6067-0415
University of Toledo, USA

ABSTRACT

Assessment is increasingly important for libraries to address, as it speaks to justification for funding and support from the larger university. Many university budget models now require departments and colleges to be self-funding, whereas the library does not have traditional revenue sources. Statistics, including retention impact, encourage faculty and staff to promote library use to their students and encourage departments and colleges to support funding the library. This chapter explores best practices for assessing social media use in the context of instruction and marketing. It outlines the reasons for implementing an assessment plan as well as the steps necessary to successfully assess social media use, starting with outlining the specific goals for social media use, all the way through review and modification of the social media plan.

INTRODUCTION

The frequent use of social media, especially among traditional age college and university students, typically defined as 18-24 year olds, is all but assumed, though specific networks and modes of use continue to be redefined. A recent study conducted by Pew Research Center found that 88% of 18-29 year olds use some form of social media, and that number only drops by 10% for the next age cohort, 30-49 year olds (2018, p.4). Social media has become an information source, and as such, the library as an educational institution has a duty to embrace social media use in order to continue serving these patrons to the best of their ability. A study by Yan, Zha, Yan, and Zhang (2016), which sought to explore students' self-efficacy in the use of digital libraries and databases, recommends that, "If students can begin to use digital libraries upon entering universities with the help of librarians, their self-efficacy in getting information would gradually develop… with the results that users can reap significant rewards…(p. 1105)." It stands to reason that a similar effect would be achieved if libraries made it a priority to include social

DOI: 10.4018/978-1-5225-8097-3.ch005

media in library instruction and other aspects of library services. Though students may have been using both digital libraries and social media prior to attending university, they would benefit from guidance from librarians to strengthen their skills, especially in judging information veracity and applicability.

The way that libraries choose to embrace this technology, however, can vary from institution to institution. Some libraries use social media as a marketing tool; some use social media as an instruction tool. Some libraries may even do both. An analysis of publications on the topic of libraries and social media conducted by Gupta, Dewan, and Pp. (2014), found that libraries use social media for a range of activities, including, "customer services, news and updates, content/collection promotion, [disseminating] research output, [making] provision of educational tools and resources, and [building] relationships both within and outside of the institution (p. 9)." However, whatever way they embrace it, these projects can have varied levels of success. This is in part because many libraries approach social media without a defined plan. Other libraries do not have the appropriate personnel infrastructure in place. Still more libraries do not have the appropriate tools to administer assessment effectively, or knowledgeable personnel in place to analyze the results.

This chapter outlines the need for an assessment cycle as it pertains to social media use, and suggests best practices for tailoring assessment to specific social media networks, tools, and program goals. With a plan in place, a direction to move in, and someone to lead the charge, academic libraries can have success with social media.

BACKGROUND

To begin, social media is defined as, "... the means of interactions among people in which they create, share and exchange information and ideas in virtual online communities and networks" (Fang, Wen & Prybutok, 2014, p.336). This is an extremely broad definition of social media, which not only encompasses familiar public networks, such as Facebook and Twitter, but also learning management systems such as Blackboard and Canvas, that may include chat, instant messaging, and discussion board features. It also includes early internet features such as message boards.

Why, then, is social media important now? Previously, such networks had limited access, whether it was due to a lack of access to technology (such as the expense associated with the first personal computers) or due to the networks themselves restricting access. After all, even Facebook was originally restricted to college students only (Rosmarin, 2006). When that major network went public, and other similar networks arose to compete with it, use of social media spread. At the same time, computers were becoming smaller, cheaper, and more use-friendly. Cellular phone technology also played a role in the rapid spread of social media use. The ubiquitous nature of social media fundamentally changed the concept of information exchange and consumption. The ability for everyone – or nearly everyone – to be connected with each other at any given time has created a rapid fire exchange of information. This rapid exchange of information can lead to problems of information overload, and the spread of misinformation. Savolainen (2015) found four barriers associated with information seeking behavior, of which information overload was one. The other barriers were, "unawareness of relevant information sources, low self-efficacy, [and] poor search skills (Savolainen, 2015, p. 619)." Libraries in general, and academic libraries specifically, have positioned themselves as experts in the field of information – as is evidenced by the title given to most departments that teach library science: the School of Library and Information Science. Librarians already assist students in overcoming the barriers of awareness, skill-learning and confidence in those skills. The next step is to help students deal with information overload. To do this, Hallis (2017) recommends that instruction, "nurture critical thinking so students can effectively evaluate, analyze and intelligently incorporate sources in their assignments (p. 373)," which can be done more effectively in unofficial sources of information like web search results and social media posts. Too often, students see the formality of databases as tacit approval from the librarians and their instructors, of the information held within and do not readily apply critical thinking to these sources. It is only natural that academic libraries would want to have a strong social media presence – to combat misinformation – and incorporate social media into their instruction offerings, to help students navigate information and avoid information overload.

At the same time, the United States in particular has seen a tumultuous economy, beginning with the Great Recession in 2008. State funding for higher education has decreased in many regions of the country, and colleges and universities have felt the pressure to 'do more with less.' One way to do this is to do comprehensive evaluation and assessment of departments, colleges, and programs. Cost-benefit analysis and return-on-investment have become educational buzz words, but both concepts had to be tailored to the educational field. There was also a return in some states to performance funding models for higher education, most notably in Indiana, Ohio, and Tennessee, driven by the economic downturn (Dougherty, Jones, Lahr, Natow, Pheatt and Reddy, 2014). The models by definition rely on statistics such as completion rates and job placements. To improve those numbers, universities rely on assessment and programmatic changes.

Even colleges and universities that have not felt economic pressure still benefit from assessment. In addition to saving money, it improves the work these institutions, which in turn can produce better outcomes for students. Libraries are not immune to the pressure to improve, evolve, and change, nor should they be.

MAIN FOCUS OF THE CHAPTER

Issues, Controversies, Problems

Assessment has become increasingly important in library and wider academic circles due in larger part to funding models and the need to justify expenses. The library is no longer considered the academic heart of the university, and must fight alongside every other unit and department on campus to maintain their relevancy in the eyes of the administration. While libraries do contribute to student learning, they cannot rely on this alone, and must also gather evidence about more subtle changes in the way students learn and how their dispositions for learning affect their behavior (Urquhart, 2018, p. 130)." in order to "think more deeply and widely about [library] value (Urquhart, 2018, p. 130)." .rely on Libraries also have to contend with the need for inflationary expenses; as more and more materials are bought through licensing agreements, these inflationary costs will rise and libraries must have data to justify the budget increase, or face a static budget and ensuing cuts to the collection.

Assessment provides a mode to generate statistics for presentation at university-level administrative meetings. Administrators, especially those who do not understand the inner workings of libraries, may respond more favorably to statistics. They answer two important questions: how many students is the library helping and what are the outcomes of these efforts to help? In essence, statistics reveal whether or not the library is contributing to the university mission on par with the level of its funding. That being said, holistic assessment need not be confined to statistical data; as Urquhart (2018) writes, "unstructured and textual data are important as well (p.126), citing a study by Dunne et al. (2014), which explored the possibilities for assessing and demonstrating impact through both qualitative and quantitative means.

Assessment also provides these benefits within the library. Different library departments have different responsibilities and some of these are easier to quantify than others. For example, an acquisitions and cataloging department has a concrete number of materials that have been processed, records that have been generated, and so on. These things have, for the most part, either been done correctly or incorrectly, and have been consistent with the demand for their services or not. How does one compare that to an outreach and instruction department, then?

When budgets are stretched thin, and individuals have to take on increasingly harder workloads, assessment can also guide the way. Assessment can show what is working and what isn't; libraries can discard what does not work and increase the use of what does work. It may even lead to the justification for new hires to spread the workload more evenly, or to capture the talent of individuals better suited for certain tasks. This assessment of human capital is an as-yet untapped area of growth for assessment in the libraries, with Town (2014) finding that there was, "very little literature on the coherent measurement of this major component of the expenditure of academic and research libraries…(p.73)."

College and university libraries should be applying assessment to all marketing and instruction plans, including those that use social media. Social media specifically should be addressed and assessed separately from larger plans because of its changing nature. Demographics of users for different platforms change regularly, and reaching students may be difficult if those in charge of the social media messaging and use are not aware of these trends.

Another trend emerging in other disciplines and worth exploring in library science is evidence-based practice. This, simply put, is the concept of tailoring what work one does around concepts and techniques that have been proven to work, and assessing new concepts and techniques to rigorous standards to provide evidence for their continued use and so that other individuals and institutions can use them as well. This trend emerged first in the medical field in the 1990s, and has since been applied to librarianship (Luo, 2018). Luo's (2018) study found that most evidence based practice in librarianship was of a practical nature, gathering evidence to fulfill a point of need, much like the research many patrons do. A culture of assessment, not only in individual institutions, but among library practitioners world-wide, could help develop evidence based practice beyond what currently exists.

SOLUTIONS AND RECOMMENDATIONS

With this emphasis on assessment, and the meteoric rise in social media use, the only answer is to start treating the library's social media use with the same rigor applied to any other thing the library does. This can be a daunting and stressful task for an unprepared institution.

One suggestion to alleviate the stress of social media is to have someone designated as a social media manager. This person would have control of all the social media accounts for the university libraries and control any access granted to other individuals for specific marketing promotions or class instruction use. They would also issue guidelines for librarians to follow if using social marketing tools that are not officially sanctioned by the university library. A person in this position should have an excellent working knowledge of different social media networks and be able to explain the differences between them, have a good attention to detail, and be willing to be aware of and involved in new social media trends.

In addition, public relations research identified nine important roles a social media manager should be prepared to take on:

1. Oversight of social media
2. Internal Collaborator
3. Policy maker
4. Policing
5. Technology tester
6. Communications organizer
7. Issues manager
8. Relationship analyzer
9. Master of metrics (Neil and Moody, 2015, p.112)

That being said, the library does not exist in a vacuum, and perhaps administrative facilitator should be added to this list. While a library specific social media manager is important to promote the library's social media goals, they will have to perform their job duties within the larger university context and serve as a liaison between the library and the university's public relations and marketing teams, to ensure that library activity is in line with university goals.

In many situations though, it may not be possible to hire a new position. In that case, the next best plan is to have a social media committee, made up of individuals who possess at least some of the attributes listed previously and can fill in those roles as a collaborative group. For those institutions who might be experiencing work overload and fatigue, getting through the formation and stabilization of another committee may be daunting, but there are practices learned from others' projects that can help alleviate the stress: encouraging input from all library staff through multiple and varied means, setting realistic timelines and celebrating when goals are met, and offering incentives and gratitude to participants (Adam, Burgess, McPhee, Olson, & Sich, 2018).

Joe (2015) speaks of the social media manager or committee in terms of branding and consistency, especially with regards to marketing, which is an important function of having someone in charge of social media. However, there is another facet to having someone in charge: they can be a point person when administrators need statistics, and can keep the lines of communication open about what kind of information would best support the library's mission. This may actually cut down on the manager or committee's work, as they will not spend valuable time hunting down data that the library will not use.

The next step in dealing with social media is to address assessment of social media the same way one would address any other new thing: an assessment cycle, as shown in Figure 1.

Originally outlined by Joe (2015), and modified for simplicity here, this assessment cycle begins with identifying the library's goals for using social media. These goals may have distinct levels, including library mission goals, departmental goals, program goals, and individual post/interaction goals. Assessment should be performed, whether formal or informal, separately for each goal, though data collected for one goal may be useful in assessing another goal. The second step after identifying goals is to do research on social media networks to find a network that suits the goal or goals in question and fits within the program or assignment. This is an important step, because there may be secondary goals (such in the case of classroom instruction) or institutional restrictions on the use of certain types of social media that may make the original plan impossible. A thoughtful consideration of these factors will prevent the librarian from focusing on what is easy and direct their attention to what is right for the project. Step

Figure 1.

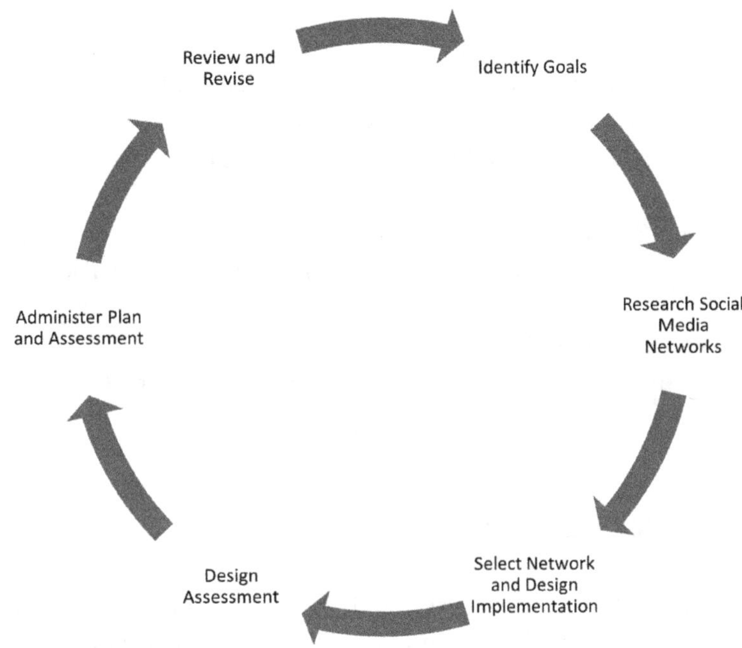

three is to select a social media network from the research step and design an implementation plan. In marketing, this would be the timeline and content; for classroom instruction this would be the lesson plan using the social media network. Step four is to design assessment, deciding whether it should be formal or informal, what information it will collect that will support the identified goals, and in the case of classroom instruction, whether the assessment will affect students' grades. Step 5 is to administer the plan and assessment. Step 6, and arguably one of the most important steps, is to review the results of the assessment and make changes as necessary. This may mean adjustments to a project while it is still on going, or making notes on observations for the next time a similar plan is implemented, depending upon the nature of the project.

Finally, assessment must be tailored to the social media used, the tools available to the librarian, and the goals that the librarian, department, or library has outlined when the plan was implemented. Assessment methods include surveys, polls, quizzes, and rubrics, as well as computer programs that can measure participation and qualitative means such as focus groups and interviews. In the classroom setting, assessment can take the form of pre and post assessments, formative assessment, summative assessments, confirmative assessments, and ipsative assessments. Formative assessments are used to identify gaps in learning, and by proxy, gaps in teaching or problems with the tools used. Summative assessments are used for measuring the effectiveness of students' learning. Confirmative assessments measure whether tools continue to be effective session after session and that students are still learning as effectively. Ipsative assessments measure performance against previous performance. Which assessment tool is chosen will depend on the goals of the project and how long the project will be carried out. Some assessments are better at assessing the social media network and whether it has performed as expected, such as formative assessment, and some are better at assessing students' learning regardless of the social media network, such as summative assessment.

Assessing social media can be as simple as an additional question or two on a quiz or survey geared toward the main topic of an assignment, such as:

- How did using [social media tool] help you with this assignment?
- Were there any problems with [social media tool] or anything you had difficulty with?
- Do you have any suggestions for social media tools that could be used in the future?

Assessment can also be more in depth, with entire surveys dedicated to understanding how students used the tool in question. In the case of a graded assignment, librarians can also assess proficiency with the tool or gauge how the use of the tool might have impacted students through rubrics. Another way to assess social media use might be to develop the same assignment with several social media tools and compare students' results. In all cases, feedback from the students will be key, as they will be the ones using the social media tool.

FUTURE RESEARCH DIRECTIONS

As social media use continues to rise, new issues and challenges will emerge. For example, the "fake news" or misinformation crisis currently plaguing major social media networks needs to be addressed by libraries. In-roads have been made into dealing with this problem, but a more defined and rigorous approach to information, which, after all, is the commodity libraries deal in, is necessary. Assessment of programs developed by libraries to combat this and other issues not only help the library that created the plan, but will help other libraries duplicate the results.

Tools for assessment that can be used for multiple platforms and to assess multiple goals should be developed and shared freely among libraries for the good of the discipline. One way to facilitate the universality of assessment tools is to use the Association of College and Research Libraries' *Standards for Proficiencies for Assessment Librarians and Coordinators*. Emmons and Oakleaf (2016) write, "Librarians who share an interest in assessment could use the *Standards* to build a community of practice around academic library assessment (p. 623)." With many librarians addressing similar goals at a variety of institutions, generic tools for popular social media platforms can easily be created. Tools for assessment may also be borrowed or reworked from other, closely related disciplines such as education and communication. Recruiting librarians who have work experience in these adjacent fields may also help. Assessment is done in many fields, and a study found that second-career academic librarians in instruction considered their prior work to be a "significant advantage," a "finding [that] was statistically significant for every skill category that was being examined, save one, communication (Bryan, 2016, p.349)." Among their surveyed skills was assessment. Assessment positive-practices can also be facilitated in the library by support from the larger university and the library administration (Farkas, Hinchliffe, and Houk, 2015)

In addition, as technology continues to develop, new social media networks will rise. On the horizon, potentially, is social media that incorporates virtual reality technology, and this is surely not the only technology that will impact social media. Libraries will need to address these changing technologies and how they change information exchange and consumption. Old problems, as well, can become new ones: bots, or social robots, found on social media sites like Twitter, have become more sophisticated, and are capable of aggregating data and posting in ways that are more human-like, making it harder for even seasoned professionals to identify them (Ferrara, Varol, Davis, Menczer, And Flammini, 2016). Evolving problems like this will make assessment even more important, as teaching style and content will need to change to help students identify these problems.

CONCLUSION

Social media is not something that the library can avoid, but using it without a plan, methods of assessment, and expected deliverables can result in brand damage, wasted time and resources, and a lowering of morale among employees. Planning, however, can be a smooth process if one employs the same structures that have helped assess other library services and programs. Assessment of social will help contribute to a larger culture of accountability and the exchange of results and proven methods will help build a better evidence-based practice among all library professionals.

REFERENCES

Adam, T., Burgess, C., McPhee, K., Olson, L., & Sich, C. (2018). Collaboratively Creating a Programmatic Information Literacy Strategy: Challenges and Opportunities. *Partnership: The Canadian Journal of Library and Information Practice and Research, 13*(1), 1–21. doi:10.21083/partnership.v13i1.4063

Bryan, J. (2016). The Preparation of Academic Librarians Who Provide Instruction: A Comparison of First and Second Career Librarians. *Journal of Academic Librarianship, 42*(4), 340–354. doi:10.1016/j.acalib.2016.05.010

Dougherty, K., Jones, S., Lahr, H., Natow, R., Pheatt, L., Reddy, V., & Mclendon, M. (2014). Performance Funding for Higher Education: Forms, Origins, Impacts, and Futures. *The Annals of the American Academy of Political and Social Science, 655*(1), 163–184. doi:10.1177/0002716214541042

Emmons & Oakleaf. (2016). The ACRL Standards for Proficiencies for Assessment Librarians and Coordinators: A New Document to Support and Strengthen Assessment Efforts in Academic Libraries. *The Journal of Academic Librarianship, 42*(5), 622-624.

Fang, J., Wen, C., & Prybutok, V. (2014). An Assessment of Equivalence between Paper and Social Media Surveys: The Role of Social Desirability and Satisficing. *Computers in Human Behavior, 30*, 335–343. doi:10.1016/j.chb.2013.09.019

Farkas, M. G., Hinchliffe, L. J., & Houk, A. H. (2015). Bridges and Barriers: Factors Influencing a Culture of Assessment in Academic Libraries. *College & Research Libraries, 76*(2), 150–169. doi:10.5860/crl.76.2.150

Ferrara, E., Varol, O., Davis, C., Menczer, F., & Flammini, A. (2016). The rise of social bots. *Communications of the ACM, 59*(7), 96–104. doi:10.1145/2818717

Gupta, B., Dhawan, S., & Pp, V. (2016). Social Media and Libraries: A Scientometric Assessment of World Output, 2003-2014. *SRELS Journal of Information Management, 53*(1).

Hallis, R. (2017). Internet outfitters: Librarians in the twenty-first century. *Library Management, 38*(6/7), 369–379. doi:10.1108/LM-02-2017-0012

Luo, L. (2018). Experiencing Evidence-Based Library and Information Practice (EBLIP): Academic Librarians' Perspective. *College & Research Libraries, 79*(4), 554–567. doi:10.5860/crl.79.4.554

Pew Research Center. (2018). *Social Media in 2018* [Complete Report]. Retrieved from www.pewinternet.org/wp-content/uploads/sites/9/2018/02/PI_2018.03.01_Social-Media_FINAL.pdf

Rosmarin, R. (2006, September 11). Open Facebook. *Forbes.*

Savolainen, R. (2015). Cognitive barriers to information seeking: A conceptual analysis. *Journal of Information Science, 41*(5), 613–623. doi:10.1177/0165551515587850

Stvilia & Gibradze. (2017). Examining Undergraduate Students' Priorities for Academic Library Services and Social Media Communication. *The Journal of Academic Librarianship, 43*(3), 257-262.

Town, S. (2014). The value of people: A review and framework for human capital assessment in academic and research libraries. *Performance Measurement and Metrics, 15*(1/2), 67–80. doi:10.1108/PMM-05-2014-0019

Urquhart, C. (2018). Principles and practice in impact assessment for academic libraries. *Information and Learning Science, 119*(1/2), 121–134. doi:10.1108/ILS-06-2017-0053

Wright Joe, J. (2015). Assessment of Social Media in the Library: Guidelines for Administrators. *Journal of Library Administration, 55*(8), 667–680. doi:10.1080/01930826.2015.1085251

Yan, Y., Zha, D., Yan, A., & Zhang, Q. (2016). Exploring the effect of individual differences on self-efficacy in getting information. *Information Development, 32*(4), 1097–1108. doi:10.1177/0266666915588795

Zha, Y., & Yan, L. (2018). Exploring the effect of social media information quality, source credibility and reputation on informational fit-to-task: Moderating role of focused immersion. *Computers in Human Behavior, 79*, 227–237. doi:10.1016/j.chb.2017.10.038

ADDITIONAL READING

Albert, A. B. (2014). Communicating Library Value— The Missing Piece of the Assessment Puzzle. *Journal of Academic Librarianship, 40*(6), 634–637. doi:10.1016/j.acalib.2014.10.001

Blevins, A., & Inman, M. (2014). *Curriculum-based library instruction: From cultivating faculty relationships to assessment.* Medical Library Association Books.

Broussard, M. (2014). Using Games to Make Formative Assessment Fun in the Academic Library. *Journal of Academic Librarianship, 40*(1), 35–42. doi:10.1016/j.acalib.2012.12.001

Butler, K., & Byrd, J. (2016). Research Consultation Assessment: Perceptions of Students and Librarians. *Journal of Academic Librarianship, 42*(1), 83–86. doi:10.1016/j.acalib.2015.10.011

Crumpton, M., & White, P. (2016). Connecting real learning with social media ROI. *The Bottom Line (New York, N.Y.)*, *29*(1), 2–11. doi:10.1108/BL-10-2015-0020

Dobbs, A. (2017). *The library assessment cookbook*. ACRL Cookbook Series.

Enis, M. (2017). Social media is an important communications channel for libraries. Experts discuss how to do it right. *Library Journal*, *142*(14), 38–40.

Hamid, S., Bukhari, S., Ravana, S., Norman, A., & Ijab, M. (2016). Role of social media in information-seeking behaviour of international students. *Aslib Journal of Information Management*, *68*(5), 643–666. doi:10.1108/AJIM-03-2016-0031

Harrison, A., Burress, R., Velasquez, S., & Schreiner, L. (2017). Social Media Use in Academic Libraries: A Phenomenological Study. *Journal of Academic Librarianship*, *43*(3), 248–256. doi:10.1016/j.acalib.2017.02.014

Howard, H., Huber, S., Carter, L., & Moore, E. (2018). Academic Libraries on Social Media: Finding the Students and the Information They Want. *Information Technology and Libraries*, *37*(1), 8–18. doi:10.6017/ital.v37i1.10160

Karak, S. (2017). Impact of awareness of library resources through electronic and social media on students: A model for library awareness. *International Journal of Information Dissemination and Technology*, *7*(4), 292–294. doi:10.5958/2249-5576.2017.00043.7

Kim, K., & Sin, S. (2016). Use and Evaluation of Information From Social Media in the Academic Context: Analysis of Gap Between Students and Librarians. *Journal of Academic Librarianship*, *42*(1), 74–82. doi:10.1016/j.acalib.2015.11.001

Malenfant, K. J., Hinchliffe, L. J., & Gilchrist, D. (2016). Assessment as Action Research: Bridging Academic Scholarship and Everyday Practice. *College & Research Libraries*, *77*(2), 140–143. doi:10.5860/crl.77.2.140

Mckee, A. (2017). Selfies, Scavenger Hunts and Scrawls: How the Vise Library Used Social Media to Increase Usage. *Computers in Libraries*, *37*(9), 4–9.

Mezick, E. (2015). Relationship of Library Assessment to Student Retention. *Journal of Academic Librarianship*, *41*(1), 31–36. doi:10.1016/j.acalib.2014.10.011

Nitecki, D., Wiggins, J., & Turner, N. (2015). Assessment is not enough for libraries to be valued. *Performance Measurement and Metrics*, *16*(3), 197–210. doi:10.1108/PMM-10-2015-0032

Oakleaf, M., Whyte, A., Lynema, E., & Brown, M. (2017). Academic libraries & institutional learning analytics: One path to integration. *Journal of Academic Librarianship*, *43*(5), 454–461. doi:10.1016/j.acalib.2017.08.008

Persson, S, & Svenningsson, M. (2016). Librarians as Advocates of Social Media for Researchers: A Social Media Project Initiated by Linköping University Library, Sweden. *New Review of Academic Librarianship*, *22*(2-3), 304-314.

Sharun, S., Edwards Thomson, M., Goebel, N., & Knoch, J. (2014). Institutions collaborating on an information literacy assessment tool. *Library Management*, *35*(8/9), 538–546. doi:10.1108/LM-03-2014-0035

Stewart, B., & Walker, J. (2018). Build It and They Will Come? Patron Engagement Via Twitter at Historically Black College and University Libraries. *Journal of Academic Librarianship*, *44*(1), 118–124. doi:10.1016/j.acalib.2017.09.016

Zhu, Q. (2016). The application of social media in outreach of academic libraries' resources and services. *Library Hi Tech*, *34*(4), 615–624. doi:10.1108/LHT-05-2016-0055

KEY TERMS AND DEFINITIONS

Assessment Plan: The method by which one will judge the efficacy of a project.

Assessment: Judging the efficacy of a project.

Community of Practice: A group of people who share a craft or a profession.

Evidence-Based Practice: Making decisions by identifying for a practice and rating it according to scientific soundness.

Justification: The action of showing something to be right or reasonable.

Learning Management Systems: Software application for the administration and delivery of educational courses.

Chapter 6
Is Anybody Out There?
Using Application Statistics and Web Analytics to Assess Social Media Reach

Junior Tidal
New York City College of Technology (CUNY), USA

ABSTRACT

This chapter will explore how social media assessment is used for library marketing. It will build upon existing literature on how other libraries quantify social media impact in promoting their services. This includes methods on how libraries can gather native application statistics from popular platforms such as Facebook, Twitter, YouTube, and Instagram. An exploration into web analytics will also be explored as evidence of social media impact. The chapter will use case-studies of the Ursula C. Schwerin Library of the New York City College of Technology (City Tech), CUNY, and how social media platforms are used to advertise library events and disseminate news.

INTRODUCTION

In the last few years, social media has made impacts in culture, politics, and most notably, libraries. Libraries and librarians are known as early technology adopters, with over 1,300 libraries possessing Twitter accounts (Emery & Schifeling, 2015). After observing 6 Midwest academic libraries, Harisson et al., make the claim that libraries "must use social media in order to retain legitimacy in today's college environment (2017)." This make sense as 68% of Americans use Facebook accessing the service on a daily basis (Smith & Anderson, 2018). As libraries utilize social media it is important to analyze if these networks are making an impact in providing their services.

This chapter will explore how social media assessment is used for library marketing. It will build upon existing literature on how other libraries quantify social media impact in promoting their services. This includes methods on how libraries can gather native application statistics from popular platforms such as Facebook, Twitter, YouTube, and Instagram. An exploration into web analytics will also be explored as evidence of social media impact. The chapter will use case-studies of the Ursula C. Schwerin Library of the New York City College of Technology (City Tech), CUNY, and how social media platforms are used to advertise library events and disseminate news.

DOI: 10.4018/978-1-5225-8097-3.ch006

BACKGROUND

There has been an enormous amount of literature related to the development of social media in libraries in the last few years. As of this writing, there are over 7,400 articles related to social media in the Library & Information Science Source electronic database. 86% of public libraries are using social media to connect with users (Dowd, 2013). It can be used for collaborative work and opens opportunities for advertising library services (Delaney & Bates, 2015). Social media tools can be a "useful discovery tool for scanning and finding users' comments" of an organization (Koontz & Mon, 2014).

Social media is useful as it can help build an online community around the library. Montana State University utilized its Twitter feed to creating more interactive postings by developing an internal social media guide, developing plans to focus on the audience, and intentional and frequent posting (Young & Rossman, 2015). Facebook was used to specifically cater to a community of young adults, by promoting materials, programming, and services, for those particular patrons (Philips, 2015). In China, libraries specifically target users of the WeChat app, a popular social media mobile chat platform, to boost and promote library services (Xu et al. 2014).

Although there is an abundance of scholarly literature on social media, there is a gap in focusing specifically on social media assessment in libraries. There are, however, articles in the larger literature that do touch upon it. Burclaff notes that when assessing social media it is important to create a strategy that identifies goals so quantifiable metrics, like click-throughs and student feedback, can be measured (2014). Libraries can also use influence, the amount of sway an organization has on its followers, or engagement, the amount of conversation a post generates, to measure the effectiveness of social media (Blowers, 2012).

MAIN FOCUS OF THE CHAPTER

The City Tech Library uses multiple social media platforms, including Facebook, Twitter, Instagram, YouTube, Flickr, and Pinterest. Each of these platforms has their own form of built-in statistics. This ranges from the complex, such as Facebook's page insights or Twitter's built-in analytics tools, to the more the simplistic like Instagram's number of likes. This chapter will look specifically at Facebook, Twitter, and Instagram.

Facebook

Facebook is a social media platform that allows its users to share information between one another, groups, and online communities. It offers a wide variety of statistics on followers visiting a library's Facebook page, using an analytics tool called Facebook Insights (see Figure 1). Administrators can access Insights through the top menu of the Facebook page.

Statistics such as page views, likes, reach, recommendations, engagements, and more are displayed. Information can be cross-referenced by date (today, yesterday, past week, and past 28 days) for comparison. There are several different metrics that Insights uses. Page views are self-explanatory. Likes indicates how many people have "liked" your page. It also displays posts from your page that appear in the user's feed that are liked. Reach is the number of people who have seen posts from your page (see Figure 2).

Figure 1. Facebook Insights displays a variety of metrics of users

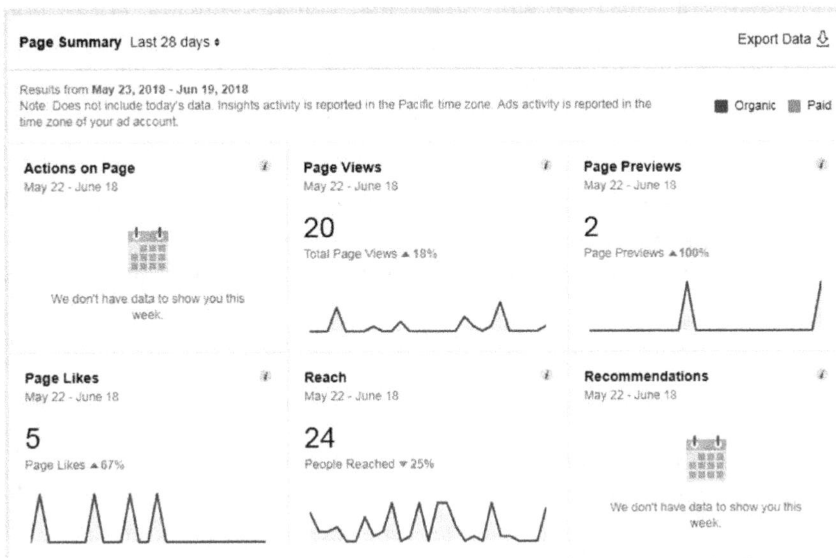

The recommendations metric indicate which users have shared your page with others. Engagement is the number of times users have liked, commented, or shared your posts.

There are other metrics that Facebook Insights records in relation to your page. Actions are user interactions that are taking place on your page. This may include clicking on directions, external websites, or phone numbers. Posts displays all the posts published on a page. It indicates when fans are online and the different types of posts, such as links, that are on your page. Thronbill and Houk point out that postings should be frequent, be highly visual, and be posted at the peak times that pages are visited (2013).

Figure 2. A display of Facebook posts and the number of users each reach

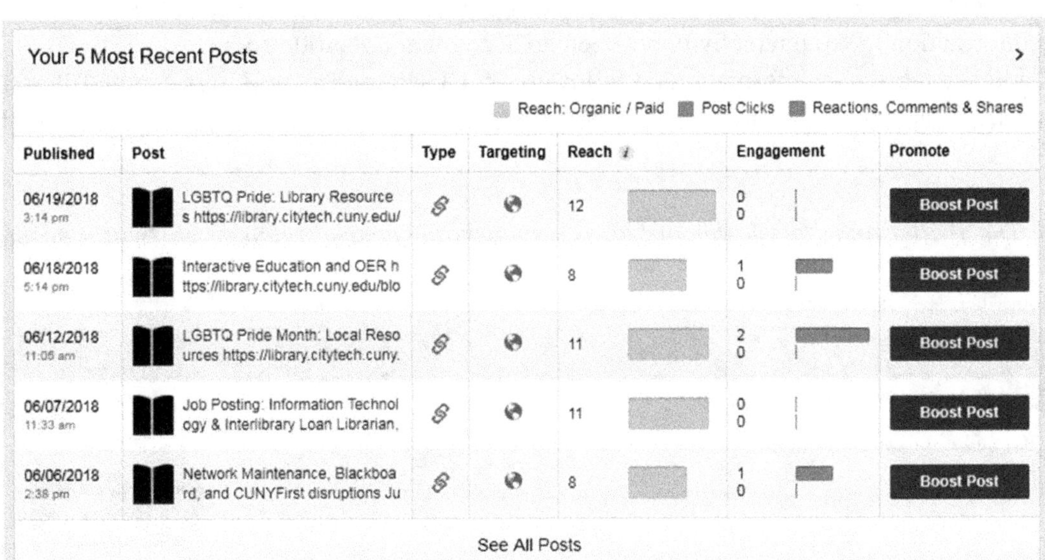

The other metric that Insights displays for posts include the top posts of pages that you are watching. This allows the comparison of your page with others that you are viewing. For example, you may be part of a consortium or branch library and you want to see what other posts they are displaying. It can also be a way to share posts from other pages you are watching.

The videos and stories categories show statistics when that type of media on your page are viewed. The people category displays demographic information about followers, as well as what country and city that they originate from. This section of Insights also shows what languages they use. The last category of the Insights page is messages, which presents active conversations between your page and users of Facebook Messenger. Facebook also has an analytics tool (https://analytics.facebook.com) that can be used to track users from your website to your Facebook page.

Twitter

Twitter is a microblogging social media platform where posts are known as "tweets." Tweets can be replied to, favored (liked), or retweeted. It is a microblogging service because the number of characters that can be posted are finite. Twitter has an analytics tool that librarians can use to see how well tweets are received. This tool also gives information on an account's followers, users who actively monitor an account.

Much like Facebook Insights, Twitter Analytics (TA) displays metrics such as the monthly number of tweets produced, tweet impressions, profile visits, mentions, and followers (see Figure 3). It can be found here - https://analytics.twitter.com/about. Impressions are the collected number of views of a tweet or conversation. Profile visits, similar to page views, are the number of times a profile has been seen by a user. Mentions indicate the number of times a profile has been referenced in an external tweet. Followers are the number of users following a Twitter account. TA also provides more in-depth information through various tabs, including the audience tab, events tab, and video and conversion tabs. All of this collected data can be exported into other formats for further manipulation.

The tweets tab displays the number of impressions a tweet has earned over a given time period. These can be filtered to display the top tweets, replies, and promoted tweets. Impressions, engagements, and engagement rate are also available for further analysis. Link clicks, retweets, likes, and replies also provides information to see interactivity between an account and its followers.

The audience tab shows information on followers of a Twitter account. Users can be filtered by all Twitter users, an account's followers, or organic audiences. These different types of users can then be

Figure 3. The Twitter Analytics dashboard gives a snapshot of metrics related to a Twitter account

compared in real-time within TA. This tab lists users' top interests, demographic information, lifestyle (interests), consumer behavior, and mobile footprint. Interests represent what topics the majority of your users favor. This can be useful for crafting specific tweets. Demographic information lists gender, household income, languages used, what country they are tweeting from, and which region or state they are from. This tab also displays what mobile carriers followers use. The consumer behavior tab displays the top products audience users have purchased.

The events tab displays trending events that are popular on the platform. Drilling down into specific events, events can show the demographics of a popular event, the number of tweets, impressions, and reach, the top tweets, and the countries that event is popular in. TA can also be used as a jumping board to create a social media campaign in relation to these events. Events can also display recurring actions. For example, the events can display #FBF. #FBF, or flashback Friday, is a popular hashtag where users post or repost a moment in their past.

In addition to those tabs, TA can also display analytics for videos posted on Twitter and conversion tags. The video tab shows the reach of an account's video. The conversion tag system is much like Google Analytics (GA), where user behavior can be tracked on a website by embedding Twitter's tracking code. This can be used to place a dollar amount to the interactions of a Twitter account on a website.

Instagram

Instagram is a photo-based social media platform which is designed specifically for mobile devices, such as smartphones and tablets. Using the built-in camera of these devices, users are able to take photos and videos posting them to their accounts along with a caption. Users can also post "stories," which disappear from the platform after 24 hours. Followers of an Instagram account can "like" posts on their feed or comment. Accounts can be made private or public, and the platform has seamless integration with Facebook and Twitter. Unless it is private, accounts do not necessarily need to be following one another to view each other's posts. These posts can be followed using hashtags, or Instagram's search interface. Instagram has also launched IGTV, which provides users with longer-format videos.

Owned by Facebook, Instagram's analytics tool is called Instagram Insights. Insights provides statistics on individual posted photos. It provides information regarding the overall interactions of an account. This feature, however, is only available for business accounts. It should be noted that standard accounts can be converted to business accounts. So, if a library has a standard Instagram account it can be altered to become a business account.

Instagram Insights, like the other native analytics tools discussed, provides numerous metrics. Individual photo metrics include the number of likes, comments, and saves of a post. Insights displays information such as interactions, discovery, reach, and impression. Interactions are similar to those in Facebook Insights. This metric is the total number of likes and comments on a post. Discovery is the number of accounts that had seen a post, including those that do not follow your account. Reach is the number of unique users that have seen your post. Impressions is the number of times a post or story has been seen.

Insights also presents the top posts based on impressions. Engagement is the total number of accounts that have liked, saved, or commented on a post. Instagram users, known as the "audience," is also analyzed within Instagram Insights. Audience metrics include age, gender, location, active hours, active days, story impressions, and top followers. These metrics are self-explanatory, but indicates an account's overall audience. They are useful for developing strategic social media campaigns, which will be discussed later.

SOLUTIONS AND RECOMMENDATIONS

Web Analytics

Application statistics are not the only tools that the modern-day social media engaged librarian has at their disposal. Google Analytics, which can be found at https://analytics.google.com and its open-source counterpart, Matomo (formerly known as Piwik and is located at https://matomo.org/) are two web analytics tools that can track social media traffic coming into a library website. This data can be used to better understand user engagement. Wright notes that "statistics provide an excellent start for assessing whether or not social campaigns are successful, but they may not give much information about problems or reasons why campaigns are not successful (2015)."

Google Analytics

In a nutshell, GA is used to gather information on web traffic for a specific website. Developed by Google, GA provides a number of metrics ranging from user engagement, referrals (where traffic is originating from), what pages on a site are visited, what pages users are exiting from, and much more. The system works by adding JavaScript to the header of a webpage. This script triggers the analytics server to record interaction data from that page. This is then processed and centralized on the GA website, where administrators can login and view the data collected from the website over a period of time.

There is an abundance of literature related to GA. Vecchione et al. used GA to better understand their users by identifying the navigation pathways used inside and out of the site (2016). It has been used to improve the design and content of library websites (Fang, 2007, Turner, 2010), develop learning objects (Betty, 2009), and understand LibGuides usage (Griffin and Taylor, 2018). There has also been literature criticizing GA due to privacy concerns. McKenzie argues that GA should not be used within libraries due to ethical and privacy concerns (2017). Cornell has replaced their installation of GA stating, "for privacy-related reasons alone, Piwik is a better web analytics solution for libraries. (Chandler and Wallace, 2016)."

GA can be used to evaluate social media reach. GA has a "Social" reports tab under the "Acquisitions" menu, that displays data from 8 different categories. This includes overview, network referrals, data hub activity, landing pages, trackbacks, conversions, plugins, and user flow.

The overview tab is the main dashboard for the social reports tab. It shows the social value of the website. It lists network referrals, the number of overall sessions of a site, and how many of those sessions originate from social media. Network referrals displays the sources and pages that users utilize on your site through social media (see Figure 4). These can be used to develop navigation schemes or prioritize campaigns for users originating from specific platforms. For instance, it can display all the sessions that had originated from Twitter and landed your blog URL. By clicking on a specific social media network within this tab, it can display the URLs that users entered through. Knowing this information, content on that page can be catered specifically for Twitter users.

Landing pages is a metric that shows what pages social media users "land" on. For example, if a user connects to the library website homepage through Facebook, this metric will display this. GA can be used to cross-reference these statistics, so it is also possible to see which of those users visited the homepage using a tablet or mobile device. With this in mind, specific webpages, if not the whole site

Figure 4. The social media page in Google Analytics show what networks are used to connect to the website

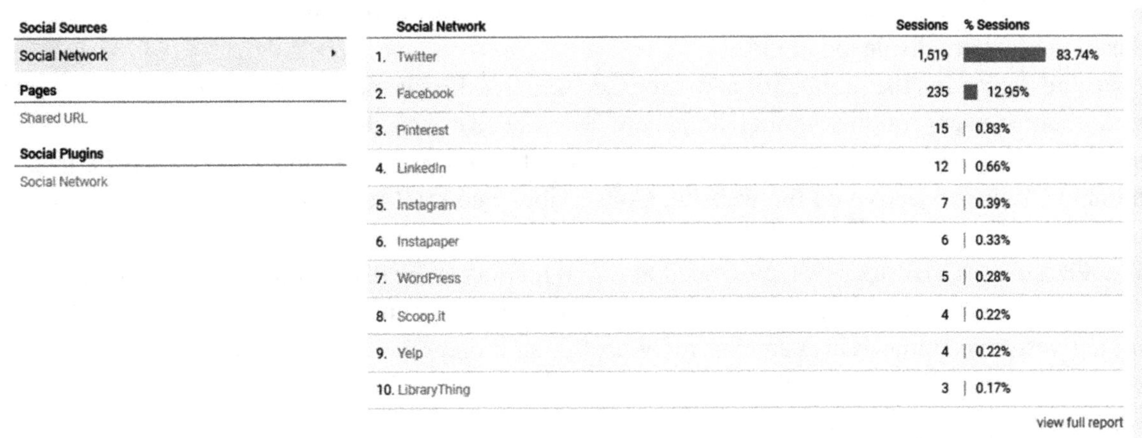

already, could be rendered mobile friendly. Again, this can be used to target specific users. In this scenario, it could potentially be Facebook users using a Smartphone.

Conversions is an analytics report show the return of investment (ROI) in social media using monetary measurements. This function requires a goal to be setup through the admin menu, where administrators can set a dollar amount. For example, one could setup a goal to have GA track every time the electronic resources page on a library website is accessed via social media and assign a dollar value to that conversion. This may be useful to show the budgetary value of social media and to justify subscriptions for electronic resources.

The social plugins is a category that displays information regarding social media buttons on the website. This system tracks when users click a social media link through that button on a webpage. If your website has a Twitter button or icon it will record the number of clicks that button receives. This is useful to see how many users are utilizing the library website to access social media platforms.

The users flow is a visualization of traffic navigating a site. It records how users enter the site, the pages they traversed, and how they exited the site. This can be useful to better understand bulk traffic. One scenario could be how successful a social media campaign is to promote a group of electronic resources. A group of electronic resources could be promoted via Twitter, and this visualization could see which specific resource is being traversed to.

Matomo

Matomo is a popular open-source alternative to GA. It offers similar features to that of GA, yet it is open-source and cost-free. It does require some technical know-how for installation. The prerequisite of running a Matomo server include a web server installed with PHP, a web parsing language, and MySQL, a popular database language. It works on the same technical principles as its Google based counterpart. A line of JavaScript code is installed into each web page of a site to track users. Matomo can be hosted, like GA, but users can install the software on the web server itself. This allows data to be stored locally ensuring user privacy.

Matomo provides reports that can be applied for social media assessment. This widget can display metrics such as visits, actions, unique visitors, users, conversions, and total revenue. Many of these are similar to the metrics displayed in GA.

Visits are defined as the number of new users accessing a site for more than 30 minutes. Actions that Matomo records users conducting include page views, site searches, downloads or clicking on external links. Unique visitors are the number of users visiting the website, omitting multiple visits. Users is the number of visitors active on the website. Conversions and total revenue are parallel to the metrics found in GA.

Visualizations of visitors cross referenced to social media can be displayed as a bar graph, pie graph (see Figure 5), a table, and even a tag cloud. This will display the most visited social media platforms within a given time-frame. This can extremely useful, as it can give comparisons to the data reported in GA. For example, GA may display uncommonly used social media platforms (see Figure 6) in their statistics, whereas Matomo may not.

The analytics system can also display insights of social media, which displays the changes in visits over a period of time. Matomo also allows URLs to be "tagged," much like GA, so specific URLs can be tracked to see what links users are clicking on to reach the site. In addition, Matomo has exporting capabilities, rendering data in CSV, XML, PHP, RSS, TSV, JSON, and HTML. This can be helpful for sharing information with other librarians and administrators. Even further, this data can be parsed for data dashboards which may be useful for annual reporting.

Figure 5. A display of visits from social media networks to the website using Matomo

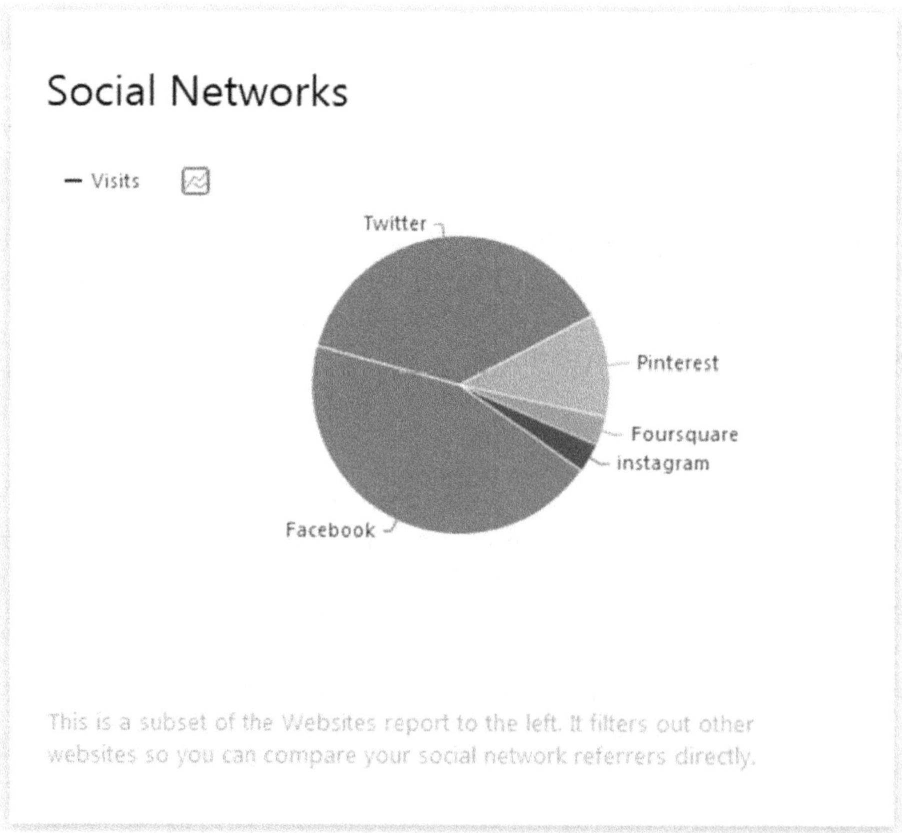

Figure 6. Matomo shows less used social media platforms

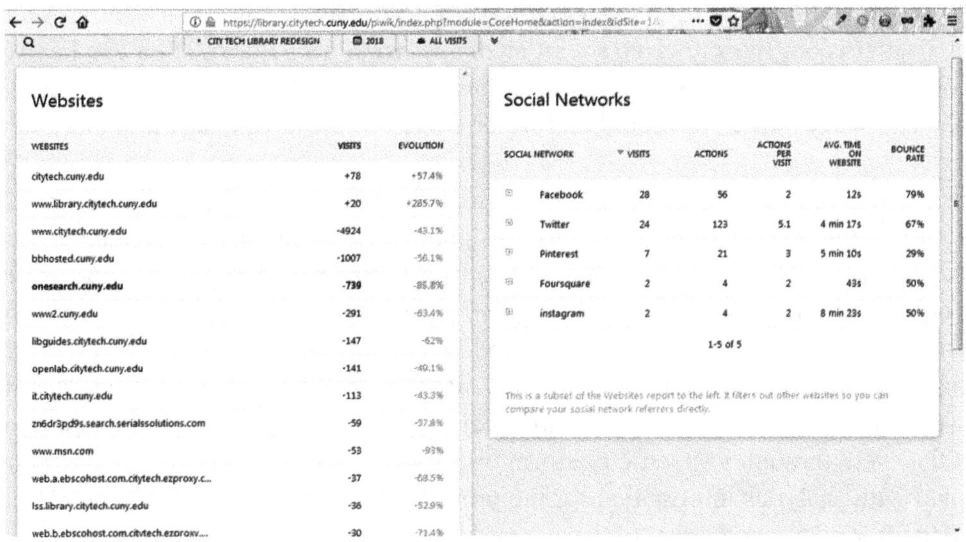

City Tech Analytics

The Ursula C. Schwerin Library has not used social media statistics to formally evaluate marketing and promotional reach. It is used more as a guideline of how things could improve. Burclaff mentions that “determining success is dependent on what you’re trying to achieve” when it comes to social media (2014). Social media strategies and goals should be developed prior to evaluating analytics. It would be difficult, if not impossible, to effectively assess a social media campaign if there were no benchmarks determined before the campaign.

Despite not using formal analytics analysis, the City Tech Library has utilized other methods to understand users’ behavior with social media. An online poll on the library website was used to determine which social media platforms the community uses. The anonymous poll was on the website for a full academic year. Although the result was a small sample of respondents (n=20), it was found that Instagram was the most popular platform, followed by Facebook, Twitter, and LinkedIn. It should be noted, however, that this does not necessarily mean our users were utilizing those platforms to visit our social media accounts. Instead, this information was used to initiate campaigns on Instagram, the most used platform.

Every semester, platforms are evaluated on an ad hoc basis. This coincides with the marketing and promotion of specific library events. The library does not have a designated social media librarian, but a formal internal committee known as the public relations, outreach, and marketing (PROM) committee. The PROM committee occasionally reviews social media statistics, such as the number of likes and which platforms referring to the library website.

GA and Matomo provides much more information that can be used to drive broad or specific social media campaigns. Some examples include better understanding website users, promoting library events, or reaching social media users not visiting the library website.

Social media analytics can find users' preferences. Using the City Tech library's analytics data, there are a number of generalities that can be derived. Over the course of a calendar year, GA and Matomo indicate that Twitter is our most referred social media network. This information can be used to target users from other platforms, such as sharing Instagram photos on Twitter or sending tweets with links to Facebook pages and events. This could be further enhanced using hashtags that are used to index a post or tweet.

Analytics can be used to strategically promote library events. For example, City Tech serves a very diverse and multicultural community. Facebook Insights indicates that there are languages other than English that users speak. This information can be useful to promote a library event specifically to speakers of those other modern languages. Inclusive library programs and events could be developed to cater to those particular users based on the statistics found in analytics.

Assessing this library event scenario is simple. Attendees can be asked how they heard about the event. A post-event survey, either through email, social media, or in-person, could enquire if they had heard about the event through a specific platform or if they speak another language. This information can be coupled with analytics information for the promotion of future events. By combining analytics and survey data, librarians can market to these target library users.

Another strategic approach to utilizing social media analytics for libraries is to reach those social media users who don't necessarily use the library at all. Twitter analytics provides a multitude of information that could be used to develop personas. Personas are a common usability method to develop archetypes based on real data. Ward notes that "personas can help us see user needs more clearly as we make decisions about how to provide services (2010)."

Deriving a persona from a combination of analytics tools can be useful to reach users who do not visit the library's website. In Figures 7 and 8, this image displays the Twitter analytics audience insight page of the City Tech Library. For instance, we can create a persona named Bob who lives in New York, speaks English and Spanish, is interested in science and uses an iPhone to access the Internet. We can also describe Bob as a male student, aged 17-22. Bob is active on social media with his mobile device, yet is easily distracted juggling a job and student life. He doesn't use the library.

Figure 7. Twitter reveals information about users through the audience insight page, such as interests

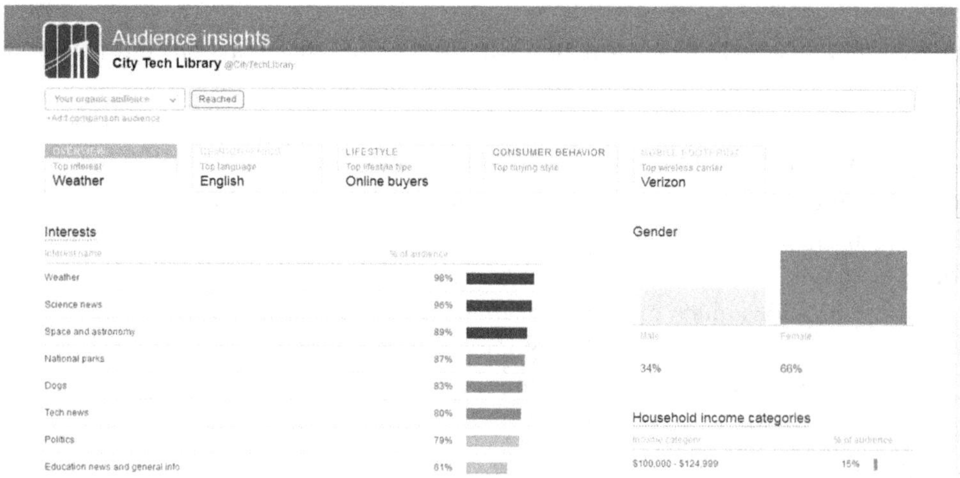

Figure 8. Audience insight shows what countries Twitter users are using the social media platform, based on IP

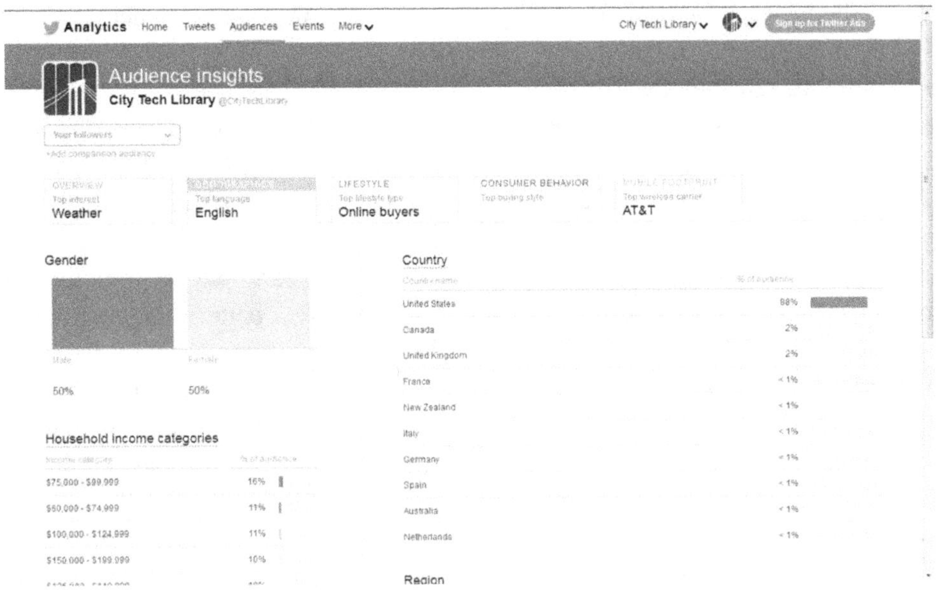

Since we have an idea of who "Bob" is, we can develop scenarios to market specifically to him. The end goal is to have Bob utilize the library website. Tweets that cater to Bob's interest in science could be one avenue to connect with him. We can construct a tweet promoting a new science-based electronic resource with hashtags that are used among City Tech students. We may also want to explore creating a bilingual tweet, since our persona speaks both English and Spanish. If there is an iPhone app for that electronic resource, which too can be promoted with a shortened URL to where it can be downloaded for Bob's consumption.

Assessing this campaign that has been developed using the Bob persona can be done by comparing it with real-world users. Similar to the event scenario above, surveys and questionnaires can be used to test users' reaction of our tweet with Bob. This can help determine if the campaign has been successful or not. For example, if these systems report that a majority of users are utilizing Facebook the most in comparison to other platforms, then campaigns can be designed to target other networks to promote library resources.

FURTHER RESEARCH DIRECTIONS: ANALYTICS IS JUST THE TIP OF THE ICEBERG

Statistics and analytics are not the only methods that a library's social media impact can be measured. These measures only provide one dimension of technological use, and at times can be quite limiting. Surveys, focus groups, and usability studies, can provide further insights into how patrons utilize social media. It is important to investigate the human aspect of how users truly engage social media to access library happenings and resources.

There are other usability techniques that can assess the performance of social media usage in libraries. As mentioned above, this can include questionnaires and surveys, focus groups, and usability testing. These research methods help round out the full picture of social media assessment. They can confirm or disprove assumptions made from analytics. More importantly, they can be used to find information that cannot be found through analytics data.

Questionnaires and surveys are useful because they can collect both quantitative and qualitative information from respondents. Likert scales can be used to discover the frequency, ease of use, and engagement of social media platforms. Besides using a persona as a point of reference for analytics data, questionnaires can be used to uncover information behind data. Data collected from surveys can be used to enhance personas and even make them more accurate. Our Bob example above notes that he doesn't use the library, but by asking a large sample of users, we can have a better understanding of why they don't use the library.

Another method of understanding users are focus groups. Focus groups are interviews with a collective of people facilitated by a stakeholder. A stakeholder could be a librarian, an administrator, a developer, or anyone who represents the library or institution. It can be beneficial for stakeholders to conduct a focus group, as interacting with users can prove or disprove assumptions about them. There is an immediacy in focus groups which may provide additional feedback with multiple participants (Battleson, Booth, and Weintrop, 2001). Focus groups may reveal insights on users' experiences with a library's social media plan, as they have with discovery systems (Brett, Lierman, & Turner, 2016), library based tutorials (Held & Gil-Trejo, 2016), and websites (Duncan, & Durrant, 2015).

Usability testing, specifically cognitive walkthroughs, can show librarians how their website works in conjunction with social media platforms. Cognitive walkthroughs are task-based heuristic evaluations of a website. Typically, a proctor will sit with a participant and have them complete a predetermined task. For example, the task could be identifying and interacting with the library's link to Facebook. The proctor can see first-hand how the user will navigate to that link and observe any obstacles from completing that task. This is coupled with the "think-aloud protocol" or TAP, where the user will discuss what they are thinking and feeling as they are navigating and attempting the task.

The TAP protocol can uncover not just usability obstacles, but can give opinions on social media embedded in the library website. Imagine a situation where users may say that the placement of social media icons in the footer is not effective. If users cannot see links to the library's social media platforms on the website, then they may be less likely to interact with them.

Once testing has ended, the website is updated to repair any usability obstacles or errors that the participant had encountered. This is re-tested again using the same task scenario, to observe the performance of the site with the repairs in place. Rubrics of success and failure rates can be applied for individual tasks to determine the effectiveness of a website in supporting a user.

Social media assessment is useful to better understand users. Utilizing it with the data gathered from usability and user experience studies can augment it to increase users, cater to their preferences, and ultimately understand them. These tools can be used to market library events and meet users where they are.

CONCLUSION

Social media assessment is an important aspect for libraries, as they digitally market their services. Native analytics within Instagram, Twitter, and Facebook can provide statistics about individual posts and generalities about users. Web analytics can further enhance this data to show how well a library's website interacts with its associated platforms. This data is useful as it can help direct campaigns, create personas, and be used to strategically communicate with users. However, analytics can only provide one piece of the bigger puzzle of how users use these services. Using other methods such as focus groups, surveys, and interviews, librarians can truly see how their community interacts with their digital presence.

REFERENCES

Battleson, B., Booth, A., & Weintrop, J. (2001). Usability testing of an academic library web site: A case study. *Journal of Academic Librarianship*, *27*(3), 188–198. doi:10.1016/S0099-1333(01)00180-X

Betty, P. (2009). Assessing homegrown library collections: Using Google Analytics to track use of screencasts and flash-based learning objects. *Journal of Electronic Resources Librarianship*, *21*(1), 75–92. doi:10.1080/19411260902858631

Blowers, H. (2012). Measuring social media and the greater digital landscape. *Computers in Libraries*, *32*(7), 27–29.

Brett, K. R., Lierman, A., & Turner, C. (2016). Lessons learned: A primo usability study. *Information Technology and Libraries*, *35*(1), 7–25. doi:10.6017/ital.v35i1.8965

Burclaff, N., & Johnson, C. (2014). Developing a social media strategy: Tweets, pins, and posts with a purpose. *College & Research Libraries News*, *75*(7), 366–369. doi:10.5860/crln.75.7.9156

Chandler, A., & Wallace, M. (2016). Using Piwik Instead of Google Analytics at the Cornell University Library. *The Serials Librarian*, *71*(3-4), 173–179. doi:10.1080/0361526X.2016.1245645

Delaney, G., & Bates, J. (2015). Envisioning the academic library: A reflection on roles, relevancy and relationships. *New Review of Academic Librarianship*, *21*(1), 3–51. doi:10.1080/13614533.2014.911194

Dowd, N. (2013). Social media: Libraries are posting, but Is anyone listening? *Library Journal.*

Duncan, A. P., & Durrant, F. (2015). An assessment of the usability of the University of the West Indies (Mona, Jamaica) Main Library's website. *The Electronic Library*, *33*(3), 590–599.

Emery & Schifeling. (2015). Libraries Using Twitter Better: Insights on Engagement from Food Trucks. In *Creating Sustainable Community The Proceedings of the ACRL 2015 Conference* (pp. 593-604). Association of College and Research Libraries: Chicago.

Fang, W. (2007). Using Google Analytics for improving library website content and design: a case study. *Library Philosophy and Practice*, 1-17.

Griffin, M., & Taylor, T. I. (2018). Employing Analytics to Guide a Data-Driven Review of LibGuides. *Journal of Web Librarianship*, 1–13.

Harrison, Burress, R., Velasquez, S., & Schreiner, L. (2017). Social media use in academic libraries: A phenomenological study. *Journal of Academic Librarianship*, *43*(4), 248–256. doi:10.1016/j.acalib.2017.02.014

Held, T., & Gil-Trejo, L. (2016). Students Weigh In: Usability Test of Online Library Tutorials. *Internet Reference Services Quarterly, 21*(1/2), 1–21. doi:10.1080/10875301.2016.1164786

Houk, K. M., & Thornhill, K. (2013). Using Facebook page insights data to determine posting best practices in an academic health sciences library. *Journal of Web Librarianship, 7*(4), 372–388. doi:10.1080/19322909.2013.837346

Koontz, C., & Mon, L. (2014). *Marketing and social media: A guide for libraries, archives, and museums*. Lanham, MD: Rowman & Littlefield.

McKenzie, J. (2017). *Ethics of using Google Analytics*. Presented to the User Experience Interest Group. Retrieved from http://summit.sfu.ca/item/17107

Phillips, A. L. (2015). Facebooking it: Promoting library services to young adults through social media. *Public Library Quarterly, 34*(2), 178–197. doi:10.1080/01616846.2015.1036710

Turner, S. J. (2010). Website statistics 2.0: Using Google Analytics to measure library website effectiveness. *Technical Services Quarterly, 27*(3), 261–278. doi:10.1080/07317131003765910

Smith, A., & Anderson, M. (2018, March 1). *Social Media Use in 2018*. Pew Internet Research Center. Retrieved from http://www.pewinternet.org/2018/03/01/social-media-use-in-2018/

Vecchione, A., Brown, D., Allen, E., & Baschnagel, A. (2016). Tracking user behavior with Google Analytics events on an academic library web site. *Journal of Web Librarianship, 10*(3), 161–175. doi:10.1080/19322909.2016.1175330

Ward, J. L. (2010). Persona development and use, or, how to make imaginary people work for you. In *Building Effective, Sustainable, Practical Assessment* (pp.477 - 483). Academic Press.

Wright Joe, J. (2015). Assessment of social media in the library: Guidelines for administrators. *Journal of Library Administration, 55*(8), 667–680. doi:10.1080/01930826.2015.1085251

Xu, J., Kang, Q., Song, Z., & Clarke, C. P. (2014). Applications of mobile social media: WeChat among academic libraries in China. *Journal of Academic Librarianship*, 41.

Young, S. W. H., & Rossman, D. (2015). Building library community through social media. *Information Technology and Libraries, 34*(1). doi:10.6017/ital.v34i1.5625

ADDITIONAL READING

Al-Daihani, S. M., & Abrahams, A. (2018). Analysis of Academic Libraries' Facebook Posts: Text and Data Analytics. *Journal of Academic Librarianship, 44*(2), 216–225. doi:10.1016/j.acalib.2018.02.004

Dority Baker, M. L. (2013). Using Buttons to Better Manage Online Presence: How One Academic Institution Harnessed the Power of Flair. *Journal of Web Librarianship, 7*(3), 322–332. doi:10.1080/19322909.2013.789333

Foster, M., Wilson, H., Allensworth, N., & Sands, D. T. (2010). Marketing Research Guides: An Online Experiment with LibGuides. *Journal of Library Administration*, *50*(5/6), 602–616. doi:10.1080/01930826.2010.488922

Guza, T. A. (2011). Washington Libraries Reveal Social Media Secrets. *Alki*, *27*(1), 19–21.

Konkiel, S., & Guichard, S. (2018). Altmetrics: "big data" that map the influence of New Zealand research. *Library Hi Tech News*, *35*(4), 1–5. doi:10.1108/LHTN-04-2018-0021

Mahmood, K., & Richardson, J. V. Jr. (2013). Impact of Web 2.0 technologies on academic libraries: A survey of ARL libraries. *The Electronic Library*, *31*(4), 508–520. doi:10.1108/EL-04-2011-0068

Rivosecchi, M. (2014). Social Media in an Academic Library: One Piece of the Puzzle. *Feliciter*, *60*(4), 45–46.

Stewart, B., & Walker, J. (2018). Build It and They Will Come? Patron Engagement Via Twitter at Historically Black College and University Libraries. *Journal of Academic Librarianship*, *44*(1), 118–124. doi:10.1016/j.acalib.2017.09.016

Sutton, S., Miles, R., & Konkiel, S. Q. (2018). Awareness of Altmetrics among LIS Scholars and Faculty. *Journal of Education for Library and Information Science*, *59*(1/2), 33–47. doi:10.3138/jelis.59.1-2.05

Vucovich, L. A., Gordon, V. S., Mitchell, N., & Ennis, L. A. (2013). Is the Time and Effort Worth It? One Library's Evaluation of Using Social Networking Tools for Outreach. *Medical Reference Services Quarterly*, *32*(1), 12–25. doi:10.1080/02763869.2013.749107 PMID:23394417

Chapter 7
Diversity and Inclusion:
How to Avoid Bias and Social Media Blunders

Shelly Black
University of Arizona, USA

ABSTRACT

The academic library profession has discussed the importance of diversity and inclusion, but has yet to explore their intersection with social media marketing. Given changing demographics and an increase in activism on college campuses, libraries must produce social media content that resonates with underrepresented groups. This chapter introduces strategies for effectively incorporating diversity and inclusion into social media and advice on avoiding mistakes. The author examines social media use at her library and lessons learned from a campaign that received criticism. The chapter concludes with challenges to practicing diversity in social media, including recruiting diverse staff and discrimination that emerges from new social media technologies.

INTRODUCTION

There has been no shortage of social media mishaps related to implicit bias. In October 2017, the soap company Dove posted an online video ad on Facebook showing a Black woman turning into a White woman. A few months later, the clothing retailer H&M featured an image on its website of a Black child wearing a hooded sweatshirt with the text "coolest monkey in the jungle." Both incidents resulted in a viral backlash against the companies online and in stores. Although academic library social media may not have the audience of multinational companies, the potential negative virality of online content requires the staff responsible for social media content to be racially sensitive.

As college campuses become more diverse, library social media managers must be intentional not only in posting engaging content that encourages people to use the library, but also in creating content which resonates with people representing different social identities and backgrounds. Photos, graphic design, videos, and messages should empower underrepresented groups, not oppress them. By reinforcing social injustice, social media can lead to a communications disaster and repercussions for the library, as well as the academic institution.

DOI: 10.4018/978-1-5225-8097-3.ch007

Libraries have long had a central role in serving diverse populations. Diversity includes, but is not limited to, race, ethnicity, gender, sexual orientation, age, physical ability, religion, socioeconomic status, and national origin. When working with groups who currently suffer from injustices, or historically have been suppressed, it is essential to practice inclusion: the act of valuing them, respecting them, and making them feel welcome. Since the 2016 presidential election, diversity and inclusion have become prominent topics within the library discourse. There have been webinars on serving immigrants and refugees, conference presentations on neutrality, topical LibGuides, and strategic plans incorporating diversity. From collection development to staff recruitment and retention, librarians and library staff are critiquing and trying to remove systemic bias and inequities. Amid these efforts, the impact of marketing, especially social media, cannot be taken lightly. Social media is public-facing, and consequently it provides the first impression of the library that many students, parents, donors, and alumni see. In a time of increased budget pressures and accountability to the parent institution, public perception can work to the benefit or detriment of the library.

Although existing literature on library social media marketing includes case studies, discussion of best practices, and a number of surveys of how different organizations have used these platforms, discussion of diversity regarding content creation is lacking. This chapter argues for embedding diversity and inclusion in social media marketing, a critical practice in times of increasing political unrest, socioeconomic uncertainty, and a change in the demographic makeup and attitudes of users.

Attempting an intersectional perspective of identity, the author presents strategies for incorporating diversity and inclusion into social media, as well as tips on avoiding mistakes. She also presents an examination of social media use at her library and the criticism received when sharing historical photos of the university. The chapter concludes with challenges staff may face while championing diversity in social media, including discrimination emerging from new social media technologies such as targeted advertising and chatbots. A lack of staff resources, including diverse members, may also pose a problem when creating diverse and inclusive content.

BACKGROUND

Since Donald Trump was elected president and took office in January 2017, higher education has been impacted by: changes in immigration policy (Ayoub & Beydoun, 2017); a growing presence of white supremacism on college and university campuses (The Anti-Defamation League, 2018; Vasquez, 2018); harassment and intimidation of professors (Levy, 2018); and legislative efforts to hinder academic freedom (H.B. 2120, 2017). The academic library is often said to be the heart of campus, and thus, not immune from these threats to the community it serves.

Students and faculty of color have been especially affected by the changes in the political climate. The Muslim Ban has instilled fear and anxiety in immigrants from the countries it targets (Ayoub & Beydoun, 2017). The rescission of the Deferred Action for Childhood Arrivals (DACA) has left many students wondering if they will be deported. Amplifying these concerns is a rise in racism on college campuses. In 2016, there were 25% more hate crimes at 6,506 institutions compared to the year before (United States Department of Education, n.d.). At the time of writing, the Trump administration is rescinding guidance documents which encourage universities to consider race when admitting students to recruit a more diverse student population (United States Department of Education, 2018).

Discrimination affecting campus communities of color is not limited to federal measures and criminal attacks on individuals. White supremacist groups, such as Identity Evropa and Patriot Front, are disseminating fliers, posters, and stickers to recruit students (The Anti-Defamation League, 2018). During the 2017-18 school year, there was a 77% increase in this propaganda at 287 universities compared to the year before (The Anti-Defamation League, 2018). The conservative, non-profit organization, Turning Point USA, has spent $2,206,000 to influence student government elections around the country (Vasquez, 2018). The group was founded by Charlie Kirk, who Trump (2018) called "a great warrior" at a White House conference on Millennial leaders. Turning Point USA also operates the Professor Watchlist website whose mission is "to expose and document college professors who discriminate against conservative students and advance leftist propaganda in the classroom" (Turning Point USA, n.d.).

Free speech and academic freedom are being tested by both legislatures and university administrators. In Arizona, the author's state, a bill was introduced to prohibit "courses, classes, events, and activities" which "promote . . . social justice toward a race, gender, religion, political affiliation, social class or other class of people" or "advocate ethnic solidarity or isolation based on ethnicity, race, religion, gender or social class" (H.B. 2120, 2017).

In August 2017, the University of Tampa fired adjunct professor Kenneth L. Storey over his Twitter post suggesting that Texas deserved Hurricane Harvey's destruction (Robertson, 2017). Then in October, Drexel University, in Philadelphia, Pennsylvania, put professor George Ciccariello-Maher on administrative leave after he posted a series of controversial tweets, including a call for "white genocide" (Jaschik, 2017). These incidents involved incendiary language and raised the question of First Amendment protection outside the classroom. They also illustrate the power of one social media post. Publishing the disclaimer, "views are my own," in the Twitter bio is no longer enough to protect one's job.

Despite the chilling effect faculty may feel online or in their classrooms, a growing resistance can be found within academia's largest population: students. Milkman (2017) observed that the post-2008 wave of activism, which includes the campus movement against sexual assault, undocumented Dreamers/DACA, and Black Lives Matter, has been led by Millennials and powered by social media. The youngest activists, responding to the February 2018 shooting at Marjory Stoneman Douglas High School in Parkland, Florida, are propelling the #NeverAgain movement for gun control and are among this year's incoming freshmen (Ducharme, 2018).

Academic libraries have also had to choose how, or when, to react to threats to those they serve. The violence at the Unite the Right rally in Charlottesville, Virginia, in August 2017 caused libraries to reconsider their role in intellectual freedom, disaster preparedness, and communications. The American Library Association (ALA), Association of College and Research Libraries (ACRL), and Society of American Archivists (SAA) released statements denouncing the violence at the rally. Although the role of professional associations is to advocate on behalf of libraries and librarians, threats to people of color, immigrants, people with disabilities, the LGBTQ community, and other marginalized groups pressure libraries to respond in both their physical and virtual spaces. A lack of response can be interpreted as tacit approval.

Furthermore, there is pressure for organizations and companies to voice their political beliefs. In July 2017, the family, personal and household care product company Procter & Gamble posted a YouTube video titled, "The Talk," which showed scenes with Black parents telling their children about the bias they will encounter while growing up (Procter & Gamble, 2017). The 2017 Super Bowl commercials, seen on television and social media, addressed immigration, equality, and gender roles (Lopez-Medel, 2017). More companies are engaging with contentious issues in their promotional content, correlating with a change in public expectation. In a survey of 1,400 respondents from 14 countries, the marketing firm Edelman (2017) found that 53% of consumers buy from or boycott brands because of their stance on a social or political issue. Similarly, when surveying 1,000 Americans from different demographics, Cone Communications (2017) noted that 87% would purchase a product because its company advocated for an issue they cared about. When studying Black Millennials, Google/Ipsos Connect learned that 70% of participants were more likely to buy from a brand that takes a stand on race-related issues (King, 2017). Although the academic library is not a for-profit company, it still has a brand and public image to manage, and its social media does not exist within a vacuum. Users scroll through their feeds where the latest news from the White House is juxtaposed with a post from the library.

However, having an overtly political position is problematic for the academic library. Communications may need to align with the parent institution, and, for the public university, its governing board. The views of donors or other stakeholders may also need to be considered. How library leadership interprets the much-debated concept of neutrality will impact social media. It is arguable whether this entails commenting on an issue, releasing a statement offering support and services to students, or staying silent.

Despite these precautions, library staff and social media managers must remember that diversity is a core value of ALA. Many libraries include diversity or inclusion among their institution's values and strategic plans. The library can support marginalized groups by creating diverse and inclusive social media content. Some libraries already practice this, but not all of them do. That is not to say librarians are not engaged with topics like diversity, inclusion, and equity on social media.

In 2016, the ALA Office for Diversity, Literacy and Outreach Services (ODLOS) created the hashtag #LibrariesRespond and encouraged libraries to share how they respond to current events on social media (Granger, 2017). They also created a section on their website featuring resources about the Dakota Access Pipeline (DAPL) protests, and immigrant, refugee, and transgender student rights (American Library Association, 2018). Public libraries have used #LibrariesRespond when posting artwork with inclusive messaging, such as "Everyone is Welcome Here" (Granger, 2017) and "Libraries Are for Everyone" (Fialkoff et al., 2018). The Mortenson Center for International Library Programs at the University of Illinois Library and ALA jointly created Project Welcome, an initiative that produced recommendations and resources on how libraries can serve refugees and asylum seekers (Project Welcome, 2018). One of the project hashtags is #LibrariesRespond. At the University of New Mexico, education librarian Sarah Kostelecky wanted to support the movement against DAPL and circulated her LibGuide listing relevant resources (Granger, 2017). Besides these examples, academic library adoption of the hashtag is less widespread, possibly due to the precautions previously mentioned.

While it may be difficult for academic libraries, individual librarians have engaged in discussions relating to current events on social media. Columbia University rare book cataloguer Matthew Haugen created the hashtag #LibrariesResist for librarians opposed to the Trump administration and shared resources on topics including civic engagement, fake news, and privacy (Flock, 2017). In response to ALA publishing a press release that conveyed it was ready to collaborate with the Trump administration, librarians used the hashtag #NotMyALA to voice their concerns (Flock, 2017). Since 2014, librarians have used #critlib to organize Twitter chats on how social justice intersects with the profession. Previous chats have addressed tribal libraries, library staff with disabilities, and homeless patrons (Critlib, 2018). In 2015, Jessica Olin and Michelle Millet started the #libleadgender hashtag to have Twitter discussions relating to gender expectations in library administration positions (Olin & Millet, 2015). These online conversations about serving and advocating for diverse communities are valuable for their participants.

They should also continue offline with all staff of the academic library, including social media managers, the marketing and communications teams, and library leadership.

The growing body of literature regarding social media marketing in academic libraries has yet to examine diversity and inclusion. Since social media became mainstream in the late 2000s and early 2010s, libraries have adopted multiple platforms including Facebook, Twitter, Instagram, and Snapchat (Collins & Quan-Haase, 2014; Robinson, Peacemaker, & Hurst, 2018). Librarians have also surveyed students on what kinds of content they want to see. Findings have included library resources and events, research tips, and updates about operations (Brookbank, 2015; Howard, Huber, Carter, & Moore, 2018; Stvilia & Gibradze, 2017). Libraries have learned more about their users and developed content strategies. Subsequently, there have been numerous case studies and books on best practices. However, social media imposes a challenge on researchers. Services regularly change their features, and new platforms emerge, resulting in literature which quickly loses its currency. Thus, this chapter focuses exclusively on the importance and benefits of creating diverse and inclusive content regardless of the platform.

KNOW YOUR AUDIENCE: WHY CREATE DIVERSE AND INCLUSIVE CONTENT?

Increasing Diversity

The latest United States Census projections predict that by 2045, people of color will outnumber the White population, and that by 2020, there will be more of the former than the latter who are 18 years old and younger (Frey, 2018). While demographics continue to shift, so will the racial attitudes of Americans. The Pew Research Center (2016) found that 61% of Americans agreed that the country needed to make changes for racial equality between Blacks and Whites. In a survey of 4,000 Americans from different generational groups, market research firm Collaborata found that Gen Z, the generation born between 1998 and 2016, were more open-minded to having friends or romantic partners of other races than Millennials, Gen X, and Baby Boomers (Kane, 2017).

The changing racial landscape has already influenced higher education marketing. The increasing cost of tuition has resulted in admissions offices putting increased focus on recruiting more students. Hence, depicting racial diversity in promotional materials has become a necessary and competitive recruitment strategy (Pippert, Essenburg, & Matchett, 2013). Although diversity is used to attract both people of color and Whites, Ihme & Stürmer (2018) found that the former perceives it as "a signal of respect and tolerance, and the latter more because they perceive such cues as a signal of intellectual stimulation and variety" (p. 67). In their study, participants were shown mock-ups of fictitious university websites and preferred the ones that emphasized diversity. Even though university marketing has become more inclusive, Pippert et al. (2013) observed that diversity was depicted by skin color—so that more Blacks were included—and that Latinx and Native Americans were still underrepresented.

Marketing has a substantial role in reinforcing stereotypes (Davis, 2018; Kendrick, Fullerton, & Kim, 2013). Historically, people of color have been invisible or discriminated against in visual media and marketing (Davis, 2018). Native Americans appear as brand mascots, Asian Americans are seen as the model minority in technical careers, Blacks are depicted as athletic or modern-day mammies, and Latinx are portrayed as sexualized. Therefore, library social media managers must be cognizant of the power of images and where their content is positioned relative to the historical legacy of bias in visual representation.

Appealing to people of color is growing in importance in the advertising industry (James, Lee, Zhang, & Williams, 2017). Some companies work with agencies that specialize in marketing to specific ethnic groups. For example, Toyota's 2018 Camry campaign was developed by four advertising agencies where three focused on Black, Asian American, and Latinx consumers respectively (Maheshwari, 2017). The growing presence of people of color in marketing content is slow, but may help establish the expectations of social media users.

It is uncertain whether audiences prefer to see marketing featuring their ethnic group or a mix of ethnicities. Studies exploring race and ethnicity have indicated that people who strongly identify with an ethnic group have responded favorably to advertisements where they are represented (Cui, 1997; Green, 1999; Torres & Briggs, 2007; Whittler & Spira, 2002). However, Torres and Briggs (2007) also found that when viewing advertisements for luxury products, even those who highly identified with their ethnicity exhibited more positive attitudes towards advertisements with White models. Since the 1960s, marketing researchers have tried to assess the attitudes of White audiences towards advertisements featuring people of color. In one study, White participants exhibited less favorable attitudes towards advertisements with Black models than advertisements with White models, regardless of prejudice (Whittler, 1991).

One reason for these inconsistencies is that racism is difficult to define or operationalize in advertising research (Morris & Kahlor, 2014). Changing generational attitudes may also impact these kinds of studies. Cooley, Brice, Becerra, and Chapa (2015) claimed young adults have become more accepting of diversity as they encounter it in schools, neighborhoods, and the workplace; subsequently, they have preferred seeing diversity in an advertisement, as opposed to advertisements designed for and targeted to specific ethnicities. When more marketing and visual content is consumed on the internet and social media, researchers need to explore how this digital medium impacts viewer perceptions of race.

Who "Likes" Your Library?

The academic library has a broad audience on social media: students, faculty, staff, alumni, donors, and the public. Social media is vital for maintaining relationships with alumni and other stakeholders (Kaplan, 2017). In 2018, 68% of U.S. adults reported being on Facebook (Pew Research Center, 2018). Despite the Cambridge Analytica data breach and its resulting public outcry, Americans continue to use Facebook. In a Reuters/Ipsos poll of 2,194 adults, half of them had not changed their Facebook usage, a quarter increased usage, and the remaining quarter had stopped using it (Kahn & Ingram, 2018). Therefore, it can be assumed that libraries will continue to find their audience on social media, whether that is on Facebook, Twitter, Instagram, Snapchat, or a new platform that future teenagers embrace. Even though social media metrics provide data on the age, gender, and location of users, the type of relationship each user has with the library is unknown. A survey of followers could be insightful but would be limited by the number of respondents. Owing to this uncertainty, social media managers who do not post inclusive content may alienate their existing and potential followers. They may also risk a public challenge to the library and the institution's reputation. Public image and branding must be considered when universities struggle to fund and recruit both researchers and students.

Today's prospective students and their parents are no longer limited to on-site campus visits. When applying to schools, virtual tours and social media aid in their decision-making process. Incoming students use social media to see what life is like on campus, to learn about events, and to read reviews by current students (Galan, Lawley, & Clements, 2015). To stay informed and engaged with the campus community, current students may follow multiple social media accounts belonging to an institution.

According to Clark, Fine, and Scheuer (2017), the higher the number of accounts a student followed, the better their relationship was with their school. Given its role in serving all students, the academic library should aspire to have social media that these students want to follow.

With increasing online offerings and electronic resources, not all patrons will visit the library in person. Neither will all the members of its social media audience, such as prospective international students, alumni, or retired employees. For these reasons, creating social media content appealing to a diverse audience is crucial. Besides the subject matter being relevant to the service and resource needs of students, faculty, and researchers, the imagery and messages should incorporate and reflect diversity and inclusion as a regular and best practice.

SOLUTIONS AND RECOMMENDATIONS

How to Create Diverse and Inclusive Content

Diverse Photography

Social media users scroll through a massive amount of information on any given day, and much is conveyed in a matter of seconds through photography. Thus, photos taken in the library should feature students who represent different ethnicities, genders, ages, physical abilities, and religious identities. If the library does not have a photographer, staff can purchase stock photos or download free Creative Commons-licensed images. However, the author recommends that stock photos be used sparingly and only within promotional collateral. Stock photos can mislead library visitors by creating a false impression. For example, they may expect the library to have a particular study area or piece of technology. Savvy viewers may prefer authentic photos taken in the library, even if they are taken on a smartphone.

When organizing a photo shoot, the marketing staff should be aware that diversity is not about numbers. Asking the one staff member of color to be in every photo shoot places a burden on them. Likewise, identifying one student of color to appear in a photo of White students reduces that student to being a prop. In discussing global marketing, Borgerson and Schroeder (2002) explained that including an underrepresented group could result in a stereotypical depiction or tokenism. Consequently, the group becomes more invisible. Library marketing staff should make marginalized people feel respected because they are giving their time to participate in a photo shoot, and the final images should not look superficial.

Recruiting people of color to appear in photos while not succumbing to tokenism can feel more challenging for academic library staff who are located in an area with low diversity. Pippert et al. (2013) discovered that some universities misrepresent their diversity and that "admissions personnel understand that since it takes diversity to recruit diversity, presenting an image of what you would like to become is important" (p. 276). Racial demographics are changing, and libraries must decide whether their images are aspirational with regard to diversity or homogeneous. The former presents a more welcoming image, whereas the latter may send the wrong message.

User-Generated Content (UGC)

One strategy for curating social media material which advances diversity and inclusion is to share user-generated content (UGC). In the author's library, located at the University of Arizona in Tucson,

Arizona, students often take selfies and photos of Starbucks-fueled study sessions, sunsets taken from the top library floors, 3D prints, and whiteboard drawings. There have even been graduation portraits and photos of yoga poses in the stacks. Unlike recruiting students of different backgrounds to appear in library photos, sharing UGC is a more organic way to incorporate diversity into library marketing. It shows followers a less staged look of the library and its visitors. In a survey of 4,578 social media users in six countries, 76% of respondents reported that they trust UGC more than traditional forms of advertising (Olapic, 2016). Additionally, showcasing posts from social media followers empowers them and strengthens their relationship with the library.

Social media managers can identify UGC highlighting the library by monitoring library-related hashtags that students self-select or posts geotagged at the library. The author always asks users for permission to share their content and has received approval for every request. This practice is particularly useful for libraries lacking full-time marketing staff or the resources for taking photos. UGC also provides insight into the most popular services or spaces.

Resources and Services Reflecting Diversity

Library resources that are promoted on social media should interest different communities. The creation of a diversity calendar may be a useful starting point for social media managers. The library can show solidarity with underrepresented groups by sharing relevant collections or databases during: months celebrating or raising awareness of diverse groups; observances of different religions; and days commemorating historical events. The author also advocates going beyond the calendar and sharing a variety of diverse materials throughout the year. Staff may wish to consult ALA ethnic affiliates for resource recommendations. The affiliates include: American Indian Library Association (AILA); Asian/Pacific American Librarians Association (APALA); Black Caucus of the American Library Association (BCALA); Chinese American Librarians Association (CALA); and National Association to Promote Library and Information Services to Latinos and the Spanish Speaking (REFORMA).

Social media posts can give visibility to underrepresented groups and still relate to library services. For example, to recognize a past Martin Luther King, Jr. Day, the author shared a link to a downloadable 3D model of King and reminded users about the library's 3D printing service. During Asian Pacific American Heritage Month, the author posted a list of streaming database films that feature Asian Americans.

Inclusive Language

Diverse and inclusive content is not limited to images, nor is it limited to visible identities. The copy—the words that accompany the images or graphic design—can empower or dehumanize different identities (Kapitan, 2017). For example, when writing about people with different abilities, people-first language is recommended. The phrase "people who are visually impaired" is preferable to "the blind" because it emphasizes the person and not the disability.

When writing about different gender identities, staff should be conscientious of a person's preferred pronouns. There is already an increasing awareness of gender pronouns and their importance on college campuses. When registering, students can indicate which pronouns they use (Binkley, 2015), and instructors address pronoun usage in class syllabi (Pettway, 2017). Gender pronouns should be honored when writing about a specific person, and binary gender pronouns ("he" or "she") should be avoided when writing about general users. Marketing staff should adopt and use other gender-neutral terms, such as "Latinx," which are being normalized by media outlets like National Public Radio.

Diction may ultimately be determined by the library's parent institution and their writing style guide. For example, university communications may not permit the singular usage of the gender pronoun "they." Thus, marketing staff must be acquainted with and help other library staff understand how the library's editorial style guide is affected.

Accessibility

Social media content should be accessible to people with different abilities. In 2017, the U.S. Department of Justice determined that the University of California, Berkeley had violated the Americans With Disabilities Act (ADA) of 1990 by not providing captioning for publicly available audio and video recordings. As a consequence, the university had to remove 20,000 multimedia files (Straumsheim, 2017). Public, and even private, universities are affected by the ADA, so academic libraries should upload subtitle files for videos on social media. Multiple publishers have reported that 85% of Facebook videos are viewed without sound (Patel, 2016), so in addition to being ADA-compliant, captioned videos may be watched by more users.

When designing graphics, there are best practices for ensuring that the content is accessible to those with deficient color vision or other visual impairments. These include: a hierarchy of text and images to guide eye movement; having enough contrast between text and background color; typographic legibility, which depends on typeface weight and scale; and typographic readability, which depends on the width of a paragraph and space between letters (The Association of Registered Graphic Designers of Ontario, 2010). The author recognizes that not all libraries have a graphic designer or professional design software. In this situation, staff can use online graphic design tools that have limited functionalities to help keep content accessible.

In larger academic libraries, the social media manager may not be involved in event or workshop planning, or creating website content, but can advocate for more inclusive practices. When promoting events, the copy should include the offer of disability-related accommodations, such as ASL interpreting. Maps should identify accessible parking and entrances with the active wheelchair symbol. If links to a website or PDF file are provided, they should be accessible to individuals who use assistive technology like screen readers. If there is a disability resource center on campus, they may offer captioning services or interpreters at no cost to the library.

Producing social media content which is inclusive and mirrors the country's population is not necessarily easy. Libraries can begin by asking who is missing in a photo or excluded by the writing or multimedia. These recommendations are not exhaustive. However, the author's impetus is to inspire library staff to make changes and to be open to learning from mistakes. Refer to the additional readings at the end of this chapter for resources pertaining to Creative Commons-licensed images, accessible graphic design, inclusive language, and other recommendations mentioned above.

Unfollows, Trolls, and Fails

In early March 2018, Heineken ran a commercial with the tagline: "Sometimes, lighter is better" (Chokshi, 2018). In the advertisement, a bartender opens a beer bottle and slides it down the bar, passing two Black women and a Black man, before reaching a light-skinned woman. After social media users, including celebrities, criticized the commercial for being racist, the company stopped running it on March 26 and apologized in an email to The Independent:

For decades, Heineken has developed diverse marketing that shows there's more that unites us than divides us. While we feel the ad is referencing our Heineken Light beer—we missed the mark, are taking the feedback to heart and will use this to influence future campaigns. (Zatat, 2018)

This Heineken advertisement offers lessons to all marketers who seek to diversify their content without resorting to tokenism or appearing biased. Even though the commercial aired on television, the video was watched online, and the criticism quickly spread on social media. This kind of viral content can also result in a loss of followers and severed relationships. In a survey of 1,000 users, Sprout Social (2017) found that 6.5% of Millennials, 17.8% of Generation X, and 9.2% of Baby Boomers would unfollow a brand's social media due to offensive content.

Libraries are not immune from controversies; they are public spaces serving various patrons. Staff must be prepared for online communications disasters that arise from both born-digital and tangible content. These have included: exhibitions of artwork that are culturally insensitive (Kandiuk, 2017); the closure of the library during a right-wing rally on campus (University of Washington Libraries, n.d.); and a pornographic video filmed in the library (Sung & Sutton, 2015).

Be Prepared

Libraries need to be familiar with online reputation management which "involves knowing how to evaluate and react to any commentary on the Web about your library" (Solomon, 2014, p. 92). Staff should monitor social media for any library-related commentary and know how to respond to different kinds of negative feedback, whether it is merited and based on something the library has done, or unmerited and from trolls. Buckels, Trapnell and Paulhus (2014) defined trolling as "the practice of behaving in a deceptive, destructive, or disruptive manner in a social setting on the internet with no apparent instrumental purpose" (p. 97). Solomon explained that trolling is "almost always an attempt to bait your library into a pointless argument" and that it is best not to respond (2014, p. 101).

When negative comments are warranted, Solomon (2014) proposed that libraries take responsibility for their mistakes and not be defensive. In the case of Heineken, their apology lacked empathy and began with a defense of their past achievements before showing accountability.

Akin to having policies for collections development, donations, meeting spaces, or artwork displayed, libraries can prepare for negative responses by having an up-to-date social media policy and crisis communications plan. It should address negative feedback, how to respond, a timeline for responding—such as within 24 hours—and define the criteria for inappropriate posts that will be removed.

#WildcatTBT

At the University of Arizona Libraries in Tucson, Arizona, the author participates in the social media trend Throwback Thursday (TBT). This campaign entails sharing historical photographs of the university from the library's Special Collections almost weekly. Photographs depict student life as well as exterior views of campus. The University of Arizona (UA) mascot is the wildcat, so in collaboration with the university's central social media manager, the author established the branded hashtag #WildcatTBT.

This hashtag helps make these posts discoverable to those wanting to learn more about UA history and to marketing staff wanting to assess the performance of the #WildcatTBT campaign.

The UA's central social media accounts have shared #WildcatTBT posts, other departments have adopted the hashtag, and the posts have received many Likes and comments. However, they have also received criticism. An Instagram user left negative comments on #WildcatTBT photographs taken in the early 20th century depicting White students. Additionally, the author received the following email from that user:

Please stop posting these ol [sic] #MakeAmericaGreatAgain white supremacist #tbt 's under the UA library Instagram account. It's embarrassing that my school doesn't understand the white narrative racist history you are constructing. You should be embarrassed and ashamed of these all white old pics. Do you know where we were in 1909? Getting raped my [sic] these white men who owned us on plantations. Getting shot by these white people taking our lands. Post about that? (personal communication, February 28, 2017)

Featuring history without unintentionally celebrating whiteness is a challenge. In the 21st century, each incoming class of freshman has had more people of color (The University of Arizona, 2014), and in 2017-18, students of color accounted for about half of the campus population (The University of Arizona, 2018). However, the university has historically had a predominantly White student body. Thus, photographs of students of color in the early 20th century are limited in quantity. The author responded to the email by providing links to previous #WildcatTBT posts featuring students of color and explaining that the library marketing team strives to show diversity. Essentially, she made the same mistake as Heineken, and the user called the author's response inappropriate.

As the first social media manager hired by UA Libraries, the author has written social media guidelines. However, at the time these #WildcatTBT comments were received, there was no documentation, and the library had never received user feedback relating to unconscious bias. Solomon (2014) recommended that libraries respond publicly to negative feedback, even if private communication has taken place; if there is no public response, other users may assume the library is ignoring the situation. However, the Instagram user had also emailed librarians, and the author was advised not to engage the individual further. A member of the library administration attempted to reach out to the user to address the concerns, but the comments remain on #WildcatTBT posts.

After receiving these criticisms, the author has endeavored to find historical photographs with students of color. The UA is a Research I institution that was founded in 1885, drawing students and faculty from around the world. Many viewers lack historical context for the university and Tucson. While the author does not want to distort the past racial makeup of the university, #WildcatTBT posts only showing White students may further make students of color invisible. Whereas the intention behind tokenism is to include people of color to make the organization appear equitable, the author's intention in posting diverse #WildcatTBT photographs is to ensure that stories about students of color are told. The lack of diversity in #WildcatTBT also calls attention to the invisibility of underrepresented groups in archives and the historical record. The author is collaborating with the archivists and librarians in Special Collections to ensure more photographs showing diversity are identified and digitized.

Over time, academic libraries generate a copious amount of content on social media. Staff should know how to make social media work for the library and not against it. Even so, a communications crisis may be inevitable, regardless of whether it relates to bias. By actively creating diverse and inclusive content and knowing how to mitigate crises, the library can establish a reputation as being an ally and supporter of diverse groups.

FUTURE RESEARCH DIRECTIONS

Technology and Discrimination

Social media platforms frequently adjust their news feed algorithms, causing a decline in the organic reach and engagement of posts. As a result, it is difficult for libraries to be seen on social media. Under these conditions, libraries will feel the need to buy social media advertising, if they do not already.

Social media advertising enables marketers to leverage user data to create relevant, targeted posts. It is more cost-effective to target a specific audience than a general one. For example, the library may seek to reach alumni or users in its city. Thus, social media platforms encourage advertisers to create segmented audiences. They can even upload customer email lists or target users who visited and clicked on their website. Using Facebook Ads Manager (2018), advertisers can currently target users on the basis of their age, gender, language, and interests relating to religion. They can also select users according to Multicultural Affinity, which is determined by the user's Facebook behavior rather than self-selected information. Multicultural Affinity categories include African American, Asian American, and Hispanic. Previously, advertisers were able to exclude one of these groups, and in doing so, may have violated laws like the Fair Housing Act and the Equal Credit Opportunity Act. Consequently, Facebook signed an agreement requiring the company to remove the ability to exclude groups by ethnicity, religion, or sexual orientation (Statt, 2018).

James et al. (2017) observed the lack of legislative efforts to regulate internet marketing to different ethnic groups, and advocated for policies such as curbing the promotion of fast food to populations with high rates of diet-related illnesses. Unlike food, housing, credit products, or jobs, library services or events may not be affected by future legislation pertaining to internet advertising. However, through the lens of diversity and inclusion, picking select groups is as discriminatory as excluding others. In this environment of information asymmetry, marketers must be wary of discrimination.

Another emerging technology that will shape the future of libraries and social media is artificial intelligence (AI). Airlines, banks, retail, and other companies employ Facebook Messenger and Twitter Direct Message chatbots as a customer service tool, and there are over 100,000 chatbots on the former (Pasquarelli & Wohl, 2017). These chatbots augment the human experience, are task-oriented, and cannot have meaningful conversations. Despite their limitations, they are convenient to both social media users and organizations wanting to relieve employees from time-consuming tasks. Social media chatbots are becoming ubiquitous.

Libraries have already used chatbots for virtual reference. For example, in 2009 Mentor Public Library in Ohio developed Emma the Catbot—an animated cat—in response to state budget cuts (Vincze, 2017). Over three years, Emma answered routine reference questions online and averaged a correct response rate of 90%. Libraries who currently use social media for reference transactions may become early adopters of the next generation of social media chatbots. Subsequently, they should become familiar with the ethical issues that have arisen with AI and their algorithms.

The Microsoft chatbot, Tay, is a well-known experiment that shows how artificial intelligence can backfire against an organization. Designed to learn human speech patterns, developers deployed Tay on Twitter in March 2016 (Wolf, Miller, & Grodzinsky, 2017). Within a day, Tay echoed the racist and sexist tweets that users tweeted at it, and Microsoft took the chatbot offline. Wolf et al. (2017) maintained that Tay's behavior was not just a programming error, but demonstrates a failure of developers to take ethical responsibility for unpredictable and experimental software. Without thorough testing, including a check for biases, libraries can find themselves implicated in the intersection of prejudice and technology.

Staff Diversity and Resources

Producing diverse and inclusive content is not without its challenges. Ultimately, diversity starts with the voices in the room. Therefore, insufficient staff diversity is a barrier to having social media that welcomes different social identities. Davis (2018) asserted that people of color are needed in marketing positions to help improve representation, reduce racism, and to avoid gaffes. However, merely hiring diverse staff is not the solution to creating diverse and inclusive marketing. In a survey of 750 professionals in the creative industry, Adobe revealed that the challenges associated with diversity extend beyond representation (Myrold, 2017). Sixty-three percent of people of color, compared to 55% of Whites, experienced barriers to success and felt less valued at work. Insufficient staff diversity is not unique to the creative industry. In Ithaka S+R's last survey, 71% of employees at Association of Research Libraries (ARL) institutions were White (Schonfeld & Sweeney, 2017). Libraries should foster an inclusive environment to recruit, retain, and combat the attrition of employees from underprivileged groups.

Because many staff members may influence social media, diverse content depends on recruiting staff from underserved populations. In a survey of 98 academic libraries, 43% used a committee to manage social media, with members representing different library positions (Robinson et al., 2018). While 47% reported having one manager who oversees all social media, 83% reported having multiple staff who could post to the same platform. If the entire staff is not committed to diversity, then even inclusive marketing may be deemed insincere. Further work could explore this relationship between library staff diversity and marketing content.

Limited staff capacity is another challenge to creating diverse and inclusive content. Academic libraries often delegate social media to multiple staff members and student interns (Robinson et al., 2018). However, a full-time employee who focuses on marketing or outreach is recommended to manage social media successfully. Dedicated time is critical to create and curate content, assess the performance of campaigns, monitor user comments, and stay apprised of constant changes and new features.

CONCLUSION

It is imperative that academic libraries strive for diverse and inclusive social media, not only because their public image is at stake, but because to do so is to serve the students, faculty, and the campus community well. Overlooking diversity in social media content is a missed opportunity. As evidenced in this chapter, changing national demographics, the political climate, and expectations of social media users necessitate content that does not oppress marginalized groups.

Social media is a newer responsibility for libraries. It requires a willingness to learn, and not just about the latest post image dimensions or character count. No matter who makes the posts, staff need to recognize that change comes from within the organization. Striving for inclusive copywriting, photography, and graphic design is a group undertaking. It also requires humility and the ability to learn from mistakes.

Libraries can be leading exemplars of producing diverse and inclusive marketing. By showing different faces, and promoting different voices, the library upholds intellectual freedom, serves a broader community, and maybe even stops the user's thumb scroll.

REFERENCES

American Library Association. (2018). *Libraries respond.* Retrieved from http://www.ala.org/advocacy/diversity/libraries-respond

Ayoub, A., & Beydoun, K. (2017). Executive disorder: The Muslim Ban, emergency advocacy, and the fires next time. *Michigan Journal of Race & Law*, *22*(2), 215–241.

Binkley, C. (2015, September 18). He? she? ze? Colleges add gender-free pronouns, alter policy. *AP News.* Retrieved from https://apnews.com/48c986c722ba4e5bb8a5a4c1f1d31df1/he-she-ze-universities-add-gender-pronouns-alter-policy

Borgerson, J. L., & Schroeder, J. E. (2002). Ethical issues of global marketing: Avoiding bad faith in visual representation. *European Journal of Marketing*, *36*(5/6), 570–594. doi:10.1108/03090560210422399

Brookbank, E. (2015). So much social media, so little time: Using student feedback to guide academic library social media strategy. *Journal of Electronic Resources Librarianship*, *27*(4), 232–247. doi:10.1080/1941126X.2015.1092344

Buckels, E. E., Trapnell, P. D., & Paulhus, D. L. (2014). Trolls just want to have fun. *Personality and Individual Differences*, *67*, 97–102. doi:10.1016/j.paid.2014.01.016

Chokshi, N. (2018, March 28). Heineken pulls 'lighter is better' ad after outcry over racism. *The New York Times.* Retrieved from https://www.nytimes.com/2018/03/28/business/media/heineken-racist-ad.html

Clark, M., Fine, M. B., & Scheuer, C. (2017). Relationship quality in higher education marketing: The role of social media engagement. *Journal of Marketing for Higher Education*, *27*(1), 40–58. doi:10.1080/08841241.2016.1269036

Collins, G., & Quan-Haase, A. (2014). Are social media ubiquitous in academic libraries? A longitudinal study of adoption and usage patterns. *Journal of Web Librarianship*, *8*(1), 48–68. doi:10.1080/19322909.2014.873663

Cone Communications. (2017). *2017 Cone communications CSR study.* Retrieved from http://www.conecomm.com/2017-cone-communications-csr-study-pdf

Cooley, D. O., Brice, J., Becerra, E. P., & Chapa, S. (2015). The effect of cosmopolitanism on multi-ethnic U.S. markets under varying conditions of diversity in advertising. *Academy of Marketing Studies Journal*, *19*(3), 119–138.

Critlib. (2018). *Previous Twitter chats*. Retrieved from http://critlib.org/twitter-chats/previous-twitter-chats/

Cui, G. (1997). Marketing strategies in a multi-ethnic environment. *Journal of Marketing Theory and Practice*, *5*(1), 122–134. doi:10.1080/10696679.1997.11501756

Davis, J. F. (2018). Selling whiteness? - A critical review of the literature on marketing and racism. *Journal of Marketing Management*, *34*(1/2), 134–177. doi:10.1080/0267257X.2017.1395902

Ducharme, J. (2018, February 24). Colleges assure prospective students that protesting for gun control will not affect their admission. *Time*. Retrieved from http://time.com/5174165/colleges-gun-control-protests-admission/

Edelman. (2017, June 18). *2017 Edelman earned brand*. Retrieved from https://www.slideshare.net/EdelmanInsights/2017-edelman-earned-brand

Facebook Ads Manager [Social network advertising tool]. (2018). Retrieved from https://business.facebook.com/adsmanager

Fialkoff, F., Chant, I., Dixon, J., Koerber, J., Murvosh, M., Pinkowski, J., ... Schwartz, M. (2018). Movers & shakers 2018: The people shaping the future of libraries. *Library Journal*, *143*(5), 20–62.

Flock, E. (2017, February 13). Why these librarians are protesting Trump's executive orders. *PBS NewsHour*. Retrieved from https://www.pbs.org/newshour/arts/librarians-protesting-trumps-executive-orders

Frey, W. H. (2018, March 14). The US will become 'minority white' in 2045, census projects [Blog post]. Retrieved from https://www.brookings.edu/blog/the-avenue/2018/03/14/the-us-will-become-minority-white-in-2045-census-projects/

Galan, M., Lawley, M., & Clements, M. (2015). Social media's use in postgraduate students' decision-making journey: An exploratory study. *Journal of Marketing for Higher Education*, *25*(2), 287–312. doi:10.1080/08841241.2015.1083512

Granger, L. (2017). Messages of inclusion: A grassroots campaign for turbulent times. *American Libraries*, *48*(5), 12–15.

Green, C. L. (1999). Ethnic evaluations of advertising: Interaction effects of strength of ethnic identification. *Journal of Advertising*, *28*(1), 49–64. doi:10.1080/00913367.1999.10673576

H.B. 2120, 53d Leg. 1st Reg. Sess. (Ariz. 2017)

Howard, H., Huber, S., Carter, L., & Moore, E. (2018). Academic libraries on social media: Finding the students and the information they want. *Information Technology and Libraries*, *37*(1), 8–18. doi:10.6017/ital.v37i1.10160

Ihme, T. A., & Stürmer, S. (2018). Emphasizing excellence and diversity cues on university websites: Additive or interactive effects on prospective students' psychological reactions? *Journal of Applied Social Psychology*, *48*(2), 59–70. doi:10.1111/jasp.12490

James, J. P., Lee, K., Zhang, M., & Williams, J. D. (2017). Ethics and policy issues for internet advertising: Targeting multicultural consumers in the digital marketing era. *Journal of Management Policy and Practice*, *18*(4), 93–106.

Jaschik, S. (2017, October 11). Controversial professor placed on leave. *Inside Higher Ed*. Retrieved from https://www.insidehighered.com/news/2017/10/11/drexel-places-controversial-professor-leave

Kahn, C., & Ingram, D. (2018, May 9). Three-quarters Facebook users as active or more since privacy scandal: Reuters/Ipsos poll. *Reuters*. Retrieved from https://www.reuters.com/article/us-facebook-privacy-poll/three-quarters-facebook-users-as-active-or-more-since-privacy-scandal-reuters-ipsos-poll-idUSKBN1I7081

Kandiuk, M. (2017). Avoiding controversy: Academic freedom and the library exhibit. *Art Documentation: Journal of the Art Libraries Society of North America*, *36*(1), 91–107. doi:10.1086/691374

Kane, L. (2017, December 4). Meet generation Z, the 'millennials on steroids' who could lead the charge for change in the US. *Business Insider*. Retrieved from http://www.businessinsider.com/generation-z-profile-2017-9

Kapitan, A. (2017, July 3). On "person-first language": It's time to actually put the person first [Blog post]. Retrieved from https://radicalcopyeditor.com/2017/07/03/person-centered-language/

Kaplan, A. (2017). Academia goes social media, MOC, SPOC, SMOC and SSOC: The digital transformation of higher education institutions and universities. In B. Rishi & S. Bandyopadhyay (Eds.), *Contemporary Issues in Social Media Marketing* (pp. 20–30). New York, NY: Routledge. doi:10.4324/9781315563312-2

Kendrick, A., Fullerton, J. A., & Kim, Y. J. (2013). Social responsibility in advertising: A marketing communications student perspective. *Journal of Marketing Education*, *35*(2), 141–154. doi:10.1177/0273475313490171

King, O. (2017, February). The case for diversity in advertising [Blog post]. Retrieved from https://www.thinkwithgoogle.com/consumer-insights/diversity-in-advertising-black-millennials/

Levy, A. (2018, January-February). State of the profession: targeted harassment—faculty report back [Blog post]. Retrieved from https://www.aaup.org/article/state-profession-targeted-harassment—faculty-report-back

Lopez-Medel, I. (2017). Using Super Bowl 2017 commercials to teach about diversity. *Journal of Advertising Education*, *21*(2), 33–44. doi:10.1177/109804821702100209

Maheshwari, S. (2017, October 12). Different ads, different ethnicities, same car. *New York Times*. Retrieved from https://www.nytimes.com/interactive/2017/10/12/business/media/toyota-camry-ads-different-ethnicities.html

Milkman, R. (2017). A new political generation: Millennials and the post-2008 wave of protest. *American Sociological Review*, *82*(1), 1–31. doi:10.1177/0003122416681031

Morris, A., & Kahlor, L. A. (2014). Whiteness theory in advertising: Racial beliefs and attitudes toward ads. *The Howard Journal of Communications*, *25*(4), 415–430. doi:10.1080/10646175.2014.955929

Myrold, J. (2017, November 2). Building the case for diversity [Blog post]. Retrieved from https://theblog.adobe.com/building-the-case-for-diversity/

Olapic (2016). *Consumer trust: usage & attitudes towards user-generated visual content*. Retrieved from http://www.olapic.com/resources/consumer-trust-usage-attitudes/

Olin, J., & Millet, M. (2015, November 4). Gendered expectations for leadership in libraries. *In the Library with the Leadpipe*. Retrieved from http://www.inthelibrarywiththeleadpipe.org/2015/libleadgender/

Pasquarelli, A., & Wohl, J. (2017, July 17). Why marketers are betting on bots. *AdAge*. Retrieved from http://adage.com/article/digital/marketers-betting-bots/309767/

Patel, S. (2016, May 17). 85 percent of Facebook video is watched without sound. *Digiday*. Retrieved from https://digiday.com/media/silent-world-facebook-video/

Pettway, A. (2017). Trans students welcome: Is your university truly inclusive? *INSIGHT Into Diversity*, *88*(4), 34–35.

Pew Research Center. (2016, June 27). *On views of race and inequality, blacks and whites are worlds apart*. Retrieved from http://assets.pewresearch.org/wp-content/uploads/sites/3/2016/06/ST_2016.06.27_Race-Inequality-Final.pdf

Pew Research Center. (2018, March 1). *Social media use in 2018*. Retrieved from http://www.pewinternet.org/2018/03/01/social-media-use-in-2018/

Pippert, T. D., Essenburg, L. J., & Matchett, E. J. (2013). We've got minorities, yes we do: Visual representations of racial and ethnic diversity in college recruitment materials. *Journal of Marketing for Higher Education*, *23*(2), 258–282. doi:10.1080/08841241.2013.867920

Procter & Gamble. (2017, July 20). *The Talk* [Video file]. Retrieved from https://www.youtube.com/watch?v=3s20ePvTaME

Project Welcome. (2018). *About*. Retrieved from https://publish.illinois.edu/projectwelcome/about/

Robertson, L. (2017, August 31). A professor tweets about Trump and Harvey. Like others, he's no longer a professor. *Miami Herald*. Retrieved from https://www.miamiherald.com/news/local/education/article170477712.html

Robinson, S., Peacemaker, B., & Hurst, E. J. (2018). *Social media best practices in academic libraries (2016)* [Survey data]. Retrieved from https://scholarscompass.vcu.edu/libraries_data/2/

Schonfeld, R. C., & Sweeney, L. (2017, August 30). *Inclusion, Diversity, and Equity: Members of the Association of Research Libraries: Employee Demographics and Director Perspectives*. doi:10.18665r.304524

Solomon, L. (2014). *Librarian's nitty-gritty guide to social media*. Chicago, IL: ALA Editions.

Sprout Social. (2017). Reasons for users in the United States to unfollow brand pages on social media as of January 2017, by age group. *Statista - The Statistics Portal*. Retrieved from https://www.statista.com/statistics/712831/brand-actions-social-media-causing-unfollows-by-age/

Statt, N. (2018, July 24). Facebook signs agreement saying it won't let housing advertisers exclude users by race. *The Verge*. Retrieved from https://www.theverge.com/2018/7/24/17609178/facebook-racial-dicrimination-ad-targeting-washington-state-attorney-general-agreement

Straumsheim, C. (2017, March 6). Berkeley will delete online content. *Inside Higher Ed*. Retrieved from https://www.insidehighered.com/news/2017/03/06/u-california-berkeley-delete-publicly-available-educational-content

Stvilia, B., & Gibradze, L. (2017). Examining undergraduate students' priorities for academic library services and social media communication. *Journal of Academic Librarianship*, *43*(3), 257–262. doi:10.1016/j.acalib.2017.02.013

Sung, C., & Sutton, J. (2015, January 20). Porn filmed in Oregon State University library. *CNN*. Retrieved from https://www.cnn.com/2015/01/29/us/feat-oregon-state-university-library-porn/index.html

The Anti-Defamation League. (2018, June 28). *White supremacist propaganda nearly doubles on campus in 2017-18 academic year* [Press release]. Retrieved from https://www.adl.org/news/press-releases/white-supremacist-propaganda-on-us-college-campuses-rises-77-percent-over-past

The Association of Registered Graphic Designers of Ontario. (2010). *AccessAbility: A practical handbook on accessible graphic design*. Retrieved from https://www.rgd.ca/database/files/library/RGD_AccessAbility_Handbook.pdf

The University of Arizona. (2014). *Diversity: By the numbers*. Retrieved from https://diversity.arizona.edu/node/146

The University of Arizona. (2018). *2017-18 fact book*. Retrieved from http://factbook.arizona.edu/2017-18

Torres, I. M., & Briggs, E. (2007). Identification effects on advertising response: The moderating role of involvement. *Journal of Advertising*, *36*(3), 97–108. doi:10.2753/JOA0091-3367360307

Trump, D. (2018, March 22). *Remarks by President Trump at the Generation Next Summit panel discussion with Charlie Kirk* [Transcript]. Retrieved from https://www.whitehouse.gov/briefings-statements/remarks-president-trump-generation-next-summit-panel-discussion-charlie-kirk/

Turning PointUSA. (n.d.). *About us*. Retrieved from https://www.professorwatchlist.org/about-us/

United States Department of Education. (2018, July 3). *Updates to Department of Education and Department of Justice guidance on Title VI*. Retrieved from https://www2.ed.gov/about/offices/list/ocr/letters/colleague-title-vi-201807.pdf

United States Department of Education. (n.d.). *Campus safety and security*. Retrieved from https://ope.ed.gov/campussafety/

University of Washington Libraries. (n.d.). *Suzzallo and Allen, Odegaard closed February 10, 2018*. Retrieved from http://www.lib.washington.edu/about/news/announcements/suzzallo-and-allen-odegaard-closed-february-10-2018

Vasquez, M. (2018, April 6). 5 takeaways from Turning Point's plan to 'commandeer' campus elections. *The Chronicle of Higher Education.* Retrieved from https://www.chronicle.com/article/5-Takeaways-From-Turning/243064

Vincze, J. (2017). Virtual reference librarians (chatbots). *Library Hi Tech News, 34*(4), 5–8. doi:10.1108/LHTN-03-2017-0016

Whittler, T. E., & DiMeo, J. (1991). Viewers' reactions to racial cues in advertising stimuli. *Journal of Advertising Research, 31*(6), 37–46.

Whittler, T. E., & Spira, J. S. (2002). Model's race: A peripheral cue in advertising messages? *Journal of Consumer Psychology, 12*(4), 291–301. doi:10.1207/15327660260382333

Wolf, M., Miller, K., & Grodzinsky, F. (2017). Why we should have seen that coming. *ACM Computers & Society, 47*(3), 54–64. doi:10.1145/3144592.3144598

Zatat, N. (2018, March 26). Heineken admits it 'missed the mark' with 'terribly racist' advert. *Independent.* Retrieved from https://www.indy100.com/article/heineken-racist-advert-apology-light-beer-missed-mark-twitter-marketing-campaign-8273791

Chapter 8
Identifiable Problems in Social Media:
Concerning Legal Awareness Within Academic Libraries

Amy D. Dye-Reeves
Murray State University, USA

ABSTRACT

The chapter serves as a primer for academic librarians on helping patrons with disabilities receive, protect, and understand disseminated content on a multitude of popular social media networking platforms. The content of the chapter provides introductory material on the Americans with Disabilities Act (ADA) and the Family Educational Rights and Privacy Act. The first part of the chapter discusses the inclusion of best practices and web accessibility applications for structuring written incorporation to help all patrons understand the expressed material within social media networking pages. The second part of the chapter discusses the importance of respecting patron privacy within FERPA guidelines. This section discusses social networking pages and best practices for helping safeguard the patron's identity concerning inadvertent HIPAA violations.

INTRODUCTION

This chapter serves as an introductory primer that provides academic librarians with detailed context on how to better assist and inform disabled patrons through social media platforms. The following paragraphs educate informational professionals concerning issues within Americans with Disability Act (ADA) and the Family Educational Rights and Privacy Act of 1974 (FERPA). As a short disclaimer, this chapter serves only as a primer that simply provides information literacy to help aid patrons with disabilities. This chapter does not serve as a directive in terms of legality issues, in which specific issues, should always be directed to the assigned university personnel within that specific institution.

DOI: 10.4018/978-1-5225-8097-3.ch008

The first part of the chapter discusses the careful consideration of social media platforms for patrons with disabilities (ADA compliance) and provides a list of applications that enhances and enriches content comprehension. The second part of the chapter discusses FERPA (Family Educational Right and Privacy Act) and provides a list of associated practices on helping patrons understand the importance non-disclosure information, such as HIPPA (Health Insurance Portability and Accountability Act) based information. The chapter ends with a recommendation section that provides a short list of professional development opportunities.

According to Merriam-Webster (2018), social media is defined as the "form of electronic communication (such as websites for social networking and microblogging) through which users create online communications to share information, ideas, personal messages, and other content (such as videos)" (Webster, 2018). In today's fast pace environment, social media is being used outside of personal correspondence. The social networking pages provide opportunities that are often being explored by corporations, pre and post-secondary education, and beyond.

Nancy Flynn (2012), *The Social Media Handbook* explains that employers must "manage social media use effectively in order to protect (their) organization's assets, reputation, and future" (Flynn, 2). However, the definition of social media should be treated as a living organism whose definition can change rapidly due to the nature of technological advancements.

The 2018 current landscape of popular social media networking sites include *Facebook, Twitter, Instagram, Snapchat and YouTube.* Each page provides a unique venue for both formal and informal conversations. According to a recent survey from the Pew Research Center (2018) revealed that a majority of adults (age 24 and older) within the United States chose *Facebook* and *YouTube* as the preferred social media platform. Whereas the younger Americans preferred a wide variety of social networking pages and used them on a frequent basis. The collected data from the Pew Research Center indicated that "some 78% of 18-24-year-olds use Snapchat, and a sizable majority of these users (71%) visit the platform multiple times a day. Similarly, 71% of Americans in this age group now use Instagram and close to half (45%) are Twitter users." (Pew Research Center, 2018). Interesting enough, *Facebook* is the most widely used social media platform where over 68 percent of adults within the United States prefer this networking page. (Pew Research Center, 2018). Another top performing networking site included *YouTube* (a popluar video sharing platform system) that uses social elements such as vlogs. Vlogs range in the promotion of consumer-based products to personal viewpoints on a multiple of subject matters. The Pew Research Center showed that over three-quarters of adults in America used this platform. Additionally, over, ninety-four percent of 18 to 24 years old utilized this particular product. (Pew Research Center,2018). This informational data allows academic librarians to consider what social networking pages might work best for both promotional and instructional service purposes.

MAIN FOCUS OF THE CHAPTER

Understanding the Americans With Disabilities Act (ADA)

The Americans with Disabilities Act (ADA) is a "civil rights law that prohibits discrimination against individuals with disabilities in all areas of public life, including jobs, schools, transportation, and all public and private places that are open to the general public. (ADA National Network, 2018). ADA prohibits any type of discrimination based on the "basis of disability in employment, state, and local government, public accommodations, commercial facilities, transportation, and telecommunications" (ADA Guide 2018—www.ada.gov/cguide.htm). Additionally, the rights of students with disabilities are protected under the Vocational Rights Act of 1973 (United States Department of Education, 2004).

This legislative act was signed into effect during the year 1990. President George H.W. Bush stated the legislation was "powerful in its simplicity" (Nolan, 2006, p. 367). The Former Attorney General Dick Thornburgh stated the ADA legislation a "great leap forward in the civil rights movement". (Thornburgh 1991, 375). The main purpose of the law allows for those with disabilities to gain the same rights and privileges as the general population. The law guarantees equal opportunities to those needing extra attention with general accommodations (such as public transportation, employment, and communication mechanisms). "University faculty members are most familiar with the reasonable accommodations requirements or appropriate academic adjustment as stated in section 504 subpart E of the Disabilities Act "(Rodriguez, 2011, p. 544). It's important to note that ADA is broken down into five different service categories: Employment, State and Local Government, Public Accommodation, Telecommunications, and Miscellaneous Provisions.

The audience's familiarity with the Americans with Disability Act often begins with Public Accommodation. This initial knowledge often begins with public signage (including public restrooms and parking regulations). A great example within academic libraries would be helping patrons remove books that are physically out of reach on higher placed shelving. The closest section on ADA compliance concerning social media would be the *Telecommunications (Title IV).* The Title IV of Americans with Disabilities Act "sets forth two major requirements to expand telecommunications services for individuals with hearing impairments: telecommunications relay services and closed captioning of all federally-funded TV public service announcements". (Explanation of the Contents of the Americans with Disabilities Act: Disability Rights Education and Defense Fund, pp. 199). The Federal Communications Center (FCC) implemented the Title V Act on August 1, 1991. Upon research, the emphasis was placed upon two issues: hearing and voice carry over recognition systems. The hearing carries over (HCO) allows the "a person with a speech disability is able to listen to the voice of the other party and, in reply, the operator speaks the text as typed by the person with the speech disability. The operator does not type the conversation." (Explanation of the Contents of the Americans with Disabilities Act: Disability Rights Education and Defense Fund, pp.200). The voice carries over (VCO) provides a person(s) with a hearing disability to "speak directly to the other party, and the operator types the response back to the person with hearing disability. The operator does not voice any conversation." (Explanation of the Contents of the Americans with Disabilities Act: Disability Rights Education and Defense Fund, pp.200). The main objective was to provide equal participation to all user groups. The congressional committees indicated the longevity of ADA stating that it must "keep pace with the rapidly advancing technology of the times". (HR Rep 101-485). The discussion on the advancement of technology eventually gave way to the ADA Amendment Act of 2008.

"In response to several Supreme Court decisions and U.S. Equal Employment Opportunity Commission (EEOC) regulations concerning the Americans with Disabilities Act (ADA), the President of the United States signed into law the ADA Amendments Act of 2008 (ADAAA). Congress signed ADAAA, which will take effect January 1, 2009, in order to correct a trend by the EEOC and Courts of decreasing the breadth of the ADA". (Race and Dornier 2009, p. 357). The original amendment of ADA was appealed due to the lack of expansive disability coverage expanding past the Courts and the Equal Employment Opportunity Commission. The term "disability" was loosely labeled and lacked extensive coverage. The current ADA and ADDAA coverage for chapter content purposes expands to the collegiate setting providing reasonable accommodations for both students and faculty members. In today's electronic environment, colleges and universities are constantly changing content management systems and library resources to accommodate all students regardless of disability status. The next section highlights how academic libraries can use auxiliary aids and assistive technologies (plain language and alternative texts) to help patrons understand posts made within social media.

Using Auxiliary Aids and Assistive Technologies (Plain Language and Alternative Text) for Americans With Disability Compliance

The personal participation for those with disabilities on social media network sites can be difficult to maneuver digitally. Therefore, technology has greatly enhanced a person with disabilities comprehension of social media postings.

The types of disabilities associated with social media technology limitations include: blindness, low vision, limited physical mobility and auditory learning. The patron experiencing a disability related to blindness will encounter the need for usage software that enables auditory readability. This software specifically reads what's on the screen (clicking links or texts) and produces the text into a Braille component for patrons with visual impairments.

The first type of technological limitations is assisting patrons with low vision disabilities. The W3C-Web Accessibility Initiative (https://www.w3.org/WAI/people-use-web/tools-techniques) provides information on utilizing software produced to help read the size of the text. This software helps reformat to a small or a larger monitor to help to enhance learning for all users.

Patrons with limited physical mobility (i.e.: arm and hand impairments) use a variety of virtual keyboards. These type of virtual keyboard includes alternative mice that help produce needed computer-based work.

The final type of incorporation system for disabled users includes a voice dictation system. The voice dictation system allows users to speak and command the conveyed text into a word processing system. The benefits include grammar checks and word prediction software to allow users to produce the best information possible. An example would be website entitled: Voice Dictation (https://dictation.io) . The website provides online speech recognition without typing.

Identifiable Problems: Using Auxiliary Aids and Assistive Technologies

The following issues play a large role in the encompassing of the development and implementation of social media pages within academic libraries.

Beginning with the United States Public Law (100-407) that denotes that any item, piece of equipment or product system whether acquired commercially, off the shelf, modified or customized, that is used to increase or improve functional capabilities of individuals with disabilities" (Public Law 100-407). Section III discusses the necessity of making reasonable modifications for users. The usage of auxiliary aids provides persons with disabilities access to screen- reader software and voice recognition over the phone or website formats.

The statue and regulations of aids are broken down into four major categories. "(1) aids and services for making aural materials accessible to individuals with hearing impairments, (2) aids and services for making the visual material accessible to individuals with visual impairments, (3) acquisition or modification of equipment or devices. (4) other similar services and actions such as furnished closed captioning and screen readers" (Legal Information Institute, 42 U.S.C 12103)

The Sub Section two of the state and regulations of aids within the major categories aligns perfectly with two major components for ADA compliance within websites. This specific sub section discusses the concepts of alternative text and plain language used within the holistic markup of the website.

Plain language provides users with the following: short logical sentences and conversational tone. This language is designed with the content in mind to help break the content down logically. The Center for Plain Language provides a five-step checklist for website organization. The five steps included "identify and describe the target audience, structure the content to guide the reader through it, write the content in plain language, use information design to help readers see and understand and work with the target user groups to test the design and content". (Center for Plain Language website, 2018). This allows users to find what is needed quickly without having to struggle with a problematic interface.

The second key component would be alternative text ("alt text). The alternative text provides a level of the descriptions associated with the image allowing the user to understand the context to their fullest possible extent. The nature of the alternative text will not alter or change the websites purpose. The text only adds a single line of coding describing the image holistically. The website designer utilizing alternative text does not need extensive training on coding. An example of alternative text can be found within the image properties of the content management system of Spring Share's product of LibGuides. The designer can add any type of alternative text associated with the image below the URL link. The alternative text features can also be found within Facebook, Twitter, and Instagram for digital incorporation. The following paragraph discusses how to help enhance the provided context for persons with limited visual and auditory disabilities.

Tackling Social Media Postings for Both the Visual and Auditory Disabled Patron

Social media does provide users with the unique opportunity to communicate in a variety of expressed manners. This includes both a verbal (example: Snap Chat) and a written form of expression (example Twitter). It's important to note that social media content can the ebb and flow of the rhythmical pattern of change can happen systematically in order to avoid unforeseen perils of possible emerging opportunities. For academic librarians, an identifiable problem would be providing accessibility for all patrons. The process begins by investigating some of the top social media websites (Facebook, Instagram, Snapchat, Twitter, and YouTube). A majority of social networking pages provides accessibility information for patrons experiencing disabilities. Table 1 provides helpful links to specific information regarding accessibility requirements for both Twitter and YouTube

Table 1. Links to accessibility requirements

Facebook	https://www.facebook.com/help/accessibility
Twitter	https://help.twitter.com/en/using-twitter/picture-descriptions
YouTube(Google Related Products)	https://www.google.com/accessibility/products-features.html

At present, Instagram and Snapchat does not provide official statements concerning accessibility. However, Instagram users can hear the words of what text looks like with the help of using alternative text. Alternative text with Instagram does not contain a word limitation like the networking site of Twitter. Therefore, disabled users can understand the image regarding the written language on their screen. The best technique would be to add the words ALT text below the hashtag information.

In terms of Snapchat, The Perkins School for the Blind does provide a 2018 guide to using Snap Chat with patrons that have low vision restrictions. This website http://www.perkinselearning.org/technology/blog/snapchat-and-low-vision) discusses the importance of both voiceover and large picture text. The voiceover application improves the quality of understanding concerning the narration of videos. The next section explores a multitude of ways to make social media understandable for those experiencing both visual and auditory disabilities.

Careful Considerations for Social Media Posts

This section provides a short chart, Table 2, discussing the problems identified within social media postings that effect both visual and auditory disabled patrons. The academic librarian might want to consider the following information before creating a social media post.

The proceeding section provides a starter set of accessibility tools concerning social media platforms to help academic librarians best serve their entire user population.

Table 2. Types of posts and accessibility considerations

Types of Posts	What content should be avoided for those with visual impairments? (think about imagery and adding alternative text (alt text)
Length of Posts (example: Word Count)	Using short and precise language for clarity of understanding. For example, in 2018, Twitter is limited to 280 characters per posts. Keep in mind that Voiceover for the visually impaired can be lengthy to hear. Therefore, the post needs to directly correspond to what is happening within that particular image.
Format (example: Content)	Think about Text vs Visual Images (Instagram vs Twitter). What format works best for your chosen content? Think about those experiencing problems with visual limitations? How might they view your content (if an image was unattached?) Would the content viewer still understand the overall message?
Visual Hashtags	The Voiceover feature (available as a downloadable attachment for the visually impaired on Google Play) will dictate the words on the screen. It's important to limit how many hashtags are being used. This can be confusing for those that cannot seem the image in front of them.
Captioning and GIFS (Images)	Within social media platforms, it's important to make note of who is being represented within a particular photo. This should include the location and other important details. A person with visual limitations needs descriptions concerning who., what, where, and how things are being represented within a particular photograph. Remember to be mindful of what is being represented and how it's being replicated with someone with visual limitations. Additionally, the moving "GIFS" can pose a problem for those with visual limitations.
Emoticons (Emoji)	Cannot be Translated using a Voiceover Audio Program. Therefore, those with visual impairments cannot understand the full context of the post with the use of emoji throughout a social media posting.

Incorporating Web Accessibility Into Social Media Platforms (ADA Compliance)

The average academic university libraries serves patrons ranging in population from hundreds to thousands on a daily basis. The services offered include: consultations, programming and instructional sessions. These are just a few services offered within most academic university units. The social media strategic personnel or administer with the university libraries will need to provide alternative methods of disseminating information. Table 3 provides a list of ADA Compliant Accessibility Tools for thoughtful implementation of future services.

Respecting Patron Privacy on Social Media Networking Pages

The following sections discuss the importance of understanding patron privacy and how to avoid the accidental posting of provided personal information to a large scale audience. The preceding paragraphs will discussion FERPA (Family Educational Rights and Privacy Act) and provide the best strategies for incorporation within an academic library setting.

Table 3. ADA compliant accessibility tools

Implementation Accessibility Tool Name	URL Address	Primary Functionality Features
DANYA This Social Media Accessibility Google Handout-DLH Holdings Corporation	https://www.youtube.com/watch?v=DKXXKtFRNlQ&t=64s	This Google Handout Video Session discusses improvements within existing and emerging social media technological tools for social media accessibility.
Easy Chirp	www.easychirp.com	Created by Dennis Lembree. This is a Third-party web-based interface aimed at Twitter users. Features shorter URLs, direct messaging, navigational and search saving tools
Tota11y- provides from the Khan Academy.	http://khan.github.io/tota11y/	Provides the website designer with possible accessibility violations through a browser-enabled plugin system.
Site Improve Accessibility Checker	https://chrome.google.com/webstore/detail/siteimprove-accessibility	Evaluates web pages for accessibility problems using Google Chrome.
Usability.Gov (provided by the Department of US Health and Human Services).	https://www.usability.gov	Provides content strategies, visual design basics, and user experience basics for providing digital content.
Wave Web Accessibility Tools	http://wave.webaim.org http://wave.webaim.org/extension/	Wave Web provides Informational Instruction on how to evaluate current accessibility within thousands of web pages. The second link provides information on web accessibility using a Browser Extension.
W3 Accessibility Testing	https://www.w3.org/wiki/Accessibility_testing	The W3 Accessibility Testing page provides a reference point for understanding usability (including Testing requirements)
Web AIM: Web Accessibly in Mind. (provided by the Center for Persons with Disabilities-Utah State University).	https://webaim.org/	The Center for Person with Disabilities (Utah State University) provides accessibility training content and up to date practices within the field of website compliance

FERPA: What Does It Mean? The Direct Effects of Social Media Compliance

"The Family Educational Rights and Privacy Act (FERPA) 20 U.S.C. § 1232g; 34 CFR Part 99) is a federal law that protects the privacy of student educational records" (US Department of Education 2018). FERPA was signed into law by President Gerald Ford on August 21, 1974, with an effective date of November 19, 1974. This law was enacted ninety days after the official presidential signage. (Department of Education 2004)

"FERPA was enacted as a new § 438 of the General Education Provisions Act (GEPA) called "Protection of the Rights and Privacy of Parents and Students," coded 20 U.S.C. § 1232g. It was also commonly referred to as the "Buckley Amendment" after its principal sponsor, Senator James Buckley of New York. FERPA was offered as an amendment on the Senate floor and was not the subject of committee consideration. Accordingly, traditional legislative history for FERPA was first enacted is unavailable." (Department of Education, 2004). It's important to note that "Congress has amended FERPA a total of nine times in the nearly 28 years since its enactment". (U.S Department of Education, 2004). The major legislative changes include the Campus Security Act (1900), Higher Education Amendments of 1992 and 1998, and the USA Patriot Act of 2001.

This federal law applies to all schools that receive any type of federal funding within the United States Department of Education Programs. The law explicitly states that "schools may disclose, without consent, "directory information" such as a student's name, address, telephone number, date and place of birth, honors and awards, and dates of attendance." (U.S Department of Education, 2018). However, the school must communicate with eligible students within a reasonable amount of time. This includes making the request for the school to disclose any type of specified directory of information.

In the digital environment, the faculty member cannot post any type of identifiable information about a student's educational progress on any social media networking platform such as Facebook, Twitter, Instagram, etc. This extends to social media within libraries concerning the sharing, posting, and publishing of any type of digital content as part of a student's educational record. FEPRA does not specifically prohibit any type of social media usage in the classroom or other related settings (Diaz et al., 2010, Lavagnino 2010). Marek and Skrabut (2017) suggest that "higher education institutions in the United States most often limit themselves to reiterating federal government statements about the requirements of FERPA and/or the specific items the school has defined as releasable, and the procedure by which the students can have some or all of these items withheld." (p.17) The standard language is well defined and broadly used and there is little incentive for institutions to "reinvent the wheel". The continued growth of technology leads to the high attention of privacy within education concerning social media as a type of record collecting. In Biegl (2012) article questioned educational privacy within legal case law and the need for revisionary changes regarding privacy regulation.

Ultimately, the academic librarian needs to consider revisiting the laws attached to FERPA ensuring complete compliance. A great starting point would be looking at the Student Privacy 101 website (https://studentprivacy.ed.gov/?src=fpco) provided by the United States Department of Education. The website includes a section for parents, students and post-secondary officials. Another important step would be discussing these types of related laws with a university lawyer and any attached university personnel concerning guidance per a university-specific social media account.

Understanding FERPA and Social Media Privacy for Disabled Patrons

This section provides an insight into helping both adjunct and faculty members at the university level concerning social media postings. The academic librarian often works with faculty members concerning specific instructional sessions and other related needs. A greater example being the digital scavenger hunt. First, this would be limited to those with visual impairments. Secondly, the academic librarian would choose to use a form of social media (i.e.: Twitter, Facebook or Instagram). Many participants may not feel comfortable with personally identifiable information being disseminated on the web to achieve a specific academic goal. Therefore, it's important for everyone to be aware of the privacy of student progress and the dissemination of information. In the past five years, faculty members have been incorporating social media tools to enhance the student learning experience. The networking pages used by faculty members include Facebook, Instagram, and Twitter. However, in 2018 most are using Snapchat and Instagram exclusively. The Pew Research Center for Internet & Technology (2018) reports that "Some 78% of 18- to 24-year-olds use Snapchat, and a sizeable majority of these users (71%) visit the platform multiple times per day. Similarly, 71% of Americans in this age group now use Instagram and close to half (45%) are Twitter users." (Pew Research Center, 2018) This technology shift allows students to collaborative groups within a flexible environment. In terms of faculty member's usage, a survey conducted by Moran, Seaman & Tinti- Kane (2011) showed that over 80 percent of all faculty members were having students complete an assignment using some form of social media. The results of this survey are not surprising concerning social media usage continues to be on the rise. Therefore, all academic professional needs to be made aware of the Family Educational Rights Privacy Act (FERPA).

The legislative law concerning FERPA protects all identifiable information concerning a student's personal academic record. The law does not specifically discuss a protocol for the digital dissemination of student records. Lavagino (2010) article entitled: "Policy as an enabler of student engagement" argued that creative course content on social platforms should not fall under FERPA law unless it's physically achieved by the course instructor, which would be considered a type of educational record. Upon implementing a social media platform, faculty members should always consult existing social media policies within the university. If none exist, the faculty member will need to consult the universities communication procedure manual. Lavagino suggests the guidelines for creation would include three inclusion categories: legal procedures, technical assistance, and educational rights. These c guidelines provide participants with additional policies, alternative assignments, constant forms, and providing faculty members with FERPA checklist for later investigation.

The audience needs to make note that FERPA does not specifically discuss or prohibit the use of social tools within digital classroom or the university library digital settings. It's important to remember that social media did not exist when FERPA was first enacted. Therefore, there is no current agreement on student postings in social media correlating to "educational records". In Lavagnino (2010) article discussed how content created on a social media platform should not fall under FERPA law unless it's archived physically by the instructor. Therefore, this case would be considered an "educational record". Faculty members using social media websites for classroom construction may not be aware of the multiple privacy issue concerns.

One major concern includes data breaches within the issued software. "These particular issues can develop into different legal and the security concerns that are related to identity management, infrastructure, risk management, legislative and regulatory compliance, integrity control, access control and other risks that are dependent on the cloud computing provider". (Almudawi, N.,2016, p.31). The invasion of data privacy can intellectually hurt both corresponding parties. The social ramifications of using a public social media platform include that of cyberbullying, profile hacking and digital identity theft. These important issues are needed for faculty members to reflect upon implantation.

According to Schwartz and Solove (2011) discusses that "congress neither revisited FERPA'S reliance on the concept of "educational records", nor created a more basic right to the block the release of student records for commercial purposes. As for universities, they remain able to sell essential student contact information to credit card companies, such as data is considered "directory information", hence not an education (al) record." (p. 1823)

Ultimately, if public information can be pieced together using "directory information", then the Family Educational Right Privacy Act would be applicable. Gross and Acquisit (2015) analyzed 4,000 Carnegie Melon University Facebook profiles and outlined the potential threats to privacy containing in the personal information included on this networking site utilized by students. These potential threats include the ability to reconstruct users' social security numbers and using information found in profiles, such a date of birth. These types of "public records" make it easy to identify any given individual. The discussed risks make it easy for third party vendors to create a digital portfolio on personal behavior.

The aforementioned statements provided context into understanding FERPA and the risks associated when students provide personal forms of information within a very public social media platform. The preceding paragraph provides best practices that will help alleviate privacy issues within social media postings.

Best Practices for Social Media Postings (Concerning FERPA and HIPAA)

The nature of this section denotes helpful tips on helping patrons not to disclose identifiable information. This can be especially important for patrons with disabilities concerning HIPAA (Health Insurance Portability and Accountability Act) First, it's important to stress and reiterate to patrons and associated staff members that social media is not concerned a private space. Therefore, an academic library should attempt to post all information from a neutral and bipartisan approach. The social media manager for the academic library should "screen" postings for any type of FERPA or HIPAA potential violations.

A suggestion for future development for academic libraries would be the creation and implementation of a social media policy. The social media policy will formalize a library's strategic guidance and will strengthen its position on social media usage. The American Libraries Association, Intellectual Freedom Committee in June of 2019 approved the Social Media Guidelines for Public and Academic Libraries. "This document provides a policy and implementation framework for public and academic libraries engaging in the use of social media" (American Libraries Association, Social Media Guidelines for Public and Academic Libraries, 2018). A section of the document entitled "Staff Responsibilities" discusses how "library staff should protect patron privacy and confidentiality whenever possible. Social media platforms should not be used to collect information about the library's users. Information shared by patrons on the library's social media should not be kept by the library or used for other purposes."

(American Libraries Association, Social Media Guidelines for Public and Academic Libraries, 2018). Delaney (2011) article entitled “Apps &Web 2.0: Legal risks from using the internet in class” provides three strategies for success: legal, technical, and educational. Each section provided alternative assignments, FERPA checklists and consent forms for future incorporation.

A final recommendation would be looking at the American Libraries Association Code of Ethics. The Code of Ethics provides a helpful reference for intellectual property and privacy concerning the ethical codes within the library profession.

SOLUTIONS AND RECOMMENDATIONS

The first solution and recommendations for social media usage and persons with expressed disabilities begins with awareness. The awareness process begins by looking at the language found within the Americans with Disabilities Act (ADA) and the Family Educational Rights Privacy Act (FERPA). The background requirements should start as a basis when considering a social media platform that would be friendly for all patrons. The complete documents can be found on the United States Department of Justice Website for ADA and the United States of Education Website for FERPA.

The second step would be looking at your specific universities handbook and communication offices concerning the proper route concerning the dissemination of information. A meeting with the university lawyer can provide additional context and a working framework for understanding the expectations and standards for specific social media networking accounts.

The third step concern is the future of technology and the rapid succession of change. Therefore, the academic librarian must continuously look for new and updated technology to help all patrons understand all given context within a social media account. A great website for ADA Compliance and social media advancement would be the Digital Gov website (https://digital.gov/index.html). The website is run by the US General Administration (an associate page with the US Government) with a section dedicated to social media and accessibility. For FERPA, the academic librarian is encouraged to look at the Protecting Student Privacy website (https://studentprivacy.ed.gov/Apps). The website is run by the US Department of Education. Each is maintained by the government and can provide insight into new laws and technology advancements to help their patrons be successful within their given environment.

CONCLUSION

The purpose of the chapter was aimed towards a primer approach to helping patrons with disabilities. The chapter discussed how the Americans with Disabilities Act and the Family Educational Act effects usability in terms of disseminating information through the means of social media. This chapter only provided best practices and suggestions for possible incorporation within an academic library setting. Therefore, this chapter is not a directive in terms of handling social media lawsuits concerning the affirmation laws. Therefore, the reader should always consider having lengthy conversations concerning legality with the assigned personnel attached to a specific university.

REFERENCES

W3C. (2018). *Accessibility Testing*. Retrieved July 18, 2018 from, https://www.w3.org/wiki/Accessibility_testing

ADA National Network: Information, Guidance, and Training on the Americans with Disabilities Act (2018). *What is the Americans with Disabilities Act (ADA)?* Retrieved July 13, 2018 from, https://adata.org/learn-about-ada

Almudawi, N. A. (2016). Cloud computing privacy concerns in social networks. *International Journal of Computer*, *22*(1), 29–36.

American Library Association. (2018). *Social Media Guidelines for Public and Academic Libraries*. Retrieved August 14, 2018 from, http://www.ala.org/advocacy/intfreedom/socialmediaguidelines

Boyd, D. M., & Ellison, N. B. (2007). Social network sites: Definition, history, and scholarship. *Journal of Computer-Mediated Communication*, *13*(1), 210–230. doi:10.1111/j.1083-6101.2007.00393.x

Center for Persons with Disabilities, Utah State University. (2018). *Web AIM: Web Accessibility in Mind*. Retrieved June 17, 2018 from, https://webaim.org

Center for Plain Language. (n.d.). *5 Steps to Plain Language*. Retrieved June 16, 2018 from, https://centerforplainlanguage.org/learning-training/five-steps-plain-language/

Charnigo, L., & Barnett-Ellis, P. (2007). Checking out Facebook. com: The impact of a digital trend on academic libraries. *Information Technology and Libraries*, *26*(1), 23. doi:10.6017/ital.v26i1.3286

Chrome Web Store. (2018). *Site Improve Accessibility Checker*. Retrieved September 10, 2018 from, https://chrome.google.com/webstore/detail/siteimprove-accessibility/efcfolpjihicnikpmhnmphjhhpicll jc?hl=en-US

Delaney, S. (2011). Apps & Web 2.0: Legal risks from using the internet in class. *Distance Education Report*, *15*(9), 5–7.

DLH Holdings Corp. (2014, May 5). *T.H.I.S Social Media Accessibility Google Hangout*. Retrieved June 13, 2018 from, https://www.youtube.com/watch?v=DKXXKtFRNlQ

Facebook Help Center. (2018). *Accessibility*. Retrieved July 8, 2018 from, https://www.facebook.com/help/accessibility

Flynn, N. (2012). *The Social Media Handbook: Rules, Policies, and Best Practices to Successfully Manage Your Organization's Social Media Presence, Posts, and Potential*. San Francisco, CA: Pfeiffer.

Google Accessibility Center. (2018). *Products and Features*. Retrieved June 5, 2018 from, https://www.google.com/accessibility/products-features.html

Gross, R., Acquisti, A., & Heinz, J. III., H. (2005). Information revelation and privacy in online social networks (The Facebook Case). *WPES'05: Proceedings of the 2005 ACM Workshop on Privacy in the Electronic Society*, 71-80. 10.1145/1102199.1102214

Jarrow, J. E. (1997). What is a reasonable accommodation? [Web log article]. *DAIS (Disability Access Information and Support).* Retrieved May 5, 2018 from, http://www.daisweb.com/

Johnson, C., & Burclaff, N. (2013, April). Making social media meaningful: connecting missions and policies. *Imagine, innovate, inspire: Proceedings of the ACRL 2013 Conference.* Retrieved June 16, 2018 from, http://www.ala.org/acrl/sites/ala.org.acrl/files/content/conferences/confsandpreconfs/2013/papers/JohnsonBurclaff_Making.pdf

Khan Academy. (2018). *Tota11y: An Accessibility Visualization Toolkit.* Retrieved September 19, 2018, from http://khan.github.io/tota11y/

Lavagnino, M. B. (2010). *Policy as an enabler of student engagement.* Retrieved May 30, 2018, from https://er.educause.edu/articles/2010/10/policy-as-an-enabler-of-student-engagement

Legal Information Institution. (n.d.). *42 U.S. Code § 12103 - Additional definitions.* Retrieved July 31, 2018 from, https://www.law.cornell.edu/uscode/text/42/12103

Lembree, D. (2018). *Easy Chirp.* Retrieved June 4, 2018 from, https://www.easychirp.com

Marek, M. W., & Skrabut, S. (2017). Privacy in Educational use of Social Media in the US. *International Journal on E-Learning, 16*(3), 265–286.

Moran, M., Seaman, J., & Tinti-Kane, H. (2011). *Teaching, Learning, and Sharing: How Today's Higher Education Faculty Use Social Media.* Retrieved from: http://www.pearsonlearningsolutions.com/educators/pearson-social-media-survey-2011-bw.pdf

Nolan, M. (2005). A Difference of Opinion: Reconciling the Court's Decision in Tennessee v. Lane. *S. Ill. ULJ, 30*, 357

Pew Research Center. (2018). *Social Media Use in 2018.* Retrieved June 10, 2018, from, http://www.pewinternet.org/2018/03/01/social-media-use-in-2018/

PUBLIC. L. (1988). LAW 100-407 and 103-218. *Technology-related assistance for individuals with disabilities.* Public, Law 100-1047, 102 STAT. 1044. Retrieved May 18, 2018 from, https://www.gpo.gov/fdsys/pkg/STATUTE-102/pdf/STATUTE-102-Pg1044.pdf

Race, P. A., & Dornier, S. M. (2009). ADA Amendments Act of 2008: The effect on employers and educators. *Willamette Law Review, 46*, 357.

REP. H. (1990). NO. 101-485 (III), 101st Cong., 2d Sess. (1990), reprinted in 1990 USCCAN 478-79. In The conference committee report also states that the phrase" clarifies that this prohibition [against discrimination] applies to any person who owns, leases (or leases to), or operates a place of public accommodation." Joint Explanatory Statement of the Committee of Conference, 101st Cong. 2d Sess.

Rodriguez, J. E. (2011). *Social Media Use in Higher Education: Key Areas to Consider for Educators.* Retrieved May 4, 2018 from, https://our.oakland.edu/handle/10323/2153

Schwartz, P. M., & Solove, D. J. (2011). The PII problem: Privacy and a new concept of personally identifiable information. *NYUL Rev., 86*, 1814.

Social Media. (n.d.). In *Merriam-Webster's collegiate dictionary*. Retrieved May 10, 2018 from, https://www.merriam-webster.com/dictionary/social%20media

Thornburgh, D. (1991). The Americans with Disabilities Act: What It Means to All Americans. *Temp. LR*, *64*, 375.

Twitter Help Center. (2018). *How to Make Images Accessible for People?* Retrieved July 17, 2018 from, https://help.twitter.com/en/using-twitter/picture-descriptions

United States Department of Education. (2004). *Legislative History of Major FERPA Provisions*. Retrieved August 4, 2018 from, https://www2.ed.gov/policy/gen/guid/fpco/ferpa/leg-history.html

United States Department of Education. (2018). *Family Educational Rights and Privacy Act (FERPA)*. Retrieved August 4, 2018 from, https://www2.ed.gov/policy/gen/guid/fpco/ferpa/index.html

United States Department of Education. (2018). *Student Privacy 101: Student Privacy at the U.S. Department of Education*. Retrieved August 4, 2018 from, https://studentprivacy.ed.gov/?src=fpco

United States Department of Health & Human Services. (2018). *Usability.Gov: Improving the User Experience*. Retrieved August 4, 2018 from, https://www.usability.gov

United States Department of Justice. (2009). *A Guide to Disabilities Rights Laws*. Retrieved August 4, 2018 from, https://www.ada.gov/cguide.htm

United States General Services Administration. (2018). *DigitialGov*. Retrieved August 4, 2018 from, https://digital.gov/

WAVE. (2018). *Homepage*. Retrieved July 18, 2018 from, http://wave.webaim.org

ADDITIONAL READING

Al-Daihani, S. M., & Abrahams, A. (2016). A text mining analysis of academic libraries' tweets. *Journal of Academic Librarianship*, *42*(2), 135–143. doi:10.1016/j.acalib.2015.12.014

American Libraries Association. (2017). *Professional Ethics*. Retrieved July 13, 2018, from, http://www.ala.org/tools/ethics

American Libraries Association. (2018). *Social Media Guidelines for Public and Academic Libraries*. Retrieved July 13, 2018, from, http://www.ala.org/advocacy/intfreedom/socialmediaguidelines

Harrison, A., Burress, R., Velasquez, S., & Schreiner, L. (2017). Social media use in academic libraries: A phenomenological study. *Journal of Academic Librarianship*, *43*(3), 248–256. doi:10.1016/j.acalib.2017.02.014

Marek, M. W., & Skrabut, S. (2017). Privacy in Educational use of Social Media in the US. *International Journal on E-Learning*, *16*(3), 265–286.

Rodriguez, J. E. (2011). Social media use in higher education: Key areas to consider for educators. Retrieved October 14, 2018, from, https://our.oakland.edu/handle/10323/2153

Stvilia, B., & Gibradze, L. (2014). What do academic libraries tweet about, and what makes a library tweet useful? *Library & Information Science Research*, *36*(3-4), 136–141. doi:10.1016/j.lisr.2014.07.001

Stvilia, B., & Gibradze, L. (2017). Examining undergraduate students' priorities for academic library services and social media communication. *Journal of Academic Librarianship*, *43*(3), 257–262. doi:10.1016/j.acalib.2017.02.013

United States Department of Education. *Family and Educational Rights and Privacy Act (FERPA).* Retrieved May 16, 2018 from, https://www2.ed.gov/policy/gen/guid/fpco/ferpa/index.html

United States Department of Justice. *Information and Technical Assistant on the Americans with Disability Act.* Retrieved May 16, 2018 from, https://www.ada.gov/

Chapter 9
Enhancing an Academic Library's Social Media Presence Using Peer-to-Peer Marketing:
The Benefits of Student Content Creators

Laurel D. Eby
San José State University, USA

Elisabeth A. Thomas
Monterey Peninsula College, USA

ABSTRACT

The San José State University Library first became involved in social media in 2011 with the formation of a social media team. The team quickly realized that maintaining an academic library's social media presence—creating original content, monitoring posts and feeds, and maximizing exposure to the library's target audience—can take a sizeable chunk of time. Additionally, it is important to understand student preferences regarding the kind of content they are interested in seeing from their university library on social media so that the time spent creating content has not been wasted. This chapter will discuss how the social media team dealt with these questions and others, such as how to adapt to the regularly changing world of social media and how to reap the benefits of hiring student assistants to help create an engaging, relevant social media presence.

INTRODUCTION

Organization Background

San José State University (SJSU) is the oldest campus in the California State University system and the first public university on the West Coast (San José State University [SJSU], 2016). The mission of the university is to "transmit knowledge to its students" and "to expand the base of knowledge through research and scholarship" (SJSU, 2018a, para. 2). The San José State University Library serves a broad

DOI: 10.4018/978-1-5225-8097-3.ch009

community with varying interests and needs. There is a diverse student body of over 32,000; the top undergraduate majors are design studies, psychology and kinesiology, and the top graduate majors are software and electrical engineering and library and information science (SJSU Institutional Effectiveness & Analytics, 2017b). The university employs over 2,100 faculty members, including professors, lecturers and librarians (SJSU Institutional Effectiveness & Analytics, 2017a). In addition to hiring faculty and staff, the university has a long-standing tradition of employing students, both to benefit students' career and academic goals and to help support the work needed for the campus to function (SJSU, 2018b, p. 4).

The Dr. Martin Luther King, Jr. Library

Located at the northwest corner of the campus in the center of downtown San José, the Dr. Martin Luther King, Jr. Library (King Library) houses both the SJSU Library and the main branch of the San José Public Library. As a joint academic and public library, it serves both the university and the City of San José communities. The services and resources provided by the SJSU Library include library instruction, one-on-one research consultations, technology lending, software training, 3D printing, digital archives, an institutional repository, and much more. Over the years, a great deal of attention has been given to providing student services but not as much to marketing those services. Finding the best solutions for marketing the library's services to the entire student population has been an ongoing challenge.

BACKGROUND: SOCIAL MEDIA IN CONTEXT

Social Media in Academic Libraries

Within the past decade, social media use in academic libraries has gone from nearly non-existent to being an essential part of most libraries' outreach and promotion strategies (Harrison, Burress, Velasquez, & Schreiner, 2017, p. 248). In his book *Tell Everyone: Why We Share and Why It Matters*, Alfred Hermida (2014) writes, "People are not hooked on YouTube, Twitter or Facebook but on each other. Tools and services come and go; what is constant is our human urge to share" (2014, p. 1). Social media is an integral part of most students' lives today — 88% of adults ages 18-29 use at least one social media site (Pew Research Center, 2018) — so it makes sense that academic libraries would eventually embrace social media as a new way to connect with their students.

Fagioli, Rios-Aguilar and Deil-Amen (2015) debunked the once-common idea that social media was a distraction for college students by finding a relationship between their community college students' GPAs, retention rates, and their activity on social media. Students who were more active on social media had higher GPAs and retention rates. There is not necessarily a direct correlation, but it can be inferred that students who are more active with their college community tend to do better academically, whether that activity is partially or solely online.

For some time, academic libraries have been exploring the benefits of utilizing social media to market their services and to communicate with their target audiences. Taylor & Francis Group summarized the current practices, perceptions, and possible future of social media in libraries in a 2014 white paper (p. 5). Libraries use social media for promotion and outreach, communicating with patrons, getting feedback, providing customer service, increasing engagement among users, and even as a collection development tool. Some challenges libraries face with social media include the time required to maintain a social media presence, the need to respond to queries in a timely manner, keeping up with the ever-changing nature of social media platforms, finding the right tone of voice, and copyright issues. Reddy & Aswath (2017, p. 3) add that some disadvantages of social media use on college campuses are its potentially addictive nature, the fact that older students may not be comfortable using it and may therefore feel socially disconnected from the college community, the fact that information disseminated on social media can be unreliable, and the potential for having one's personal information stolen.

Social Media at the SJSU Library

This chapter is a case study chronicling the successes, challenges, and reassessments faced by the San José State University Library's social media team. It explores the benefits of including student assistants as content creators on social media and discusses the ways in which the library's social media team has endeavored to understand what types of content students find engaging.

The SJSU Library first became involved in social media in 2011 with the formation of a social media team made up of a mix of faculty librarians and library staff. The university library initially joined Facebook, Twitter, and Google+, and in 2012 added YouTube and started a joint Pinterest account with the San José Public Library. In 2014 the social media team added Instagram and Tumblr to the mix.

Being responsible for an academic library's social media presence — creating original content, monitoring posts and feeds, and figuring out how to maximize exposure to the library's target audience — can take a sizeable chunk of a librarian's time. A great deal has been written about academic libraries and their usage of social media, but there is no one-size-fits-all solution to the question "What type of content should we post, and on which platforms?" Every academic library is different, just as every student population is different. Figuring out what a library's specific target audience will find interesting and helpful can be extremely difficult.

In 2016, the SJSU Library formed a marketing team made up of student assistants, with one of their main objectives being to assist the social media team in creating content for the library's social media accounts. The hope was that the student employees would provide a voice for marketing the library's services that would capture their fellow students' attention while simultaneously gaining valuable experience in a work setting related to their career interests.

CHALLENGES OF CREATING AND MAINTAINING A SOCIAL MEDIA PRESENCE

The Ever-Changing Landscape of Social Media

Since the SJSU Library made its first foray into social media, many changes have required the library's social media team to reassess the way they maintain its online presence. New platforms have arisen, while the popularity of existing platforms has waxed and waned. Occasionally social media platforms change the way they work, as with the change in Facebook's algorithm in 2013 (Brookbank, 2015, p. 233). Intended to ensure that users only saw what was relevant to them, one consequence was that posts by organizational Facebook pages (such as those for libraries) were no longer viewed as often.

The members of the social media team had no prior experience in marketing; consequently, they had to learn by trial and error how best to use social media to promote the library. In addition, protocols have changed over the years as the team experimented with what kinds of content to post and how best to interact with online users. Issues the social media team has grappled with include:

- Understanding student preferences regarding the kind of content they are interested in seeing from their university library on social media.
- Staying on top of which platforms are currently popular with the library's key demographic — college students — and which seem to be losing favor.
- Maximizing the effectiveness of social media posts with a minimal investment of time.
- Adapting to the regularly changing world of social media.

Workload Required for Social Media

Creating content for social media is sometimes seen by library administration as an assignment that does not require much time, is not a high priority, and is not necessarily "real work." In fact, if done correctly, social media is a marketing tool that reaches a large number of students, faculty, and staff. Social media will not sustain itself, however, without dedicated people creating content and managing the platforms to some degree on a regular basis. The outreach librarian and web services librarian at the SJSU Library, both members of the social media team, regularly monitor the library's social media accounts for any communications from users, including any questions or complaints that need to be addressed.

With limited time available to devote to creating content for social media, however, it is necessary to choose only those platforms that resonate with the library's patrons, and as with any other service offered by the library, the social media strategy should be regularly assessed and changed as needed. Brookbank (2015) stated, "Remaining stagnant is a recipe for becoming irrelevant in the constantly changing and evolving world of social media" (p. 232). In some cases, it has been necessary to abandon a platform completely. For example, Google+ never became very popular with the SJSU student population, so the social media team eventually decided it no longer made sense to spend time creating content for it. Likewise, the team realized they did not have the bandwidth to keep up with creating new content for Tumblr, so they stopped supporting that account as well. In the case of Pinterest, the interests of the university library and the public library diverged so much that this online partnership did not thrive. In 2013 the two parties agreed to disband the joint Pinterest account and the SJSU Library created its own Pinterest account with the intention of using it to showcase the library's special collections.

Understanding Student Preferences

College students generally separate their personal lives from their academic lives on social media (van Beynen & Swenson, 2016). They tend to use social media primarily to keep in touch with family and friends, to share photos, and to interact with classmates. Students are typically less interested in academic uses of social media, but Brookbank (2015) found that they do use social media to find out about new things and to keep up with what is happening on campus (p. 239). These are areas in which the library could post content that would capture the interest of college students.

Students also value information from their peers and their instructors, especially information needed to accomplish an academic task (Kerney & Bailey, 2016). Academic librarians undoubtedly would like to think that they are included in the definition of "instructors," but it is not likely that students would see librarians as instructors when grades are not a factor. Fagioli et al. (2015) state that, if students who do well academically post quality information online, other students are more likely to get engaged online too.

Some ways SJSU students interact with the library are by "liking" images, commenting on the library's posts, and tagging the library in their posts. For a while the members of the social media team wondered whether there was enough interaction between the library and its users. Observations were made that were consistent with Fagioli et al. (2015) who noted that students' online habits vary quite a bit, given that some students are actively engaged while others prefer being passive observers. They noticed that, in a college community, passive engagement can be just as beneficial as active engagement.

Content must be relevant to students not simply because of who they are but also based on what time of the semester it is. A post about late-night tutoring offered in the library will not connect with students at the beginning of the semester but might garner a lot more attention approaching midterms or finals. Van Beynen and Swenson (2016) found that posts about library services and resources received the most attention at the beginning of the semester, during midterms, and shortly before and during finals (p. 47). They also found that when they posted photos of an event right as it was starting, students who were perhaps between classes or who just needed a break would spontaneously decide to attend the event.

SOLUTIONS AND RECOMMENDATIONS

Hiring a Library Student Marketing Team

Student assistants are essential to the daily functioning of an academic library. They work in every department, processing and shelving books, working as assistants to administration and librarians, setting up event rooms and classrooms, checking out items, working with patrons, and troubleshooting technology issues. Library employees can work much more efficiently with a well-selected team of student assistants.

During the fall of 2016, the outreach librarian was tasked with hiring a student assistant marketing team. The new university library dean wanted to have student ambassadors who could promote the library to their peers. Details were left to the outreach librarian to create a successful team. After contacting similar student marketing groups on campus to gain insight into what was needed, four undergraduate students from different academic disciplines were hired to make up the first student assistant marketing team: a writer from the Department of English and Comparative Literature, a marketer from the School of Journalism and Mass Communications, a photographer/videographer from the School of Art & Design Photography, and a graphic designer from the Department of Design. The marketer and the writer took the lead on most social media content, with the photographer/videographer and the graphic designer contributing video and visuals.

New student assistants are hired each year to replace those on the team who have graduated. As part of the interview process, student candidates are asked to bring either a portfolio or other samples of their work. Depending on the position they are interviewing for, these are either written or artistic works from class assignments or prior work experience. A semi-structured interview is conducted that includes questions about experience with social media and preference of platforms. The interviewers are looking for students who respond professionally and show a high level of interest in the subject.

Great care is taken in the selection of the student assistants in order to form a team that works well together, feels invested in the content they are creating to market the library's services and resources, and can be trusted to post content directly onto the library's social media accounts without having it reviewed first. Student selection is based on their past work, school experience, knowledge of the subject, and future career goals. These positions are intended not only to support the library but also to give the students an opportunity to gain career experience, which benefits all parties and gives the students more of an investment in the content they produce.

There is no formal social media training when new students are hired. Rather, as part of the student marketing team orientation, each new student assistant takes part in an informal group discussion with the outreach librarian and other members of the team. Topics of discussion include what kind of content to post, professionalism, accessibility, and the importance of written and image copyrights.

While the outreach librarian oversees the students to ensure accuracy and clarity in post content, the students take an active, leading role in finding events and services that should be promoted, and in creating and posting relevant content to social media. They take ownership over learning more about the services provided by the library and relaying this information to their fellow students. The members of the social media team regularly monitor the library's social media accounts and respond to questions or comments, but do not review content created by the student team before it is posted. It is felt that the marketing team needs the freedom to create content they feel will best connect with students and should not have to worry about getting approval for every post. Giving the students this freedom also saves time for the librarians and the social media team, which they can use to focus on other work.

Diverse Voices

Taylor & Francis Group (2014, p. 3) found a difference in opinion among librarians regarding finding the right tone of voice on social media and whether a library's social media accounts should have a professional branded look or a less formal, more personal look. Over the years, the social media team has tried various approaches to voice and branding, realizing in the end that they wanted the library's social media presence to have a balance between a uniform look across platforms and a voice that embraces the diversity of opinions and experiences of the SJSU and King Library communities.

At conferences and in other discussions in library marketing communities, many people mention the importance of having a formal writing style and one professional "voice" (Bussell & Hagman, 2017, p. 153). They believe that, if student employees create social media content, an approval process should be implemented to make sure the content is accurate and professional. Though one voice may be ideal for a library in a professional business setting, colleges and universities have diverse student populations, and a library should reflect that diversity while still maintaining an academic writing standard.

The University of Liverpool Library, in Liverpool, England, advocates for having a variety of employees from throughout the library get involved in social media. "In many academic libraries, it is common for a limited number of people to be responsible for managing social media but from the Liverpool experience the recommendation to other institutions would be to take the opposite approach. Large groups can help generate ideas and ensuring members represent the complete library service means that people's interests, and therefore content, is varied and interesting" (Chatten & Roughley, 2016, p. 255). University of Liverpool employees developed a policy on creating and maintaining social media that is intended to provide guidelines without diminishing creativity. They recommend using an informal style on social media that sounds like it is coming from humans, not robots, and state that, while it is important to be as accurate as possible, one should not be afraid of making mistakes (Chatten & Roughley, 2016, p. 252).

The SJSU Library embraces the use of multiple voices in their social media presence for several reasons:

- It reflects the diversity of the university population.
- It includes many employees' ideas and experiences.
- It saves time and spreads the workload around.
- It creates a community and gets users engaged with the library.
- It gives everyone an opportunity to contribute.

It is, of course, possible that something inappropriate or incorrect will be posted, so it will always be necessary for the social media team to regularly monitor the library's social media accounts.

The SJSU Library's social media team has always encouraged their colleagues to contribute to the library's social media presence. For example, if a library employee posts photo of the library from their own personal account and uses the hashtag #sjsulibrary, the team will repost it to the library's accounts. Additionally, an iPod Touch was purchased for anyone in the library to borrow and use to post photos to any of the library's social media accounts. Having this iPod available is helpful, for example, when there is an after-hours event in the library that members of the social media team are unable to attend. Employees can also email anyone on the team with a request to post content.

In contrast to other libraries that closely monitor what student assistants post and have an approval process for content created, the SJSU social media team has followed a method similar to that used by Allers (2015, p. 13), allowing employees to step back from overseeing daily posts and instead look at the overall social media plan. This strategy has been successful for a few reasons. First, one of the criteria for hiring students is professionalism and trustworthiness. The students are expected to do their background work to ensure the accuracy of what they post, and they are invested in the work they do and product they create. Second, the librarians and managers created the student marketing team specifically to promote peer-to-peer marketing of the library's services and resources. The students on the marketing team are the library's ambassadors and need to be able to connect with students in a way that appeals to them. Allers writes that some of the most popular posts made by her student social media team were those they posted while walking around campus (p. 15). Lastly, one goal in hiring the marketing team was to help take on some of the burden of maintaining the library's social media accounts. It would defeat the purpose if the social media team had to closely monitor the content the students create.

Time-Saving Tools

Seeking to minimize the time required to keep the library's various social media accounts updated before the creation of the student marketing team, the members of the social media team looked into ways to automate posting and to make it easier to add to more than one platform at a time. One of the first tools used was If This Then That (IFTTT), which allows users to create conditional statements called applets that trigger when a certain action happens. The first applet the team created specified "*If* a photo is tagged #sjsulibrary by any user on Instagram, *then* post it to the SJSU Library's Facebook account."

In this way the members of the social media team hoped to harness the creativity of San José State students and other library users to provide interesting content as well as to get them to feel engaged with and connected to the library. An Instagram widget on the home page of the library's website would show photos tagged #sjsulibrary, so the social media team encouraged students to tag their photos in order to see them on the website. The team also held a contest during the Great California Shakeout (an annual statewide earthquake drill) in which students who tagged their photos #sjsulibrary during the drill

Figure 1. An example of applets from If This Then That

would be entered in a drawing to win a $25 gift card. This contest generated a great deal of interest, and undoubtedly introduced many students to the library's Instagram account.

Creating content this way worked well for a while, but in June 2016, Instagram changed their API (application programming interface) so that third party apps such as IFTTT could no longer access other users' photos (Cook, 2016). As a result, the API that pulled users' photos into the widget on the library's website no longer worked, nor did the IFTTT applet that would post photos to the library's Facebook and Twitter accounts. IFTTT applets would now only work on the library's own Instagram photos. The social media team realized that they would need to begin investing more time in actually creating original content for the library's social media accounts. Members of the team were concerned that they would need to log out of their own Instagram accounts in order to post anything to the library's account; fortunately, they discovered that it is easy to toggle between accounts in the Instagram app. This enabled them to post photos to the library's Instagram account and then easily switch back to their own accounts. The team continues to use IFTTT to automatically post the library's Instagram photos to Twitter and Facebook.

After the change in the Instagram API, the social media team discovered an app called Repost, which can be used to repost another user's Instagram photo to the library's account. Members of the social media team will occasionally look through photos tagged #sjsulibrary and repost ones that are interesting (always giving credit to the original poster). This app helped make up for the loss of the IFTTT applet for Instagram photos tagged #sjsulibrary by others, even though it became necessary to repost photos manually.

Another tool the social media team uses is Hootsuite. Hootsuite is a social media management system that allows the social media team to schedule posts in advance for several accounts at once. Using Hootsuite enables the team to plan out a series of posts about upcoming events or information students may need at particular times during the semester. Scheduling posts in advance takes some of pressure off the team to remember to post at regular intervals. In addition, Hootsuite has a dashboard for monitoring important social media streams by keyword, hashtag, username, or location. In addition to #sjsulibrary and @sjsulibrary (the library's official hashtag and username), the social media team also monitors keywords such as "sjsu," "library," and "san jose." In this way, they are able to monitor what people are saying about the library, even if they do not specifically tag the library.

Figure 2. The dashboard of Hootsuite, showing the library's Facebook feed

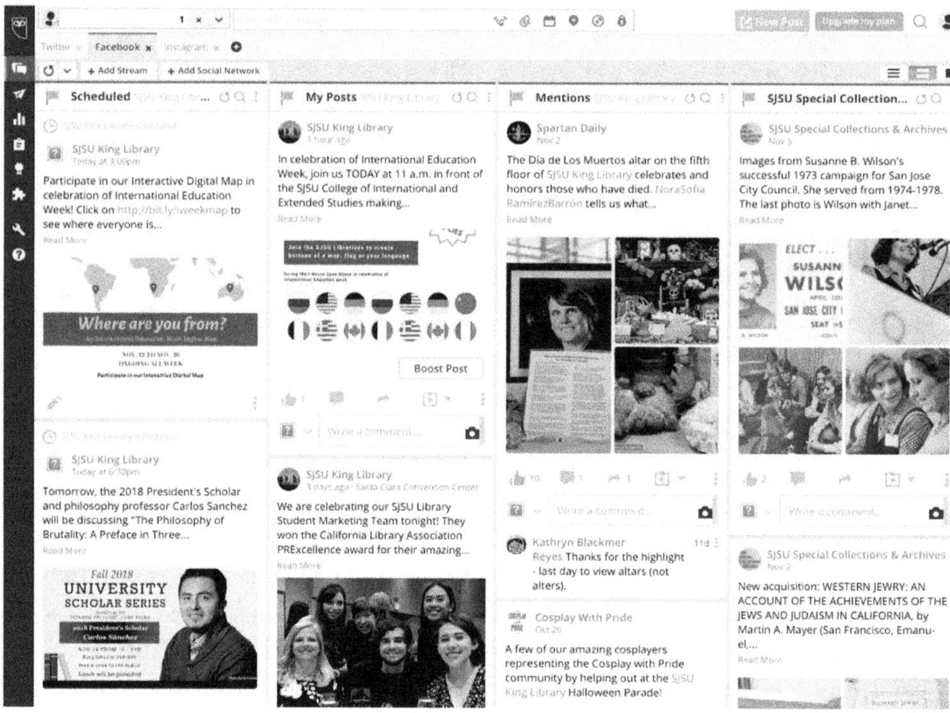

Finding Insights Through Statistics

Because the social media team initially had little or no experience in either marketing or using social media in an academic setting, they were unsure how to assess the successes and failures of the library's social media platforms. Add to this the fact that each platform has its own way of tracking analytics, and it was quite a learning curve for the team. The team began gathering statistics in October 2012, just over a year after they had established the library's social media presence. The primary statistics gathered were the number of total likes/followers.

Of the three social media platforms still regularly maintained by the SJSU Library, Facebook and Twitter continue to have the most followers/likes, with Twitter outpacing Facebook in the last couple years. Instagram is quickly catching up, however, going from 54 followers after one year to over 1,100 just four years later.

Table 1 shows the number of likes/followers of the SJSU Library's Twitter, Facebook, and Instagram accounts each year starting in 2012. Twitter and Instagram have gained followers at a higher rate than Facebook over the last two years — the number of Twitter and Instagram followers has increased approximately 50%, while the number of Facebook followers has only gone up by 24% in the same time frame. This trend is supported by Pew Research Center's data on social media use. Table 2 shows the percentage of adults ages 18-29 in who said they use each platform (Pew Research Center, 2015, 2016, 2018). The 2018 Pew Research report was the first year to break the 18-29 demographic down into two age groups, 18-24 and 25-29, and the difference in the 18-24 demographic is even starker. The percentage of young adults aged 18-24 who said they use Instagram in 2018 is 71%, which is nearly as many as those who say they use Facebook (80%).

Table 1. Number of likes/followers of SJSU Library social media accounts

	2012	2013	2014	2015	2016	2017	2018
Twitter	288	556	832	888	1262	1618	1905
Facebook	400	689	850	1184	1366	1556	1722
Instagram	n/a	n/a	n/a	54	550	768	1133

Table 2. Percentage of social media users age 18-29 (Pew Research Center)

	2014	2016	2018
Twitter	37%	36%	40% (45%*)
Facebook	87%	88%	81% (80%*)
Instagram	53%	59%	64% (71%*)

* 18-24 age group; in 2018 Pew split the 18-29 demographic into 18-24 and 25-29

In the social media team's experience, posts that include images tend to be more popular among students. Lidwell, Holden, and Butler (2010) write that pictures are more easily recognized and remembered than text, a phenomenon known as the picture superiority effect (p. 184). Standing, Conezio, and Haber (1970) conducted a study in which college students were shown a total of 2,560 photographs for 10 seconds each over the course of four days. They were then shown a series of two photos at a time, one of which they had seen before and one they had not, to test their recall. The students chose the correct photo an average of 90% of the time, even up to three days after initially viewing the photos (p. 73). Images on social media may also mitigate loneliness, according to Pittman and Reich (2016). They found that the more image-based social media platforms (such as Instagram and Snapchat) a person uses, the happier and less lonely they perceive themselves as being (p. 164). Pittman and Reich theorize that images give the sense that one is communicating with an actual person, not just an interface (2016, p. 164). Taylor & Francis (2014) mention that images resonate more quickly on an emotional level, and state, "With information overload continuing to be a problem, a continued move towards greater use of image-based social media channels by librarians is highly likely" (p. 12). Considering the above-mentioned advantages of images, it is not surprising that in the 18-24 demographic, 71% say they use Instagram and 78% say they use Snapchat (Pew Research Center, 2018), both of which are image-based platforms. Snapchat was not even mentioned in the Pew Research Center Social Media Update for 2014.

Students seem to favor posts with interesting photos of the library or other areas of the SJSU campus or information about library services or events presented in a humorous or eye-catching way. The marketing team promotes services and resources with these preferences in mind. Figure 3 shows two of the library's most popular tweets from 2018. The first post, in honor of César Chávez Day, shows the Arch of Dignity, Equality, and Justice, a monument to Chávez on campus. The second post is an artistic shot of a rainy sidewalk outside the library. The majority of popular tweets from 2018 contain photos, including original photos posted by the library, reposts of photos other users took of the library, and photos of events and library services

Figure 3. Two of the SJSU Library's top Tweets from 2018

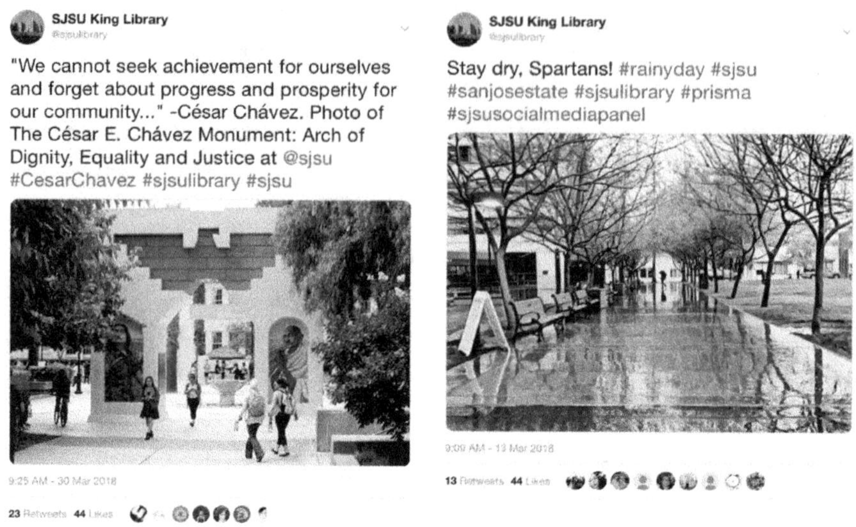

Likewise, the top Facebook posts from 2018 were photos or videos of the library itself and library services and events. Figure 4 shows two of the library's most popular Facebook posts of 2018. The first, posted on the first day of the semester, is a humorous photo on a subject every San José State student knows well — the difficulty of finding parking at the beginning of the semester. The second is a photo of the oldest building on campus, Tower Hall, which just the day before had been completely covered in ivy.

Figure 4. Two of the SJSU Library's top Facebook posts from 2018

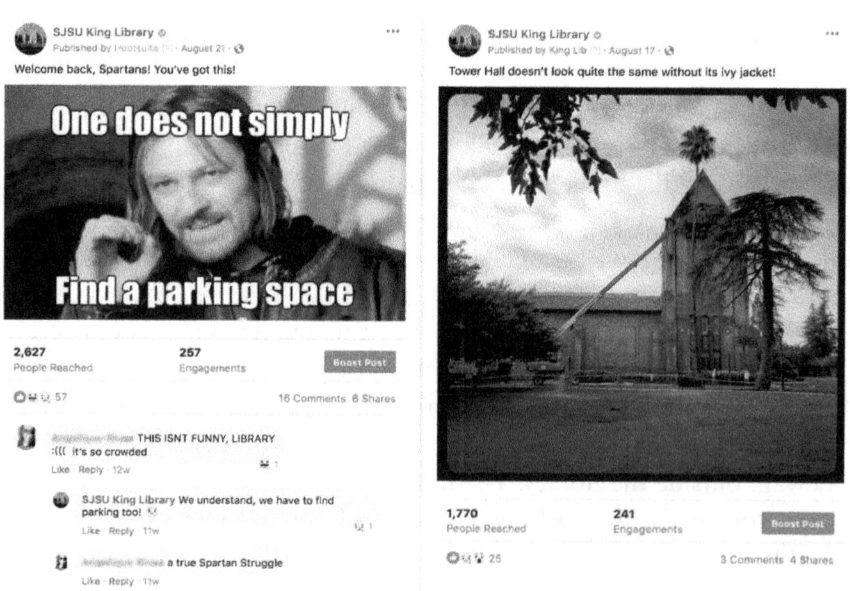

UNEXPECTED BENEFITS

Having student assistants create content for social media and using the aforementioned tools have both been very beneficial in solving time management issues and helping the social media team understand students' social media preferences. There have also been unexpected benefits for the student assistants that the authors feel are important to discuss when recommending including student employees in a library's marketing strategy.

Student Learning in the Workplace

The SJSU Library Student Marketing Team earns financial compensation for their work, but they also gain valuable work experience that directly relates to their career goals, helping them become more invested in their work assignments than they might be otherwise. Kuh's *High-Impact Educational Practices* (2008), endorsed by the Association of American Colleges & Universities as beneficial to student learning, retention, and engagement, come into play as the student assistants create content for the library's social media accounts. The ten high-impact practices are:

- First-Year Seminars and Experiences
- Common Intellectual Experiences
- Learning Communities
- Writing-Intensive Courses
- Collaborative Assignments and Projects
- Undergraduate Research
- Diversity/Global Learning
- Service Learning, Community-Based Learning
- Internships
- Capstone Courses and Projects

These practices can take different forms in the academic world. Four come into play when employing students to create and maintain the library's social media presence: Learning Communities; Collaborative Assignments and Projects; Service Learning, Community-Based Learning; and Internships.

Learning Communities encourage students to integrate education across courses and get them involved in related issues outside of the classroom. Though the original intent is to have students take two or more related courses and work with one another and with their professor, this practice can still apply to students seeking answers regarding library services from their peers and finding solutions through the marketing team on social media. The members of the marketing team are the library's online ambassadors, answering questions for and marketing academic services to their peers.

The Collaborative Assignments and Projects practice relates to learning to work and solve problems collaboratively with others, and to listen to and learn from others. The students on the library marketing team are required to work collaboratively with each other and with the social media team to create original content for social media and other library marketing materials. This collaboration gives them valuable experience working with their peers and with their supervisors to reach a common goal.

Similar to Learning Communities, Service Learning, Community-Based Learning is based on experiential learning with members of the community, the idea being to give students direct experience in the field they are studying, where they can actually apply what they are learning in a real-world setting and feel that they are giving back to their community. Bussell and Hagman (2017) explain that people new to a job do not simply absorb all of the information given to them through work training but also relate it to prior knowledge. They work to solve new problems using prior experience.

Lastly, the Internships practice is the most relevant practice for this chapter. Students gain experience in a work environment that is related to their career interests. Service Learning is focused on benefiting the community, while Internships focus on giving students real-life experience in the workforce. The students on the library marketing team are engaged in work directly related to their fields of study: the English major writes copy, the design major creates graphics, the photographer/videographer takes photos and videos, and the marketer creates marketing campaigns, for the library's social media accounts as well as for other library marketing materials. This is real-world experience that will aid them in their job searches after graduation. Additionally, as student assistants graduate and leave the library, the outreach librarian includes the current members of the team and if possible the graduating students in the process of hiring replacements. The current and graduating students on the marketing team take turns asking predetermined questions and adding more questions to the discussion during the interviewing process. In this way, the marketing team students gain more job skills and have a say in who joins the team. The outreach librarian makes sure that each new candidate meshes with the team and can be trusted in adding content to social media. The student assistants on the marketing team have expressed how vital it was for each of them to be an integral part of the creative process, a process they took very seriously. The marketing team is allowed to keep soft and hard copies of the work they have created to use in their portfolios, and the outreach librarian can become an internship advisor if class assignments can be fulfilled through the workplace.

These high-impact practices are mentioned to show the benefit of giving students more leadership roles in the library. Providing students an opportunity to acquire experience that relates directly to their field and to connect what they have learned in class to the real world helps prepare them for their future careers.

During extremely busy periods in a library, student assistants may be viewed simply as worker bees rather than persons in a learning environment. Bussell and Hagman (2017) explained how they redesigned their student assistant positions to include student learning components in order to give students job experience that they could apply outside the library, to encourage a learning environment, to create leaders, and to give students work they could feel invested in. Bussell and Hagman (2017) found that, instead of simply giving students tasks to work on, giving them more leadership in figuring out and analyzing their roles allowed the students to make more decisions, to learn from their successes and failures, and to gain more knowledge that would help them in the future.

Supervisors need to create a balance between making sure work is done accurately and concisely and letting student assistants learn from their working experience (Bussell & Hagman, 2017, p. 155). Rules regarding copyright and accessibility were given as examples of things students must learn and perform correctly. Supervisors should create a set schedule of meetings in order to stay on top of the work and be available for any questions (Chatten & Roughley, 2016, p. 255). The workload for supervisors will be greater during the beginning of the semester when new student assistants start the job but should lessen as students start to work independently (Bussell & Hagman, 2017, p. 153). Bussell and Hagman (2017) state that it is important and at times difficult to create a working environment between a supervisor and the student assistant that is both trusting and flexible enough to allow the student to grow with the position. Student assistants need to feel that they have opportunities to communicate their opinions (p. 152).

CONCLUSION

Creating an engaging social media presence for an academic library is a long-term project that must be regularly maintained and periodically assessed. It is necessary to keep up with the constantly evolving nature of social media and to understand the interests of the library's target audience, the students. Gaining the perspective of the students on the Library Student Marketing Team has greatly benefited the library's social media accounts in that regard.

The SJSU Library social media team has a few recommendations to offer other academic libraries hoping to enhance their library's social media presence:

- Make use of time-saving tools, such as Hootsuite and IFTTT, that can lessen the workload required to maintain social media.
- Use statistics to understand which platforms are the most popular and what kind of content garners the most interest.
- Engage colleagues and students in creating content for social media, which not only decreases the workload required to maintain social media but also mirrors the diversity of the target audience.
- When employing students to help support the library's social media presence, give them relatively free rein, which not only enables them to create content most likely to be of interest to their fellow students, but also gives them valuable experience in their chosen fields.

ACKNOWLEDGMENT

The authors would like to thank their colleague Silke Higgins for meticulously recording the SJSU Library's social media statistics over the first few years of the social media team's existence.

REFERENCES

Allers, M. (2015). Creating a successful student social media team. *Campus Activities Programming, 48*(5), 12–15.

Brookbank, E. (2015). So much social media, so little time: Using student feedback to guide academic library social media strategy. *Journal of Electronic Resources Librarianship, 27*(4), 232–247. doi:10.1080/1941126X.2015.1092344

Bussell, H., & Hagman, J. (2017). From training to learning: Developing student employees through experiential learning design. In P. McDonnell (Ed.), *The experiential library: Transforming academic and research libraries through the power of experiential learning* (pp. 147–159). Chandos Publishing. doi:10.1016/B978-0-08-100775-4.00011-X

Chatten, Z., & Roughley, S. (2016). Developing social media to engage and connect at the University of Liverpool Library. *New Review of Academic Librarianship, 22*(2-3), 249–256. doi:10.1080/13614533.2016.1152985

Cook, J. (2016, June 4). Instagram made a change that stopped lots of third-party apps from working. *Business Insider*. Retrieved from https://www.businessinsider.com/instagram-made-a-change-that-stopped-lots-of-third-party-apps-from-working-2016-6

Fagioli, L., Rios-Aguilar, C., & Deil-Amen, R. (2015). Changing the context of student engagement: Using Facebook to increase community college student persistence and success. *Teachers College Record, 117*(12), 1–42.

Hermida, A. (2014). *Tell everyone: Why we share & why it matters*. Toronto: Doubleday Canada.

Kuh, G. D. (2008). *High-impact educational practices: What they are, who has access to them, and why they matter*. Washington, DC: Association of American Colleges and Universities.

Lidwell, W., Holden, K., & Butler, J. (2010). Picture superiority effect. In *Universal principles of design: 125 ways to enhance usability, influence perception, increase appeal, make better design decisions, and teach through design* (p. 184). Beverly, MA: Rockport Publishers.

Pew Research Center. (2015). *Social media update 2014*. Pew Research Center. Retrieved from http://assets.pewresearch.org/wp-content/uploads/sites/14/2015/01/PI_SocialMediaUpdate20144.pdf

Pew Research Center. (2016). *Social media update 2016*. Pew Research Center. Retrieved from http://assets.pewresearch.org/wp-content/uploads/sites/14/2016/11/10132827/PI_2016.11.11_Social-Media-Update_FINAL.pdf

Pew Research Center. (2018). *Social media use in 2018*. Pew Research Center. Retrieved from http://assets.pewresearch.org/wp-content/uploads/sites/14/2018/03/01105133/PI_2018.03.01_Social-Media_FINAL.pdf

Pittman, M., & Reich, B. (2016). Social media and loneliness: Why an Instagram picture may be worth more than a thousand Twitter words. *Computers in Human Behavior, 62*, 155–167. doi:10.1016/j.chb.2016.03.084

Reddy, A., & Aswath, L. (2018). Emerging trends in library marketing and engagement through digital media. *KIIT Journal of Library & Information Management, 5*(1), 1–6.

San José State University. (2016). *SJSU timeline*. Retrieved from http://www.sjsu.edu/about_sjsu/history/timeline/

San José State University. (2018a). *San José State University mission*. Retrieved from http://www.sjsu.edu/about_sjsu/mission/

San José State University. (2018b). *Student employment guide for hiring departments*. Retrieved from http://www.sjsu.edu/up/all_forms/student_forms/index.html

SJSU Institutional Effectiveness & Analytics. (2017a). *Faculty quick facts*. Retrieved from http://www.iea.sjsu.edu/Faculty/quickfacts/

SJSU Institutional Effectiveness & Analytics. (2017b). *Student quick facts*. Retrieved from http://www.iea.sjsu.edu/Students/QuickFacts/

Standing, L., Conezio, J., & Haber, R. (1970). Perception and memory for pictures: Single-trial learning of 2500 visual stimuli. *Psychonomic Science*, *19*(2), 73–74. doi:10.3758/BF03337426

Taylor & Francis Group. (2014). *Use of social media by the library: Current practices and future opportunities*. Retrieved from https://librarianresources.taylorandfrancis.com/library-insights/white-papers/use-of-social-media-by-the-library/

van Beynen, K., & Swenson, C. (2016). Exploring peer-to-peer library content and engagement on a student-run Facebook group. *College & Research Libraries*, *77*(1), 34–50. doi:10.5860/crl.77.1.34

ADDITIONAL READING

Anderson, C. L. (2012). LibraryPalooza: A marketing case study. *New Library World*, *113*(1/2), 55–64. doi:10.1108/03074801211199040

Ellis, L. A., & Peña, A. (2015). Crowdsourcing as an Approach to Customer Relationship Building in Academic Libraries. *College & Undergraduate Libraries*, *22*(3–4), 273–295. doi:10.1080/10691316.2015.1076364

Fasola, O. S. (2015). Perceptions and acceptance of librarians towards using Facebook and Twitter to promote library services in Oyo State, Nigeria. *The Electronic Library*, *33*(5), 870–882. doi:10.1108/EL-04-2014-0066

Foster, M., Wilson, H., Allensworth, N., & Sands, D. T. (2010). Marketing Research Guides: An Online Experiment with LibGuides. *Journal of Library Administration*, *50*(5/6), 602–616. doi:10.1080/01930826.2010.488922

Gaha, U., & Hall, S. (2015). Sustainable Use of Social Media in Libraries. *Codex*, *3*(2), 47–67.

Ismail, M. (2014). Marketing Academic Libraries -- Marketing is Communication with Our Users. *Against the Grain (Charleston, S.C.)*, *26*(1), 68–69.

McKee, A. (2017). Selfies, Scavenger Hunts, and Scrawls: How the Vise Library Used Social Media to Increase Usage. *Computers in Libraries*, *37*(9), 4–9.

Vucovich, L. A., Gordon, V. S., Mitchell, N., & Ennis, L. A. (2013). Is the Time and Effort Worth It? One Library's Evaluation of Using Social Networking Tools for Outreach. *Medical Reference Services Quarterly*, *32*(1), 12–25. doi:10.1080/02763869.2013.749107 PMID:23394417

Watson, A. M. (2017). Manage Your Social Media in 5 Minutes a Day. *Public Services Quarterly*, *13*(1), 41–47. doi:10.1080/15228959.2016.1268942

Young, S. W. H., & Rossmann, D. (2015). Building Library Community through Social Media. *Information Technology and Libraries*, *34*(1), 20–37. doi:10.6017/ital.v34i1.5625

Zhu, Q. (2016). The application of social media in outreach of academic libraries' resources and services. *Library Hi Tech*, *34*(4), 615–624. doi:10.1108/LHT-05-2016-0055

Section 3

Further Examples of Social Media Use

Chapter 10
"Is There Anybody There?": Engaging With Open University Distance Learners

Helen Clough
The Open University, UK

Karen Foley
The Open University, UK

ABSTRACT

The Open University (UK) Library supports its distance-learning students with interactive, real-time events on social media. In this chapter the authors take a case study approach and concentrate on the examples of Facebook and Livestream to illustrate how live engagement events on social media have helped to build communities of learners in spaces they already occupy, raise the visibility of the library's services and resources with staff and students, and foster collaboration with other departments, while also being effective mechanisms for instruction. The chapter concludes with the library's plans for the future and recommendations for other academic libraries wishing to run live engagement events on social media.

INTRODUCTION

The Open University UK (OUUK) is, in terms of student numbers, the largest academic institution in the United Kingdom (UK), and the UK's only university dedicated to distance learning, with 174,000 students, most of whom are studying part-time. The vast majority of undergraduate qualifications have no prerequisite study requirements, which appeals to students who had poor experiences of secondary education, those who were not able to access higher education in early adulthood, or those who have disabilities that prevent them from studying on campus at a brick university (The Open University, 2018a).

The OUUK Library was set up at the same time as the university to support the research and teaching needs of academic staff on campus, with a physical building (shown in Figure 1) and print resources that only students who chose to travel to the campus could access. In addition to the physical library, an online library was launched in 2000. Prior to that time, OUUK students were provided with all of

DOI: 10.4018/978-1-5225-8097-3.ch010

the content they needed to complete their studies via television and radio broadcasts, videos and DVDs, and printed module material; there was no requirement to search for external content, and therefore no tradition of academic library use.

As a digital institution, the OUUK uses a range of online platforms to connect with students. The virtual learning environment (VLE) is the main way to access module material, and Adobe Connect is used for tutorials. Livestream, a service that allows customers to broadcast live video content through the Internet, is also used, and the OUUK is active on social media in a number of ways. Facebook and Twitter are the most used social media platforms, and in addition to the institutional accounts, some of the faculties and support services – such as the Careers and Employability Service and the Library – have their own accounts. The Library was an early adopter of social media both within the institution and across the UK higher education sector, and has a culture of experimenting with online technologies in order to reach out to students. The main driver for this is to raise the visibility of the Library and offer support and teach library skills to students in the online spaces they occupy, such as Facebook. There is an additional institutional driver of building communities of students in order to combat the isolation of distance learning and improve retention and progression. An added benefit of being innovative in order to raise the visibility of the Library with students is that this also raises the Library's profile across the institution and fosters collaboration with faculties and other professional service departments; indeed, the authors first met each other via working together on a Livestream event! Social media as a mechanism for teaching library skills is evidenced throughout this chapter; and the question about whether or not it is an effective one is identified as an area for potential future research.

The online library has opened up opportunities for embedding online library resources and information literacy skills into the OUUK curriculum. The authors touch on this aspect of the service, but the main focus of this chapter is on how the Library has had to think creatively in order to support and engage with students whose experience of the Library is as a virtual entity (if they are aware of its existence at all). It adopts a case study approach drawn from the OUUK Library's use of Facebook and involvement with the institution's Student Hub Live Livestream events, and addresses the following objectives:

- Reaching out to distance learners in spaces they occupy
- Building communities of learners
- Raising the visibility of the Library's services and resources
- Fostering collaboration with other departments.

BACKGROUND

The Open University UK

The Open University UK (OUUK) is the leading expert in flexible higher education (www.open.ac.uk). The university is open to all and has a commitment to widening participation. This means that anyone can study an entry-level module. The student population is diverse: young, mature, full-time, part-time, UK-based and international students choose to study with the OUUK. The university is also the largest provider of higher education for people with disabilities (23,630 students declared a disability in 2016/17). The specific nature of part-time distance learning and the associated barriers were explored by Butcher (2015) and Butcher & Rose-Adams (2015). They found that the flexibility offered by distance

Figure 1. Library building at The Open University campus in Milton Keynes, UK
Source: Helen Clough

learning appeals in particular to those whose personal circumstances prevent any other mode of study, and therefore enables these excluded groups to access higher education.

The OUUK specialises in distance learning, and in addition to the printed and virtual module material supplied to them, students have access to synchronous online tutorials (delivered through Adobe Connect, at the time of writing) and also a range of online forums. Students are supported in their learning with personalized feedback from their tutor. While some modules have face-to-face residential events, the majority of students will never visit the university campus, and many will study alone. The impact of this largely isolated study, which requires motivation and self-discipline, is that many students do not learn about additional services or avenues of support such as the Library. Unlike students at a brick university, who can converse face-to-face with their peers before lectures, or have a spontaneous conversation with their lecturer or a librarian, OUUK students may not be in regular contact with other students or staff. When faced with challenges that impact on their study they can withdraw, interpreting the challenge as a failure on their part. However, many students face similar issues, so they can gain a sense of relief when they understand that they are not alone or unusual. For this reason, it is important that the OUUK facilitates communication networks for students who wish to actively engage with their peers. In addition to tutorials and forums, the OUUK has Facebook and Twitter accounts, and the Open University Students Association (OUSA) arranges physical and virtual events for students. There are also many student-initiated social media groups that are not moderated by the OUUK, which indicates that for some students, engaging with their peers is important.

Embedding Library Content and Skills Into the Curriculum

Since 2000 and the launch of the online library service to students, embedding online library resources and digital and information literacy (DIL) skills into OUUK modules and qualifications has been a strategic priority for the Library (Goodfellow & Reedy, 2014). To enable this, librarians work closely with the academics who write modules, identify suitable library resources, write skills activities, and refer to the DIL framework (Goodfellow & Reedy, 2012) when discussing learning design, assessment, and skills development. The DIL framework promotes skills that are embedded into the curriculum and are linked to assessment rather than 'add-ons' because most OUUK students have limited study time (76% of OUUK students work full or part-time during their studies) and, in common with students at other institutions, they are assessment driven (Gibbs, 2006).

The OUUK distance learning model involves the delivery of the majority of learning and teaching via the VLE, so the DIL skills teaching needs to be virtual too. There are two main types of skills activity: the first are DIL interventions (both asynchronous and synchronous), which are targeted at module or qualification level and the students encounter them as part of that week's required activities. The second are generic, standalone materials that interested students can dip into. An example of the second type of resource is 'Being digital' (http://www.open.ac.uk/libraryservices/beingdigital/), an open-access collection of short, introductory level activities, loosely mapped to the DIL framework. The topics cover how to be effective online, including using social media.

The Library's Live Engagement Team

As part of both the module-specific and the generic, standalone DIL skills resources, the Library's Live Engagement team design and deliver synchronous online teaching events. During the team's most recent peak period, from September until the end of December 2017, they delivered 62 synchronous online teaching sessions via Adobe Connect, with over 3,100 attendees in total. Most of these sessions were held in the evening or at weekends, and recordings were made available for those unable to attend live.

At this point it is worth explaining the background to the Live Engagement team, and how the establishment of this group freed up librarian resource for innovation. Previously the OUUK Library had a team of subject librarians, solely dedicated to a particular discipline, doing everything from working with modules to staffing the enquiry desk to online teaching. In 2015, in common with some other UK academic libraries such as the University of Manchester Library (Hoodless & Pinfield, 2016), the OUUK Library moved to functional, task-based teams in order to become more responsive and flexible in a rapidly changing higher education environment. At the time of writing, each librarian works within two or three of the four functional teams (Academic Liaison, Authoring, Enquiry Services, and Live Engagement), which enables teams and individuals to develop specialisms, and – particularly within the Live Engagement team – has freed up time and resource for experimenting with online technologies and new ways of engaging with the OUUK community.

There is evidence that the module-targeted live engagement events run via Adobe Connect can have a positive impact on the student experience and student success. For example, the introductory module in the Law qualification saw a 95% reduction in the number of student referrals to study skills support as a result of the Library's help with referencing via a synchronous training session and asynchronous forum. The Live Engagement team felt that live events delivered via social media could also have a positive impact on student success by reaching out to a different audience, one that would not think to attend a library session, by delivering skills tuition in their preferred online spaces. The team were already actively monitoring the Library's Facebook and Twitter accounts and answering queries from staff and students, as well as assisting the Library's communications team by creating copy for social media campaigns, so running live events was the next logical step.

CASE STUDY 1: FACEBOOK

At the time of writing, two thirds of the UK population are active social media users, and Facebook is by far the leading social media platform, with 71% of the market share (Statista, 2018a and 2018b). There is no available data on how many OUUK students are active on Facebook, although the Open University Facebook group (which is a closed group) has 20,400 members as at mid-2018 and features multiple posts a day; some asking for help, advice and reassurance, and some celebrating success and achievement. The Live Engagement team are members of this group; they approached the moderators and asked to be added so that they could monitor posts and intervene if they felt they could offer advice about the Library. Many OUUK students are active on Facebook and they are also using it for peer support; gathering in groups to discuss their subjects and share study tips and advice. In a small student survey as part of an internal OUUK research project, 28 out of 141 students (20%) reported that they visited OUUK-related Facebook groups when studying (Ellis, E., Gallagher, A., & Peasgood, A., 2017).

One of the key pedagogic drivers for the use of new and emerging technologies at the OUUK is reducing the isolation felt by distance learners (The Open University, 2015). The hope is that by enabling and building active online communities of learners, and encouraging students to engage with and support their peers, there will be a reduction in the dropout rate.

There are examples across the university where staff are exploring the possibilities of social media in a distance learning context. Some of these were shared during an internal social media 'Unconference' event in 2017 where practitioners across the university, including the Library, shared their experiences and findings (The Open University, 2017). In a 2016 paper, OUUK researchers wrote about the 'Friday Thinker' where academics facilitate discussion with students on contemporary social science issues on the Faculty of Social Science's Facebook page. They found that this approach made a contribution to overcoming isolation and creating an academic community of learners (Callaghan & Fribbance, 2016). Another approach piloted by the university in 2016 was using Twitter to supplement teaching on a large population science module. Initial analysis revealed a high level of engagement and positive qualitative feedback (Dresden & Hidalgo, 2017).

A review of the literature reveals that many academic libraries are using Facebook as a community building and information sharing tool. For example, an analysis of the social media postings at six academic libraries in the United States (US) revealed themes around community outreach and advocacy, providing an inviting environment, and access to content (Harrison, Burress, Velasquez, & Schreiner, 2017). However, there is a lack of literature around academic libraries engaging with Facebook as a platform for teaching. A report by Taylor & Francis in 2014 stated that the use of social media as a teaching and learning tool was not a high priority for librarians but was likely to be an emerging trend in the coming years (Taylor & Francis, 2014).

Within this wider institutional and professional setting, the Live Engagement team have used Facebook to teach DIL skills in two ways; they started off with real-time text chat events and then moved to video events when Facebook Live was launched.

Real-Time Text Chat Events on the Library's Facebook Page

The Live Engagement team ran their first live text chat event on the OUUK Library's Facebook page (https://www.facebook.com/OULibrary/) in March 2016. They chose to do a 'Question and Answer' (Q&A) session on referencing in response to the large number of students who contact the enquiry desk for help with this topic. The event was run on a weekday evening because internal research showed that this is when OUUK students tend to study. The hour-long event was advertised as an opportunity to ask questions of librarians and an OUUK tutor. Involving a tutor in the delivery of the event added an academic perspective, and this cross-departmental collaboration remains important to the team because it is a great way to benefit from expertise in other departments while raising the internal visibility of the Live Engagement team and the Library's services and resources.

The event was widely publicised to both staff and students on all available communication channels, including Twitter and Facebook, and the Library paid to boost the visibility and reach of the event on Facebook. In the days and weeks before the event the team kept posting to the event page. For example, each moderator introduced themselves and posted a picture. They also ran polls and asked students if they had any particular questions on the topic; this kept the event visible on Facebook news feeds. Students were encouraged to use the 'Going' or 'Interested' buttons for the event so that the Live Engagement team could gauge how popular it might be and therefore how many moderators were needed, and this also meant that students were reminded of the event on their Facebook news feed.

The event started with an icebreaker question (Figure 2) in order to get students feeling comfortable, remind them that they were talking to real people, and encourage them to talk to each other.

Five members of staff were involved in the event: four Live Engagement librarians and a tutor. There were three discussion threads posted 20 minutes apart, each containing different prompts, and each with a librarian or tutor assigned to moderate and respond to questions. The most recent thread was pinned so it appeared at the top of the page. The fourth librarian acted as overall moderator and time keeper. On reflection, this way of organizing the event over-complicated matters and people were posting all over the event page. The team kept back-channel communication open (in this case, Facebook's messaging system) so they could talk to each other and assign questions, and had a back-up communication plan in case of technical problems.

Figure 2. Screenshot from a Facebook chat event on referencing, March 2016
Source: https://www.facebook.com/events/511732965676869/

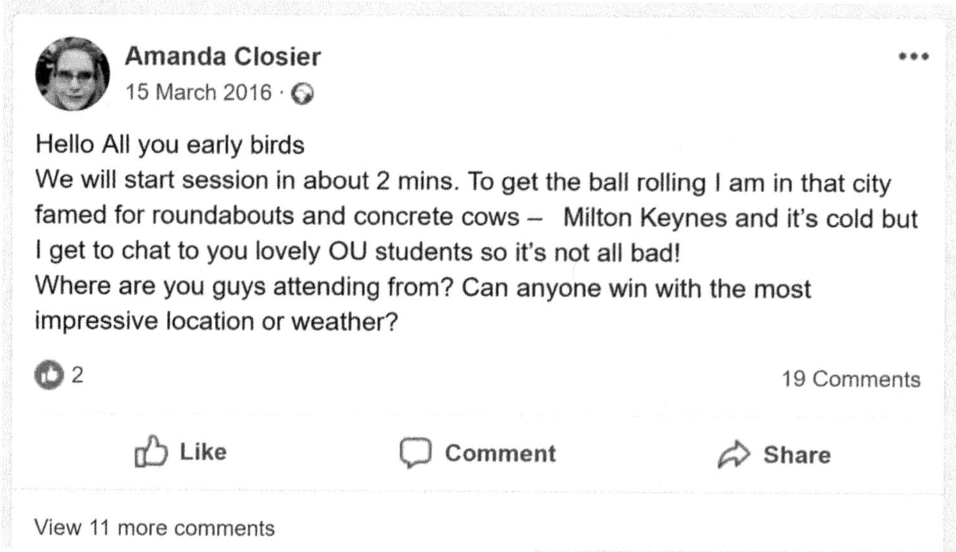

277 individuals expressed an interest in attending, there were 403 live viewers, and 54 individuals posted to the page during the event, either asking questions or replying and conversing with others. An example of how these events can help to build communities of learners and counteract the isolation of being a distance learner can be seen in the following interaction: Student A asked the question 'What is referencing?' and a librarian replied with the official definition, but then Student B replied and the two students started chatting with each other:

Student B: *Good luck with your studies! What are you doing?*
Student A: *Health and social wbu[1]? And thank you, this is my first year starting from September, so I'm kinda trying to get the background (Anonymous, personal communication, March 15, 2016)*

The students continued chatting in the thread, sharing their personal stories and learning journeys and offering encouragement:

I wonder where your journey will take you! all the best and don't give up! (Anonymous, personal communication, March 15, 2016)

This thread ended with the two students agreeing to direct message each other.

The morning after the event a member of the Live Engagement team read through all the comments on the event page and responded to any that were missed or were posted after the event finished. The team also held a debrief session where they evaluated how it went and what they might do differently next time. It was agreed to keep the event page and discussion threads visible, so that those who were unable to attend or who found it difficult to follow live (like the following student) could refer back to it:

Thank you for this session. As a student studying for a qualification in online and distance education it is interesting to experience different learning environments! This one seems a reasonable way of meeting the needs of a lot of people at once, but hard to keep up with it all. At least the messages are all still here so we can go through them slowly at a later date. thanks again. (Anonymous, personal communication, March 15, 2016)

A week after the event, the 'Insights' tool on Facebook revealed that 8,600 individuals had been reached, 2,000 of these in the week following the event, which shows the value of keeping the page and discussion visible. It should be noted that the Library's Facebook page is publicly accessible and so these events are available to all Facebook users, not just OUUK students. With over 25,000 followers this makes it a powerful tool for raising the visibility of the Library to potential students and throughout the higher education sector.

Since that first event, the Live Engagement team have run more text chat events on Facebook. Some of them were arranged to coincide with a calendar event. For example, the team ran a chat on 'Preserving your digital identity over the festive season' in December 2016, and gave tips on Facebook privacy settings and preventing everyone from seeing all of your Christmas party photos. Some were arranged due to an identified need, for example, the Library and the Disabled Students' Group of the institution's Students' Association collaborated on an event in a closed group in order to raise the visibility of the Library's services to disabled students. However, none of the subsequent text chat events has had the reach of the referencing event. This is most likely due to the nature of the topic, which is perennially popular amongst OUUK students. On reflection, the team felt that the referencing event was slightly chaotic and difficult to manage due to the different threads and need to refresh the screen, and if they ran it again they would have only one discussion thread. However, the team also felt that it was incredibly rewarding to see evidence of students supporting and connecting with each other, which was also found during Student Hub Live events discussed later in this chapter.

Facebook Live Video Events

Facebook Live was launched to all users in April 2016 and the Live Engagement team were keen to experiment with the new tool. There are other social media platforms that offer live video, such as Periscope on Twitter, Instagram Stories, Snapchat and YouTube, but the Library had a large existing audience on Facebook and a tradition of using the platform for live teaching events, such as the referencing event. The team decided to run a 30-minute Q&A session on Facebook Live in December 2016. They set up the Facebook event page and promoted it as described previously for text chat events, but they also filmed and edited a 40-second trailer, put it on YouTube and used it heavily in promotion. At the time of writing, 20 months after the trailer was uploaded, there had been 1,400 views (The Open University Library, 2016).

On the day, they used a lapel microphone plugged into a mobile phone on a tripod, with one librarian in front of the camera and one librarian behind the camera. The librarian behind the camera controlled the recording, monitored the comments using a laptop, and relayed questions to the librarian on camera. There were also two other members of the team logged in remotely monitoring the event, relaying questions via the instant messaging back-channel and posting links. Figure 3 shows the behind the scenes technical set-up.

To ensure that the recording of the event was accessible to deaf and hard of hearing students and available to follow without sound, the Live Engagement team downloaded the video recording after the event and created captions and a transcript using Amara (https://amara.org/en/). The captions were added

Figure 3. Behind the scenes at a Facebook Live recording
Source: Helen Clough

to the Facebook recording and the video was also uploaded to YouTube for ease of sharing and embedding in the Library website (http://www.open.ac.uk/library/training-and-events/facebook-live-events). The event was watched live by 23 viewers, which was initially disappointing when compared with the 403 live viewers during the referencing chat event. This could have been due to the less specific nature of the topic, or the video medium. However, the team were encouraged by the engagement that happened after the event. At the time of writing, the recording of the event had received 264 views on Facebook and a further 121 on YouTube. One of the comments on the video provided qualitative evidence of the usefulness of the pilot to at least one student:

I watched this session the day after. Excellent presentation and so valuable for my next TMA[2] in A335 (Anonymous, personal communication, December 2, 2016)

The team were keen to build on the moderate success of the Q&A session and run a series of shorter live videos on a more engaging topic. Following the US presidential election in 2016, there was a lot written about the use of social media platforms to spread misinformation (for example, Lewis, 2016) and the role of librarians in teaching critical thinking skills and media literacy in order to increase awareness of 'fake news' (for example, Batchelor, 2017). In response to this, the International Federation of Library Associations and Institutions (IFLA) produced an infographic, 'How to Spot Fake News', with eight simple steps to evaluate news (IFLA, 2018). The Live Engagement team felt that this was an important and engaging topic, especially in the lead-up to the UK general election in June 2017. Therefore, in May 2017 they planned and delivered a series of 5-minute long Facebook Live videos on 'fake news', based around the IFLA infographic, and broadcast during Friday lunchtimes, branded as #FakeNewsFridays (The Open University Library, 2017).

There were four events, with a different librarian writing and rehearsing a short script to deliver live to camera on two of the eight IFLA steps. The technical set-up was exactly the same as the Q&A, with a mobile phone on a tripod and a librarian behind the camera pressing the record button. In a change from the previous Q&A, no interaction was invited from viewers during the live broadcast. On reflection, the team felt that while using Facebook Live enabled them to quickly create timely video assets that could be reused, the lack of live interaction and engagement with and between viewers was a disadvantage. As previously mentioned, one of the drivers of offering these outreach events on Facebook is to build communities and enable students to interact with staff and each other. In addition, due to the fact that the videos were live and done in one take, they were unpolished. The team felt that for standalone video assets it would be preferable to film multiple takes and edit them into a single, more polished asset using video editing software.

Despite the lack of live interaction, there was subsequent engagement after the event via views and shares on Facebook, Twitter and YouTube. At the time of writing, the four videos had received over 1,000 views each on Facebook and hundreds more when they were uploaded to YouTube. The team attributed the popularity of these videos to the timely choice of topic. There was subsequent interest in these recordings from academics who wished to use them as standalone learning objects in teaching material.

After the #FakeNewsFriday events, the Live Engagement team reflected on the advantages and disadvantages of Facebook Live. The first advantage they identified was that it was a great tool for engaging students in an online space where they already were. At the OUUK there is some anecdotal evidence that students do not want staff infringing on their online spaces, so this use of Facebook Live could also be seen as a disadvantage. However, because most OUUK students will never visit the physical library space on campus it is important that the Library is visible where the students gather online and is offering events on a platform they are comfortable and familiar with. As already mentioned earlier in this chapter, Facebook is by far the leading social media platform in the UK, so it makes sense to use it to engage with OUUK students and promote the Library to other potential learners too. When the team have run text chat events on Facebook, like the referencing event described previously, there have been a few negative comments from non-Facebook users about the choice of platform. One of the big advantages of Facebook Live is that someone without a Facebook account can view it via a direct link to the video. Finally, the team commented on how easy it was to film and quickly share the recording using a mobile device.

As previously stated, one of the unanticipated benefits of experimenting with Facebook Live and being an early adopter was the conversations it stimulated across the institution and the wider sector, raising the visibility of the Library and fostering collaboration. For example, the Live Engagement team were asked to cascade training on Facebook Live to the Careers and Employability Service, and one of the authors of this chapter co-wrote and delivered a workshop on Facebook Live at the Social Media in Higher Education conference with a senior lecturer who was also experimenting with using this tool with students.

CASE STUDY 2: STUDENT HUB LIVE

Student Hub Live has been effectively used by the Live Engagement team in two ways: to showcase the Library's services and resources to OUUK students, and to teach specific DIL skills such as referencing and evaluating information. The Live Engagement team have also benefitted from participating in live events, developing confidence at an individual level and also inspiring Live Engagement work in other formats such as Facebook. The nature of these Student Hub Live extracurricular events, which are both university driven and faculty specific, has enabled the Live Engagement team to collaborate with other areas of the institution, supporting discipline-specific activities and also filling DIL gaps that were not covered elsewhere. This section explains the platform and the Live Engagement team's use of it. The main kinds of event are considered in more detail, and the extent to which the Library sessions fit within the wider programme is discussed. The implications for the specific OUUK student demographic are addressed in the final part of this section.

Student Hub Live: Concept and Development

The Student Hub Live (http://studenthublive.open.ac.uk) is the OUUK's live, interactive online platform to support both students and staff in an academic community. The Student Hub Live (SHL) uses Livestream technology and synchronous digital interfaces to deliver learning to a wide audience who engage online in real-time. Instead of delivering lectures, which are often recorded or streamed using these kinds of technology in brick universities, SHL showcases OUUK content and staff in an accessible and informal way, always incorporating the voice of the audience. Using a 'breakfast TV' style approach to create engaging content that is both informative and fun, SHL broadcasts using Livestream from a studio on campus (shown in Figure 4). SHL was shortlisted in the Times Higher Education awards 2016 in the 'best support for students' category, and won the innovation category at the University Association for Lifelong Learning (UALL) awards in 2018 (https://www.uall.ac.uk/uall-awards-2018).

Figure 4. The Student Hub Live studio
Source: The Open University, 2018

SHL was developed in 2014 to welcome new OUUK students to the university with orientation events, but has since developed to include skills sessions, dissemination of research and academic debate. SHL programmes on Livestream range in length from two hours to two days. 'Sessions' are parts of the overall programme on Livestream and are typically 25–60 minutes in length, depending on their objective. Student attendance at SHL events is optional and varies widely depending on promotion and marketing, and also the nature of the event. The 'study skills bootcamps' have been very effective, with approximately 2,000 students logging on to view before their modules start.

The events are made interactive through the use of a chat box, widgets (interactive voting tools) and also email and Twitter. The questions and feedback from the audience are fed into the discussion through the 'hot desk' (shown in Figure 5), a part of the set in the studio that is staffed by a range of students and members of staff. The chat box provides a very rich source of information that can be used to understand more about the experience of participation, and some of the quotations from the chat box are used in this chapter to support particular points that are made.

A catch-up service on YouTube is available for those unable to attend live, and, at the time of writing, the channel had 848 subscribers and 68,433 total views over the two-year period since it was set up.

SHL is a OUUK initiative that offers students an extracurricular space in order to engage in activities outside their modules. The scaffolding of academic community and the opportunity to take part in additional learning events is important for student success. Much research has found that students who engage in activities outside of the core requirements and who feel part of a community are more successful in their studies (Trowler, 2010).

This quotation from a student consultative forum sums up the value that participation in this event has for this student.

Finally, I wanted to say that I appreciate the work of Karen and Student Hub Live. Although it takes a light hearted approach at times, I really appreciate what SHL is trying to achieve. It is the only place

Figure 5. The 'hot desk' at SHL
Source: The Open University, 2018

where I can see and hear OU staff talking about their work in a meaningful way and giving people a chance to ask questions on the spot. SHL is a great opportunity to allay anxieties about study and provide interesting information about courses. Although it cannot replace the human contact of tutors and tutor groups - I can't emphasize enough how important real, human contact is to learning - but it does provide a window on the OU and OU study which is not otherwise available. (Anonymous, personal communication, date unknown)

While SHL is primarily for students, a secondary benefit is that it gives OUUK staff access to students in a way that was not possible beforehand, since many academics are not directly involved with face-to-face teaching. This not only offers an opportunity to connect with student concerns, but also provides an opportunity to deliver teaching in a very different format. The SHL team work with presenters to produce content that is inspirational, fun and engaging, and very often that means doing something that has not been done before.

Library Involvement in Student Hub Live

The Live Engagement team were involved early on in SHL, delivering sessions that raised awareness of Library services and resources and informing students about topical issues relating to DIL skills. For this chapter, the team were asked to reflect on their first experience of being on live camera for SHL. A common theme that emerged was being brave enough to try something new:

In my case it was just being brave the first time - it's always hard facing the unknown. The first SHL I was terrified...I felt like a rabbit in the headlights. After a bit I realised we were talking about stuff I knew...No session since has ever felt that terrifying! I would say once you get over the initial fear and being filmed is no longer an unknown, it becomes much easier. (Live Engagement librarian, personal communication, August, 2018)

The other themes that emerged were:

- Preparation; knowing the talking points and rehearsing
- Doing it regularly to build confidence
- Doing it in pairs in case one person dries up
- The importance of watching the recording on continuous improvement
- The importance of positive feedback from peers and managers in building confidence.

The team have delivered a range of sessions at SHL that can be broadly categorized into the following areas: what is an online library; referencing; online skills (including fake news, trust, and managing digital identity); and evaluation frameworks. Measuring the impact of these sessions is challenging because they are part of programmes that reach between 400 and 8,000 students, with durations of anywhere between two hours and two days. Many students log on to live events at times that suit their availability. However, it appears that some students do specifically log on with the aim of watching library sessions, as this student wrote when they logged on and the previous session was overrunning by two minutes:

I thought referencing was 14.30 - 15.00 did i miss this? (Anonymous, personal communication, February 22, 2018)

Students who do not attend live events can watch recordings on catch-up, and the unique views from the YouTube channel at the time of writing show that of most interest is 'Referencing' (471 views), followed by 'Managing your digital presence' (242 views) and then 'Evaluation Frameworks' (194 views). While students enjoy learning about what the Library has to offer, the skills content appears to have most value to them. This is in keeping with the participation in the events overall, with the skills sessions attracting higher attendance both live and on catch-up.

The Live Engagement team arrange their own tie-in events to coincide with SHL and use their appearance on SHL as an opportunity to promote these. This cross-promotion works well:

'Do you know if there will be a training session with the Library team soon? Before the courses start' (Anonymous, personal communication, February 22, 2018)

What Is an Online Library

General introductory 'What is an online library' sessions have been included in SHL programmes such as the Open Day (for new and prospective students), and the orientation events (for all new students). The purpose of these sessions was to showcase the resources and support that students could access from the Library. Many of these sessions have been delivered live; however, they have also been replayed in the non-live part of the programme, when the studio takes a break from livestreaming video but students can still talk to each other using the chat box. These sessions target new students, but many continuing students are not aware of the support that the Library offers, and so the secondary objective is to raise awareness of this.

Referencing

Referencing is a common concern for both new and continuing OUUK students. Despite some differences in certain discipline areas such as Law, the OUUK uses a version of Harvard referencing called OU Harvard. Internal research conducted by the Library found that many students struggle with knowing when to reference, and also how to apply this bespoke style. The referencing sessions that have been part of SHL programmes have been well received by students, and, as has previously been mentioned, feature most highly in terms of views on the YouTube channel.

Referencing sessions have been included in the 'study skills bootcamps' which prepare students for study, and they have also featured in specific skills programmes such as 'Improving your study skills and academic practice event' on February 2018. For some of these sessions the Live Engagement team designed and delivered the content in collaboration with academic colleagues.

Students appear to be enthusiastically engaged with the content:

'Wow, would love to know some of those plagiarism stories' (Anonymous, personal communication, February 22, 2018)

During a discussion about common knowledge, students were engaged, reflecting on when they had not referenced because they thought something was common knowledge:

Something to take from that is if you're not sure check with your tutor as I agree with you that common knowledge does vary from people to place to content and subject! Use your tutors folks. I say it's always better to ask a silly question than make a silly mistake:) (Anonymous, personal communication, February 22, 2018)

And many felt able to share their referencing concerns with other students:

No clue how to reference:/ (Anonymous, personal communication, February 22, 2018)

i spending as long checking references than what i do on the essay lolol (Anonymous, personal communication, February 22, 2018)

I have downloaded and printed all the info and examples from library but as i have a tracking issue, as in transferring info from paper to screen i tend to miss things (Anonymous, personal communication, February 22, 2018)

Students responded with reassurance and were supportive of each other:

don't worry, that's about my extent of knowledge on referencing lol (Anonymous, personal communication, February 22, 2018)

that's where I get lost, but I agree with [panellist] if you're unsure make sure to reference or just check with your tutor:) (Anonymous, personal communication, February 22, 2018)

Asking for recommendations and sharing tips is a common activity at SHL events, and the Library sessions are no exception:

I understand referencing takes a lot of time so can we use an App to help? (Anonymous, personal communication, February 22, 2018)

I use Zotero but you still need to check the reference generator to ensure it is correct style and all information has been added (Anonymous, personal communication, February 22, 2018)

Online Skills

One of the most popular videos on catch-up is the 'Managing your digital presence' session, which focuses on digital literacy and the use of Facebook. As described previously, many students gather in groups on Facebook, and in this session, students discussed how to locate groups and also the benefits and pitfalls of belonging to such groups:

My Facebook module groups have kept me sane and made the experience a whole lot less lonely' (Anonymous, personal communication, September 5, 2016)

Facebook groups have been so useful and you meet great people (Anonymous, personal communication, September 5, 2016)

Facebook groups for modules are a fantastic way of getting support as long as you don't worry too much about people who are well ahead of you on the module. Just working at your own pace is the way to go (Anonymous, personal communication, September 5, 2016)

Based on the advice from the Live Engagement team, students also echoed where caution was necessary:

you should always be cautious with Facebook groups, people are not bound by OU computing conduct (Anonymous, personal communication, September 5, 2016)

Evaluation Frameworks

The Library recommends frameworks such as PROMPT (http://www.open.ac.uk/libraryservices/being-digital/objects/87/index.htm) and 'Who, Why, When' to students when they need to evaluate the extent to which material can be trusted. The Live Engagement team have developed a range of sessions using evaluation frameworks, and the most popular one was included in the critical thinking programme shown in Figure 6. Drawing on several 'fake news' stories they used frameworks to ascertain what could be trusted.

This went down very well with students who drew on their own examples of fake news stories:

Spinach and Popeye is an example. There was a 'spinach mountain' so the government promoted spinach, when other greens were equally nutritious (Anonymous, personal communication, September 19, 2016)

Figure 6. Live Engagement librarians talk about fake news in the SHL studio (The Open University, 2016)
Source: https://youtu.be/QFR1UjV5kSE

And also commented on the relevance of identifying untrustworthy sources based on their own experiences of media:

unfortunately that's how a lot of research is reported (Anonymous, personal communication, September 19, 2016)

Serious point - urban myths are perpetuated by other media who should know better. In Guardian there is increasing criticism from commentators that stories and opinion pieces are using Twitter feeds as source and reference. (Anonymous, personal communication, September 19, 2016)

Students also talked about how they evaluated information, echoing many of the key teaching points communicated by the Live Engagement team during the session.

It always helps to read the introduction to see whether the sources give relevant information for your topic (Anonymous, personal communication, September 19, 2016)

when I am getting sources of information from newspaper articles and magazines online, I always read information on the author who wrote the article and evaluate whether the information is useful for me (Anonymous, personal communication, September 19, 2016)

Benefits to the Library

SHL has provided another mechanism for the Live Engagement team to showcase Library services and resources to students and also to support DIL skills development through fun, interactive events that are popular with students. Additional benefits to the Library include increased visibility within the institution, which helps to raise awareness and foster collaboration. Indeed, this book chapter is an example of cross-departmental collaboration; the authors are a member of the Live Engagement team and the SHL project leader.

The Live Engagement team are also often asked to contribute to discussions about good academic practice, take part in an interactive panel quiz show, and develop specific sessions for particular cohorts of students, for example humanities students or postgraduates. The skills that they have developed in front of the camera and the knowledge that they have about students makes the Live Engagement team ideal participants; however, their willingness to collaborate and desire to constantly innovate is what is most appreciated by the SHL organisers.

In addition to the live content, the SHL team create short videos that are used as breaks between live sessions. The Live Engagement team has featured in several of these, including a tour of the Library. These videos are included within SHL programmes to raise awareness and have been useful assets that the Live Engagement team have used elsewhere on social media.

The Value of Extracurricular Events

OUUK students who attend live events like SHL appear to gain a lot from the experience; however, while this is one of only a few live events, it is one of many sources of information. Considering the care with which core skills are embedded into module content, and the range of information that is readily accessible to students, the question about why students would want to join or catch up on a live event highlights the value of these types of activity.

When considering some of the challenges that are encountered in part-time distance learning, it is unsurprising that students find value in talking to peers and members of staff in an informal way, and the expression of support from others has been evident in some of the quotes from the chat box. Students with busy lives and other responsibilities may not always be able to engage fully with their module material, and they may skip over certain activities that they consider either challenging or irrelevant. The high engagement with generic, skills-based content at SHL could indicate that students want to develop these skills, and that they require something in addition to the material they already have access to. Another explanation for the high viewing figures may be that students feel validated in attending events that are both fun and have a clear benefit to their study. However, although this explanation would hold for live events, it does not explain the high levels of catch-up viewing.

Students attend to learn, but also appear to find altruistic value in sharing ideas that have worked well for them – such as referencing tools and strategies – and they engage in sessions that have relevance and meaning to their lives. The Live Engagement team present the teaching points in an engaging way, and their examples are always topical. This is particularly important for live interactive events for two reasons: people will contribute when the discussion is meaningful and they feel able to add their own experiences and viewpoints, and participants can log off when they lose interest.

Discussions about digital presence, particularly regarding Facebook, have been useful in highlighting the benefits and limitations of these spaces, which are not all monitored by the OUUK. The strategy to acknowledge these spaces and use DIL skills to support students in them has meant that the Library is positioned as relevant and useful.

FUTURE RESEARCH DIRECTIONS

Due to temporary resourcing issues in the 2017/18 academic year, the Live Engagement team had to put a hold on using Facebook for student engagement to concentrate on meeting existing module-targeted online teaching commitments. At the time of writing, the team are back to full strength and keen to continue running events on social media and experimenting with different platforms. Facebook use in the UK among those aged 16 to 24 years is decreasing in favour of other sites such as Instagram and Snapchat (Statista, 2018c). This indicates a need to investigate other social media platforms in order to stay ahead of the trend. Facebook will still remain a valuable platform for the Library, however, because the age demographic of OUUK students is wide and the median age of new undergraduate students is 28.

A lesson learned during past investigations into different social media sites is that the Library does not necessarily need to have a separate account on a platform in order to make an impact. In 2016 the Library partnered with the OUUK Communications team to run a pilot with the institution's main Instagram account, providing regular content with the pre-agreed hashtag #OULibrary in order to create a library sub-community. It was judged to be a success by both departments due to the Communications team having a regular stream of content to post and the Library remaining visible on the main account without the pressure to maintain and monitor a separate channel (Bateman, 2017). This example of cross-departmental collaboration and resource sharing is something the Library is keen to continue.

As discussed earlier in this chapter, the OUUK Library is gathering evidence of the impact of module-targeted online training sessions on the student experience and academic success. A future area of research may be to explore how live engagement with students on social media impacts on the student experience, and whether it is an effective instruction mechanism. This could be done via feedback surveys or by using the Library's student panel (http://www.open.ac.uk/library/library-information/library-services-student-panel), which is made up of around 500 current OUUK students from a wide variety of backgrounds, ages and study levels who have been invited to be on the panel for one year and take part in research activities.

CONCLUSION

The OUUK Library uses various online platforms to teach digital and information literacy skills to the institution's distance learners. The Live Engagement team have a particular remit for designing and delivering synchronous events and experimenting with new tools and platforms. The reason for experimenting with new platforms is in order to reach out to a different audience who might not think to attend a Library-branded session, delivering skills and raising the visibility of the Library's services and resources in students' preferred online spaces. The team have reflected on their experiences with Facebook and SHL and now plan their events around audience interaction, picking topics that will engage students and encourage communication and peer support. This contributes to the institutional driver to build communities of students in order to combat the isolation of distance learning and improve retention and progression. An added benefit of being innovative in order to increase the visibility of the Library with students is that this also raises the Library's profile across the institution and fosters collaboration with faculties and other professional service departments.

To conclude, the authors recommend that other academic libraries who wish to use social media to hold live engagement events that build communities of distance learners consider the following steps:

- Choose an enticing topic with relevance to students' studies. Think about:
  - Popular questions at the enquiry desk
  - What is in the news
  - What will help students save time and be more efficient.
- Choose a time of year and time of day that will have maximum impact.
- Choose a platform that allows for interaction both with the hosts/presenters and between the students.
- Promote the event heavily via relevant communication channels – but especially via social media – in order to be visible to the audience the event is trying to reach. Think about:
  - Producing audio-visual assets such as short trailers
  - Selling the benefits of attending by linking the topic to students' study concerns
  - Paying to boost the visibility and reach of events on Facebook.
- Encourage interaction between students by having icebreaker questions/polls. For example:
  - What is the weather like where you are?
  - What are you studying?
  - How are you feeling today?
  - Where do you usually study? Why not post a picture?
- Prepare well. For text-based events, have pre-prepared responses to cut and paste. For video-based events, write a script, rehearse, and anticipate possible questions.
- Have a plan, but be flexible and allow for spontaneity.
- Make recordings of video events available afterwards and use in future promotional materials.
- Allow time and resource to make events accessible to disabled users. Consider having live captioning, or add captions and transcripts afterwards.

ACKNOWLEDGMENT

The authors would like to thank Amanda Closier, Jo Parker and Beccy Dresden for their help with preparing this chapter.

REFERENCES

Batchelor, O. (2017). Getting out the truth: The role of libraries in the fight against fake news. *RSR. Reference Services Review*, *45*(2), 143–148. doi:10.1108/RSR-03-2017-0006

Bateman, R. (2017). *InstHEgram: A 'Uni'-versal Guide to Instagram in Higher Education.* Retrieved from https://leanpub.com/instHEgram

Butcher, J. (2015). *'Shoe-horned and side-lined'? Challenges for part-time learners in the new HE landscape*. Retrieved from https://www.heacademy.ac.uk/knowledge-hub/shoe-horned-and-side-lined-challenges-part-time-learners-new-he-landscape

Butcher, J., & Rose-Adams, J. (2015). Part-time learners in open and distance learning: revisiting the critical importance of choice, flexibility and employability. *Open Learning: The Journal of Open, Distance and e-Learning, 30*(2), 127-137.

Callaghan, G., & Fribbance, I. (2016). The use of Facebook to build a community for distance learning students: a case study from the Open University. *Open Learning: The Journal of Open, Distance and e-Learning, 31*(3), 260-272.

Dresden, B., & Hidalgo, R. (2017, September). *Beyond the VLE forum: using Twitter to build community and currency into distance-learning modules*. Paper presented at the Association for Learning Technology Annual Conference, Liverpool, UK. Retrieved from https://altc.alt.ac.uk/2017/sessions/beyond-the-vle-forum-using-twitter-to-build-community-and-currency-into-distance-learning-modules-1760/

Ellis, E., Gallagher, A., & Peasgood, A. (2017). *Study behaviours in an increasingly digital world: Learning habits, top tips and 'study hacks' questionnaire survey*. The Open University. Retrieved from http://oro.open.ac.uk/50433/

Gibbs, G. (2006). How assessment frames student learning. In C. Bryan & K. Clegg (Eds.), *Innovative Assessment in Higher Education* (pp. 23–36). London: Routledge.

Goodfellow, R., & Reedy, K. (2012). *Digital and Information Literacy Framework*. Retrieved from http://www.open.ac.uk/libraryservices/pages/dilframework/

Goodfellow, R., & Reedy, K. (2014). 'You've been frameworked': Evaluating an approach to digital and information literacy at the Open University. *Journal of Learning Development in Higher Education, 7*. Retrieved from http://oro.open.ac.uk/41547/1/Reedy.pdf

Harrison, A., Burress, R., Velasquez, S., & Schreiner, L. (2017). Social Media Use in Academic Libraries: A Phenomenological Study. *Journal of Academic Librarianship, 43*(3), 248–256. doi:10.1016/j.acalib.2017.02.014

Hoodless, C., & Pinfield, S. (2016). Subject vs. functional: Should subject librarians be replaced by functional specialists in academic libraries? *Journal of Librarianship and Information Science*. Retrieved from http://journals.sagepub.com/doi/abs/10.1177/0961000616653647

IFLA. (2018). *How To Spot Fake News*. Retrieved from https://www.ifla.org/publications/node/11174

Lewis, H. (2016, November 17). Did fake news on Facebook swing the US election? *New Statesman*. Retrieved from https://www.newstatesman.com/world/2016/11/did-fake-news-facebook-swing-us-election

Statista. (2018a). *Total number and the share of population of active social media and mobile social media users in the United Kingdom (UK) in January 2018*. Retrieved from https://www.statista.com/statistics/507405/uk-active-social-media-and-mobile-social-media-users/

Statista. (2018b). *Market share held by the leading social networks in the United Kingdom (UK) as of January 2018*. Retrieved from https://www.statista.com/statistics/280295/market-share-held-by-the-leading-social-networks-in-the-united-kingdom-uk/

Statista. (2018c). *Which one of these social networking sites or apps do you use most often?* Retrieved from https://www.statista.com/statistics/308712/main-social-networking-site-preference-in-the-uk-by-age/

Taylor & Francis Group. (2014). *Use of social media by the library: Current practices and future opportunities*. Retrieved from http://www.tandf.co.uk/journals/access/white-paper-social-media.pdf

The Open University. (2015) *Learning and Teaching Vision and Plan 2025: Learning now and for the future*. Retrieved from http://www.open.ac.uk/about/main/sites/www.open.ac.uk.about.main/files/files/ecms/web-content/Learning-and-Teaching-Vision-and-Plan.pdf

The Open University. (2017). *Open University Social Media Unconference 0.1 October 11th 2017*. Retrieved from https://sites.google.com/view/ousocmed/home

The Open University. (2018a). *Facts and figures*. Retrieved from http://www.open.ac.uk/about/main/strategy-and-policies/facts-and-figures

The Open University Library. (2016, November 14). *Facebook Live Trailer December 1 2016* [Video file]. Retrieved from https://youtu.be/z0DSR9vDKPs

The Open University Library. (2017, May). *#FakeNewsFriday playlist* [Video file]. Retrieved from https://youtu.be/PJCDj0iUc08

Trowler, V. (2010). *Student Engagement Literature Review*. Retrieved from https://www.heacademy.ac.uk/system/files/studentengagementliteraturereview_1.pdf

ADDITIONAL READING

Callaghan, G., & Fribbance, I. (2018). Facebook and Informal Learning. In J. Baxter, G. Callaghan, & J. McAvoy (Eds.), *Creativity & Critique in Online Learning: Exploring and Examining Innovations in Online Pedagogy* (pp. 81–102). Cham, Switzerland: Palgrave Macmillan. doi:10.1007/978-3-319-78298-0_5

Closier, A. (2018). How the Open University library uses Facebook Live to reach, engage and support students. *ALISS Quarterly*, *13*(2), 1–14.

Closier, A., & Clough, H. (2018). Walking the talk: Using digital media to develop distance learners' digital citizenship at the Open University (UK). *The Reference Librarian*, *59*(3), 129–133. doi:10.1080/02763877.2018.1468848

Foley, K., & Fribbance, I. (2018). Student Connections: Livestreaming and Creating Community via an Annual Student Conference. In J. Baxter, G. Callaghan, & J. McAvoy (Eds.), *Creativity & Critique in Online Learning: Exploring and Examining Innovations in Online Pedagogy* (pp. 169–189). Cham, Switzerland: Palgrave Macmillan.

Foley, K., Middleton, D., & Fribbance, I. (2015). *From despair to somewhere: activating students in a distance learning environment.* Practice and Evidence of Scholarship of Teaching and Learning in Higher Education.

Harrison, A., Burress, R., Velasquez, S., & Schreiner, L. (2017). Social Media Use in Academic Libraries: A Phenomenological Study. *Journal of Academic Librarianship, 43*(3), 248–256. doi:10.1016/j.acalib.2017.02.014

Smith, A. (2016). *Teaching by Twitter: Extending the classroom via Social Media?* Paper presented at CompTIA EMEA Member and Partner Conference, London, UK. Retrieved from http://oro.open.ac.uk/47622/

Weinbren, D. (2014). *The Open University: A History*. Manchester, UK: Manchester University Press.

ENDNOTES

1 What about you?

2 TMA is Tutor Marked Assignment and A335 is the code for an English Literature module.

Chapter 11
Using Social Media to Enhance Information Literacy:
The VCU Libraries #VetYourSources Campaign

Sue Robinson
Virginia Commonwealth University, USA

Laura W. Gariepy
Virginia Commonwealth University, USA

ABSTRACT

Academic librarians have long been committed to developing their students' abilities to assess the quality and credibility of various types of information. A combination of increasing public discourse about evaluating every day information and librarians' commitment to empowering students to be responsible consumers of information led Virginia Commonwealth University (VCU) librarians to develop the #VetYourSources campaign, focused on enhancing undergraduate students' skills for evaluating information in academic and day-to-day contexts through social media. This chapter details the design, planning, and execution of the campaign, as well as future directions.

INTRODUCTION

Librarians in higher education devote notable time and energy to developing their students' abilities to assess the quality and credibility of various types of information. The importance of evaluating sources as a learning outcome was clearly articulated in the Association of College and Research Libraries' (ACRL's) *Information Literacy Competency Standards for Higher Education* (2000), and continues to be prominently featured in the new *Framework for Information Literacy for Higher Education* (Association of College and Research Libraries, 2017). In the wake of the 2016 United States presidential campaign and election, the American public has been more attuned to accuracy, misinformation, and bias in news media outlets than at any time in recent history. As a result, librarians have been well positioned over the

DOI: 10.4018/978-1-5225-8097-3.ch011

past several years to use their expertise to educate students and members of the general public on how to evaluate news and other types of information. A search of the academic library literature quickly reveals librarians' efforts to enhance students' skills in evaluating information through instruction, outreach, events, and online learning (Batchelor, 2017; Burkhardt, 2017; Johnson, 2019; Musgrove, Powers, Rebar, & Musgrove, 2018; Wade & Hornick, 2018).

At the same time, academic libraries continue to explore meaningful ways to engage social media to connect with library users. Most libraries use social media to create posts intended to help library users by increasing their awareness of library initiatives, alerting people to learning opportunities, and inviting the academic community to library-sponsored events (Taylor & Francis Group, 2014; Wan, 2011). However, the literature does not reveal examples of libraries using social media to enhance users' information literacy skills, or to connect them to a robust suite of resources that might help them do so. It was the combined interest in leveraging social media for educational initiatives plus evidence of the increased need to assess the quality of sources that led Virginia Commonwealth University (VCU) librarians to develop the #VetYourSources campaign, focused on connecting undergraduate students to ideas and materials that will help them enhance their skills for evaluating information in academic and day-to-day contexts.

For the past several years, VCU Libraries (VCUL) has had a robust social media presence and an active information literacy program focused on undergraduate students. However, VCUL had not used social media as a vehicle to enhance information literacy in the past. Like most academic libraries, VCUL's social media presence has been and still is often focused on publishing about services, resources, collections, and events (Taylor & Francis Group, 2014, Wan, 2011). The idea of using VCUL social media platforms in order to enhance information literacy -- specifically by addressing "fake news" and related concepts -- arose in a brainstorming conversation with members of the VCUL public relations (PR) team and several librarians. As a result, librarians and the PR team initiated the #VetYourSources campaign, which began in February of 2017 and is still ongoing.

The overall purpose of the campaign is to point VCU Libraries social media followers, and especially undergraduates, toward high-quality resources that help them improve their skills in evaluating information. The initial campaign took place in spring 2017 and was reprised with less frequent posting in spring 2018. It is planned to continue as an ongoing theme of social media postings during the 2018-19 academic year. In this highly practical chapter, readers will become familiar with:

- The need for the campaign
- The social media environment and information literacy objectives at VCU Libraries
- The process for designing the campaign conceptually
- The planning and execution of the campaign, including the process of developing content for Facebook and Twitter, and assessing success through engagements and impressions
- The in person events offered to complement the social media campaign
- Methods used to enhance social media accessibility
- Future directions for the campaign

BACKGROUND

The Need for the Campaign

In December of 2016, a group of librarians and representatives of the VCUL PR office met to discuss social media plans and ideas for the spring semester. On the heels of the 2016 presidential election, the group was keen to respond to the nation's interest in combating misinformation and misleading news. Although librarians expressed some distaste for the phrase "fake news," which they believed oversimplified the phenomenon of biased or misleading information, it was acknowledged that this phrase seemed to strike a chord with the American people. The creation, dubious origins, and circulation of intentionally false news stories arose as themes for public discussion and further investigation in late 2016 and beyond, with "fake news" as the catchall phrase representing these issues.

VCU librarians had also grown increasingly concerned about students' inability to recognize reliable sources. Around the same time as the 2016 presidential election, the Stanford History Education Group (2016) released a report that described middle school, high school, and college-aged students' abilities to evaluate information in a real-world context with a disheartening word: "bleak" (2016, p. 4). Students were unsuccessful in various forms of evaluating information online. For example, they struggled to identify native advertisements and evaluate claims made on social media. The authors stated that they were "taken aback by students' lack of preparation" to evaluate information at all levels of schooling and in all scenarios assessed (p. 4). This is consistent with Coiro, Coscarelli, Maykel, and Forzani's (2015) findings that 7th graders used a set of "unacceptable or superficial criteria" to evaluate websites. Similarly, Amsbary and Powell (2003) found that the indicators that adults used when evaluating the of credibility of websites -- such as whether or not the site author had a PhD and how many links were listed -- were not necessarily signs of source quality.

Metzger emphasized in 2004 the increasing importance of equipping students to evaluate information online, due to the proliferation of information available through this medium at that time, and because nearly anyone can be an author. These issues have only intensified in the 14 years since Metzger's publication, in which individuals' use of websites and social media for the purposes of news consumption have grown considerably (Shearer & Gottfried, 2017). Findings from these studies, experience in working with students on a daily basis, and the growing national conversation around the importance of news literacy and individuals' abilities to separate fact from opinion demonstrated clearly to VCU librarians the need to amplify efforts to enhance students' abilities to assess the credibility of sources.

Social Media at VCU Libraries

VCU is a large, urban research university with 32,000 students on two campuses in Richmond, Virginia. All aspects of social media use at VCU are governed by University Relations, the unit that maintains VCU's social media guidelines (Virginia Commonwealth University, 2018). In the library system, all social media activity and channels are coordinated in compliance with VCU's social media guidelines by the VCUL PR Office and specifically, a full-time communications and Public Relations director. In general, VCUL uses a collaborative, flexible, but strategic approach to social media, with people from different library departments taking responsibility for certain roles and for certain content types for

Facebook, Twitter, YouTube, blogs, and other platforms. Each of VCUL's 18 platforms/channels has a written content strategy, consistent with best practices for public relations (Peacemaker, Robinson, & Hurst, 2016). Specific campaigns and projects are guided by a project plan or creative brief, in alignment with best practices for social media management (Steiner, 2012).

Although VCUL does not have proscriptive metrics for the level of activity or engagement expected to be seen on individual accounts, the PR officer monitors social media platforms to ensure that they are active with regular postings, or they are retired. Combined activity levels on Facebook and Twitter – the libraries' most active platforms with the greatest number of followers – typically range from 10-30 posts per week.

In the past, The PR office developed social media campaigns that promoted services and collections and offered tips for how to make the most of the libraries at VCU. General messaging on VCUL social media channels generally fell in the vein of helping library users and researchers through increasing their awareness of library initiatives, alerting people to learning opportunities and inviting the academic community to library-sponsored events. These types of social media use are consistent with other libraries' practices, as well (Taylor & Francis Group, 2014; Wan, 2011). Historically, VCU Libraries had not focused its social media presence on knowledge-building tied to a core teaching mission until this campaign -- namely to enhance students' abilities to evaluate information sources by connecting them to resources and content that would related to assessing academic and day-to-day sources.

Information Literacy at VCU Libraries

Teaching librarians at VCU view their work as very closely tied to student success, including enhancing students' lifelong learning abilities. One of VCUL's strategic areas of focus is *Learning and Teaching*, which includes specific references to innovation in teaching and using technologies in teaching. (Virginia Commonwealth University Libraries, 2017). VCU librarians in the department of Teaching, Learning, and Information (TLI) are heavily focused on enhancing undergraduate students' information literacy skills through teaching and research assistance and enjoy close relationships with faculty who teach core curriculum classes focused on research and writing. Librarians' roles as teachers and facilitators of the research process are tightly integrated into the undergraduate curriculum.

Following the adoption of ACRL's *Framework for Information Literacy for Higher Education* (2016), TLI librarians worked with faculty in core curricula to align learning outcomes to frames that were identified as most important for new students, including *Searching as Strategic Exploration*, *Research as Inquiry*, and *Authority is Constructed and Contextual*, the latter of which most closely aligns with the goals of the #VetYourSources campaign. In order to advance student learning in this area, librarians spend time in undergraduate courses focusing on differentiating between types of sources and understanding methods for evaluating them.

As the social media presence at VCU Libraries grew more robust over the years, TLI librarians intermittently considered the potential for including content related to information literacy on social media platforms. The 2016 presidential campaign and subsequent inauguration, both rife with themes of misinformation and distortion of information were the catalyst for TLI librarians and the VCU Libraries PR office to bring this idea to life.

MAIN FOCUS OF THE CHAPTER

Designing the Initial Campaign

As a result, a group of VCUL librarians and PR professionals agreed to develop a social media campaign intended to point VCU Libraries social media followers, especially undergraduates, toward high quality resources that would help them improve their skills in evaluating information. In order to draw attention and to sufficiently address even a small portion of the complexities of evaluating information, it was agreed that a thoughtful and intentional campaign was warranted, as opposed to simply a series of posts on the topic. Two principals were identified to take lead roles on the project. The first was the Head of Teaching, Learning, & Information at VCUL, who is responsible for oversight of the integration of information literacy into the undergraduate curriculum. The second was VCUL's Director of Communications and Public Relations. From the beginning, the principals expected to gather input from numerous librarians across the organization and from PR staff.

In early conversations, the group agreed to these general concepts to guide the campaign:

- Librarians should drive the content. The voice needed to be authoritative in terms of library expertise and offer a substantive information stream that would be led by/managed by librarians, not the PR office. The PR office would take lead on accompanying artwork, developing a process for creating and publishing posts, and adjusting wording of posts to achieve the casual yet professional language sought in all VCUL social media posts.
- Partisanship or perceptions of political bias must be avoided. Maintaining the libraries' identity and credibility as an unbiased source of information was crucial, particularly during such a politically fraught time.
- Timeline must be aggressive. The principals agreed that the campaign could start no later than February of 2017 (less than two months from the initial conversations about the idea), and that a substantial amount of crafted content must be developed by the first day of the campaign in order to ensure routine and high-volume posts. The principals also concurred that creating, reviewing, revising and publishing posts must be done quickly and with high priority, often in turnarounds of a couple of hours or a couple of days.

Planning and Executing the Campaign

In December 2016 and January 2017, the principals of the campaign developed a project plan/creative brief that spelled out goals, timeline, audience, and approach with a launch date of mid-February. Developing a plan of this sort is consistent with how VCU Libraries generally approaches planning for a platform and best practices for social media in libraries (Steiner, 2012). To work quickly and remain flexible, they agreed that the creative brief needed to be pliable and in constant evolution. Through developing and revising the brief, the principals defined the scope and tactics for the campaign, which are explicated in this section.

The campaign name and hashtag -- #VetYourSources -- was one in the same. #VetYourSources was selected as the title of the campaign as opposed to variations on "fake news," "alternative facts," or other phrases that immediately conjured specific political figures, movements, or orientations. However, it was understood that such phrases may be inevitable at times throughout the campaign given the prevalence of both terms in national conversations in libraries and journalism groups about evaluating information. The concept of "vetting" sources fit well with the learning outcomes VCU librarians have developed with teaching faculty that focus on the *Authority is Constructed and Contextual* frame of the *Framework for Information Literacy for Higher Education* (2016). The overall goal of the campaign was to respond to the current interest in evaluating online information and increase students' ability to assess information in day-to-day and academic contexts. The audience would be primarily undergraduates. The principals agreed that instead of creating a large amount of new or original content in the form of videos, websites, etc., to point to during the campaign, they would rely instead primarily on materials already available through VCUL and other institutions. An existing VCUL research guide on evaluating sources was refreshed and received a custom URL to match the campaign (go.vcu.edu/VetYourSources; see Figure 1).

Given the timeliness of the national conversation about false and misleading news, the core planning team agreed that time was of the essence for the success of the campaign. The principals selected mid-February of 2017 as the beginning of the campaign, tentatively expecting to develop posts with the #VetYourSources hashtag through mid-April, with the understanding that if it was successful then the project may be continued in some way. As it turned out, the initial iteration of the campaign continued through early May. Principals agreed that the tone on social media should be advisory and designed to encourage independent ability and, as is the case with all of VCUL social media posts, professional yet approachable.

Figure 1: Flagship website for #VetYourSources campaign with custom URL (go.vcu.edu/VetYourSources)
Source: VCU Libraries

The principals determined that the development of some original artwork to brand the campaign would increase ability to promote it both on social media through some consistent images, and in real life through a series of posters throughout VCU's two main research libraries. (see Figure 2 and Figure 3 for examples of the key imagery). Recurring message points that were used on original artwork that was used for physical posters in library buildings and on social media were: *Search for answers; Examine endlessly;* and *Find out for yourself.*

The planning team identified two platforms and four primary social media channels for posting:

- **Twitter Accounts**: @VCULibraries (1664 followers) and @VCUCabell (1867 followers).
- **Facebook Accounts**: VCU Libraries (1194 likes) VCU James Branch Cabell Library (2160 likes).

VCU Libraries accounts represent the entire library system at VCU, while the others are associated with James Branch Cabell Library, one of two major research libraries at VCU with a strong emphasis on undergraduate services. Twitter and Facebook were selected as the two most optimal platforms for this campaign based on the fact that they have the largest number of followers of VCUL social media accounts, and because they allow posts comprised of both text and different forms of media, which is most ideal for the types of posts we envisioned for the campaign given our desire for textual explanation and visual impact.

For the duration of the 2017 campaign, the principals set a goal of publishing five to ten Tweets weekly, and two to three Facebook posts weekly. Content posted on Facebook was occasionally similar to that which was posted on Twitter, but not identical. It was also determined that the campaign would kick-off with a Twitter blitz -- 12 Tweets in 12 hours -- in February, shortly after the university published a news

Figure 2: Original artwork for #VetYourSources campaign
Source: VCU Libraries; illustrator Jeff Bland

Figure 3: Original artwork for #VetYourSources campaign
Source: VCU Libraries; illustrator Jeff Bland

article about the campaign's imminent beginning (McNeill, 2016). For the reprise of the campaign in spring 2018, the posting schedule was more relaxed, which is discussed in more detail later in this chapter.

Developing Content for Twitter and Facebook

Employing crowdsourcing to generate ideas for postings, the Head of TLI and Director of PR used Google Docs as a shared space to collate background information and fodder for potential posts, and to create and hone the posts themselves. The Head of TLI reached out to other VCU librarians for content ideas, although she did not expect others to actually write or organize the content for posting. The idea was to tap librarian brain power for ideas but not to require anyone other than the principals to focus much measurable time on the project.

Keeping the core of the project team nimble -- just two people -- was a boon to success. The principals had a sense of ownership and could work together informally and efficiently, sometimes trading multiple emails daily and populating content in the shared documents as they became aware of materials that may make useful or timely original posts or reshares on Twitter and Facebook accounts.

The small size of the #VetYourSources team, however, did pose some limitations. After the initial surge of pre-planned and edited posts at the campaign's onset, other deadlines and day-to-day workplace demands eroded some focus. Available time--even if all that was required was 15 minutes a day--could slip away easily. Although the planning team achieved their stated goals to post routinely and with fairly high volume on both Twitter and Facebook, a disciplined approach of actively monitoring relevant social media channels for content every day would have likely yielded more good content.

The Head of TLI focused on harnessing suggestions from librarians across the organization to craft the initial iterations of posts, ensuring content was clear and based in the expertise of information professionals. She also monitored library channels for ideas and information to share. The Director of PR, who has deep background and contacts in journalism, monitored mass communications channels for examples and resources that could be shared. Many new resources emerged during the campaign from some of the nation's most reputable sources in professional journalism education. Notably, the American Press Institute (API) created a fact-checking team that published a weekly e-newsletter packed with inspiration and examples.

Throughout the campaign, the editing process was collaborative with both principals wordsmithing and adjusting tone. The PR director refined posts with a focus on character counts, adding artwork or gifs and revising language for the professional yet approachable tone used for social media at VCUL.

Posts were scheduled using Hootsuite and Facebook, usually set several days in advance of publication to guarantee that they would go up even if other priorities took the principals' attention away from the #VetYourSources campaign for a few days. Some posts were published on an ad hoc basis in real time when information surfaced that was worthy of resharing or retweeting immediately. The images used were generally in the public domain. Sources tapped included Giphy, Creative Commons, and Wikimedia. Copyrighted material was used only with permission and attribution. As previously mentioned, original artwork was also created to serve as the visual hallmark of the campaign.

Other than the posts themselves, VCU Libraries created very little original content for this campaign. The most significant investment of time, which was still only a few hours of work, was in refreshing the flagship website of the campaign, which was an online research guide (go.vcu.edu/VetYourSources, see Figure 1) about evaluating sources. The bulk of the revision consisted of making sure the guide focused on evaluating academic as well as day-to-day information equally; prior to the campaign, it had minimal focus on evaluating every day types of information such as news. The principals linked to the online guide or portions of it several times throughout the campaign. They also used other extant VCUL materials in posts, including a video on evaluating websites (see Figure 4), materials on how to discern peer-reviewed articles from others, and more. However, content in most posts relied on a rich stream of materials from a growing circle of librarians, professors, fact-checkers, and watchdogs in journalism and media circles. As a rule of thumb, posts always included textual explanation crafted by the #VetYourSources principals paired with some other type of media, be it an article, website, video, image, or infographic. Many of our most popular posts featured infographics (see Figure 5).

The principals monitored major media outlets for content, as well as other libraries websites and social media channels. They focused particularly on the American Press Institute, which debuted a weekly fact-checking blog, and Poynter.org, associated with the prestigious Poynter Institute for Journalism which launched the International Fact-Checking Network in 2015 (https://www.poynter.org/tags/international-fact-checking-network). A number of organizations introduced media awareness projects during spring 2017, which also made for rich content. For instance, International Fact-checking Day debuted in April. The principals also relied on their own Googling skills of searching for information relevant to the campaign, and carefully vetting its quality for inclusion. The principals located germane content from many academic libraries, as well.

Throughout the course of the campaign, most posts could be grouped into these three categories regarding their purpose:

Figure 4. This Tweet serves as an illustrative example of the posting formula of approachable, encouraging text coupled with a form of media on evaluating information. The linked video was produced by VCU Libraries.

Figure 5. High performing post with 3,615 impressions. Infographic developed by the International Federation of Library Associations and Institutions (IFLA) and used under a Creative Commons license.

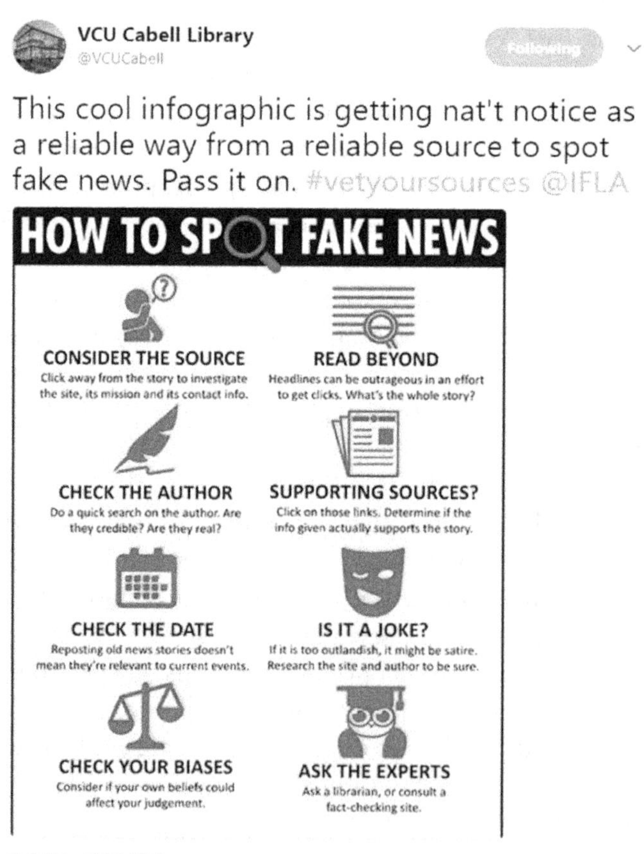

1. To develop skills for evaluating news and other day-to-day information
2. To develop skills for evaluating academic information
3. To encourage metacognition in the process of evaluating resources (Fitzgerald, 1999), in which followers were urged to consider their own perspectives and biases as they pertain to the way they interact with information.

The third category, which was focused on the role of metacognition -- the process of thinking about thinking -- in the information evaluation process (Fitzgerald, 1999), is typically not addressed in heuristics for evaluating information that academic librarians often espouse such as the CRAAP test (California State University, Chico, 2010) or CARS test (North Hennepin Community College, 2017). In fact, critics of these types of checklist approaches to evaluating information describe them as overly mechanistic, leaving little room for critical thinking in general (Meola, 2004). The principals became particularly interested in filling this perceived gap by crafting posts focused on confirmation bias, people's ability to disregard factual information, and other such content (see Figure 6).

ASSESSING SUCCESS THROUGH IMPRESSIONS AND ENGAGEMENTS

Because the campaign was organized and executed so quickly, the principals were unable to devote significant time to developing an assessment plan. Although this was acknowledged as an unfortunate outcome of the aggressive timeline for implementation, it was agreed that the it was more important to move forward with the campaign than to delay for the purposes of developing a robust assessment roadmap. In addition, the principals recognized that while the goal of the campaign was to connect students to information that would help them enhance or think differently about how they evaluate sources, there

Figure 6. High performing Tweet that illustrates emphasis on confirmation bias, a metacognitive component of evaluating information. Engagement was 43. Confirmation bias cartoon © 2018, Kris Straub. Used with permission.

was no practical way to evaluate the extent to which social media followers' thoughts or behaviors were changed by the #VetYourSources campaign. Instead, it was determined that success could be most effectively measured by considering the overall reach of posts in the campaign, thereby defining success as the extent to which posts made it into users' feeds and timelines.

During the initial iteration of the campaign from February - May 2017, VCU Libraries produced many posts under the #VetYourSources hashtag. On Twitter, more than 200 posts were shared, liked, or acknowledged by more than 35 different Twitter accounts (including the @VCUCabell and @VCU-Libraries accounts). Thirty-three (33) posts were posted on the VCU Libraries Facebook page, and 17 were posted on the James Branch Cabell Library Facebook page.

The primary method of analyzing impact on social media was through Twitter as opposed to Facebook since the majority of posts were created for and shared on the @VCULibraries and @VCUCabell Twitter accounts. The principals considered both impressions and engagements in assessing the success of the campaign. According to Twitter (2018), engagements and impressions are defined as follows:

- **Engagements**: Total number of times a user interacted with a Tweet. Clicks anywhere on the Tweet, including Retweets, replies, follows, likes, links, cards, hashtags, embedded media, username, profile photo, or Tweet expansion.
- **Impressions**: Times a user is served a Tweet in timeline or search results.

Because the PR Office and others involved in maintaining the VCUL social media presence had not previously run a campaign of this nature on VCUL social media channels, the organizers did not set specific goals for impressions and engagement. Instead, the project managers took an exploratory approach to analyzing impressions and engagement on both the @VCULibraries and @VCUCabell Twitter accounts. They focused on a comparison of average number of impressions/engagement for all Tweets posted during the #VetYourSources campaign (whether they were associated with the campaign or not) as compared to the Tweets that were part of the campaign. The principals assumed that such a comparison would offer insight into the reach of the #VetYourSources campaign compared to VCUL's routine social media presence, and potentially serve as a baseline for understanding average Twitter user engagement overall.

As detailed in Table 1, the average number of impressions from February to May of 2017 for all Tweets on the @VCULibraries Twitter platform was 553 with an average of nine engagements. On the @VCUCabell Twitter account, average number of impressions was 663, with 17 engagements. These numbers suggest that users interact with content more on the @VCUCabell platform than the @ VCULibraries channel. Accordingly, the focus of the discussion in this section is on analytics from @ VCUCabell account, although some examples of posts and related insights from the @VCULibraries account are also included.

#VetYourSources Tweets on the @VCUCabell account from in spring 2017 had, on average, more impressions but slightly less engagement than non-#VetYourSources Tweets. However, some of the highest impact posts (see Figure 5 and Figure 7) of the #VetYourSources campaign far exceeded average impressions and engagements. These posts also illustrate the style and type of content often featured in #VetYourSources Tweets.

The campaign's online research guide (see Figure 7) received 1,099 hits during spring semester. That was roughly 20 percent more traffic than the previous fall semester, before the campaign began. The highest one-day use for the guide was on the first full day of the campaign in February, with 105 visits.

Table 1. Analysis of Tweets February 1, 2017 - May 3, 2017: Impressions and engagements

	VetYourSources Tweets		Non-VetYourSources Tweets		All Tweets	
	Imp.	**Eng.**	**Imp.**	**Eng.**	**Imp.**	**Eng.**
@VCULibraries	519		575	7	553	9
@VCUCabell	667	12	661	20	663	17

Figure 7. Most impressions (11,944) and engagement (442) of the campaign

Although the principals did not engage in formal analysis of Facebook posts, they anecdotally observed average to higher than average engagement with #VetYourSources posts from Facebook followers. One opportunity that Facebook afforded that Twitter did not was the ability to address slightly more complex concepts with more text in the post, which allowed the planning team to develop posts that were more instructional in nature (see Figure 8).

Overall, the analysis of impressions and engagement on Twitter that indicated comparable or higher impressions and engagements when compared with other Tweets in the same time period (see Table 1), the anecdotal observations of average or higher than average engagement on Facebook, and the increased usage of the research guide on evaluating sources (see Figure 1) are markers of the campaign's success, particularly since it was VCUL's first foray into posting information literacy-focused content on social media. Concise, highly visual information such as infographics were among the most high-performing

Figure 8. Facebook post illustrating use of instructional text. Source: From L.M. Glackens' "The Yellow Press" (1910)

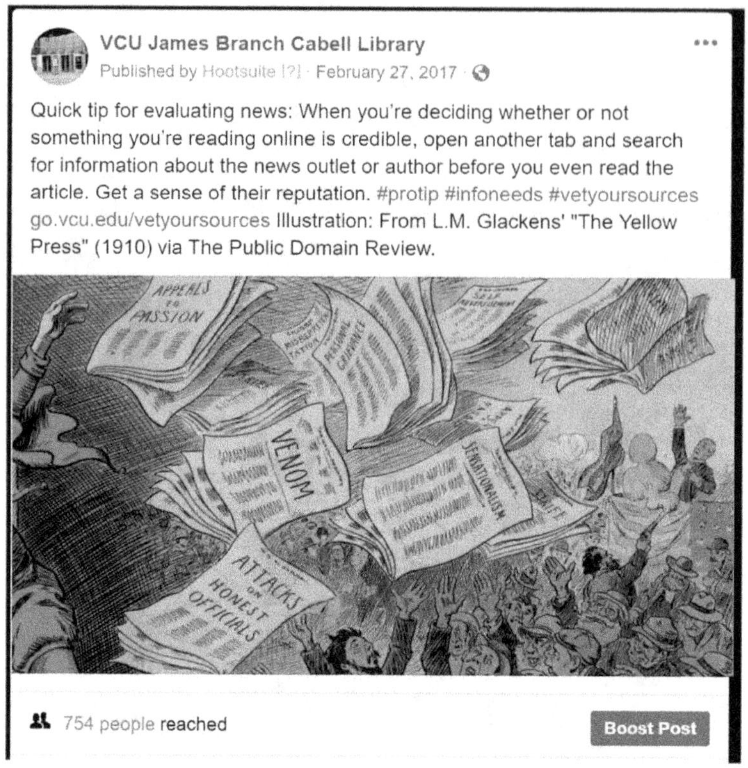

posts (see Figure 5 and Figure 7), but those in which response was invited -- such as asking people to share their tips for vetting sources -- fell very flat.

However, there are notable limits to the extent to which the type of assessments we engaged in can be meaningful indicators of success. Observations and analytics about social media followers' engagement with #VetYourSources posts do not give insight to the extent to which the campaign increased undergraduate students' ability to assess and evaluate information. Instead, the best assertion to be made based on analytics is that the campaign's content was as successful and in some cases more successful in reaching VCUL social media followers (specifically on Twitter) when compared with the overall corpus of social media posts on VCUL accounts. From a practical perspective, it is unlikely that the principals will be in a position to invest more resources into assessing impact of the campaign in the future beyond comparative examinations of analytics provided by the social media platforms. Although it would be fascinating to better understand the extent to which the campaign changed user thoughts and behavior, assessments of this nature would simply not be practical given the time required for such an undertaking. In addition, analytics, broadly speaking, are considered to be a legitimate and appropriate way to measure success of social media posts and campaigns (Dodson, 2017).

As the campaign progressed, at least five academic libraries and one high school started using the #VetYourSources hashtag and adding their own content. The principals considered this another indicator of the campaign's success.

A Real World Presence

As the campaign began in February of 2017, the organizers became increasingly interested in having a real world presence associated with #VetYourSources and began to consider what types of events would dovetail with the overall goals of the campaign. VCU's Robertson School of Media and Culture invited VCUL to co-sponsor a lecture featuring a former network journalist-turned professor who was speaking about the challenges of journalism in the Trump era. The #VetYourSources campaign hashtag was used to promote the well-attended event.

In addition, The Head of Teaching, Learning, and Information planned and implemented a faculty-focused event about to teaching as it relates to teaching students to evaluate sources. The late April event was a faculty-librarian conversation about pedagogy and critically assessing information. Nearly 40 people participated, two-thirds faculty and one-third librarians. The agenda for the event was:

- 30 minutes of socializing and networking
- 30 minutes of remarks to open discussion about pedagogy and evaluating sources
- One hour of small and full group discussion

The discussion portion of the event touched on particular struggles students experience when vetting their sources, such as their tendency to gravitate toward sources that confirm their position and difficulty in understanding what type of information resource to consult for specific purposes. Faculty also discussed pedagogical strategies for increasing students' skills in evaluating sources, such as asking them to evaluate sources using multiple source evaluation checklists such as the CRAAP test (California State University, Chico, 2010) and CARS test (North Hennepin Community College, 2017). One faculty member indicated that understanding and avoiding confirmation bias is an explicit lesson in his courses, and another indicated that he spends time helping his students understand the difference in scientific articles between assertions and observations. Discussion also ensued about the importance of transferring skills from an academic to a day-to-day context, including the importance of allowing students to use and become familiar with high-quality, non-academic sources when appropriate in the classroom.

No formal assessment of the faculty event was conducted. The fact that the event ran over its scheduled time due to active faculty participation coupled with positive feedback after the meeting summary was sent to attendees suggest that faculty found it valuable to exchange ideas about teaching students to vet their sources. Librarians appreciated the insights from faculty about their challenges and priorities for facilitating student learning in this area. In addition, the in-person events offered throughout the #VetYourSources campaign in spring 2017 allowed librarians to generate new ideas for the types of content to include in future iterations of the #VetYourSources social media campaign.

Enhancing Social Media Accessibility

Midway through the campaign, beginning in fall 2017, VCU's university social media administrative leadership issued new directions and guidelines regarding improving accessibility for visually impaired information consumers, noting in VCU's Social Media Content policies (2018) that:

VCU is committed to fostering a safe and inclusive environment that ensures equal access to education and related services to everyone affiliated with the VCU community. The university is continually making efforts to reduce barriers to access for individuals with disabilities and this includes university information shared on VCU-owned social media sites.

The policy goes on to say that all videos must be captioned, and that "Useful information about VCU programs, activities and services on graphics or images shared to VCU-owned accounts will need to be accessible to assistive technology (e.g., infographics, text on photos and flyers)."

The principals decided to not only meet the University's requirements for accessibility, but exceed them. VCU Libraries social media administrators developed internal workflows for captioning what few videos did not already have captions and were owned by VCU, and for adding image descriptions to Twitter and Facebook posts. To meet enhanced accessibility goals, #VetYourSources posts that contained text-dense images or infographics were transcribed and linked as a PDF from the post or Tweet. This ensured that screen readers would be able to interpret the information. The hashtag -- originally used as #vetyoursources -- was changed to "camel case" with uppercase letters starting each word (#VetYourSources), also in an effort to be more compatible with screen readers.

An Ongoing #Vetyoursources Social Media Campaign

Based on the initial success of the campaign as evidenced by impressions and engagements, and the principals' belief that it was important for this to be an ongoing area to which VCUL devoted attention, the campaign was reprised in Spring 2018 at a level that could be more realistically sustained as an ongoing campaign. The scope of content was the same, and posts were a blend of both reprising popular posts from the first campaign, as well as new content. Goals were one Facebook post per week, and two to three Tweets. This more ad hoc approach to posting #VetYourSources content will continue as part of the larger fabric of VCU Libraries' social media presence in 2018-2019 and beyond.

FUTURE DIRECTIONS AND LESSONS LEARNED

The need for #VetYourSources thinking is not abating. A recent study from the Pew Research Center (Mitchell, Gottfried, Barthel, and Sumida, 2018) demonstrates that many American fail to discern fact-based news statements from opinion-based news statements. The #VetYourSources campaign is a useful instrument both for reaching undergraduate students to enhance their skills for evaluating sources, and also to raise awareness that this aspect of information use is an area that VCU librarians can contribute to within university curricula. In addition, the time librarians spent reflecting on the type of information worth sharing in some cases led them to engage with materials that they subsequently used to shape their approach to teaching.

Journalistic organizations are exploring ways to be more transparent and open about their reporting processes and revealing to readers what is unknown and what questions are unanswered. This aligns closely with librarians' work. A recent essay published by the American Press Institute (Rosenstiel and Elizabeth, 2018) suggests that news gatherers need to help their readers better understand how journalists do their work. The essayists suggest a move from a "literacy" objective of understanding news information to one that has "fluency" as the goal. Rosenstiel and Elizabeth (2018) state:

Literacy suggests someone is either capable or incapable of performing a task — in the same way one either can or cannot read. That doesn't aptly describe what is going on with news. People consume news constantly, even at an early age. The issue is whether they recognize the characteristics of good reporting — such as thoroughness, good sourcing, strong evidence, the difference between hearsay and eyewitness evidence and more. The metaphor of fluency, by contrast, describes the process of mastering something you can already do. Fluency also is something you can accomplish on your own, through conscious effort.

The principals plan to approach the 2018-19 campaign in largely the same way they have in years past, although perhaps with a more pointed focus on fluency versus literacy. At the same time, it is important to remain aware that many undergraduates do, in fact, need support to understand the basics of evaluating news and academic information. The principals will rely on a small "lead team" taking point on the content development, while crowdsourcing ideas from others as they have in the past. Additional approaches and practices under consideration for the overall campaign include:

- Using interest in the #VetYourSources campaign as an entry point into additional curricula focused on evaluating information in day-to-day and academic contexts. This could take the form of in-person instruction, consulting with professors on assignment development, or creating additional online learning materials that support students' ability to evaluate sources.
- Partnering with journalism faculty to engage more students and create new content.
- Involving VCU Libraries' student advisory groups as advocates for the campaign and encouraging them to follow and share on their personal platforms.
- Continuing to promote shared use of the hashtag #VetYourSources and also inviting libraries' free use of our images and posters, which are available for download on VCU Libraries Flickr.
- Continuing to use the #VetYourSources poster images in on-campus digital screens.

Specific objectives for reach, impressions and engagements for #VetYourSources posts going forward have not been set. Although the team leads for the campaign acknowledge that more intentional approaches to assessing the social media campaign would be interesting and informative in determining the extent to which the campaign was truly successful, it is unlikely that the assessment strategy will change dramatically going forward. To invest significant resources in assessing this particular set of posts/Tweets would be counter-intuitive in terms of time spent given the relatively minimal amount of effort the campaign will require to maintain on a regular basis, since it is just one component of the overall VCUL social media presence. Instead, the level of engagement and impressions of content under the #VetYourSources hashtag will be examined in the context of broader analyses of users' engagement with VCUL's social media presence. We will remain attentive to both numbers of people reached and engagement.

This attention will be filtered through VCUL's overarching view of social media "performance" that could be integrated more closely in future planning. The VCUL PR office is of the thinking that some information is meant simply to be seen or "consumed" in the constant stream of information sent to phones and tablets and laptops, and that consumption is enough. The reader gleans the information he/she needs (the library hours are changing, an event is scheduled, a tour is available, this research tip can save you time, this LibGuide might help you.) Not every piece of information published cries out to be shared with others, reacted to, or engaged with. So, just because engagement with some #VetYourSources posts is not high does not necessarily mean the information was not read/consumed or not found to be useful by the consumer. In these cases, Twitter's metric of impressions and Facebook's reach counts can be useful indicators of how many people may have seen the post. When engagement is high, the content likely does have high salience to the user or it might just be interesting, provocative, or amusing enough to warrant sharing with followers.

In considering other future directions for the campaign, the team leads for the #VetYourSources campaign realize that an opportunity was lost in failing to formally assess the faculty conversation about evaluating sources that was offered in April of 2017. In the future, components of the campaign, including but not limited to what is posted on social media, will benefit from explicit goal setting and an assessment plan of some type. Assessment of the campaign in general will be balanced with the overall investment of time, energy, and anticipated impact of any future components of the campaign to ensure that assessment is informative but also practically manageable.

CONCLUSION

The high quality of materials published, commendable analytics, and potential for elevating students' awareness of sources that can guide them in evaluating sources all illustrate the overall success of the #VetYourSources campaign. It was and is a successful endeavor in exploring how social media can be used for educational purposes in academic libraries, which is not a common endeavor according to the literature. It is the hope of the campaign's planning team that sharing the planning and execution of the process might aid other libraries in developing similar educationally-focused social media campaigns.

REFERENCES

Amsbary, J. H., & Powell, L. (2003). Factors influencing evaluations of web site information. *Psychological Reports*, *93*(1), 191–198. doi:10.2466/pr0.2003.93.1.191 PMID:14563048

Association of College and Research Libraries. (2000). *Information Literacy Competency Standards for Higher Education*. Chicago, IL: American Library Association.

Association of College and Research Libraries. (2016). *Framework for Information Literacy for Higher Education*. Chicago, IL: American Library Association.

Batchelor, O. (2017). Getting out the truth: The role of libraries in the fight against fake news. *RSR. Reference Services Review*, *45*(2), 143–148. doi:10.1108/RSR-03-2017-0006

Burkhardt, J. M. (2017). Combating fake news in the digital age. *Library Technology Reports*, *53*(8), 1–33. https://doi-org.proxy.library.vcu.edu/10.5860/ltr.53n8

California State University, Chico. (2010). *Evaluating information: Applying the CRAAP test*. Retrieved from https://www.csuchico.edu/lins/handouts/eval_websites.pdf

Coiro, J., Coscarelli, C., Maykel, C., & Forzani, E. (2015). Investigating criteria that seventh graders use to evaluate the quality of online information. *Journal of Adolescent & Adult Literacy*, *59*(3), 287–297. doi:10.1002/jaal.448

Dodson, I. (2016). *The art of digital marketing: The definitive guide to creating strategic, targeted, and measurable online campaigns*. Hoboken, NJ: Wiley.

Fitzgerald, M.A. (1999). Evaluating information: An information literacy challenge. *School Library Media Research, 2,* 1-34.

Johnson, M. (2018). Fighting "fake news: How we overhauled our website evaluation lessons. *Knowledge Quest*, *47*(1), 32–36.

McNeill, B. (2017). *To combat 'alternative facts,' VCU Libraries launches campaign to encourage students to #VetYourSources*. Retrieved from https://news.vcu.edu/article/To_combat_alternative_facts_VCU_Libraries_launches_campaign_to

Meola, M. (2004). Chucking the checklist: A contextual approach to teaching undergraduates Web-site evaluation. *portal. Libraries and the Academy*, *4*(3), 331–344. doi:10.1353/pla.2004.0055

Metzger, M. J. (2007). Making sense of credibility on the Web: Models for evaluating online information and recommendations for future research. *Journal of the American Society for Information Science and Technology*, *58*(13), 2078–2091. doi:10.1002/asi.20672

Mitchell, A., Gottfried, J., Barthel, M., & Sumida, N. (2018). *Distinguishing between factual and opinion statements in the news.* Retrieved from http://assets.pewresearch.org/wp-content/uploads/sites/13/2018/06/18110034/PJ_2018.06.18_fact-opinion_FINAL.pdf

Musgrove, A. T., Powers, J. R., Rebar, L. C., & Musgrove, G. J. (2018). Real or fake? Resources for teaching college students how to identify fake news. *College & Undergraduate Libraries*, *25*(3), 243–260. doi:10.1080/10691316.2018.1480444

North Hennepin Community College. (2017). *CARS checklist.* Retrieved from https://www.nhcc.edu/student-resources/library/doinglibraryresearch/cars-checklist

Peacemaker, B., Robinson, S., & Hurst, E. J. (2016). Connecting best practices in public relations to social media strategies for academic libraries. *College & Undergraduate Libraries*, *23*(1), 101–108. doi:10.1080/10691316.2016.1134244

Shearer, E., & Gottfried, J. (2017). *News use across social media platforms 2017.* Retrieved from http://www.journalism.org/2017/09/07/news-use-across-social-media-platforms-2017/

Stanford History Education Group. (2016). *Evaluating information: the cornerstone of civic online reasoning*. Retrieved from https://stacks.stanford.edu/file/druid:fv751yt5934/SHEG%20Evaluating%20Information%20Online.pdf

Steiner, S. K. (2012). *Strategic planning for social media in libraries. The Tech Set, #15*. Chicago, IL: American Library Association.

Taylor & Francis Group. (2014). *Use of social media by the library: current practices and future opportunities*. Retrieved from https://librarianresources.taylorandfrancis.com/library-insights/white-papers/use-of-social-media-by-the-library/

Twitter. (2018). *About your activity dashboard: What is the Tweet activity dashboard?* Retrieved from https://help.twitter.com/en/managing-your-account/using-the-tweet-activity-dashboard

Virginia Commonwealth University. (2018). *Social media guidelines*. Retrieved from https://socialmedia.vcu.edu/for-social-admins/

Virginia Commonwealth University Libraries. (2017). *Creating the 21st century research library at VCU: Strategic framework 2014-2017*. Retrieved from https://www.library.vcu.edu/media/vculibrary/documents/strategic-framework/Strategic-Framework.pdf

Wade, S., & Hornick, J. (2018). Stop! Don't share that story!: Designing a pop-up undergraduate workshop on fake news. *The Reference Librarian*, *59*(4), 188–194. doi:10.1080/02763877.2018.1498430

Wan, G. (2011). How academic libraries reach users on Facebook. *College & Undergraduate Libraries*, *18*(4), 307–318. doi:10.1080/10691316.2011.624944

Wiley, J., Goldman, S. R., Graesser, A. C., Sanchez, C. A., Ash, I. K., & Hemmerich, J. A. (2009). Source evaluation, comprehension, and learning in Internet science inquiry tasks. *American Educational Research Journal*, *46*(4), 1060–1106. doi:10.3102/0002831209333183

ADDITIONAL READING

Bridges, L. M. (2012). Librarian as Professor of Social Media Literacy. *Journal of Library Innovation*, *3*(1), 48–65.

Copenhaver, K. (2018). Fake news and digital literacy: The academic library's role in shaping digital citizenship. *The Reference Librarian*, *59*(3), 107. doi:10.1080/02763877.2018.1484412

Ellis, L. A., & Peña, A. (2015). Crowdsourcing as an Approach to Customer Relationship Building in Academic Libraries. *College & Undergraduate Libraries*, *22*(3–4), 273–295. doi:10.1080/10691316.2015.1076364

Kooy, B. K. (2016). Building Virtually Free Subject Area Expertise through Social Media: An Exploratory Study. *College & Research Libraries*, *77*(4), 423–454. doi:10.5860/crl.77.4.423

Neely-Sardon, A., & Tignor, M. (2018). Focus on the facts: A news and information literacy instructional program. *The Reference Librarian*, *59*(3), 108–121. doi:10.1080/02763877.2018.1468849

Pendell, K., & Armstrong, A. (2014). Psychology guides and information literacy: The current landscape and a proposed framework for standards-based development. *RSR. Reference Services Review*, *42*(2), 293–304. doi:10.1108/RSR-10-2013-0052

Wissinger, C. L. (2017). Privacy Literacy: From Theory to Practice. *Communications in Information Literacy*, *11*(2), 378–389. doi:10.15760/comminfolit.2017.11.2.9

Woxland, C. M., Cochran, D., Davis, E. L., & Lundstrom, K. (2017). Communal and student-centered. *RSR. Reference Services Review*, *45*(1), 79–99. doi:10.1108/RSR-03-2016-0023

Chapter 12
What's Old Is Marketable:
Creating a Social Media Plan for Special Collections and Archives

Leigh Rupinski
Grand Valley State University, USA

ABSTRACT

This chapter will provide direction to special collections and archives looking to craft a social media strategy by including steps to guide archivists and librarians through the planning process. It will provide an adaptable approach to engaging special collections and archives' audiences with the unique treasures in the collection holdings and in initiating conversations about the opportunities and challenges associated with social media at their respective institutions. This chapter will also assist archivists and librarians in creating a practical framework to make informed decisions for their social media accounts, in crafting goals that advance their organizational mission and values, and in making social media outreach sustainable by considering questions of purpose, audience, platform, messaging, tone, content, and assessment.

INTRODUCTION

Although social media is widely used by businesses, celebrities, and institutions as an essential component of outreach and marketing, special collections and archives often do not have the staff, time, or budget to dedicate solely to outreach efforts. These limitations can make creating and sustaining social media accounts a constant struggle. Without a strategy in place, staff members may find themselves frustrated and burned out on committing the necessary time and energy to support an active social media presence for their organization.

Managing successful social media accounts requires careful examination and planning prior to implementation. By thinking through the goals and planning for potential issues, archivists and librarians can create documentation to guide their institution's social media usage. Potential issues may include crafting a code of conduct for managing reputation or brand, ensuring a consistent institutional voice, considering inclusivity and accessibility, and posting appropriate content. Special collections and archives at

DOI: 10.4018/978-1-5225-8097-3.ch012

larger institutions may be able to refer to greater academic or library-wide policies, while others may need to start from scratch. Social media can often blur the lines between personal and professional, so establishing these guidelines up front will help minimize potential confusion and conflicts down the road.

By writing an outreach plan, archivists and librarians can work through the practicalities of establishing and effectively managing social media at their institution. Documentation creates a place for logistical information, such as who will be responsible for overseeing the accounts, as well as the necessary background to understand how and why decisions were made. Since social media evolves at a rapid pace, it is essential to record the context and rationale behind current choices to allow for informed strategic growth.

In this chapter, archivists and librarians involved in crafting social media plans will examine the intended purpose of creating accounts, the target audience(s) for the accounts, and which platform(s) best suit the institution's needs at this time, drawing on examples from Grand Valley State University Special Collections and Archives' social media plan. A plan will also include a clear vision for why the account was created, criteria for evaluating content to post, the account's personality or tone, and metrics for success. Complicating social media usage is the fact that a "one size fits all" approach does not apply. Metrics for success must be defined by each individual organization; what works for one institution may not be relevant to another. Despite this variance, advanced planning and tracking of goals and progress can provide a useful means of assessment for organizations looking to grow their social media reach over time.

BACKGROUND: HISTORY OF SOCIAL MEDIA IN SPECIAL COLLECTIONS AND ARCHIVES

In recent years, special collections and archives have begun to pay increased attention to the importance of dedicated marketing and outreach, which has led to the rise of positions with these responsibilities interwoven in their makeup. Palmer and Stevenson (2011) noted the increasing role of outreach in everyday archival workloads, while simultaneously acknowledging that these kinds of activities "can often be undertaken in an *ad hoc* and nonstrategic manner" due to limited budgets and available expertise (p. 4). While outreach has recently been considered integral to maintaining successful archives, few archivists had the time, background, or funding to create strategic, sustainable, ongoing outreach programs.

Archivists have long argued for treating outreach as part of an archivists' normal workload rather than "a series of haphazard short-term projects undertaken as time and money permit" (Ericson, 1990-91, p. 115). In fact, outreach supports all other facets of the archival workflow, including acquisition and description (Ericson, 1990-91, p. 115). Successful outreach activities may increase awareness of the purpose of archives at an institution, which in turn aids archivists in bringing in new donations or transferring material from institutional departments. Posting photographs or documents on social media can help identify people or interpret difficult-to-read handwriting, which in turn improves archival metadata. In truth, outreach encircles the entire archival workflow, supporting it from start to finish.

Social media extends outreach further than archivists in the 1990s could imagine; archives have positioned themselves towards building collaborative online spaces that not only justified their existence, but destroyed stereotypes of dusty old basements, and created new representations of archives as vibrant and relevant in the modern world. One of the advantages of social media tools "is their ability to reach a self-selected, interested audience, without requiring expensive overhead or extensive experience" (Crymble, 2010, p. 129). This makes social media an attractive outreach strategy on several fronts.

There is no associated cost to writing a post or a tweet, and, given the right settings, no limit to who can interact with that content.

Many libraries and archives did not begin embracing social media's marketing potential until 2008 to 2010, with the rise in popularity of Facebook and Twitter (Hopman, 2012, p. 3). Even then, archival institutions lagged behind museums and libraries in integrating social media into their outreach activity (Bountouri & Giannakopolous, 2014, p. 511). Despite the slow initial acceptance of social media as a worthwhile tool, archivists and librarians have since embraced many of the more popular platforms as a means of communicating further and more innovatively than ever before.

In fact, social media continually challenges archivists to rethink previous outreach strategies. In contrast to other prevalent types of outreach, such as exhibits and guest speakers, social media expands the audience for archives beyond the serious scholar, historian, or academic researcher. Instead, social media builds on the ability of the archives to reach students, alumni, and other individuals who, although they may never physically visit the archives, are still interested in archival materials (Chute, 2000, p. 36; Palmer & Stevenson, 2011, p. 7). Thinking more broadly allows archivists and librarians to engage with their materials in new ways that move beyond traditional academic research and help solidify the relevancy of special collections and archives in their academic communities.

Many studies have been conducted on the popularity of various platforms for special collections and archives, with Facebook and Twitter continuing to lead the pack (Chu & Du, 2012; Hopman, 2012; Washburn, Eckert, & Proffitt, 2013). Hopman (2012) found, however, that of 185 survey respondents, 54% did not use social media due to lack of time, and 51% because of staffing limitations (p. 2). While the desire and need to integrate social media outreach work more intentionally into practice exists, it seems archivists find themselves continually stymied by inadequate resources.

In 2017, the work of two full-time archivists at Grand Valley State University Special Collections and University Archives split along "front-facing" and "backend" lines by dividing the University Archivist position into two new ones: an Archivist for Public Services and Community Engagement and an Archivist for Collection Management. While other academic archives employ similar models to address outreach and engagement needs, they remain a relative minority. While this kind of solution may be ideal to allocate responsibility for outreach work, it is not practical at every institution, particularly smaller ones. For special collections and archives without dedicated outreach positions, it is important to remember the advantages of engaging in the time-consuming work of maintaining social media accounts, including promotion of library services, quick dissemination of news, and increasing direct interactions with users.

For many organizations, the perceived benefits of using social media tools outweighed the costs, which were found to be minimal, if not non-existent (Chu & Du, 2012, p. 72). However, multiple authors have noted the importance of strategic multi-platform approaches to make the most of social media's potential (Crymble, 2010; Rodgers, 2018). While the idea of managing one platform, let alone several, may feel overwhelming, creating a social media plan will help guide the work and ensure a more focused—and consequently time-saving—approach. No matter how well thought out the plan is, however, adaptability is necessary to stay aligned with users' needs and interests and the inherently trendy nature of social media itself.

Why Social Media?

Essential to any successful marketing strategy is to understand the goals behind it. Chute (2000) identifies goals of any outreach program, including "promoting a positive attitude" toward the institution, collection recognition, and demonstration of the value of staff members and materials alike (pp. 43-44). Crymble (2010) asks, "What is the most effective and efficient way of promoting our holdings without overextending our resources?" (p. 126). With limited time and budgets, archivists and librarians should grapple with these questions before launching any sustained outreach program. The key advantage of social media as an outreach strategy is its low cost. At the time of publication, accounts on popular platforms such as Facebook, Twitter, and Instagram required no contractual obligation for usage. A simple email and password combination unlocks significant audience reach for any institution.

Social media offers distinct benefits to archives and academic libraries looking to engage users on minimal budgets. In their survey, Bountouri and Giannakopolous (2014) found that 88% of respondents believed that social media provided more direct contact with users while also improving the overall public image of their organization (p. 515). It offers a way for archives and libraries to promote their activities, resources, and services while allowing for a continuous connection and dialogue with their users (Canty, 2012, p. 43).

The archivists at Grand Valley State University Libraries initiated distinct social media accounts for Special Collections and University Archives in 2017, with the advent of the new Archivist for Public Services and Community Engagement position. Previously, no promotional work was done consistently for Special Collections and University Archives. Occasionally digital collections materials, such as images from the University Photographs collection, were tapped for a post on the Libraries' or University's social media platform(s), but there was no consistent sharing schedule or plan. Special Collections and University Archives vied for promotion with the other four library locations that make up Grand Valley State University Libraries. Creating their own distinct social media channels, however, allowed the archivists to control and target the messages surrounding the unique collection materials. It also helped the archivists coordinate with the University Libraries' user-centric focus, by providing a low-threshold opportunity to engage users through a variety of storytelling means with a minimal outlay of resources.

At its core, sustained, consistent social media usage is all about user-focused service. It connects archives and libraries to their communities and provides an avenue to directly engage with the interests of their users.

MAIN FOCUS OF THE CHAPTER: CREATING A SOCIAL MEDIA PLAN

Utilizing social media effectively for an academic library or archives differs noticeably from managing a personal account. Organizational accounts require active cultivation and attention, and creating a social media plan can establish standards for consistency, tone, and content. A secondary, but no less important, benefit of creating a social media plan for any institution is to provide a reference point for colleagues and administrators, who may only be familiar with personal social media usage, to understand the amount of thought and time that goes into a successful and sustained social media presence. While portions of the plan may cover marketing goals, the plan's primary objective is to provide clarity of purpose, standards for post content, key messages, and success metrics. A well-crafted plan considers the why behind using social media as an outreach strategy. An effective vision will make it easier for responsible staff members to identify target audience(s) and the platforms most suited to achieving that vision, while also establishing the criteria for evaluating and creating the content to be posted.

Defining a Target Audience

In the face of increasing and ongoing funding restrictions, archivists must actively and continually validate their existence, which includes expanding the customer base beyond the stereotypical academic scholar (Chute, 2000, p. 33). For academic archives in particular, collection holdings may be relevant and impactful to anyone associated with the institution, from prospective and first-year students to faculty and upper level administration (Chute, 2000, p. 37). That leads to a tremendously broad range of possibilities for an institution to engage with online.

Before creating a social media account, it is essential to think about "who" the institution is trying to reach. At an academic institution, it is likely that other institutional accounts already exist. Does the target audience completely overlap with an account already in existence? For special collections and archives, an associated institutional library may already run an account that reaches the same audience. In that case, a special collections and archives specific hashtag on the library's main account may be the best use of time and resources. If the audiences diverge enough, however, a separate account may be necessary to adequately represent the desired messages and promote the collection materials. Crystal Rodgers (2018) believes in the value of special collections and archives developing their own social media presence, as it allows for content tailored specifically to the interests of their audiences and connects the institution to the greater community surrounding those interests (p. 4). Responsible staff members should carefully consider the workload balance when deciding whether or not to pursue a separate social media presence.

For most academic special collections and archives, target audiences may include students, alumni, and faculty/staff—at the institution and beyond—outside researchers, genealogists, nearby historical societies, and even other special collections and archives. The revolutionary opportunity afforded by social media is the ability to change the traditional audience away from "serious" historians or researchers to a more general audience (Palmer & Stevenson, 2011, p. 7). For many academic institutions, students and researchers will likely be the primary audience groups, but anyone can be interested by special collections and archival content.

While posts can be aimed at any audience, or combination of audiences, it is beneficial to prioritize one or two groups. Try looking at the institution's overall strategic plan or available demographic information to understand which users to focus on (King, 2015, p. 17). For Grand Valley State University Special Collections and University Archives, the institution's emphasis on teaching places primacy on connecting with undergraduate students and faculty in the classroom, by bolstering collection holdings that tie specifically to coursework. Chute (2000) wisely points out that students, even those in programs traditionally aligned with library and archives research, often fail to use archival resources simply because they do not know the archives actually exist (p. 37). Social media offers an opportunity for special collections and archives to reach students where they are already interacting. Increasing student awareness can translate into increased alumni awareness as those students graduate, which can also lead to increased interactions for events, exhibitions, and even donations down the road. By drafting the majority of posts with that audience in mind, the content becomes more focused and, consequently, more interesting for the desired audience to read.

This does not mean, however, that every post must be written for the primary audience. As noted previously, special collections and archives have numerous interested audiences. Ericson (1990-91) argues that "the fact of the matter is that everyone is interested in archival records—in history; it is just that most people do not realize it" (p. 118). Social media platforms offer an opportunity to reach out more broadly to "everyone," so long as the archivist or librarian can educate them as to why these unique materials are interesting, appealing, or important.

Closely interconnected to content selection, social media offers the ability to crowdsource metadata for archival documents as well. At Grand Valley State University, the archivists have successfully identified past students and faculty members by posting old University photographs to Instagram and Facebook. This makes the social media accounts collaborative spaces of co-creation, where students, alumni, or anyone interested can make connections and begin to see themselves reflected in the archival records.

Choosing a Platform

Once an audience group has been determined, archivists and librarians can examine which platforms the target group is most actively engaged with before creating any accounts. If accounts are already in existence, but perhaps languishing, the institution may wish to reevaluate whether or not that platform still reaches the appropriate audience. Additionally, it is important to keep in mind that an effective social media strategy will likely involve multiple platforms working in tandem. This ability to pick and choose where to post, or to modify a post for multiple platforms, is beneficial to the many kinds of content special collections and archives possess (Rodgers, 2018, pp. 4-5).

Crymble (2010) wisely cautioned that the first, and perhaps most important, aspect of social media "is that not all tools perform all jobs equally well" (p. 129). Each platform is used by different age groups at different rates, has different engagement rates, and supports content types differently. As the primary audience may vary by platform, the posts and content need to be adapted accordingly (King, 2015, p. 17). In fact, social media is, by its nature, trendy and constantly evolving. What is in fashion one year may be well on its way out by the next. This does not mean, however, that these platforms hold less value as outreach tools. For the present, social media remains a critical avenue of disseminating information.

The two largest platforms for academic archives and libraries continue to be Facebook and Twitter. In her survey of 185 archives and special collections, Hopman (2012) found that 83% of institutions used Facebook and 54% used Twitter (p. 2). More broadly speaking, the Pew Research Center reported that Facebook and YouTube dominate the social media landscape, with younger Americans embracing Instagram, Snapchat, and overall platform variety (Smith & Anderson, 2018). The key to choosing which platform (or platforms) is right for an institution lies in knowing where the desired audience is "hanging out" (King, 2015, p. 7). Meeting the targeted audience where they already spend time gives the institution a distinct advantage towards actually achieving its goals and getting its account noticed.

According to the Pew Research Center, a national survey of 2,002 adults found that Facebook continues to be America's most popular social networking platform with nearly 68% of United States adults using the platform (Smith & Anderson, 2018). Facebook's popularity allows for the largest potential audience reach for special collections and archives. The platform easily supports photos, videos, and extensive text blocks, all of which are ideal for promoting the varied types of archival content. For assessment purposes, statistics are readily available. The paid promotion side of Facebook has grown more dominant in recent years, however, leading to a more business-like model. This has made it difficult to get content in front of non-followers without sinking money into advertisements, which can be at odds with special collections and archives' budgets. Another factor to consider is the Cambridge Analytica privacy breach in 2018 that broke user confidence in the platform, driving some users away completely (Perrin 2018).

In contrast, Twitter is ideal for brief text, high levels of engagement in conversation with users, and easy hashtag searches. The short content lifespan, however, means more frequent posts are necessary to stay on user's feeds. Furthermore, overall user growth has been slow, if not stagnant at times, for the past few years (Twitter, 2018). Twitter's strength, however, lies in its ability to connect communities with a sense of immediacy heightened by the short content lifespans and frequency of posts—an urgency that is not replicated on other platforms like Facebook. Special collections and archives can take advantage of that to engage in timely discussions of events or issues. For example, "live tweeting"—writing posts concurrent to experiencing an event—a guest speaker or educational workshop can initiate conversation on relevant topics to the institution and extend the reach of an event.

One interesting distinction between these two dominant platforms is the tension between professional and personal. On Facebook, archives and libraries have been creating business pages that mix news, promotion, and user engagement, but remain separated from the personal pages of staff members. Twitter, on the other hand, thrives on blurring the lines between the business identity and the personal (Canty, 2012, p. 48). This encourages staff members to take a more opinionated approach to content. If an institution desires to engage in conversations about archival theory or current issues in collecting and description, Twitter is the place to be.

As Lisa Bunker (2017) notes, image-focused social networking sites are the fastest-growing platforms and offer the power of imagery to convey not only what is going on but also the meaning or emotions behind it (p. 9). Instagram stands out as the platform of choice for visual content, with high levels of engagement from its youthful user base. Despite its visual appeal, Instagram does not support links and is almost completely dependent on mobile devices. Statistics are currently only available through associated Facebook accounts. However, Instagram is one of the only platforms experiencing user growth. Of U.S. adults, 35% now report using the platform, an increase of seven percentage points from a similar survey conducted in 2016 (Smith & Anderson, 2018). The Pew Research Center further highlights that Instagram use is especially high among younger adults. Roughly 71% of online adults between the ages of 18-29 use Instagram (Smith & Anderson, 2018).). Instagram's emphasis on visual media meshes well with the unique materials in special collections and archives holdings, and its younger user population suggests the ability to reach student audiences most effectively. Instagram provides a visual space to highlight collection holdings that are often visually appealing, such as book covers, old-fashioned handwriting, memorabilia, and, of course, photographs and film clips.

Important to note, however, is that the majority of social media users indicate that they are active on multiple platforms; for example, 73% of Twitter and 77% of Snapchat users also indicate that they use Instagram (Smith & Anderson, 2018). A typical American maintains accounts with three of the most popular social networking sites (Smith & Anderson, 2018). Engaging on multiple platforms maximizes the chances of having content seen and shared by multiple audiences. While it may seem simplest to blast the same content across all the major platforms, institutions need to be careful not to cause content fatigue. Followers who keep seeing the same content are far more likely to unfollow an institution's account on one or all of the platforms to avoid the tediousness of scrolling through repetitive posts. Instead, think strategically about what gets posted where and why. Tailor posts to best fit each site, by adding visuals or changing caption language, or simply skip sharing content on platforms that do not reach the target audience for that particular post.

Crafting the Message

Ultimately, social media serves as one of many tools in the outreach toolbox. As such, the messaging does not have to include *everything* the institution wishes to communicate; however, a focused set of key points can help guide content creation.

Simply put, the message is the purpose behind the post. Thoughtful message statements can help keep social media accounts focused. While room remains for interpretation, playfulness, and serendipity, having set messaging goals will help ensure consistent tone and set expectations for account followers. On their blog, popular social media management platform Hootsuite advocates for three basic principles to help with content marketing, all of which can be adapted for special collections and archives.

First, Hootsuite's CEO, Ryan Holmes, suggests, "Be the show not the commercial" (2014). In other words, spend time thinking about creating value for the audience, not just traditional direct selling methods. It is less valuable for academic archives and libraries to spend time creating catchphrases and slogans, or beautiful graphics advertising services, than it is to show those services in action and demonstrate the benefits to your audience.

Secondly, Holmes (2014) writes, "At the heart of effective content marketing is risk and originality." Think further than what everyone else is doing. While that may be the best jumping-off point, keeping it fresh and experimenting with new ideas, new tools, or new angles is what will keep audiences intrigued. Finally, Holmes (2014) recommends to "Tell stories with heart." Everything is more resonant to audience members if they can feel the emotions behind the item. Archives, in particular, are built on everyday stories. Engage with them!

Messages are intended to be guidelines for creating post content, not the post themselves. Archivists at Grand Valley State University have worked to develop a set of messages that guide their social media posts. For each general concept presented below, there is a sample message drawn from Grand Valley State University's Special Collections and University Archives' 2017-2018 social media plan and corresponding post ideas. The sample messages are intended to be general and fairly broad, to accommodate a wide variety of content that can speak to each point; the goal is not to limit ideas, but to provide an intentional framework to guide content selection and captioning.

1. **Focus on the Audience:** What is essential for the target audience to know about the institution? Another way to frame this question might be to think about common misunderstandings. For example, at Grand Valley, Special Collections and University Archives is housed in a separate building from the main library and only recently shifted to the peer-to-peer service model in the reading room that had been the norm at other library locations. These differences have led to confusion about the purpose of the building and its status as an official library space.
    a. **Sample Message:** Special Collections and University Archives is part of the University Libraries system, and upholds the same student focus in its services.
    b. **Sample Post Ideas:** A photograph of the student employees at the reference desk with a caption noting open hours or a helpful research tip; interview with a student researcher about their experience; reminders of Library-wide or University-wide events and initiatives, like Open Access week or exam week.
2. **Promote Collection Holdings:** What areas does the institution specialize in collecting? What makes the institution unique? This is also an avenue to encourage donations or transfers of records

from other departments. Educate the audience about how materials are acquired, why, and what happens to them after acquisition.

   a. **Sample Message:** Special Collections and University Archives has an abundant collection of holdings related to a wide variety of topics and continue to acquire new materials.
   b. **Sample Post Ideas:** The unboxing of a recent acquisition; photographs of collection items; behind-the-scenes photos of archival processing; video of archivist or student employee removing staples properly or housing photographs.

3. **Information Literacy:** How do special collections and archives intersect with greater information literacy needs for students? Is the institution integrated into curricular courses? Does it run workshops on information literacy or primary source literacy? Special collections and archives often support classroom visits from a wider variety of disciplines than non-specialists may realize.
   a. **Sample Message:** Primary source literacy is an important component of information literacy as a whole, and Special Collections and University Archives is actively promoting building those skills in the classroom.
   b. **Sample Post Ideas:** Video clip of instruction session; sneak peek of materials pulled for an upcoming class; "Did You Know?" trivia related to an upcoming lesson or about using primary sources in general.
4. **Services of the Institution:** What kinds of services does the institution provide to its users? Social media is a perfect place to post reminders for upcoming events, advertise exhibitions, or seek input on generating new outreach ideas from the target audience.
   a. **Sample Messages:** Special Collections and University Archives strives to create unique experiences, exhibitions, and events for the community; Special Collections and University Archives is open for research use and encourages community interaction with materials and spaces.
   b. **Sample Post Ideas:** Advertisement promoting an upcoming guest speaker or event; "mini-exhibit" highlighting key collection items placed in a physical exhibit; polls asking about event attendance; photograph of an event with questions asking audience members for their favorite moments.
5. **Staff Expertise:** What areas do your staff members specialize in? Are there particular conversations online that you want to engage in, such as open educational resources and open access, or other trending professional topics? Do you want to share knowledge about how to preserve digital records or share behind-the-scenes processing tips?
   a. **Sample Message:** Special Collections and University Archives staff members are experts in the field and have knowledge to share.
   b. **Sample Post Ideas:** Participation in #AskAnArchivist Day answering questions about what archivists do, or the kinds of materials in the archives and how to care for them; tips for preserving personal records; behind-the-scenes videos of caring for collection items; trivia about types of rare materials held in the collections.

It is powerful organizationally to have crafted messages ready to share, even if the posts themselves may address these ideas rather indirectly. By understanding what the institution wants to communicate, staff, and any potential student employees or interns, have a measuring stick for comparison to check that content is appropriate and supports the overall vision for the account.

Determining Personality

Just as essential as the actual messages are how they are communicated to the audience. Unlike personal accounts, institutional accounts may wish to craft some general guidelines for creating a consistent tone. Will the account use the pronoun "I" or maintain the plural "we" for a more inclusive outlook? How formal should the language used in a post be? An account that leans too heavily on humor can be at odds with prestigious artifacts, while one that never cracks a joke can be seen as too stuffy.

Special collections and archives need to consider the voice of an account upfront, regardless of how many people are involved in content creation. How much does the account's personality rely on the person responsible at any given moment (Palmer & Stevenson, 2011, p. 18)? If that responsibility is spread between staff members, the tone may feel inconsistent and even contradictory to followers. This is not to suggest that variation is not desirable or natural, but rather that set standards create a template for anyone to follow, including potential student employees who may be involved in creating content. A workaround for a team-based approach to posting is to create a style guide for posts that can specify use of active or passive voice, conversational language, jargon, and more.

David Lee King (2015) pointed out, "Social media tools were created for people to connect, which requires a highly casual, conversational writing style. If your social media content sounds like a brochure or an ad, you will be ignored" (p. 18). King (2015) further suggested aiming for a "business casual" conversational tone that could be achieved by reading content captions out loud prior to posting; "If it doesn't sound like something you'd actually say to a friend or a coworker, rewrite," he advised (p. 18). Think, for example, of a post advertising an upcoming exhibition. Consider the difference between "Please visit Exhibit A in the Archives Gallery at your earliest convenience" and "Drop by the new Exhibit in the Archives Gallery between classes!" One sounds like a formal invitation that can be intimidating to younger audiences, in particular, while the second option clearly aims for a friendly approach and signals an understanding of busy student schedules.

Again, it is important to keep the target audience in mind. If the target audience is professionals or faculty and staff, business casual may be the appropriate tone to strike. If, however, the target audience is college-aged first year students, think about adding a little bit more informality or sprinkling in emojis more liberally. Resist the urge to try to be as "hip" as possible, but do consider how to come across as approachable and authentic. One of the major barriers to student use of archives is the perception of restrictive rules, formality, and stuffiness. How can your institutional personality on social media help combat that stereotype? Every institution should strive to find a comfortable balance of message and tone.

Finally, most large academic institutions will have established guidelines about professionalism and respectful interactions with users online. For example, Grand Valley State University's Communications Team maintains a quick reference guide with suggestions related to confidentiality, responding to feedback, and transparency, as well as understanding relevant policies, such as copyright and FERPA. If an institution does not have any policies of their own, investigating larger institutions' policies may provide helpful starting points to creating documentation on these topics.

Creating and Evaluating Content

After narrowing down key messages, archivists and librarians can dig into what kinds of content they want and need to promote. This will likely affect platform choices. For example, Twitter does not support images as easily as Instagram. Similarly, the history of a new acquisition, or links to a collection finding aid, may not be suited to Instagram's visual nature, but will read quite easily on Facebook. For cross-posting purposes, the same content can be approached from various angles and tailored to fit each platform's restrictions and strengths.

Traditionally, libraries have used social media largely for marketing purposes. In their international survey, Chu and Du (2012) found that "the two most reported purposes for which libraries used social networking tools were promotion of library events (e.g. exhibitions, competitions, talks, seminars, workshops, tutorials, training courses) and dissemination of news (e.g. events alert, library updates)" (p. 69). A similar survey found that 66% of institutions posted information about their dates of establishment, size of collections, information access policy, hours, and daily news (Bountouri & Giannakopolous, 2014, p. 513). Using the marketing approach as the only purpose for social media might limit the way users could engage with archives and special collections' holdings.

Thinking beyond the box, other types of content could include behind-the-scenes views of what goes on in the "hidden" spaces of the institution. These kinds of insights can help followers, especially millennials, become more comfortable visiting the spaces in person and asking for help (Bunker, 2017). For example, a tutorial on how to access materials in the Reading Room posted on Facebook might lessen that initial fear of entering an unfamiliar space.

Connecting collection materials to current events bridges the gap between historical and contemporary, allowing users to see the relevance of archives (Rodgers, 2018). In what ways can the unique assets of the institution be leveraged not just to promote, but also to educate potential users? Grand Valley State University's Special Collections and University Archives frequently posts snippets of behind-the-scene preparation for class visits to highlight that the archivists offer instructional services to faculty looking for hands-on experiences with primary sources for their students.

Other popular post ideas include "unboxing" videos of recent acquisitions, favorite collection items of staff members, sneak peaks of exhibition design, or clips of past promotional videos for the institution.

When choosing the kinds of content to post, it is helpful to consider several questions:

1. What is the goal of the post? Does it tie into the key messages? Remember to post for the target audience, not for personal taste or to please a supervisor.
2. Is it tailored to the desired audience? Check for obscure references, jargon, and tone.
3. What is essential for the audience to know? Keep it simple; social media is not the place to overwhelm the audience with information, but it can be a stepping-stone for interested users to click and learn more.
4. Does it encourage interaction? Add in necessary keywords, hashtags, or links to encourage further engagement.
5. Would a visual help? As Ericson (1990-91) points out, "we need to *show* people, not tell them" why these materials are interesting, useful, or relevant (p. 120). In almost every case, adding a visual is a good idea.

David Lee King (2015) stated, "The easiest way to turn followers into engaged fans… is to create compelling, interesting content" (p. 16). Creating content that tells stories and engages audiences will take trial-and-error. What works for one institution may not work for another, and what works one year may fall flat with the audience by the next.

When creating content for image-dependent platforms, such as Instagram, archivists and librarians should consider the overall look and feel of their feed. While much of this will depend on the kinds of materials the institution holds, it is worthwhile to think about the feed's cohesiveness. Should there be varied black-and-white and color images, or one consistent palette? Will there be visuals of the institution's staff at work or just collection materials?

Thinking about the visual aspects of the platform can prevent stranded content, such as a lone color photograph in a feed of gorgeous black-and-white images, or a single behind-the-scenes video amidst a series of diary snippets. If the institution includes a split between types of materials, also consider how to balance the perspective of available resources. For example, Grand Valley State University's Special Collections and University Archives juggles both sides of its identity on social media by including both rare books and archival photographs in the same feed. Although the overall look and feel of the feed matters, the focus of using images in the first place is to connect with users. Accordingly, ask questions such as: "Does the image complement the topic, such as a groundbreaking video for the anniversary of the institution's founding, or does it compel people to click, like, or want to share?" In other words, is the image intriguing or stimulating enough to prompt audience members to want to know more?

A critical element of creation is necessarily engagement. How will this post or this content encourage interaction with the institution's materials? Remember to actively solicit ideas and feedback from the audience. Social media provides direct access to users' ideas, suggestions, and questions. Encourage audience participation by asking questions about service needs, posting fun trivia polls, or providing some kind of call to action (King, 2015, p. 19). Again, it may take a good bit of trial-and-error before any of these methods inspire a significant amount of feedback. Remember to set expectations realistically and revise them as the account grows.

Another strategy to generate relevant content is to simply ask the audience prior to posting. If the target audience is college-aged students, ask student employees what they would like to see posted. Student employees or interns can also be used to create appealing content by photographing materials, creating graphics, or researching and writing content. Be sure to have a staff member review and edit any student-created content prior to posting, however, to check it matches the desired tone and messaging and to correct any glaring grammatical or content errors. Student employees at Grand Valley State University frequently photograph material for social media or provide selections of digitized material they feel fit a particular topic for the archivist to choose from for a post.

When it comes to images, it is important for staff to resist the urge to achieve complete perfection. One of the drawbacks of social media culture is the tendency to over-cultivate a flawless façade. While this may work on personal accounts or for business brands, academic institutions with historic or rare materials have an obligation to use filters and editing wisely. It is important to properly represent the collection materials themselves, rather than heavily filtered or cropped renderings of them. In other words, if overly manipulating, cropping, or otherwise changing an image, provide an explanation or disclaimer. There is a certain element of trust implicit in being custodians of historical items and information, and that trust should be respected in interactions with your audience.

On a related note, it can be useful to demonstrate the challenges of archival work and caring for old materials instead of focusing solely on the positives and successes. Is there material that was improperly stored and needs preservation work? Discuss it in a video or explain how it could or could not be remedied. Providing a more accurate depiction of the work that goes on in special collections and archives creates a more authentic and trustworthy feel, while easing user perceptions of rules and rigidity that still dominate stereotypes of libraries and archives.

Making Connections

A critical component of a successful social media strategy is not only making connections with the audience through post engagement, but also making connections with other institutions and taking advantage of opportunities for collaboration.

Following and "liking," other accounts are good ways to begin understanding how similar or aspirational institutions are using social media. What kinds of content are they posting? What hashtags do they use with the most response? That is not to say that an organization should simply duplicate what others do, but it does make a good starting point to begin creating the organization's own social media presence. Making these connections with other institutions that have similar collections can help advertise holdings to an already interested audience, as well as promote collaboration possibilities, relevant events or exhibitions, and potentially create opportunities for community partnerships (Rodgers, 2018, p. 20). Scrolling through social media accounts that the institution account follows should be a regular occurrence to generate new ideas for creating connections with the audience.

Similarly, browsing other institutions' Instagram and Twitter accounts for popular hashtag ideas can be beneficial. On Instagram, archives formed a community around the hashtag #ArchivesOfInstagram while libraries use the similar #LibrariesOfInstagram or #IgLibraries. There are multiple hashtags for every day of the week, from the popular #ThrowbackThursday (or #TBT) to more select ones such as #ManuscriptMonday, #TravelTuesday, #WednesdayWisdom, and #ForeEdgeFriday. In addition, some institutions will sponsor particular contests for a month on Instagram and Twitter. In 2018, the National Archives began hosting a popular #ArchivesHashtagParty on the first Friday of every month with changing themes that have included content prompts such as #ArchivesDanceParty and #ArchivesRoadTrip.

As Ericson (1990-91) astutely observes, "No human being is able to resist celebrating an anniversary divisible by twenty-five" (p. 118). Adding national holidays, institutional anniversaries, and other key events to a social media calendar can make for quick and easy post inspiration. The popular #OnThisDay hashtag, often abbreviated as #OTD, is well-suited for archival holdings such as event posters, campus building construction dates, birthdays of significant figures in campus lore, or publication dates for books.

Unfortunately, simply creating an account does not guarantee that the target audience will find it. Some additional promotion and marketing will be needed to forge those connections. One way might be to include social media buttons on the organization's home page, or to add icons to responsible staff member's email signatures. At a larger institution, archives and special collections can ask to be added to lists of "official" institutional accounts. Local professional organizations may curate similar lists. It is good practice to follow other accounts run by the institution's various departments or student groups, prominent campus figures, and nearby institutions, such as local public libraries or historical societies, to begin building a follower base and attract the desired audience.

Measuring Success

Creating a social media presence is far from a "one size fits all" process. Each individual institution will need to decide what an effective social media plan looks like, and how to measure its success. In the beginning, success might simply mean consistent posting to start building a social media presence. Most institutions, however, will want to track the metrics on their account right away to gage what posts are connecting with audience members and what content is missing the mark.

Each institution will need to decide what metrics they are most interested in based on the goals for its accounts. If the institution is most interested in awareness, look at metrics like reach to gage how far post messages are spreading; if the institution is most interested in engagement, look at metrics for retweets, comments, link clicks, and other forms of active interaction with the post. Facebook Insights tracks useful metrics to help an institution work with Facebook's often-changing algorithm rather than "sending content into the void and hoping someone will see it" (Seybolt, 2018). Insights tracks audience demographics, location and gender breakdowns, as well as post reach, views, most popular times for audience members to log on, and likes and comments. These statistics provide guidance into which posts are most popular, when the best times to post online for audience interactions are, and more. Special collections and archives can take advantage of available analytics to better position themselves for success.

No matter which set of metrics the institution focuses on, it is important to be specific about the desired goals. For example, if the institution wishes to grow the number of account followers or increase post interactions and engagements, specify reaching 500 followers, or reaching 100 followers from the target audience group. This provides clearly measurable targets to evaluate how well goals are being met that can be supported by the metrics.

Beyond the conventional data outlined above, the intangibility of social media makes it difficult to judge how effective it is as an overall outreach strategy. Someone might interact with social media, but not realize its relevancy for months or years before inquiring further. For example, a freshman might see a post about a particular collection holding at the beginning of the year that becomes useful to them in an end-of-year assignment. In a similar vein, social media might provide a first experience with what exactly Special Collections and Archives contain that then leads to someone visiting an exhibition or making a donation (Ericson, 1990-91, p. 118). The "success" is not immediate, but it is correlated.

Another approach might be to take a holistic view of outreach activity. Ericson urges archivists and librarians to examine what they are doing to engage with users and place less overall emphasis on how effective each avenue is on its own (as cited in Chute, 2000, p. 43). Due to the indirect nature of many outreach activities, it may be more valuable to examine the full picture rather than try to pick individual threads apart. A user may be motivated to visit an exhibit for a variety of reasons, none of which could easily be pinpointed as *the* factor, but the end result is the same: they came in the door. This approach can also reduce stress and anxiety for staff members, particularly those without solely outreach-related duties, and encourage them to think more broadly rather than fixate on reaching specific numbers. Thus, while short term pay-offs might be limited, social media outreach is a long-term investment in the future of the institution.

RECOMMENDATIONS FOR CONTINUED SUCCESS

In his analysis of Twitter and Facebook use in archives, Adam Crymble (2010) noted that 71% of respondents complained that time overwhelmingly prevented them from integrating more social media tools into their outreach programs (p. 128). Chu and Du's 2012 survey of academic libraries produced similar results, concluding that the most pressing challenge to successfully implementing social media was inadequate time and manpower (p. 70).

While it may be impossible to totally eliminate these constraints, there are ways minimize them. One of the easiest is to create a posting schedule or content calendar—and then stick to it. At Grand Valley State University, the responsible archivist uses a simple Outlook calendar to track ideas and relevant hashtags.

Some platforms, such as Facebook, allow posts to be written and saved for publishing at a specified later date and time. If the institution uses multiple accounts and takes advantage of cross-posting opportunities, content management sites, such as Hootsuite, allow for content to be written and scheduled to post later on multiple platforms. This can help not only manage time on a regular workday, but also creates a potential workaround for holiday breaks or staff vacations when the account might otherwise languish.

Additionally, spreading the responsibilities across staff members might be an effective solution depending on staffing levels and institutional needs. A team-based approach can provide an easier way to cover all parts of the organization's work as well as divide staff time spent on social media across the week (King, 2015, p. 24). Similarly, while one full-time staff member might be responsible for the social media presence, student employees can contribute to the work. Although this work should always be checked over by staff, students and volunteers can take photographs, perform necessary research on collection items, generate ideas, and demonstrate procedures or pose with items.

Even beyond these limitations, the nature of social media itself demands a different mindset to effectively take advantage of it as an outreach tool. As Scott Young and Doralyn Rossmann (2017) point out, focusing solely on social media as a marketing tool limits the platform to a type of broadcasting network, missing the point of the "social" element; instead, social media must be seen as a "tool for conversation, community, and social good" (p. xv). Thus, the challenge is to use social media platforms effectively in ways that promote virtual participation and collaboration focused on user-centered needs and interests (Canty, 2012, p. 41). Ultimately, social media creates a new channel for a more conversational, informal connection with users not only to promote archives and libraries and all they have to offer, but also to expand interaction beyond the confines of "traditional" scholars or the physical barriers of location. Thus, social media allows archivists and librarians to expand their mindsets and think more exhaustively about whom their target audience *could* be. Focusing on the possibilities of the online realm rather than the restrictions of the physical can be empowering for archives staff, in particular, who are often limited by having to entice users into monitored reading rooms.

At its core, social media's nature is to be social. Thus, any effective plan will be at intrinsic odds with the spontaneity and authenticity of the channel itself. Little, Lopez, McCullough, and Parmer (2017) stated, "The tension between bureaucratization of social media activities and the need to be flexible in order to follow our audience is ever present" (p. 44). That tension may never fully be resolved, but its existence will continually challenge staff members who manage social media for their institutions.

Ultimately, a social media plan is only as effective as the goals each institution sets out to achieve. Thinking through all of the aforementioned components of the plan provides a solid foundational document that explains the rationale behind staff members' decision-making and outlines the vision for the social media outreach strategy. A vision or mission statement helps to clarify the "why" question that plagues all outreach activities in as succinct a manner as possible. As Lisa Bunker (2017) points out, the answer to that question needs to be more user-centric than "We need to be there" or "The director insists" (p. 5). Those might be inciting reasons to begin investing social media as an outreach strategy, but they will not evoke the necessary inspiration and commitment to make the plan a success for long. Thus, the vision statement should include a concise description of social media's purpose and benefit to the institution.

From there, staff members should focus on creating a breakdown of the institution's goals that explains not only what those goals are, but also what strategies can be taken to ensure those goals are reached and the metrics for success. A good starting point for writing effective goals is the S.M.A.R.T (Specific, Measureable, Attainable, Relevant, Time-Specific) structure. Hootsuite provides a social media goal template that walks through each letter of the S.M.A.R.T acronym with several examples to help create more effective goal statements (LePage, 2017). Goals can be very simple or multi-faceted and complex, depending on the nature of the institution and its needs.

For example, when first implementing social media at Grand Valley State University Libraries, the archivist set a goal of increasing awareness of Special Collections and University Archives in the University community and greater academic library community through active participation in social media. The goal was then broken down into strategies, or actionable steps, that demonstrated exactly how it would be accomplished. In this case, the strategies were fairly simple, as no previous social media presence existed. Accordingly, the initial strategy was to establish the requisite platforms. Other strategies included developing a content calendar to encourage regular postings, implementing popular hashtags, participating in library and archive hashtag challenges, and following other institutional accounts. Finally, the plan lays out how success will be measured: was the account created, was content posted regularly, did it gain the desired number of followers, and so on. A more complex goal might be to boost engagement. With that goal in mind, strategies might include experimenting with platform features, leveraging partnerships in new ways, or making use of contests, giveaways, and other promotions. Success might be increasing the number of likes on a post, or the number of comments, or simply how many new features were tried out during a particular timeframe.

Outlining goals in this way can provide archivists and librarians with manageable steps for success. Not only does this diminish some of the limitations identified earlier, but it also allows administrators to see very clear, concise plans and metrics to justify the time and effort involved in cultivating an active social media presence.

FUTURE TRENDS

Social media has rapidly become an essential component of outreach strategies for academic institutions, at least in part because of its affordability in a sector that continually suffers from tight budgets and understaffing. As with all technology, however, social media is constantly evolving. Facebook updates its Newsfeed display, Instagram adds a new video feature, Twitter expands its character limit, and all the while, another new platform lurks around the corner waiting for its moment to surge into popular consciousness. With popularity liable to change at any moment, social media plans may only be effective for so long. As new platforms rise, and old platforms change, future researchers may wish to explore how best to make plans as flexible as possible for these inevitable transitions. Given the relative newness of social media networking as a whole, there is a great deal of potential for future longitudinal studies of social media plans' effectiveness and adaptability. As social media evolves, new opportunities for study will doubtlessly arise with every new platform and audience engagement feature.

CONCLUSION

Despite its relative youth as an outreach tool, social media has proven to have enduring value for archivists and librarians looking to connect with their audiences in new and innovative ways. Although always changing, social media's defining characteristic is its emphasis on engagement and connection. For special collections and archives, this provides an opportunity to look beyond the restrictions of space and material frailty to reach a wider audience where they are already interacting. Social media provides special collections and archives with the opportunity to communicate directly with their diverse audiences and build community outside of the reach of the physical building or traditional research users.

Special collections and archives can customize their social media tools to best suit their individual institutional needs at relatively low cost, a distinct benefit in an age of shrinking budgets and staffing levels. Although the newness of social media tools and the inability to simple copy other institutions can be intimidating to staff, archivists and librarians are well positioned to maximize the potential of social media for promotion and education purposes. Outreach as a whole has taken on greater importance to increase awareness of special collections and archives' services and collection holdings, as well as demonstrate the overall value of maintaining these materials in the first place.

In order to maximize staff time, creating a social media plan allows for flexibility while maintaining consistency. Creating a schedule for who posts, when, and what type of content can make integrating social media activity into regular workflows a smoother process. Drafting a vision statement and creating achievable goals at the outset will provide direction when selecting content, training student employees, and making strategic decisions for future expansion into different platforms. Ultimately, the plan functions as guiding documentation to walk through necessary decisions to make social media as functional and efficient for responsible staff members as possible.

REFERENCES

Bountouri, L., & Giannakopoulos, G. (2014). The use of social media in archives. *Procedia: Social and Behavioral Sciences*, *147*, 510–517. doi:10.1016/j.sbspro.2014.07.146

Bunker, L. (2017). Picking a platform and finding a voice. In S. Young & D. Rossmann (Eds.), *Using social media to build library communities: A LITA guide* (pp. 1–28). Lanham, MD: Rowman & Littlefield.

Canty, N. (2012). Social media in libraries: It's like, complicated. *Alexandria (Aldershot)*, *23*(2), 41–53. doi:10.7227/ALX.23.2.4

Chu, S., & Du, H. S. (2012). Social networking tools for academic libraries. *Journal of Librarianship and Information Science*, *45*(1), 64–75. doi:10.1177/0961000611434361

Chute, T. (2000). Selling the college and university archives: Current outreach perspectives. *Archival Issues*, *25*(1/2), 33–48.

Crymble, A. (2010). An analysis of Twitter and Facebook use by the archival community. *Archivaria*, *70*, 125–151.

Ericson, T. L. (1990-91). Preoccupied with our own gardens: Outreach and archivists. *Archivaria*, *31*, 114–122.

Holmes, R. (2014, July 21). Want to win with content marketing? Stick to these 3 basics. *Hootsuite*. Retrieved from https://blog.hootsuite.com/want-to-win-at-content-marketing-stick-to-these-3-basics/

Hopman, R. (2012). *2012 survey results: Social media use in archives and special collections*. Retrieved from http://rebeccahopman.com/index/wp-content/uploads/2014/09/2012 surveyresults.pdf

King, D. (2015, January). Managing your library's social media channel. *Library Technology Reports, 51*(1), 5–35.

LePage, E. (2017, June 27). 7 social media templates to save you hours of work. *Hootsuite*. Retrieved from https://blog.hootsuite.com/social-media-templates/

Little, L., Lopez, A., McCullough, J., & Parmer, R. (2017). From broadcast to conversation in an academic library. In S. Young & D. Rossmann (Eds.), *Using social media to build library communities: A LITA guide* (pp. 28–45). Lanham, MD: Rowman & Littlefield.

Palmer, J., & Stevenson, J. (2011). Something worth sitting still for? Some implications of Web 2.0 for outreach. In K. Theimer (Ed.), *A Different Kind of Web: New Connections Between Archives and Our Users* (pp. 1–21). Chicago, IL: Society of American Archivists.

Perrin, A. (2018, September 5). Americans are changing their relationship with Facebook. *Pew Research Center*. Retrieved from http://www.pewresearch.org/fact-tank/2018/09/05/americans-are-changing-their-relationship-with-facebook/

Rodgers, C. (2018). Labor of likes: Developing a social media strategy for archives. *Archival Outlook, 45*, 20–21.

Seybolt, B. (2018, April 4). A beginner's guide to Facebook analytics. *Hootsuite*. Retrieved from https://blog.hootsuite.com/facebook-analytics-insights-beginners-guide/

Smith, A., & Anderson, M. (2018, March 1). Social media use in 2018. *Pew Research Center*. Retrieved from http://www.pewinternet.org/2018/03/01/social-media-use-in-2018/

Twitter. (n.d.). Number of monthly active Twitter users worldwide from 1st quarter 2010 to 1st quarter 2018 (in millions). *Statista - The Statistics Portal*. Retrieved June 4, 2018, from https://www.statista.com/statistics/282087/number-of-monthly-active-twitter-users/

Washburn, B., Eckert, E., & Proffitt, M. (2013, August 16). Social media and archives: A survey of archive users. *OCLC Research*, 3-32. Retrieved from https://www.oclc.org/research/ publications/library/2013/2013-06r.html

Young, S., & Rossmann, D. (2017). Introduction. In S. Young & D. Rossmann (Eds.), *Using social media to build library communities: A LITA guide* (p. xv). Lanham, MD: Rowman & Littlefield.

ADDITIONAL READING

ALA Intellectual Freedom Committee. (n.d.). Social media guidelines for public and academic libraries. In *American Library Association*. Retrieved from http://www.ala.org/advocacy/sites/ala.org.advocacy/files/content/smg2018.pdf

Garofalo, D. (2013). *Building communities: Social networking for academic libraries*. Cambridge, United Kingdom: Chandos Publishing. doi:10.1533/9781780634012

Gharib, M., & Frohlich, D. (2015, December 9). Why you need a digital plan for success. In *NPR social media desk*. Retrieved August 19, 2018, from https://socialmediadesk.tumblr.com/post/ 134862056031/why-you-need-a-digital-plan-for-success

Hager, J. D. (2015). To like or not to like: Understanding and maximizing the utility of archival outreach on Facebook. *The American Archivist*, *78*(1), 18–37. doi:10.17723/0360-9081.78.1.18

Llewellyn, G. (2016, March 25). Content marketing strategy lessons from Buzzfeed. In *Smart Insights*. Retrieved from https://www.smartinsights.com/content-management/content-marketing-strategy/content-marketing-strategy-lessons-buzzfeed/

National Archives Social Media Strategy 2017-2020. (2017). In *National Archives*. Retrieved August 19, 2018, from http://usnationalarchives.github.io/social-media-strategy/

Theimer, K. (Ed.). (2011). *A different kind of web: New connections between archives and our users*. Chicago, IL: Society of American Archivists.

Yakel, E. (2006). Inviting the user into the virtual archives. *OCLC Systems & Services: International digital library perspectives, 22*(3), 159-163.

Chapter 13
Expanding the Awareness and Use of Library Collections Through Social Media:
A Case Study of the Library of Congress International Collections Social Media Program

Anchi Hoh
Library of Congress, USA

ABSTRACT

The Library of Congress houses more than 164 million items in various formats, languages, and subjects. Found among its treasures are the international collections. The Library's four area studies divisions—African and Middle Eastern (AMED), Asian, European, and Hispanic—reading rooms provide access to many of these resources. In 2016, the four area studies divisions launched a collaborative social media program to encourage the use of the library's international collections by domestic and global online audiences. The program adopted the 4 Corners of the World blog and the Library of Congress International Collections Facebook page as interactive social media tools. This chapter will examine the interdivisional initiative through its purpose, target audience, content focus, platform selection, management and operation, audience interaction, and current status. Next, the chapter will discuss challenges and opportunities facing the four divisions. Finally, the chapter will offer recommendations for other libraries that are interested in establishing a similar program.

DOI: 10.4018/978-1-5225-8097-3.ch013

INTRODUCTION

For nearly 200 years, human communication has experienced several revolutions due to inventions like the telegraph, telephone, computer, and Internet. Between 1990 and 2006, we witnessed the important advent of broadband technology, which allowed for the high-speed, simultaneous Internet transmission of voice, data, and video signals (Britannica Academic, 2018; Dewing, 2010). During the same time, we saw the emergence of social media platforms, including YouTube, WordPress, Facebook, and Twitter.

These developments denote a remarkable milestone with long-lasting impacts in the history of human communication. Social media has changed the way people network and share information. It has permeated all aspects of our daily lives. This translates into an evident marketing opportunity for both public and private organizations that aim to engage the public for commercial or nonprofit purposes (Britannica Academic, 2017.).

In 2014, eMarketer Pro surveyed American organizations with 100 or more employees. Eighty-eight percent of the organizations were using social media to market products or services (Bennett, 2014). Social media and libraries appear to be a natural fit because social media aids libraries in sharing information broadly and easily by reaching "users who may not have considered the library as a resource for their information needs" (Canty, 2012, p. X). According to a special report by the American Library Association (2011):

libraries are also making voracious use of social media ... to connect with patrons and to market programs and services. More than 90 percent of the respondents in a survey of library administrators/managers, librarians and other staff called Web 2.0 tools important for marketing and promoting library services. (p. 6)

According to Mickoleit (2014), in the public sector:

presence and activity on social media is no longer a question of choice for most governments as those new platforms empower individuals and non-traditional interest groups. Politicians were first to react to these changes by using platforms such as Twitter, Facebook and blogs to rally support. Government institutions are slowly catching up and increasingly experiment with social media. (p. 2)

To establish more effective communication and to better serve constituents, members of the U.S. Congress were early adopters of social media. From 2009-2013, more than 78% of individual members had an official Twitter; more than 87% had a Facebook account. By 2016, Congressional committees were using social media extensively (Straus & Glassman, 2016).

The U.S. Federal Government views social networking as an effective means of improving public services through direct interaction with constituents. In April 2010, social media was standardized through an Office of Management and Budget (OMB) memorandum through the Social Media, Web-Based Interactive Technologies, and the Paperwork Reduction Act (U.S. OMB, 2010). The act was based on a 2009 OMB memorandum, M-10-06, titled Open Government Directive. Since then, the Federal Government has developed comprehensive strategies and guidelines for the Executive Branch agencies to address all aspects of its social media practices. These include the adoption of plain language (U.S. GPO, 2010), public participation, performance measurement, and privacy protection.

In early 2007, the Library of Congress made its social media debut. Established in 1800 as part of the Legislative Branch, the Library is the oldest Federal cultural institution. Recognized as the largest library in the world, it has a fast-growing collection of digital resources and more than 164 million items in a variety of formats, languages, and subjects. In addition to acquiring and preserving, its mission aims to provide access to its collections (Library of Congress, n.d., 2010). Through social media, the Library can fulfill its mission of providing access to a considerable audience.

In addition to its large collection of Americana, one of the Library's most prized features is its unparalleled international collections. The Library's international collections, which are made of hundreds of languages and scripts, consist of a large corps of foreign publications acquired through gifts, exchanges, donations, and purchases by the Library's six overseas offices. These acquisitions are often from foreign countries and territories in which the publishing industry may not be as developed or stable as in western countries due to their political or economic conditions. Thus, the Library's international collections are considered among the most comprehensive in the world. The Library's four area studies divisions—African and Middle Eastern (AMED), Asian, European, and Hispanic—offer reader services in their respective reading rooms. These division reading rooms are some of the main access points to global resources.

In 2016, the four area studies divisions launched a social media collaboration program to introduce the 4 Corners of the World: International Collections and Studies at the Library of Congress blog (https://blogs.loc.gov/international-collections/2016/04/hello-from-the-4-corners-of-the-world/) (or 4 Corners) and the Library of Congress International Collections Facebook page (https://www.facebook.com/libraryofcongressinternationalcollections/) (or International Collections). The interdivisional program is one of the latest social media initiatives at the Library. This is the first time in the Library's history that social media has been used to systematically and directly publicize the Library's international collections to a broad audience.

The interdivisional management model and the sheer size of the social media market make this social media program an unprecedented adventure. For instance, the program offers useful lessons for academic and research libraries that plan on pursuing broader public engagement. This chapter will provide an overview of the Library's tradition of sharing its resources through new technologies. It will then focus on the Library's area studies divisions and international collections to establish a sense of the scope and importance of the resources. It will discuss reasons why social media is an essential tool in achieving the Library's mission to share its unique collections. The remainder of the chapter will focus on the development of the Library's international collections social media program by exploring its purpose, social media tools, target audience, content focus, management and operation, audience interaction, and current status. Finally, it will discuss challenges and opportunities facing this program, as well as recommendations for academic and research libraries that aim to establish similar programs.

BACKGROUND

Using New Technologies to Share Resources

The Library has always been an early adopter of new technologies to achieve its institutional mission. During the formative years of the Internet (1987-1991), the Library used computer networking to share information and services with a broader audience. A major networking endeavor was the Linked Systems Project (LSP), a cooperative effort among the Library, the now defunct Research Libraries Group, Inc., and OCLC, Inc. Through this initiative, the organizations shared bibliographic data via computer-to-computer links (Library of Congress, 1989). Another major project, American Memory, was launched in fiscal year 1988, "to explore ways to deliver some of the Library's unparalleled resources to a wider audience, particularly to schools and libraries nationwide, using new technologies" (Library of Congress, 1990, p. 22). In the following fiscal year, the Library began discussions about:

Internet (a planned supernetwork), access to library utilities, pilot projects of a state consortium of libraries, university versus library networks, compatibility of standards and protocols, and the role of the librarian and the technologist in an evolving network. Success in such endeavors will set the stage for forging one national information network. (Library of Congress, 1990, p. 75)

In the early 1990s, the Library digitized manuscripts and rare materials from its collections. Digitization became an effective way to preserve fragile and rare materials. Digitized versions were accessed by users more easily, broadly, and frequently without preservation concerns. According to the *Annual Report of the Librarian of Congress for the Fiscal Year Ending 30 September 1995* (1996), in 1994, the Library established the National Digital Library (NDL) program to "make elements of the Library's Americana collections accessible to the American people through digital conversion and electronic distribution" (pp. 23-24). In the following year, the Library's "Newspaper and Current Periodical Reading Room created the Library's first Reading Room World Wide Web (WWW) home page" (Library of Congress, 1996, p. 61). Other divisions soon began offering more of the Library's resources on the Library's website. In 2000, the Library began exploring digital reference services, which were designed for "all users anytime and anywhere through an international digital network of libraries and of similar services and organizations" (Library of Congress, 2001, p. 75). Today, digital reference services continue to thrive and complement in-person reference services available in the Library's 21 reading rooms.

The Library's four area studies divisions have also utilized the latest available technologies to more effectively serve the Library's international collections for the public. In 1994, the Hispanic division unveiled the *Handbook of Latin American Studies CD-ROM,* which provided access to a large corps of records covering more than 60 years of scholarship in this subject field (Library of Congress, 1996). In the following decade, the four area studies divisions joined the Library in digitizing apace rare materials from their collections and making them available via the Library's website or other storage media. In 2004, in collaboration with the National Library of Egypt, the African and Middle Eastern Division (AMED) presented a new initiative, the Global Gateway, which initially focused on digitizing rare Arabic materials (Library of Congress, 2005). It later expanded to become a portal featuring the Library's international collections with the participation of all four area studies divisions and other relevant divisions in the Library, as well as showcasing external resources from major repositories worldwide.

Library of Congress and Social Media

The invention of social media, as well as its subsequent widespread popularity, continues to motivate the Library to use this new technology for "sharing knowledge through online resources, public programs, and publications" (Library of Congress, n.d., p. 6). The Library also uses social media tools (i.e., listservs, blogs, wiki, etc.) for internal staff communication. However, this group of tools is out of scope for this chapter. The Library's external social media use meets several goals and objectives, including (Library of Congress Web Governance Board, 2013):

1. Increasing public awareness of the Library's resources through users' discoveries and shared content
2. Effectively meeting user needs by presenting resources and expertise at the point of need

These goals and objectives coincide with the reasons why libraries use social media, including "ease of use, communication with patrons, marketing and promotion, and a way to improve customer service" (Canty, 2012, p. 4).

As a Legislative Branch agency, the Library is not required to follow the Office of Management and Budget's (OMB) memorandum on social media. In 2010, the Library established an institution-wide governing authority, the Web Governance Board (WGB), which was chaired by the deputy librarian. The WGB brought together technology and content specialists from across the institution to map out strategies and identify resources to enhance the Library's online presence. Social media was a key emphasis of the study. The WGB's social media working group established application and review processes to oversee the institution's social media operations and handle ethics, copyright, and technological issues. Subsequently, a comprehensive set of policies, regulations, guidelines, and processes have been developed. The Library negotiated user agreements with social media platforms to formalize relationships and to comply with government regulations concerning legal, management, operational, and other requirements. A new social media initiative must enter an application process with careful planning and assessments. Several layers of management review occur before final approval.

Some of the Library's initial offerings were through blogs (https://blogs.loc.gov/loc/), Flickr (https://www.flickr.com/photos/library_of_congress/), and YouTube (https://www.youtube.com/user/LibraryOfCongress). In the following decade, the Library's social media engagement expanded to 17 blogs, 7 Facebook pages, and 11 Twitter accounts. To date, the Library has a strong presence on many popular social media sites, such as Instagram, Medium, and Pinterest. It also offers several mobile apps and podcasts about its collections and public programs.

The Library's social media tools are managed by a singular office or division and designed with specific audience types, subject matters, and scopes. Regarding the adoption of tools, a division/office considers a set of factors, such as preferences of the communities served, effectiveness of particular tools, and a division's priorities and resource availability. During the application process, divisions are required to justify these factors in their business plan. The following are examples of divisions/offices that use social media functions to achieve their missions.

- **The American Folklife Center:** One of the largest ethnographic archives in the world, this division manages the Folklife Today blog (https://blogs.loc.gov/folklife/) and a Facebook page (https://www.facebook.com/americanfolklifecenter) for those who are "interested in folklore, folklife, and oral history" (Fenn et al., n.d.).
- **The Business, Science and Technology Reading Room:** This division handles respective reference questions using the Library's collections. It also operates the Inside Adams blog (https://blogs.loc.gov/inside_adams/).
- **The Geography and Map Division:** This division holds more than 6 million items in the forms of map sheets, atlases, microfilms, globes, aerial photos, and images. It manages the Worlds Revealed (https://blogs.loc.gov/maps/) blog and the Library of Congress Maps (https://twitter.com/LOCMaps) on Twitter.

- **The Law Library of Congress:** The largest law library in the world, this division is on Facebook, Twitter, YouTube, and iTunes. It serves legal communities domestically and internationally (http://www.loc.gov/law/).

Until 2015, the Library's social media content mostly showcased the Americana collections for an American audience or for those interested in American studies. The four area studies divisions provide access to the Library's unparalleled international collections and reference services. In 2016, the four area studies divisions launched a social media collaboration program with the 4 Corners blog and the International Collections Facebook page. As the titles suggest, these two outlets are dedicated exclusively to featuring the Library's international collections.

The Library of Congress International Collections

To understand the need and purpose of an international collections social media program, it would be helpful to review the background of the Library's international collections. This section will also discuss the roles and responsibilities of the Library's area studies divisions.

The Library's international collections are a rich and diverse assortment of research materials in hundreds of languages published in a variety of formats. The roots of the international collections can be attributed to Thomas Jefferson's Library, the purchase of which was authorized by Congress for the reestablishment of the Library in 1815 after the Library's original collection in the U.S. Capitol was burned down during the 1814 British invasion. Jefferson's collection originally contained 6,487 volumes. Many of these were collected from dealers in several European cities during his tenure (1784-1789) as minister to France (Haltzel, 2014). The collection's subjects include Persian history, the Koran, and Italian and European cultures and civilizations (Allen, 2013). Jefferson's statement, "There is, in fact, no subject to which a member of Congress may not have occasion to refer," continues to be the guiding principle for the Library's collection development (The Library of Congress, n.d., para. 1).

Following the purchase of Jefferson's collections, the Library's collections on European and Hispanic studies developed steadily (Haltzel, 2014; Hebert, 2010). Jefferson's original collection contained volumes on the Middle East, Africa, and Judaica. These became the foundation for the Library's Near East and Hebraic collections. In the next 150 years, the Library's foreign language collections began to take shape as some of the world's major research resources outside those respective regions. The following is a list of dates, in chronological order, related to the establishment of the key foreign language collections:

- In 1842, the earliest group of Southeast Asian books arrived as part of a collection obtained in Singapore by Lt. Charles Wilkes of the U.S. Naval Exploring Expedition (The Library of Congress, 2018b).
- In 1869, the Chinese collection began when the Library received 10 works in 933 volumes from Emperor Tongzhi (1862-1874) (The Library of Congress, 2018b).
- In 1875, the Japanese collection began when the governments of the U.S. and Japan reached an agreement for the exchange of government publications (The Library of Congress, 2017c).
- Between 1893 and 1901, two Mongolian manuscripts and one xylograph were donated to the Library by William Woodville Rockhill, American scholar and diplomat (The Library of Congress, 2017a).

- In 1901, the Tibetan collection began with a corps of xylographs and manuscripts acquired by William Woodville Rockhill during his travels in Mongolia and Tibet between 1888 to 1892 (The Library of Congress, 2017b).
- In 1904, the foundation of the Library's South Asian collection was laid with the purchase of the collection of German Indologist Dr. Albrecht Weber (1825-1901) (The Library of Congress, 2017e).
- In 1912 and 1914, the Hebraic collection further developed through Jacob H. Schiff's gifts and the purchase of the private collection of Ephraim Deinard, a well-known bibliographer and bookseller (The Library of Congress, 2010).
- In 1950, the Korean collection began with the start of the Korean War (The Library of Congress, 2017d).

In many countries and regions, print remains the primary publishing format. Therefore, the Library continues to collect print foreign publications. International digital collections have also developed rapidly through a host of activities, including purchases, donations, database subscriptions, Web archiving, digitization, and digital conversion.

Four Area Studies Divisions: Responsibilities and Services

The Library's various offices were established to fulfil the responsibilities of developing, managing, and serving its international collections. In 1978, after several reorganizations, four area studies divisions were created and named: (1) African and Middle Eastern (AMED); (2) Asian, (3) European; and (4) Hispanic. The key functions of the four divisions include:

- **Collection Development and Management:** In collaboration with the Library's acquisitions and bibliographic access directorate, overseas offices, and other divisions, the four divisions' reference specialists and recommending officers develop the Library's print and digital foreign language collections. AMED and the Asian division have custodial responsibilities of managing their respective collections in vernacular scripts. These include housing, preserving, and serving the collections. The European and Hispanic divisions do not manage collections in their respective languages because the collections are housed and managed as part of the Library's general collections, which contain items in both English and European languages.
- **References Services:** While the Library's main clientele is members of Congress and congressional staff, as the de facto national library with an international reputation, the Library's collections serve the American people and welcome international researchers. Readers may access collections in reading rooms, submit reference questions via the digital Ask-A-Librarian tool, or request permitted items through interlibrary loans via affiliated libraries. The four divisions routinely work with other Library's special format reading rooms to promote user access to foreign publications in the forms of maps, posters, photographs, films, and audio recordings. Examples of these services include the geography and map division, the prints and photograph division, and the motion picture, broadcasting, and recorded sound division.
- **Public Services:** In addition to providing user reference services, the four area studies divisions perform the following:

- Establishing and Maintaining Culture, Diplomatic, and Scholarly Connections: The language expertise of the four area studies divisions' reference staff is a useful tool in aiding the Library in connecting with international organizations, including other national libraries, embassies, foreign academic institutions, and think tanks.
- Organizing Public Programs: To promote the use of its vast collections, the Library organizes public programs to engage scholarly communities and the public. Targeting initiatives include book displays, book talks, concerts, exhibitions, film screenings, lectures, symposia, and other activities. Some programs are organized or cohosted by the four divisions in coordination with internal or external organizations. All programs are recorded and posted as webcasts (video recordings that could be viewed on the Library's website or YouTube channel). These webcasts become a part of the Library's collections.

The four area studies divisions' main mission is to help the Library develop its global collections and serve the public with these invaluable resources. The wide and global acceptance of social media offers a new means in accomplishing this mission.

INTERNATIONAL COLLECTIONS' SOCIAL MEDIA PROGRAM

Purpose

According to the Pew Research Center (2018), in 2005 only 5% of American adults were on social networking sites. By 2018, a median of 69% of American adults use social media. Globally, the Pew Research Center surveyed 39 countries and found that an average of 53% of adults from those countries use social networking sites (Gramlich, 2018). Middle Eastern and North African countries reach 68% and Latin American countries reach 59%. The survey also showed that a median of 75% of adults from the 39 countries are either on the Internet or own a smartphone. This suggests that the number of global social media users may continue to trend upward.

Concurrently, more of the Library's digital resources have been made available to the public through the Internet and the Library's social media enhancements. In late 2015, the Library's four area studies divisions (i.e., AMED, Asian, European, and Hispanic) began discussing, in more concrete terms, the possibility of accessing the vast market of global social media users who could become patrons of the Library's online digital resources. The discussions were initiated and led by AMED Chief Mary-Jane Deeb (2018).

To promote our collections and reach out to people around the world ... Even if they could not come to the Library in Washington, DC, they could still reach us and access some of our collections online, view our programs, and get an idea of some of our exceptional collections.

In early 2016, a series of interviews with area studies staff and the Library's other social media program managers was conducted by the international collections social media program's responsible staff. The purpose of speaking with staff was to identify the social media content focus. Social media managers shared their experiences in managing social media. Subsequently, a proposal was made for the four division chiefs' review. Discussions were held to build consensus on a collaboration model and to make operational decisions on issues focused on how to present the area studies collections in a balanced manner, how the four divisions should coordinate, what the workflow looks like, etc.

A few months later, the four divisions launched a collaborative social media program to showcase and introduce the Library's international collections to users from around the world. The program included the 4 Corners blog and a Library of Congress International Collection Facebook page. The following subsections look at the content, management, and operations of this program. They also discuss challenges and opportunities.

Social Media Tools

The first task of the program considered and identified valuable social media tools. This decision impacts the realization of an organization's goals and objectives. To evaluate the suitability of a social media tool, the four area studies divisions' decision makers considered a suite of internal and external factors.

Internal factors include:

- **Time and Staff Resources:** Some tools are designed to encourage more frequent content postings and user interactions. Choosing one tool over another may affect the level of staff time and engagement in social media activities.
- **Staff's Insight of Their User Communities:** Attendance at public service offerings, conferences, and workshops gives the division's staff members an in-depth understanding of the communities they interact with and/or serve. Therefore, staff have valuable insight into their users' preferred social media platforms and communication purposes.
- **Content Creation and Publishing Frequency:** Social media requires consistent content feeds to interest and engage users. It is important to establish a publishing schedule with regular feeds. It is also imperative to consider an ideal pace for the content creation timeline and publishing schedule.

External factors include:

- **Organizational Goals:** A social media platform must be analyzed to determine its effectiveness in reaching an organization's goals.
- **Public Use:** One factor to consider is the public's level of use and acceptance of a social media platform.
- **Availability and Limitations of Services:** All services may not be available. For example, some may be limited by the service agreement between a social media company and user organization.

In the case of the Library's international collections' social media program, it was determined that a blog and a Facebook page would be the most suitable for its intended audience. Having reached more than 160 million individuals by 2012 (Canty, 2012, p. 3), blogging is considered a genre that bridges "multimedia HTML documents and text-based computer-mediated communication" (as cited in Heyd, p. 152). It can "be taken as a cue and starting point in order to summarize some of the central insights from research on blogs within a social media context" (Heyd, 2017, p. 152). In the blog's text, one or more links to relevant online content may be incorporated. These links can encourage the discovery of additional Library resources.

Furthermore, blogs drive traffic to a website as the site's pages are indexed. This, in turn, increases findability through search engines (DeMers, 2015). This format also fosters conversations and encourages direct communication with constituents (ExecutiveGov, 2010). Unlike an academic article, a blog post is intended for the public rather than academics or researchers. Thus, it tends to be shorter than an academic piece and is written in plain English to convey the blogger's personality. At the same time, blog posts give an author space to discuss or present a topic in a concise and effective style (Library of Congress, 2016).

In addition to benefitting the reader, a blog enriches staff's knowledge of their collections, which enables them to better serve the user. As Chief of the European Division Grant Harris (2018) stated:

Few of our posts can be written quickly. We start with knowing there's a good story behind an item or collection … it still takes research to verify the particulars before we commit to putting this on the Web. In the process, we learn more about the collections than we can squeeze into a post. I see the posts as a way to deepen our knowledge. In some cases, it might lead to lengthier pieces that go deeper than posts in describing the collections … it's possible to write a post and a longer description in tandem, with the post linking to that description.

According to the Pew Research Center (2018), the share of adult social media users in the U.S. is 73% YouTube, 68% Facebook, 35% Instagram, 29% Pinterest, 27% Snapchat, 25% LinkedIn, 24% Twitter, and others. Since 2012, Facebook continues to be the most used social media platform. Globally, according to Facebook's company Website, in March 2018, the average daily active users amounted to 1.45 billion. It is recognized as the most popular social networking site with 2.2 billion monthly active users. YouTube's share of users is 1.9 billion, Twitter is 336 million, Snapchat is 255 million, and Pinterest is 200 million (Statista, 2018). The large number of domestic and international Facebook users makes it an attractive market to introduce the Library's international collections.

Facebook posts use less than 120 words. Posts should be concise and contain visually striking images complying with copyright regulations.

When considering users of different social media platforms and levels of engagement, the combined efforts of the blog and Facebook tools would reach a broad and diverse audience. In addition, they engage both scholars and members of the public.

In terms of publishing frequency, comparatively Facebook and blogs require less postings per daily and per week than, say, Twitter (Lee, 2014; Patel, 2016). Thus they require less staff time and resources to maintain and are thought to be more manageable when considering overall staff workload in the four area studies divisions.

In comparison to private organizations, government agencies often comply with stricter rules and regulations related to social media. Thus, paid advertisements or other promotion mechanisms through Facebook do not apply to the International Collections Facebook page.

Primary Audience

The pool of social media users presents a great opportunity to introduce the Library's international collections. Defining and narrowing down target audiences will help determine content, format, and writing styles to achieve better results. It could also inform outreach strategies and affect outcomes.

After analyzing approximately 100 academic blogs, Mewburn and Thomson (2013) determined that most blogs are intended for five reader categories: (1) academics; (2) researchers; (3) students; (4) professionals; and (5) the educated public. Regarding the 4 Corners blog, primary target audiences included individuals like members of Congress, staffers, researchers, scholars, teachers, college and high school students, librarians, other professionals, and members of the public with specific interests in international studies or global affairs. Target audiences may also be educational, cultural, academic, research, professional institutions, government agencies, and libraries.

Facebook permits the use of multimedia to present information. Users can write a post without inserting images (or vice versa), create a photo album, cross-post blogs, create event announcements, or upload videos and/or stream a live video event. While the International Collections Facebook page does not have plans to upload videos or create live video events, the area studies divisions' public programs are all recorded as "webcasts," which are then shared via links in posts so that users may click on the links to view those webcasts on the Library's website or YouTube channel. These Facebook functions warrant careful consideration regarding how to best present content and how to identify audiences.

The four divisions identified target audiences of the International Collections Facebook page, potential content focus, and suitable content formats. The target audiences fit the following categories: (1) researchers, scholars, and librarians (including individuals, groups, and communities of special subjects or research interests on Facebook); (2) students at high school, college, or higher level; (3) educators of all levels; (4) organizations like libraries, universities, federal agencies, think tanks, embassies, etc.; and (5) the public. These five categories may be local, remotely located, or on short-term visits. Local audiences reside in the greater Washington, DC metropolitan area. Due to their physical access to the Library, this audience can attend public programs in person. Remotely located audiences may live more than two or three hours away from the Library or reside overseas. The audience would most likely access the Library's digital resources. Table 1 presents the crosswalk between audiences, content focus, and presentation formats.

Content

The international collections social media program publishes posts pertaining to the following:

- **International Collections:** These posts include noticeable items, new acquisitions, collection finding aids, etc.
- **Public Programs:** These programs are publicized through weekly events on the 4 Corners blog and the events category on the International Collections Facebook page. Most of the public programs are recorded webcasts (video recordings that could be viewed on the Library's website or YouTube channel). These are accessible on the Library's Website and YouTube channel. To bring public awareness to these resources, the four divisions publish periodical blog posts and weekly featured webcasts on Facebook to highlight the webcasts.
- **Interviews:** Interviews with the Library's subject experts, interns, and researchers are featured, as well as guest blogs. The Library's area studies subject experts and reference staff are intimately familiar with their respective collections. They are also the recommending officers for developing invaluable resources. Interns and researchers use the Library's international collections to complete assignments or research. Therefore, they use this forum to share how they use and locate information in the collections.

Table 1. Target audience, content focus, and format

Audience	Content Focus	Facebook Format
Scholars, researchers, and librarians (including Facebook groups and communities based on subjects or interests)	• Collections with a focus on scholarly interests • Reference services • Research orientations (for locals) • Digital resources and projects (e.g., program webcasts, Web archives, etc.)	• Cross-posts of blogs • Online audio/webcast recordings • Event announcements of exhibitions, programs, research orientations, etc.
• Students (at the college and high school levels)	• Collections with a focus on: o Course work o Online trending topics, pop culture, etc. o Current affairs o Cultures and languages o Country in the news • Research orientations (for locals)	• Images of a blog, collection items, exhibitions, programs, etc. • Online audio/webcast recordings • Collection-related trivia quizzes • Announcements of exhibitions, programs, etc.
• Educators of all levels	• Collections • Reference services • Public programs/exhibitions (for locals)	• Images of a blog, collection items, exhibitions, programs, etc. • Online audio/webcast recordings • Announcements of exhibitions, programs, etc.
• Organizations: libraries, universities, research centers, think tanks, embassies, etc.	• Collections • Research orientations (for locals or visiting groups) • Reference services • Digital resources and projects • Visits of foreign dignitaries • Collaborations	• Blogs • Photo(s) of visits of VIPs or delegations (with permissions) • Images • Online audio/webcast recordings
Public	• Public programs/exhibitions (for locals) • Personal stories tied to a collection	• Event announcements of exhibitions, programs, etc. • Images • Online audio/webcast recordings • Trivia quizzes

Source: (African and Middle Eastern Division, 2016).

- **Announcements:** Social media posts can capture unique collection items that the area studies divisions can share with special visitors or foreign dignitaries. Internship and fellowship opportunities may also be shared through social media.

On a weekly basis, the 4 Corners blog highlights an international collection or collections. The blog is a joint collaboration of the four area studies divisions. To balance content and frequency, each division contributes one post per month. Posts range between 500 and 1,500 words. This results in four posts on the international collections and studies. This frequency is considered manageable because each post requires a considerable amount of time to write, edit, and format before publishing. Furthermore, social media work is one of the many assignments completed by reference staff. In addition to this work, the staff focus on reference services to Library patrons and recommended materials for the Library's collections. With competing priorities, staff time invested in social media activity must be kept at a reasonable level so that the assignment does not impact their main duties.

In addition to collections-centered posts, the blog publishes a weekly calendar of events to announce public programs organized by the four area studies divisions. Announcements also include blogs related to newly released webcasts for those who could not attend the events in person.

It was determined that two to three weekly posts would be shared on the International Collections Facebook page. This frequency engaged users while creating a manageable schedule for staff's writing and review. To highlight unique collection items, each division is tasked with preparing one Facebook post per month with at least one image. Images must be cleared of copyright restrictions. These short Facebook posts (no more than 120 words) take less time to create and edit. Therefore, a division may choose to submit more than one post per month.

In addition to collections-related posts, the Facebook page publishes a weekly featured webcast to introduce the Library's webcasts, announcements of public programs, and posts to coincide with special occasions (i.e., holidays, anniversaries, world events, etc.).

Table 2 shows a weekly blog and Facebook publishing sample schedule.

Interaction With Members of Intended Audience

Maintaining regular contact with blog subscribers and social media users is essential to retaining audiences and expanding the user base. From the user's perspective, a blog or Facebook page offers information, provides a platform to connect with others, and offers opportunities to communicate. Therefore, maintaining a social media publishing schedule and moderating reader comments on a daily basis are key to engagement.

To encourage users to respectfully interact on social media, the 4 Corners blog and the International Collections Facebook page follow the Library's comment and posting policy (Library of Congress, 2017, February):

Table 2. Sample of a social media weekly publishing schedule

Day	Social Media	Responsible Division	Content
Monday	4 Corners blog	One of the four area studies divisions	A blog post discussing one of the four content areas (i.e., collections, public programs, interviews, event announcement)
Tuesday	International Collections Facebook page	One of the four area studies divisions	"Featured Video Tuesday" Webcast
Wednesday	Facebook	One of the four area studies divisions	A cross-post of Monday's blog
Thursday	Facebook	One of the four area studies divisions	A post showcasing a collection or item
Friday	Blog	All	A weekly calendar of upcoming public programs organized or cohosted by the four divisions
Saturday/Sunday	None	None	An activity is not scheduled unless a post has been prescheduled to coincide with a special occasion on the weekend

Source: (African and Middle Eastern Division, 2016).

We welcome your participation and comments on the Library's blogs and social media and in our Webinars and online forums. Our online sites are governed by the general rules of respectful civil discourse. You are fully responsible for everything that you post.

The Library of Congress does not discriminate against any views. Nevertheless, the Library may monitor any user-generated content as it chooses and reserves the right to remove content for any reason whatever, without consent. We do not verify the identity of participants. Here are some of the rules we follow:

- *Please stay on topic. We will remove content that is clearly off-topic.*
- *We will remove content that contains abusive, vulgar, offensive, racist, threatening or harassing content, personal attacks of any kind, or offensive terms that target specific individuals or groups.*
- *We will remove spam and content that promotes services or products, or that involves political campaigning or lobbying.*
- *We may remove content that contains personal information (whether your own or someone else's), including home address, home or cell phone number, or personal e-mail address, in order to protect privacy.*
- *Gratuitous links to sites and repeat submissions of the same (or very similar) contributions are viewed as spam and may result in the content being removed.*
- *Do not post anything that you do not have the right to post. We will not post comments that appear to post material without permission, and we will follow a notice and takedown procedure for complaints of copyright violation under the Digital Millennium Copyright Act.*
- *We will only post content from participants over 13 years of age.*
- *Communications made through social media posts, e-mail, Webinars, and messaging systems will in no way constitute a legal or official notice or comment to the Library of Congress or any official or employee of the Library for any purpose.*
- *All user-generated content is released into the public domain unless the participant clearly states otherwise, so do not submit anything you do not wish to broadcast to the general public.*
- *Users who do not comply with these standards of conduct may be blocked.*

Readers often send reference questions in their comments. Post contributors who are either area or reference specialists respond with information that can be of interest to others. Readers are also encouraged to submit queries via the Library's digital reference system, Ask-A-Librarian, to ensure timely responses and user privacy.

Management and Operation

Managing a social media program requires continuous investments of staff resources to produce steady content feeds and to grow a broad user base. The interdivisional collaboration model is ideal because it affords staff opportunities to write about their collections at a manageable frequency. This ensures the richness and diversity of content to appeal to a large audience of varied cultural backgrounds and languages. These readers may not otherwise follow the Americana content on the Library's main Facebook page.

Each division is represented by two coordinating staff members. The eight members form a social media committee. Two members of the committee, who serve as the responsible content authors (RCAs), coordinate the committee's activities, review published content, and liaise with the Library's oversight body, the WGB's social media working group. The RCAs are "authorized and trained to create and publish content, including content created by others, to a social media project." (Library of Congress, 2018c). This group works to convey guidelines and address unforeseen issues and/or concerns. The division coordinators work with the committee and their respective division to plan content and arrange their division's internal submission and review process to complement the general workflow. The general workflow is shown in Figure 1.

During the infancy of the international collections social media program, the committee met twice a month to address issues related to setting up the program. In fiscal year 2018, as the program operation stabilized, the committee met once a month to discuss contemporaneous operational issues, including content planning, staff training on writing for social media, and marketing strategies.

The area studies divisions' blog and Facebook page follow a general workflow with five key phases:

1. **Phase One, Plan:** During this phase, the social media committee discusses and plans two to three months of content. Staff writers are assigned.
2. **Phase Two, Review/Edit:** Available drafts undergo an editorial review and supervisory review for accuracy and readability. Accompanying images are reviewed for suitability and copyright status. Selected images must best represent the collection or topic. The Library's general counsel provides guidance on the use of images and other legal matters. Scanned images and photographs by staff must meet visual quality standards established by the social media committee.
3. **Phase Three, Publish:** After a draft is finalized and approved, its images follow the RCA's format. It is published according to the schedule.
4. **Phase Four, Moderate Reader Comments:** Once a post appears on the 4 Corners blog or the International Collections Facebook page, the RCAs monitor it for performance, reader comments, and reference questions.
5. **Phase Five, Report:** After reviewing the posts' performance statistics, the RCAs share details with division coordinators and staff. Each month, the RCAs submit qualitative reports for the Library's monthly social media analytics reports. At the end of each fiscal year, the Library requires that an annual assessment be submitted for each social media account. This is an opportunity to review if a social media operation meets its established goals and objectives. Using lessons learned from the prior fiscal year's assessments and reports, the social media committee begins a new work cycle at the beginning of each fiscal year. This cycle aims to enhance the four divisions' social media work (see Figure 1). Assessment questions include:
    a. Does the number of published posts meet or exceed the established annual target?
    b. How many readers subscribe to the blog?
    c. How many followers and/or likes are on the Facebook page?
    d. Is it an efficient internal workflow?
    e. Does the publishing frequency need to be adjusted?
    f. Did we reach the intended audience?

Figure 1. Area studies social media program workflow
Source: (African and Middle Eastern Division, 2016)

Training

The 4 Corners blog and the International Collections Facebook page offer area studies staff an opportunity to introduce the Library's international resources and expertise services to the public. Therefore, it is essential to familiarize staff with writing for the Library's social media platforms. To achieve this goal, the following strategies were adopted:

- **Blog Checklist for Authors:** This checklist covers the length of a post, tone, style, image requirements, release permissions for guest authors and photographs, submission deadlines, etc.
- **Formula for Writing Facebook Posts:** This formula provides a step-by-step guide for staff interested in writing about an item.
- **Staff Orientation:** Orientations establish a better understanding of the value of the Library's social media work. For instance, the four area studies divisions organized several staff orientations since the beginning of the program. One session, which hosted a colleague from the Library's Office of Communications, offered background information on the Library's path to social media adoption. The Library's Office of the General Counsel held an orientation to discuss social media ethics. Additional staff workshops were held to share experiences on preparing social media posts.

In addition, the area studies social media committee holds periodic discussions with other Library social media managers to share experiences, exchange ideas, and seek opportunities for collaborative writing and cross-posting content.

Measuring Effectiveness

Thoughtful planning and careful implementation can ensure a social media program's efficiency. However, it is equally important to measure a program's impacts and/or success. Scholars have noted difficulties in evaluating the return on investment or success in social media. While the numbers of likes, follows, shares, and subscriptions are easily obtained, it is important to consider reader engagement, including comments, clicks on links, and referrals from search engines (Canty, 2012). Indirect factors (i.e., reading room visits, Website or Webpage visits) may need to be considered to gain an understanding of the effects of social media.

The Library measures its social media effectiveness by reviewing the number of users, global reach, and anecdotal reporting. The following information is related to the inception of the 4 Corners blog in April 2016 and the International Collections Facebook page in October 2016.

- The blog has published more than 230 posts and garnered more than 10,300 subscriptions.
- The Facebook page has published more than 450 posts and received more than 5,200 likes and follows.
- The blog and Facebook page have been accessed by users from more than 56 countries. The darkened countries in Figure 2 and Figure 3 contain users who accessed the blog and the Facebook page.

Figure 2. 4 Corners blog accessed by users from 56 countries
Source: (Library of Congress, 2018a)

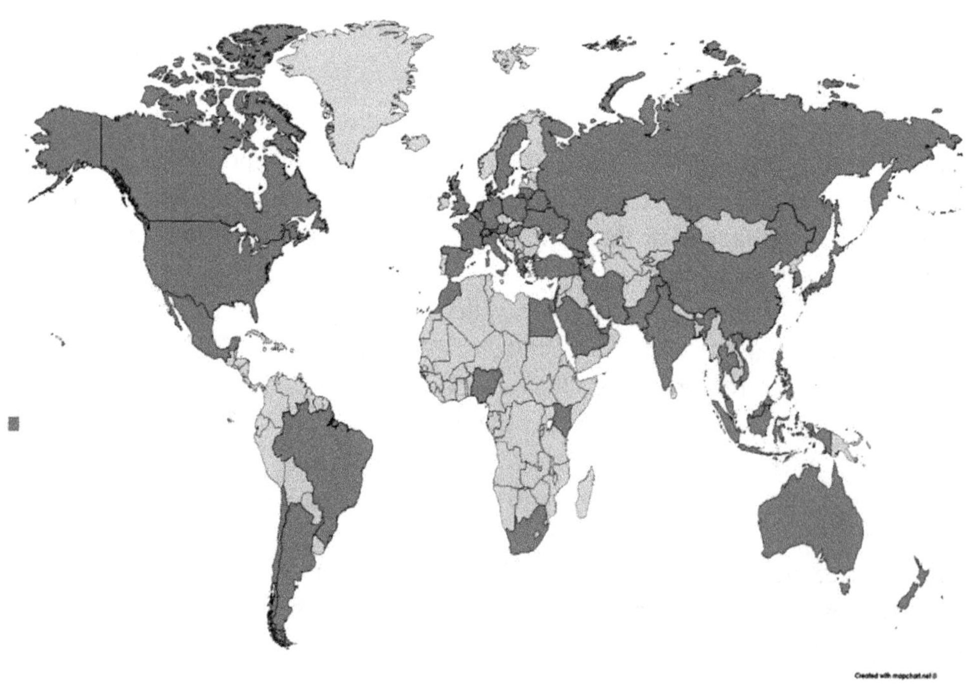

Figure 3. International Collections Facebook page accessed by users from 57 countries
Source: (Library of Congress, 2018b)

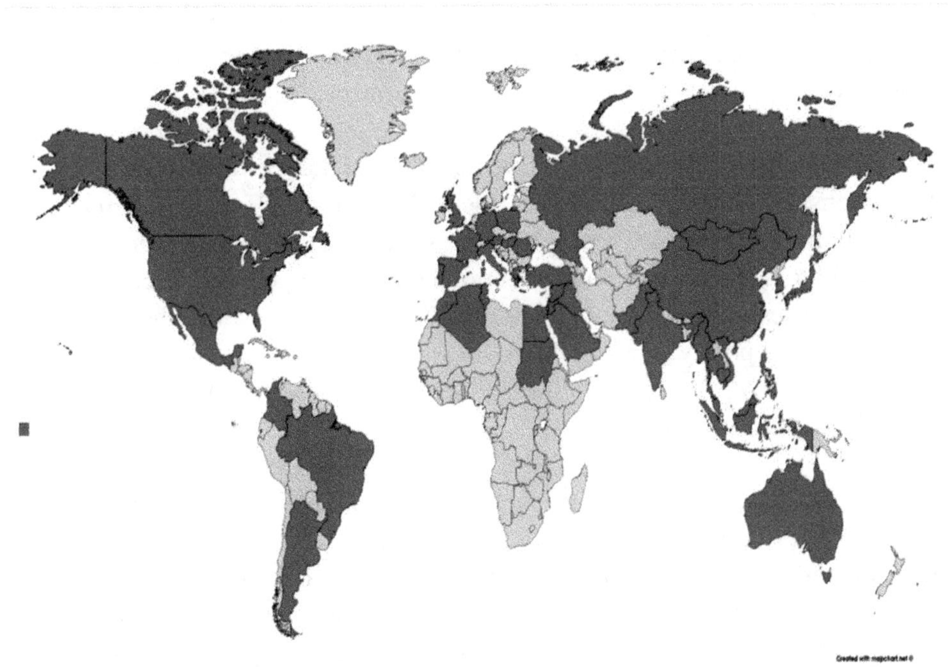

Users were not asked how they knew about the collections. Therefore, the four area studies divisions had to collect anecdotal information concerning social media effectiveness. Thus, reference librarians are now asked to note when reference questions are received via Ask-A-Librarian.

The area studies division chiefs provided feedback on influences of the international collections social media program. According to Deeb (2018):

resurrected videos of programs that were held some years ago ... keeping it alive and useful for teachers and students alike.

The number of users referred from social media to the area studies divisions' Web resources also increased as evident in the counts of Webpage and Webcast views. According to Chief of the Asian Division (Shao, 2018):

The use of social media helps to keep our collections and services relevant to users of all age groups. At a time when social media becomes a paramount channel to disseminate and share information, it is important for reference librarians to leverage on its powerful reach. During the past two years, we've garnered thousands of impressions on highlighted collection items and activities, which in turn contributes to increased traffic to our Website and greater use of the Ask-a-Librarian link.

The Chief of the European Division (2018) noted:

On one hand, our posts have made our collections and services more known. This happens in various ways. Sometimes we're promoting an item or a small collection. Sometimes we're describing a larger collection or depth of a collection. Anyone reading several of our posts will start to understand how deeply universal our collections are. Just as important, of course, is that readers will also sense the depth of our expertise.

Collaboration with the Library's other social media platforms have extended the use of the Library's international collections. For instance, a blog post titled "Rabindranath Tagore: A Great Indian Poet and Writer," originally published by the 4 Corners blog, was cross-posted by the Library's Poetry Office's From the Catbird Seat blog. It received much attention because the post was used as part of a school's teaching materials. As a result, many students used the blog post to access the Library's collections pertaining to Tagore and his poetry.

Challenges and Opportunities

An internal challenge confronting the Library's international collections social media program relates to encouraging more area studies divisions' staff to participate in content contribution to the blog and Facebook page. Area studies reference staff are not required to use social media. Blogging and Facebook use may be unfamiliar to some staff who are not social media users and thus could be intimidating. To overcome these obstacles, the area studies social media committee organized regular workshops and orientations to enhance knowledge about the Library's social media. These offerings also provide instructions on writing for social media. Sharing the program's success stories and performance statistics related to staff contributions can encourage others to emulate such success.

Raising public awareness and promoting the use of the Library's resources have been one of the Library's critical missions. These tasks are more easily obtained through social media due to its convenience and economical mechanisms to build consistent, long-term relationships with large groups of users regardless of time or geographic boundaries (Achen, 2016). An associated challenge is strategically publicizing the 4 Corners blog and the International Collections Facebook page. Academic or university libraries target their students, faculty members, and a university community as the base audience (Rauh & McReynolds, 2016). However, the Library's public-facing area studies social media resources welcome researchers and the public. One strategy aims to market the Library's tools at research orientations, professional conferences, and public programs.

It is important to acknowledge that the International Collections Facebook page is connected to a public institution without a marketing budget. Therefore, it relies on nonpaid or organic reach vs. paid Facebook advertisements. The area studies social media committee contacted organizations or academic/research subject groups on Facebook whose communities could benefit from the Library's area studies resources. When reaching out, they also asked for permission to cross-post content on their pages. However, it is important to carefully vet selected Facebook pages for legitimacy, relevance, and appropriateness.

Undoubtedly, social media has become a widespread and powerful communications tool. This is demonstrated through its considerable impact on social and political movements, global events, and national elections in various countries. Its usefulness in spreading and sharing information will likely continue. As the Library's international collections social media program continues, additional social media tools may be considered for future use. (Deeb, 2018)

RECOMMENDATIONS

Mickoleit (2014) noted that the return on investment of social media in government can be applicable to all organizations, including research and academic libraries:

The purpose and returns … are not as clear as they are for political personalities. This leads to uncertainty among government institutions about how to best leverage social media and about the implications for strategic objectives and day-to-day operations. (p. 2)

This reveals the importance of program planning, assessment, and management that an organization or a library should conduct while considering investing resources in social media. In the case of the Library's international collections social media program, it is essential for the four area studies divisions to be aware of the relevant policy, regulations, and guidelines that govern the application and use of social media. Social media program managers must recognize limitations impacting outreach strategies, such as restrictions on paid marketing options. Thus, to plan an effective program, the following items should be addressed regarding planning, management, operations, and evaluation.

1. How does social media help to achieve the institution's missions and goals?
2. Can the institution's goals and objectives be met without social media? Can they be met through other means and/or tools?
3. What are the objectives and purposes of the organization's use of social media?
4. What governing authorities apply to this work?
5. What social media tools are most suited and effective to meet the organization's objectives and purposes?
6. Who is the target audience?
7. What content should be published? How often? Who should write the content?
8. What are the anticipated outcomes?
9. What are the performance targets and milestones?
10. How should the social media program be managed and operated?
11. How much time and resources should be invested in social media? Is that reasonable, given other demands?
12. What does the workflow look like? How is the work divided? Who is involved? What are the roles and responsibilities?
13. What are the requirements for moderating user comments?
14. Are there copyright and ethics requirements and/or other standards to follow?
15. Are there plans for promoting the organization's use of social media?
16. How will the organization build consensus and gain long-term cooperation from stakeholders and involved offices?
17. What knowledge and skills are required of participating staff and content contributors?
18. How do you engage staff and encourage content contribution?
19. What are the standards for receiving high-quality content and visual materials?
20. How often will the organization monitor performance? What will be monitored?
21. Should there be joint campaigns across social media platforms?
22. What lessons are learned from user interactions? How will these lessons improve content?

23. How will the organization measure progress against established benchmarks, milestones, and final outcomes?
24. Should posts be archived? What are the requirements?

The following observations apply to organizations or libraries that plan on using social media to market or publicize their resources or services.

First, enough full-time manpower must be available to properly manage the content publishing cycle. If not, the interdepartmental collaboration model, as demonstrated by the Library's international collections social media program, may be ideal because the continuous demand for content could be fulfilled by a larger number of staff. Juggling competing priorities would be less of a concern.

Second, a large amount of staff participation will promote the organization's social media platforms. Staff members gain ownership of their posts, which encourages them to widely share those posts.

Third, the Library's general social media experience shows that it takes time to build a large social media following. Operating an open-ended initiative is ideal because it allows more time to build and maintain user relationships. However, an open-ended program requires a sustainable operation related to content and staffing. In the case of the Library's program, the content featured on the 4 Corners blog and the International Collections Facebook page are evergreen, valuable resources for many generations. In terms of staff participation, it is essential to build an inclusive program to motivate staff. Staff should receive training and updates to equip them with knowledge and skills, as well as keep them interested and engaged. It is equally important to remain flexible regarding technology. Organizations must be willing to make strategic adjustments as needed.

CONCLUSION

The Library's international collections social media program's blog and Facebook page have made it easier for researchers and the public to discover, learn about, and use the Library's international resources. Through this open-ended initiative, the four area studies division staff will continue to make discoveries through the collections and write related posts to share with researchers and the public. It is expected that:

the number of subscribers will increase significantly in the future … more and more countries from around the world will want to join to find out what treasures we hold from their regions in our collections. (Deeb, 2018)

Social media will continue to play an indispensable role in building communities and facilitating the sharing of information. Its use by organizations, including libraries, will continue to broaden. Shao (2018) noted that:

this should be a dynamic component of the Library's digital strategy and commitment.

Disclaimer: Anchi Hoh is Program Specialist in the African and Middle Eastern Division of the Library of Congress. The opinions expressed here are of her own and do not represent the Library of Congress.

REFERENCES

Achen, R. M. (2016). Examining the influence of Facebook fans, content, and engagement on business outcomes in the National Basketball Association. *Journal of Social Media for Organizations*, *3*(1), 1–16.

African and Middle Eastern Division. (2016). *Social Media Communications & Business Plan*. Washington, DC: Library of Congress.

Allen, E. (2013, February). *Inquiring minds: Exploring Jefferson's universe*. Library of Congress Blog. Retrieved from https://blogs.loc.gov/loc/2013/02/inquiring-minds-exploring-jeffersons-universe/

American Library Association (ALA). (2011). *The state of America's libraries: A report from the American Library Association*. ALA. Retrieved from http://www.ala.org/news/sites/ala.org.news/files/content/mediapresscenter/americaslibraries/state_of_americas_libraries_report_2011.pdf

Bennett, S. (2014, October 20). 88% of companies are using social media for marketing. *Adweek*. Retrieved from https://www.adweek.com/digital/social-media-companies/

Britannica Academic. (2017). *Media convergence*. Retrieved from academic.eb.com/levels/collegiate/article/media-convergence/439212#

Britannica Academic. (2018). *Broadband technology*. Retrieved from academic.eb.com/levels/collegiate/article%20/broadband-technology/471920

Canty, N. (2012). Social media in libraries: It's like, complicated. *The Journal of National and International Library and Information Issues*, *23*(2), 41–54. Retrieved from https://www.researchgate.net/publication/249371034_Social_Media_in_Libraries_It's_Like_Complicated

DeMers, J. (2015). The top 10 benefits of blogging on your website. *Forbes*. Retrieved from https://www.forbes.com/sites/jaysondemers/2015/05/28/the-top-10-benefits-of-blogging-on-your-website/#6ce3b5a31177

Dewing, M. (2010). *Social media: An introduction*. Library of Parliament Information and Research Service. Retrieved from http://publications.gc.ca/collections/collection_2010/bdp-lop/bp/2010-03-eng.pdf

ExecutiveGov. (2010). *The five best government blogs and the six reasons why they work*. Retrieved from http://www.executivegov.com/2010/01/the-five-best-government-blogs-and-the-six-reasons-why-they-work/

Fenn, J., Hall, S., Harris, M., Saylor, N., Shankar, G., Stefano, M., … Winick, S. (n.d.). About [Blog post]. *Folklife Today*. Retrieved from https://blogs.loc.gov/folklife/about/

Gramlich, J. (2018, April). *5 facts about Americans and Facebook*. Pew Research Center. Retrieved from http://www.pewresearch.org/fact-tank/2018/04/10/5-facts-about-americans-and-facebook/

Haltzel, M. H. (2014, February). *Library of Congress: An illustrated guide*. European Collections. Retrieved from https://www.loc.gov/rr/european/guide/intro.html

Hebert, J. R. (2010, July). Hispanic and Portuguese Collections: Introduction. *Library of Congress: An illustrated guide*. Retrieved from http://www.loc.gov/rr/hispanic/guide/intro.html

Heyd, T. (2017). Blogs. In C. Hoffmann & W. Bublitz (Eds.), *Pragmatics of social media* (pp. 151–172). Berlin, Germany: De Gruyter Mouton. doi:10.1515/9783110431070-006

Lee, K. (2014). The social media frequency guide: how often to post to Facebook, Twitter, Linkedin, and more. *Fast Company*. Retrieved from https://www.fastcompany.com/3029019/the-social-media-frequency-guide-how-often-to-post-to-facebook-twitter-linkedin-a

Library of Congress. (1989). *Annual report of the Librarian of Congress for the fiscal year ending September 30, 1988*. Washington, DC: Library of Congress. Retrieved from https://hdl.handle.net/2027/mdp.39015082937049

Library of Congress. (1990). *Annual report of the Librarian of Congress for the fiscal year ending September 30, 1989*. Washington, DC: Library of Congress.

Library of Congress. (1996). *Annual report of the Librarian of Congress for the fiscal year ending 30 September 1995*. Washington, DC: Library of Congress.

Library of Congress. (2001). *Annual report of the Librarian of Congress for the fiscal year ending September 30, 2000*. Washington, DC: Library of Congress. Retrieved from https://hdl.handle.net/2027/mdp.39015082936801

Library of Congress. (2005). *Annual report of the Librarian of Congress for the fiscal year ending September 30, 2004*. Washington, DC: Library of Congress. Retrieved from https://hdl.handle.net/2027/mdp.39015082937098

Library of Congress. (2010, November). *Library of Congress strategic plan fiscal year 2011-2016*. Washington, DC: Library of Congress. Retrieved from http://lcweb2.loc.gov/master/libn/about/documents/strategicplan2011-2016.pdf

Library of Congress. (2016). *Area Studies Blog Post Guidelines*. Author.

Library of Congress. (2017). *Annual report of the Librarian of Congress for the fiscal year ending September 30, 2016*. Washington, DC: Library of Congress. Retrieved from https://www.loc.gov/portals/static/about/reports-and-budgets/documents/annual-reports/fy2016.pdf

Library of Congress. (2017, February). *Comments & posting policy*. Retrieved from https://www.loc.gov/legal/comment-and-posting-policy/

Library of Congress. (2018a, July). *4 Corners of the World Blog Dashboards, April 2016-July 2018*. Author.

Library of Congress. (2018b, July). *International Collections Facebook page Insights, October 2016 to July 2018*. Author.

Library of Congress. (2018c, October). *Library of Congress Rules and Regulations*. Washington, DC: Library of Congress.

Library of Congress. (n.d.). *Library of Congress Strategic plan FY2016 through FY2020: Serving the Congress and the nation*. Washington, DC: Library of Congress. Retrieved from https://www.loc.gov/portals/static/about/documents/library_congress_stratplan_2016-2020.pdf

Library of Congress Web Governance Board. (2013, March). *Social media strategy to support the library's web strategy*. Author.

Mewburn, I., & Thomson, P. (2013). Why do academics blog? An analysis of audiences, purposes and challenges. *Studies in Higher Education, 38*(8), 1106–1119. doi:10.1080/03075079.2013.835624

Mickoleit, A. (2014, December 22). *Social media use by governments: A policy primer to discuss trends, identify policy opportunities and guide decision makers* [Working paper]. Paris, France: OECD. Retrieved from doi:10.1787/5jxrcmghmk0s-en

Patel, N. (2016). How frequently you should post on social media according to the pros. *Forbes*. Retrieved from https://www.forbes.com/sites/neilpatel/2016/09/12/how-frequently-you-should-post-on-social-media-according-to-the-pros/#7c4eb4e9240f

Pew Research Center. (2018, February). Social media fact sheet. *Internet and Tech*. Retrieved from http://www.pewinternet.org/fact-sheet/social-media/

Rauh, A. E., & McReynolds, S. J. H. (2016). Telling our story: A case study of a collaborative departmental blog at Syracuse University Libraries. *New Review of Academic Librarianship, 22*(2-3), 315–324. doi:10.1080/13614533.2016.1181664

Statista. (2018). Most popular social networks worldwide as of July 2018, ranked by number of active users (in millions). *The Statistics Portal*. Retrieved from https://www.statista.com/statistics/272014/global-social-networks-ranked-by-number-of-users/

Straus, J. R., & Glassman, M. E. (2016, May 26). *Social media in Congress: The impact of electronic media on member communications* [CRS report]. Washington, DC: Congressional Research Report. Retrieved from https://fas.org/sgp/crs/misc/R44509.pdf

The Library of Congress. (2018a, May). *Southeast Asian collection*. Asian Reading Room. Retrieved from http://www.loc.gov/rr/asian/SoutheastAsianCollection.html

The Library of Congress. (2018b, January). *Chinese collection*. Asian Reading Room. Retrieved from http://www.loc.gov/rr/asian/ChineseCollection.html

The Library of Congress. (n.d.). *Selected special collections: Thomas Jefferson's Library*. Rare Book & Special Collections Reading Room. Retrieved from https://www.loc.gov/rr/rarebook/coll/130.html

U.S. Government Publishing Office (GPO). *Public Law 111-274-Plain Writing Act of 2010*. Washington, DC: U.S. Government Publishing Office. Retrieved from https://www.gpo.gov/fdsys/pkg/PLAW-111publ274/content-detail.html

U.S. Office of Management and Budget (OMB). M-10-06: Open government directive [memorandum]. By P. R. Orszag. Washington, DC: Executive Office of the President OMB, December 2009. (n.d.). Retrieved from https://www.whitehouse.gov/sites/whitehouse.gov/files/omb/memoranda/2010/m10-06.pdf

U.S. Office of Management and Budget (OMB). Social Media, Web-Based Interactive Technologies, and the Paperwork Reduction Act [memorandum]. By C. R. Sunstein. Washington, DC: Executive Office of the President OMB, April 2010. (n.d.). Retrieved from https://obamawhitehouse.archives.gov/sites/default/files/omb/assets/inforeg/SocialMediaGuidance_04072010.pdf

ADDITIONAL READING

Alhabash, A., & Ma, M. (2017, January/March). A tale of four platforms: Motivations and uses of Facebook, Twitter, Instagram, and Snapchat among college students? *Social Media + Society*, 1-13.

Bacon, M. (2017). How libraries use social media. *Techsoup*. Retrieved from http://forums.techsoup.org/cs/community/b/tsblog/archive/2017/10/12/how-libraries-use-social-media.aspx

Coleman, B., Petitt, S., & Buning, M. (2018). Social media use in higher education: Do members of the academy recognize any advantages? *The Journal of Social Media in Society*, *7*(1), 420–442.

Eisenlauer, V. (2017). Social Network Sites/Facebook. In C. Hoffmann & W. Bublitz (Eds.), *Pragmatics of social media* (pp. 225–242). Germany: De Gruyter Mouton. doi:10.1515/9783110431070-009

Hendricks, D. (2013, May 8). Complete history of social media: then and now. *Small Business Trends*. Retrieved from https://smallbiztrends.com/2013/05/the-complete-history-of-social-media-infographic.html

Litt, E., & Hargittai, E. (2016, January/March). The imagined audience on social network sites. *Social Media + Society*, 1-12.

Manca, A., & Whitworth, A. (2018). Social media and workplace practices in higher education institutions: A review. *The Journal of Social Media in Society*, *7*(1), 151–183.

Poushter, J., Bishop, C., & Chwe, H. (2018, June). *Social media use continues to rise in developing countries but plateaus across developed ones: Digital divides remain, both within and across countries*. Pew Research Center. Retrieved from http://assets.pewresearch.org/wp-content/uploads/sites/2/2018/06/15135408/Pew-Research-Center_Global-Tech-Social-Media-Use_2018.06.19.pdf

Tan, C. (2018). *Regulating content on social media: copyright, terms of service and technological features*. London, UK: UCL Press. doi:10.2307/j.ctt2250v4k

United States Office of Personnel Management. (2017, July). *Social media policy*. Retrieved from https://www.opm.gov/news/social-media-presence/social-media-policy.pdf

Chapter 14
Social Media Use in Academic Libraries:
Applications and Implications in a Developing Country

Goodluck Ifijeh
Covenant University, Nigeria

Julie Ilogho
Covenant University, Nigeria

Juliana Iwu-James
https://orcid.org/0000-0001-5141-1457
Covenant University, Nigeria

Happiness Chijioke Michael-Onuoha
https://orcid.org/0000-0003-2996-6979
Covenant University, Nigeria

Ifeakachuku Osinulu
Covenant University, Nigeria

ABSTRACT

Social media use has become the norm in information services delivery. It holds the unique advantage of delivering service to users through social interaction. This chapter discussed social media use in academic libraries in a developing country: Nigeria. It examined the concept and definition of social media; it also discussed trends in social media usage in libraries. The chapter further outlined the types of social media tools used in libraries. It discussed the peculiar challenges of social media use in Nigeria and proffered solutions.

DOI: 10.4018/978-1-5225-8097-3.ch014

INTRODUCTION

Social media, a term which is sometimes referred to as social media tools, has gained so much popularity over the past few years. In a study, Jacka and Scott (2011) argued that there is no single definition of social media. But some authors have tried to define the term. Social media can be said to be a medium of communication that is virtual, participatory and collaborative. Kaplan, and Haenlein (2010) defined social media as 'a group of internet-integrated applications that build on the ideological and technological foundations of Web 2.0 (the platform) and that allow the creation and exchange of User Generated Content (the ways in which people make use of social media). Social media is an evolution of word of mouth that scaled up by leveraging the persuasiveness of the internet. Its major components are social networking, microblogs, blogs, RSS feeds, widgets, linking and posting, content rating, book marking sites, audio podcasting and video podcasting (Sajithra & Patil, 2013). Social media has been defined as website and applications used for social networking. It is sometimes said to mean the same thing as social network even though some authors have tried to differentiate social media from social network (Hartshorn, 2010). Social media is primarily used to transmit or share information with a broad audience, while social networking is the act of engaging people with common interest to associate together and build relationships through community (Cohen, 2009; Hartshon, 2010). Bedell (2010) opines that social media is a simple system, a communication channel; it is not a location that you visit. Social networking is a two-way communication, where conversations are at the core and through which relationships are developed (Edosomwan et al 2011).

Social media have evolved over the years into what is obtainable presently and in recent times. The use of the telegraph to transmit and receive messages over long distances was the experience in 1792 (Ritholz, 2010) as cited by Edosomwan et al, 2011. Then, in the 1800s, the radio and telephone were used for social interaction (Rimskii, 2011; Wren, 2004). Phone phreaking was a popular term in the 1950s, a term used for the rogue searching of the telephone network. Phreaks were able to hack into corporate unused voice mailboxes to host the first blogs and podcasts (Borders, 2010). During the 1960s, the public saw the advent of email (Borders, 2010). It was originally a method to exchange messages from one computer to another, which are online (Mwangi & Wagoki, 2016). Although, there has been a lot of debates as to whether the email is social media, Sajithra and Ratil (2013) opined that the introduction of Email marked the beginning of the much more collaborative social media years later, even though Edosomwan et al (2011) opined that social media started with the telephone and not computer.

The 1970s witnessed further social media development; Multi-User Domain, a real-time virtual world with role-playing games, interactive fiction, and online chat have since emerged. The process of managing email list was automated and christened LITSERV in the 1980s. Internet Relay Chat (IRC) was introduced in the late 1980s to ease the group discussions in a chat as well as data transfer. The 1990s witnessed the birth of private internet service providers which gave rise to personal websites, discussion groups and chat groups. This brought about the need for online media etiquette standard known as netiquette to serve as a control mechanism. The first social networking site, classmate.com was introduced in the mid-1990s. This was closely followed by the invention of blogs in the 1990s. The need to generate user contents gave rise to Web 2.0 (a term commonly associated with web applications) which was created in the late 1990s; this sprang into the early 2000s.

A web 2.0 site gives its users the free choice to interact or collaborate with each other in a social media dialogue as creators of user-generated content in a virtual community. These include social networking sites, blogs, wikis, video sharing site etc. This was closely followed by Web 3.0 which could be described as an extension of Web 2.0's participatory technologies and social networks into 3D space. This has also evolved into Web 4.0, sometimes referred to as the semantic web. The impact of social media in various fields, including librarianship relies on how well an organization's goals are matched with digital technologies as well as the needs of its target (Sajithra & Ratil, 2013). Kaplan and Haenlein (2010) classified social media into six types: collaborative projects, blogs, content communities, social networking sites, virtual social worlds and virtual game worlds.

Social media can be used by individuals and organizations or institutions as a very powerful tool for disseminating information. The library as an institution employs social medial tools for promoting its services and resources. One of the challenges institutions in the information era face is how to harness the potentials of social media tools and get the best results. Social media can be used in a variety of communication methods broadly summarized as broadcast messages, response to enquiries and then conversation between institution and users. Regardless of the approach taken, there are compelling reasons for libraries to engage with social media. Social media offer librarians a way to reach out to their users who may not have considered the library as a resource for their information needs.

One important question that may be asked is: how are social media tools being used by some major libraries across the world? A 2010 survey by the Society of Chief Librarians in the UK found that internet users trust library staff more than most other providers of online support and information, and public library staff are second only to doctors in terms of the trust placed in them by seekers of information. The core of the work of librarians is information sharing; this survey results suggest librarians are in a unique position to implement and exploit social media to their (and their users) advantage (Canty, 2012).

Social media can give a competitive edge in a time of major technological change and competition from other information channels. Libraries need to demonstrate the value of their proposition. Social media give librarians a way to reach out to their users who may not have considered the library as a resource for their information needs (Islam & K. Tsuji, 2016).

Background

Information and communication technology (ICT) has brought great changes in the way individuals, organizations, society and the world at large conduct their day- to – day activities. ICT has not only made creation and access to information very easy, it has made communication of useful information to any part of the world smarter and seamless. Though there are various definition of ICT, the concept may be described as the various technologies (applications, equipment, devices or tools) deployed in the transmission and communication of information. In this regard, social media can be viewed as ICT networking tools designed for social interaction. Boyd and Ellison (2007) defined social network sites as web-based services that allow individuals to (1) construct a public or semi-public profile within a bounded system, (2) articulate a list of other users with whom they share a connection and (3) view and traverse their list of connections and those made by others within the system. The nature and nomenclature of these connections may vary from site to site. Chu and Du (2013) opined that social networking can encompass almost all collaborative environments employing web 2.0 technologies. The original aim of web 2-0 technologies is collaboration among users. It proffers solutions in the use of the internet for interactive purposes engaging tools like blogs, wikis, RSS (Really Simple Syndication), podcasting, social bookmarking, social networking, feeds, and Google (Churchill 2007 as cited by Chu & Du 2013). Any website designed to allow multiple users to publish content of themselves is a social networking site (SNS). The amazing thing about these websites/tools is that they are free, hence users are allowed to create personal pages with content in diverse forms such as images, texts, music, videos etc. Members of the sites are also able to share web pages with friends, search for friends with similar interests and interact for as long as they so desire leading to establishing long and lasting relationships.

Boyd and Ellison (2007) stated that websites vary in terms of features and membership. In other words not all the websites are all-encompassing. Some websites allow photo/video sharing, others blogging, and private messaging while some others are for content sharing. Wikis, blogs, chat rooms, instant messengers, message boards and social bookmarking are web 2.0 technology applications that have been used to facilitate members' interaction and thus are referred to as social networking tools (Jones & Conceicao 2008 as cited by Chu & Du 2013). Burkhardt (2010) posits that the use of social media is all about sharing, learning, ability to have conversations and give same back.

Current trends from literature show that social media use in developed countries is in a very advanced stage; though social media use in developing countries was initially low, it began to steadily increase due to proliferation of mobile devices and internet (Poushter, Bishop & Chwe, 2018). Poushter, Bishop and Chwe (2018) reported that internet use among 19 developing countries increased to a median of 64% in 2017, compared to the 42% increase witnessed in year 2013 and 2014. The same report revealed that a median of 87% was sustained for 17 developed countries who indicated occasionally using the internet. The trend in developing countries applies also to Nigeria. In 2017, it was reported that about 75% of Nigeria's population use the social media for various purposes (Amaefule, 2017).

A major advantage of social media tools lies in their ability to reach a large number of a targeted population within a very short time. It is not surprising therefore that social media tools have become very useful in disseminating library and information services. The use of social media provides tremendous values to the library. Canty (2012) posits that social media can be powerful information dissemination tools and offer a way for libraries to promote their activities, resources, and services while allowing a two-way dialogue with stakeholders. It is also not enough to have these social media but they must be used to enable users appreciate their values. Palmer (2014) supported this assertion by saying that any value created for an organization through social media comes not from any particular platforms but from how they are used. The potential value of social media for academic libraries was recognized comparatively earlier on with the term 'Library 2.0' (referring to the application of web 2.0 online tools to library functions) being coined by Casey in 2005 (Harinarayana & Raju, 2010; Mahmood & Richardson, 2011; Palmer, 2014). Stuart (2010) notes that libraries use social media platform to make their services public. Libraries also use Web. 2.0 technologies to extend their services to students outside the traditional library buildings (Muhamad & Khalid, 2012; Andrea et al, 2010; Matthews, 2006). The traditional library as it is known, confines library users to a particular place or location, but with the introduction of Web. 2.0 technologies to library operations, it is now possible for users to enjoy library services anywhere in the world. On the international platform, libraries have adopted social media tools in marketing and disseminating information services. For example, libraries in the United States, Canada and countries in Western Europe have since adopted social media tools like Facebook, Youtube, Twitter, Flickr and others in carrying out library and information services with great success (Chu & Du, 2013)

Like every other developing country, the adoption of any ICT-based platform is not without challenges in Nigeria. Social media use by Nigerian libraries have been relatively poor, when compared with trends in developed countries. Though a large number of the Nigerian population including librarians and library users are active on social media platforms through mobile technology devices, libraries as organizations are not well equipped with necessary facilities that will facilitate effective and efficient social media use for information service delivery. However, this does not imply that these services do not exist; the crust of the matter is that social media usage in Nigerian libraries is still at infancy stage when compared with their counterparts in developed countries. A review of literature reveals that academic libraries are in the forefront of social media adoption in the country. Amuda and Adeyinka (2017)'s study revealed that social media networks are widely adopted for the delivery of library services by professional librarians in South-West Nigeria. The most popularly used social media in the region include Facebook, Blog, LinkedIn, Twitter, Myspace, Delicious and Flickr, with Facebook being the most used social media network (Olajide, Otunla & Omotayo, 2017). Respondents in this study affirmed that reference services, communication, dissemination of information and news are the major driving motivation for using social media in their respective academic libraries in South-West Nigeria. In this same region, librarians in federal universities make use of social media for the delivery of library services (Adewoyin, Onouha, & Ikonne, 2017). From the study of the latter, the popular social media network used among librarians in this part of the country include: Facebook, WhatsApp, YouTube and Instant message 39.8% most of the time. Olajide, Otunla and Omotayo (2017) also discovered from their study that libraries loved to use visual social media like YouTube, VIMEO and Pinterest, while social media specifically designed for library (e.g. Library Thing and Ning) were not being used. It was also observed from the study that most libraries maintained one social media platform. Again the investigation revealed that collaboration among libraries using social media was poor. In one study titled "Social Media for Library Outreach and Collaboration by Librarians in Private Universities Libraries in South-South Nigeria (Odiachi & Omorodion, 2018), it was revealed that South–South Nigeria Private Universities prefer to use Facebook, WhatsApp, Twitter, Blogs and LinkedIn and that their level of use is very high compared to other social media tools.

TYPES OF SOCIAL MEDIA USED IN LIBRARIES

There are various types of social media tool used in academic libraries. The different types of social media tools or platforms include but are not limited to Facebook, LinkedIn, Google+. Others include Twitter, Tumblr; the photo sharing include Instagram, Snapchat, Pinterest; the video sharing include YouTube, Facebook live, periscope, Vimeo etc. While some of these platforms are popular among Nigerian Libraries and librarians, others are not.

Colburn and Hanes (2012) and Palmer (2014) affirmed that the use of twitter and Facebook seem to be the most commonly observed social media application for libraries. Winn, Rivosecchi, Bjerke, and Groenendyk (2017) during a study on the 'big four' academic libraries in Montreal stated that during the 2015/2016 academic session, the four libraries used five different social media sites: Facebook, Instagram, Pinterest, Twitter, and YouTube.

For the purpose of expanding knowledge, it is important to discuss some social network platforms and applications relevant to libraries.

Facebook

This is a popular social media tool that can be used to reach library audience/users irrespective of where they are. According to Alexa topsites (1996), Facebook is the most visited website in the world with close to one billion users across the world. There are different types of user account under Facebook. They may seem to be serving different purposes; yet they share the same features. They include profiles, groups, and pages. Aharony (2012) as cited by Palmer (2014) posits that to use Facebook, a library would typically create a Facebook page, while Facebook users have a personal profile that allows them to describe themselves and their interests and through this locate and connect with other users and interest groups. There are diverse ways and methods of using these social media such that users are able to maximize their benefits and are also maximally served. Facebook can be used to provide reference services, share information and broadcast news concerning the library. As at today, Facebook is the number one choice social media used by libraries all over the world, including libraries in developing countries like Nigeria (Vassilakaki & Garoufallou, 2014).

To make use of Facebook, a Facebook account must be consciously created using the link Facebook.com. Palmer (2014) averred that individual users, requests to be 'friends' with other users, and if a request is accepted, this connection allows enhanced interactions between the two-users. Now, all the library need do if they know any Facebook account, is send a friend request to these accounts and wait for the requests to be accepted after which interaction has begun. The interactions also referred to as communication takes place on each user's 'wall'. On the 'walls', messages are sent or posted, and replies are made via comments. Users can also 'like' a post or show other emotional feelings by the use of 'emojis' displayed on the posts. Emojis are small digital images used to express one's emotions or feelings during an electronic communication.

Libraries can take advantage of the Facebook feature called 'newsfeed'. The newsfeed is a part of the Facebook where activities of what user's friends have sent or responded to are harvested. It is the main place where all activities on the page are recorded and this notifies a Facebook user of how his/her post is being appreciated or turned down. So libraries can from newsfeed harvest the way they are being appreciated or know what users think about what is posted about them. Once a Facebook user likes a page or a message is shared, any other message(s) the account user sends subsequently, these 'friends' will automatically be able to view the posts. So for a library, when a Facebook user searches out your social media page, likes or expresses his/herself same friend will receive all library services posts deposited on that library's Facebook wall.

Facebook is a very good platform to market whatever the library does. It helps deliver better customer service, promote your library, and drives traffic to your library website and events. One can also be assured that once the Facebook page remains active with relevant contents post from the library, the audience will grow naturally because they will always stop by to check for new, relevant and educative posts and most likely share same on their walls for their friends to read and when their friends are reached, your audience increases and a community is formed.

According to Chen et al (2012), libraries have reported that both twitter and Facebook are used because the features they provide work in related but different ways. The amazing thing about Facebook and twitter is that both platforms can be linked together in order to increase the total reach of libraries social media contents. Saylor, Schnizer, Alee, and Blumenthal (2011) asserted that it is possible to configure twitter and Facebook to automatically route updates in one system to the other, and this has been reported to be useful for libraries that use both systems concurrently.

Twitter

Twitter is a social media tool for communication. Canty (2012) refers to it as a platform possibly better than other platforms which exemplify the ability to enable a rapid two-way dialogue. He added that library use of twitter suggests it is a popular platform for reaching out to communities. There are various services the library can engage in, using twitter. Canty (2012) listed such as operational issues like Library opening and closing hours; showcasing activities of the library; advertising new additions to the library collections; responding to questions and also giving feedback. The way twitter is used actually varies across libraries. Some may choose to adopt a conversational approach while others could go for a conventional 'top down' broadcast medium.

Dickson and Holley (2010), and Kim and Abbas (2010) asserted that twitter is a particular and rapidly growing microblogging service where users can post quick and frequent short messages (up to 140 characters) called tweets. They explained that these tweets may contain links to other online material such as photos and websites, to their 'followers' who have subscribed to their twitter account. Audience can further be reached by the use of hashtags on twitter. The hashtag becomes active when a program or event publicizes a hashtag for its participants to use in order to participate in the event and to enable them collate their tweets by the use of such named hashtags. One event can have as many participants as possible if the few audience reached 'retweets' the content of the sending account. Palmer (2014) averred that except for the content of tweets from protected accounts, all tweets are effectively broadcast to 'the world' and are publicly discoverable via a search. Twitter can be used in the readers' services section to broadcast messages to users on the arrival of new books, and can be used to send notices to borrowers to return borrowed books and many more services provided by the library.

Flickr

This is a photo sharing site. Pictures of events could be shared here include community development visits and others. It is a great channel to display photographic collections (Canty, 2012). Pictures and library images are posted, and shared for the knowledge of library users.

Pinterest

This social media tool is relatively new. It was founded in 2010 (Canty, 2012). It acts like a virtual pin board. It is used in organizing, sharing, images around themes, hobbies and activities such as social events. Libraries can use Pinterest to publicize events like library week and orientation by displaying images and pictures of previous events.

YouTube

This social media tool is great for demonstrating products. It is used to post videos and sometimes static images.

Videos could be streamed and posted on the library website. The key indicator in YouTube is the number of subscribers (Canty, 2012). The number of subscribers shows how much people like the content and wish to maintain contact with the channel. The YouTube channel can be promoted in such a way that users are urged to subscribe to the channel. This is done by the use of prompts and hints. When the library does this successfully, it indicates better engagement and shows that the library has succeeded in building up following viewers and not random viewers.

Ongoing library events can be captured or recorded in camera and shared for a later view. The video could be on the tour of the library. It could augment for fresh students who usually miss the physical library orientation embarked on during school resumptions. The video will help them to get to know the library and the services made available for all library users. Canty (2012) averred that it is more difficult to post decent quality videos than static images. He added that YouTube could also contain contents like interviews, recorded presentations of full conferences. The library can as well add its university's programme like inaugural lectures, special visits, and if there are Vice Chancellors' visits to the library in various institutions depending on the extent to which such activities are allowed to be on the internet.

Blog

Before now, social media tools such as blogs and wikis were seen as ideal channels to disseminate information about a library and her services. Cooper and May (2009) as cited by Collins and Quan-Haase (2014) recorded that the implementation of a blog at a small academic library in Alabama served as an important tool in reaching out to students regardless of their involvement on campus and previous experience with the library. Blogs are considered relevant social media tool because they can be used to send latest happenings in the library. A survey was carried out by Draper and Marthea (2008) and it was discovered that 265 academic librarians used the blog tool overwhelmingly to market the library services. There are some potential library users who may not be aware of the existing resources and services in the library, these social media applications/tools are used to get them to connect and have access to what is made available.

In summary, a lot of libraries tend to adopt different web 2.0 tools but implementation of those tools in different libraries differs. Some libraries prefer to use blogs and RSS feeds as they are seen as being more popular than being interactive. Others use Facebook and twitter. A study conducted by Xu, Ouyang, and Chu, (2009) on the impact of web 2.0 in 81 University libraries in New York revealed that 34 libraries incorporated one or more web 2.0 applications for various purposes. Many of the web 2.0 tools were used as web-based extensions of traditional library services such as reference, news updates and the like. The tools enable librarians to retain custodianship of information and have authority over user account. (Kim & Abbas 2010).

CHALLENGES OF SOCIAL MEDIA USE IN NIGERIA

A developing country (also called less developed or underdeveloped country) is a sovereign state that is not yet highly industrialized compared with other countries and has a low human development index. These countries are found mainly in Africa, South America and parts of Eastern Europe and Asia. In our contemporary world, developed countries which are geographically located in Europe, North America and parts of Asia are highly industrialized and have an edge in science and technology. They also possess greater levels of wealth, with very stable governance structure. Due to their low level industry, human development and socio-economic bases, developing countries are far behind their developed counterparts in terms of ICT acquisition, accessibility and application. As earlier alluded, most developing countries like Nigeria have peculiar challenges in the execution of ICT-based projects. These challenges also affect social media use. Note that some of the challenges outlined here may also be experienced in developed countries, but the enabling environment and policies provided by the Government in these countries have helped libraries to deal with the issues easily.

The challenges of social media use include the following:

Digital Divide and Lack of Infrastructure

Digital divide maybe defined as a technological gap with regard to access to, use of and impact of information and communication technologies among a group of people either within a country or between two or more countries. The gap between countries is termed global digital divide. It is a disparity in the availability, accessibility and deployment of ICT infrastructure between the industrialized or developed and underdeveloped countries. The concept has gained importance because it carries educational and socio-economic inequality consequences. Ogunsola and Okusaga (2006) posited that the line of demarcation between the developed and developing countries is not income (criteria of wealth) but technology (criteria of skill). Digital divide is anchored on inequalities which the emergence of and access to ICTs have either inherited or widened. Indicators show that there is a significant difference between developed and developing countries in terms of availability, affordability, access and use of ICTs. In its report in 2010, the International Telecommunication Union (ITU) observed that 72% of the population in developed countries are internet users, while just 21% of the population in developing countries are internet users (ITU, 2010). Nigeria falls in the developing countries' bracket.

The digital divide is measured through the digital opportunity index (DOI). DOI is an internationally accepted ICT indicator developed to measure and capture technological divides. The digital opportunity index classifies and measures the divide in three categories – opportunity, infrastructure and utilization. Opportunity encompasses accessibility and affordability. Infrastructure include network indicators and availability of facilities. Utilization relates with ICT usage and quality. Ogege (2010) observed that developing countries like Nigeria had very low scores and performed very poorly in the global digital opportunity index indicator released by the International Telecommunication Union (ITU) in 2005. No developing country appeared in the digital opportunity index first 25 top economies. This implies that developing countries are inherently disadvantaged as far as availability and access to ICT infrastructure and electronic resources are concerned. Consequently, it is more expensive and difficult for academic institutions in developing countries to acquire, access and maintain ICT infrastructure and facilities required to manage electronic resources like e-journals.

Nigeria, like other developing countries does not have basic infrastructure needed as foundation on which to run electronic facilities. Poor electricity supply is a common occurrence in Nigeria. It is common place in the country for individuals and institutions to purchase and maintain power plants due to irregular electricity supply from the national grid. Access to adequate bandwidth to run efficient internet system is also a major challenge. Academic institutions and libraries in Nigeria have a lot of hurdles to cross in terms of infrastructure in their quest for access to electronic resources and platforms including social media networks.

Copyright Violations and Plagiarism

The concept of 'cut and paste' is an old long issue and has grown easier over time. The use of intellectual property of others without permission, copying data and circulating/reposting text, quotes, ideas, music, pictures etc. is a popular culture on social media and has become a great source of worry and concern for copyright violations and plagiarism. Ifijeh (2014) warns that this may pose a challenge to Librarians who are not well knowledgeable in the process of establishing originality of idea/content before making information accessible on social media. Rapier (2015) opines that committing copyright or trademark infringement via social media is oftentimes unintentional. Nevertheless, infringing on copyrights has consequences for the librarian, the library and even their users.

Lack of Authentication

Librarians are not just supporting researchers, they carry out researches too. The issue of gathering content for research purposes on social media is faced with a lot of hurdles. There is need for caution in social media data usage, interpretation and generalization. Bright, Margetts, Hale and Yasseri (2014) in their study about using social media and its role in social research and analysis, reported that data sources from most social media are very difficult to authenticate and interpret in isolation. They blamed the situation on the unmitigated number of social networking sites available, continuous changes in user interface; unreliable information sources. This makes it hard for the librarians or library users to utilize them for research. They further recommended the benchmarking of all social media data be against other sources.

Time Consuming

Librarians already have their hands full with their routine duties of cataloguing and classification, collection development etc.; these duties in themselves are time consuming. Collins and Quan-Haase (2012) and Cvetkovic (2009) assert that social media adoption and use by librarians will significantly consume more time and effort. Creating additional time for constantly responding to chats, postings, updates and the likes can be overwhelming for any librarian. Frustrations may set in when Library users queries are not attended to as at when due.

Inadequate Computer Skills

Users of social media are sometimes faced with technical difficulties that cannot be overlooked. Significant computer skills are required for effective use of social media. Herrick and Burriesci (2009) recognize that social media platforms like Wiki require users to know how to use computer markup languages to edit or modify their inputs. Baro, Idiodi and Godfrey (2012) and Mahmood and Richardson (2013) also observed that librarians needed requisite skills for tagging, bookmarking and incorporating social media into their Public Access Catalog. Ezeani and Igwesi (2012) revealed that lack of awareness and training among the library professionals in Nigeria has drastically contributed to the non-use of social media in the library environment. Thanuskodi (2012) submits that librarians who lack adequate social media skills are oftentimes discouraged from adopting and adapting the technologies. Many librarians, considering their training may not possess needed skill to function effectively in this area .This, as observed by Tyner (2010) has prompted academic libraries to hire persons who possess requisite skills in social data analytics and create job titles like web services Librarian or social media librarian for them.

Identity Fraud

Social media often requires a record of personal data input during profile creation/ new sign ups; as expected, this provides enough identifying information about a user to the public. This has turned social media to a one stop shop for information about subscribers. Identity thieves are known for stealing the real identity of an individual and thereafter, create synthetic identities compiled from elements of the data stolen from a user personal information that social media users have on the social networks, exposing the real owners to different levels of risk. Fear of becoming a victim can stand as an impediment to the adoption of social media by librarians. Facebook has tried to reduce this menace by introducing picture guard and picture watermark which are not foolproof but the trend has been on the increase. Mansfield-Devine (2015) apprises that social media providers are not doing enough to create awareness and protect users against identity theft.

Social Media Distractions

The original intent of joining a network may be for information dissemination, user enquiry, academic purposes etc. but often times there are distractions. Herrick and Burriesci (2009) explains that law librarians and law students are often times faced with distractions. They blame the situation on availability of personal data, games, advertisements, captive debates, interesting updates and pictures which can serve as distractions to the users.

Reduced Productivity

Bryson and Forth (2007) define productivity as the output a worker, firm or country generates per unit of labor and capital inputs. Productivity can be measured based on hours spent on a given task. Leftheriotis and Giannakos (2014) posit that internet connectivity and access is commonplace in today's workplace, whether provided by the organization or the individual. According to them, this is responsible for reduced productivity of employees. They argue that social media is rich in time occupying activities and apps e.g. status updates, gaming, betting, chatting etc., persons may spend time on these things instead of performing tasks that are work-related. In order to curb the huge loss of official resources and maintain productivity level, Aguenza, Al-Kassem, and Som, (2012) reported that many organizations and more than half of U.S. employers reportedly block access to social media at work.

Privacy and Confidentiality Issues

Fernandez (2009) maintain that confidentiality is one of the foundations on which librarianship is built and that libraries are trusted for placing value on privacy. The library is supposed to protect confidentiality of users. The history of internet usage or social networks visited by any user should remain confidential and not revealed for any reason. This privacy right is entrenched in ALA intellectual freedom manual, which describes an information seeker's privacy right as "the right to open inquiry without having the subject of one's interest examined or scrutinized by others" (ALA Office for Intellectual Freedom. American Library Association, 2013). McHone-Chase (2009) observes that the challenge is that libraries do not have a social media policy in their libraries. They do not know what confidentiality policies covers and what it does not cover.

Inadequate Understanding of Data Protection Rights

Signing up to a social network of choice is quite easy but it has been revealed that many SM users do not bother to read the policy details, some have a poor understanding of data protection rights guiding the social networks of their choice. Senthil, Saravanakumar, and Deepa (2016) blames this on a dearth of technical makeovers. The assertion that many social media users are not aware of what violates their rights and those of others is a major concern as expressed by Romansky (2014) who strongly believes that data protection rights is an object of serious discussion. Kosta, Kalloniatis, Mitrou and Gritzalis (2010) decry the incautious attitude with which users reveal personal information on social network sites; they blame this on the lack of awareness and understanding of the potential threats and dangers lurking that may arise as a result of this. Bonneau and Preibusch (2010) outlined the lack of awareness on vague terms of agreement, the unnecessary use of legal jargon, the length and content of formal privacy policies as reasons for inadequate understanding of data protection rights among social media users.

Social Media Addiction

According to Ashwini and Samuel (2012), the need to be connected with friends, family, collaborators, co-workers, and classmates has inadvertently led to increased and extensive use of social media. This has also led to Social media addiction which is a growing social problem. Erfanmanesh and Hossseini (2015) compared social media addiction to addictions to substance like alcohol and drugs.

Emotional and Ergonomic Issues

Hansraj (2014) revealed that Surgeons have discovered that people spend 700 to 1400 hours a year looking down as a result of their mobile phones. Slouching has been revealed by the surgeons to affect the body posture, especially the hands, eyes back and other parts of the body. The Surgeons linked poor body posture to chronic pain, cervical scoliosis, breakdown of cervical tissues, headaches and other neurological problems, depression, constipation, and heart disease

Social Media-Induced Techno Stress

Brooks and Califf (2017) postulate that interacting and alternating between multiple social media platforms and technologies while also trying to complete work related tasks simultaneously for a long period of time usually leads to stress.

Information Overload

Bawden, Holtham and Courtney (1999) describes information overload as occurring when information received becomes a hindrance rather than a help. Social media is plagued by rapidly-expanding number of information feeds. Social media users are inundated by sometimes irrelevant innumerous information, sometimes the same information sent over and over again. When the person is overloaded with information, consequently, this affects the time to effectively process the information, the ability to take decisions, and even the final quality of the decision. (Benselin & Ragsdell, 2016).

Cyberbully

Behind a keyboard or phone, young people and adults are emboldened to bully others. Posting hurtful negative remarks or rumors on social media sites for the world to see. Unlike traditional websites, social media comments cannot really be deleted since third party and others who have access may save and continually have the information. These harmful or hurtful information when released has the potential to affect the health, mental, psychological and social well-being of an individual. Many have committed suicide as a result of this (Garett, Lord, and Young, 2016).

Lack of Awareness and Perceived Usefulness

Baro, Idiodi and Godfrey (2012) also noted that many librarians in developing countries like Nigeria are not aware of social media networks. They opine that so many of them do not know how to use web 2.0s to affect their services. Similarly, De Rosa, Cantrell, Havens, Hawk, Jenkin, Gauder, and Cellentani (2007) discovered that many librarians were avers to social media. They saw it as a distraction.

In the same vien, Charnigo and Barnett-Ellis (2007) reported in their survey of academic librarians attitudes about Facebook, that the majority of librarians studied considered Facebook outside the scope of professional librarianship.

Lack of Cyber Knowledge

According to Christie (2017) cyber security is an intimidating subject for most librarians. And that libraries have had their systems breached and infected with malware through social media. Profile hacking and malwares (viruses, Trojans and worms) are some of the most common challenges posed by cyber attackers on social media. Khan and Bhatti (2012) posit that librarians in developing countries lack adequate cyber knowledge and advice that librarians cannot identify their vulnerability and take steps to clamp down on cyber attackers without adequate cyber knowledge.

Poor Academic Performance

While some researchers (Ahmed & Qazi, 2011; Akanbi & Akanbi, 2014) argue that social media usage has no significant impact on academic performance of students in developing countries like Nigeria, other studies (Paul et al., 2012; Burak, 2012; Rouis et al., 2011; Bányai et al., 2017) revealed a drastic drop of grades/poor academic performance among students as a result of heavy social media usage.

Cost Implications

There are cost implications for purchasing and maintaining needed infrastructure in terms of bandwidth requirements of social media, computers and mobile devices, training staff to be active, steady power supply. Many academic libraries are grappling with budget cuts and may see this as unnecessary expenses.

SOLUTIONS AND RECOMMENDATIONS

Bridging the Digital Divide and Provision of Infrastructure

Bridging the digital divide in any nation requires the commitment of the government at the national, state and local or district level. The government must take ICT acquisition as a top priority. This would require allocation of a substantial amount of the nation's budget on the acquisition of ICT infrastructure and facilities and training. There should be an appropriate fiscal policy and discipline on ICT development on a short and long term basis. The initial step would be to import required facilities. However, on the long run, persons would need to be trained abroad who would return back home as indigenous ICT specialists. The indigenous ICT specialists would help to assemble facilities locally, thus reducing the cost of acquisition. Alternatively, foreign ICT specialists may be invited to help train selected individuals locally. Either way, the objective is to make ICT facilities readily available, accessible and very importantly cheaper to acquire.

One big challenge of developing nations is political instability. There is incessant change of government. Unfortunately, each government comes with its own agenda; thus projects started by a particular government are abandoned by subsequent ones. Therefore, to forestall any hitch on the long term plan for ICT acquisition and training, there is need to formulate and legislate a national ICT policy document. Legislating the ICT policy document would compel any government to implement its stipulated contents at any point in time.

Fortunately, the governments of many developing countries are becoming much more interested in ICT acquisition. A few like India and Malaysia are progressing very fast towards attaining self-dependence status.

Provision of Funds and Eradication of Corruption

As earlier noted, cost implication is a major challenge to social media use in developing countries. The situation has become worse in the face of current global economic recession. Libraries and their parent organizations should begin to look for alternative means of generating funds rather than depending on government subventions and allocations. They should seek funds from corporate bodies, multinationals, philanthropic individuals and donor agencies. In this regard, the Carnegie Corporation and MacArthur Foundation in the United States have contributed immensely to the development of higher institutions and libraries in developing countries in terms of ICT deployment. Institutions and libraries should take advantage of the opportunities provided by these bodies to subscribe to electronic journals, as well as acquire necessary facilities to use them.

Institutions and libraries can also take advantage of consortia platforms to reduce cost of acquiring ICT facilities. Consortium provides opportunities to negotiate for cheaper prices on the basis of number. However, efforts must be made to ensure that such consortia are sustainable on the long run. Furthermore, the alumni base of institutions can also be exploited for better funding. This would require the institutions making appeals to their graduates or alumni to make donations towards projects in their alma mater.

No matter the funds provided, if corruption is not eradicated, no laudable objective can be achieved. Governments at all levels in developing countries should take up the responsibility of fighting and eradicating corruption. Like the example of Nigeria, special anti-corruption agencies should be set up to apprehend and prosecute corrupt officials in both public and private sectors. Severe penalties should be meted on convicts to serve as a deterrent to others.

Awareness Creation and Promotion of Information Literacy Programs

Libraries and librarians should offer effective current awareness service to users, by informing users of innovative services and resources available on the library's social media platforms. Kiscaden (2014) discovered that many library users are not aware of tools available to create their own service. According to him, lack of awareness presents a barrier to adoption of ICT-based services. The onus is still on librarians to make individual users responsible for subscribing to various social media platforms.

For effective current awareness services, the Liaison librarians should be responsible for the development and delivery of professional/ specialized information services to support for faculty staff and students. To be effective, they can do the following:

- **Join Research Cluster:** The library needs to maintain close collaboration with faculty, and students' research cluster to identify areas of need that could be addressed by the librarian. In agreement, Federer (2013) opine that librarians possess the required expertise that researchers can harness to help them create better research output especially: performing database searches, locating materials relevant to their research, providing links to critical information in e-journals and citation assistance.
- **User Education/ Awareness:** Foote and Rupp-Serrano 2010 touting the need for awareness, believe that discoverability is paramount for the usage of e-resources. The library is expected to provide adequate platforms for user education/ awareness campaigns. There are different methods of educating users about new developments and services. Through seminars, workshops, YOU-Tube videos, formal and informal training and retraining for the faculty and students on how to carry out better and efficient online searches. Users need to know what the library has as per content, browser requirements, issues concerning location/ access points. Some libraries create information slides, some send links of their social media platforms to the network of faculty and staff. Creating this awareness will result in increased usage and downloads.

Training Programs for Librarians

Sequel to the challenges earlier discussed, there is need for ICT and social media training programs for librarians. Workshops and seminars on ICT skills acquisition would enhance librarians' use of ICT facilities in general and social media in particular. Training programs would also help address critical social media issues like copyrights, privacy and data protection rights, authentication, identity theft, time management and others. These trainings could be organized and facilitated by libraries, Library Associations, Government and non-Governmental agencies.

FUTURE RESEARCH DIRECTIONS

Global trends indicate that social media platforms are effective tools and channels through which libraries can reach their users. Researches carried out in developing countries like Nigeria show that the adoption of ICT related services including social media have been slow due to ICT challenges peculiar to these nations. These peculiar challenges in developing countries have been perennial; there is a need to properly investigate the remote causes of these challenges, with a view to proffering lasting solutions. Therefore, future research directions should focus on dealing with state of social media usage among librarians and library users, formulation of correct hypotheses to test various variables responsible for usage or non-usage of social media platforms as well as uncover remote challenges and proffer lasting solutions.

CONCLUSION

This chapter has dealt with the emergence and concept of social media and their usage among faculties in Nigeria. The chapter outlined the important roles social media use could play in academic libraries. Challenges militating against social media usage in Nigeria (which are generally peculiar to developing countries) were examined and solutions were proffered.

From the aforementioned discussions in the chapter, it is clear that social media usage have come to stay in academic libraries. Authorities of institutions, libraries and other relevant agencies in Nigeria must of necessity make provisions for the full adoption of social media in order to align with global trends. Libraries and librarians should realize that the world has gone digital; they either adapt to the changing academic environment or they will be sidelined and become irrelevant in the scheme of things. They should take personal responsibility for digital and information literacy and be empowered to take full advantage of the opportunities provided by social media tools.

REFERENCES

Adewoyin, O.O., Onuoha, U.D., & Ikonne, C.N. (2017). *Social Media Use and Service Delivery by Librarians in Federal Universities in South-West, Nigeria*. Retrieved from https://digitalcommons.unl.edu/libphilprac/1641/

Aguenza, B. B., Al-Kassem, A. H., & Som, A. P. (2012). Social Media and Productivity in the Workplace: Challenges and Constraints. *Interdisciplinary Journal of Research in Business, 2*(2), 22–26.

Ahmed, T., & Qazi, F. (2011). A look out for academic impacts of social networking sites: A student based perspective. *African Journal of Business Management*, *5*(12), 1–6.

Akanbi, M., & Akanbi, A. (2014). Influence of social media usage on self-image and academic performance among senior secondary school students in Ilorin west Local Government, Kwara State *Int. Res. J. Pure Appl. Phys.*, *24*, 42–50.

ALA office for Intellectual Freedom. (2010). *Intellectual Freedom Manual* (8th ed.). Chicago: ALA Editions.

Amaefule, E. (2017). *75% of Nigeria's Online Population Use Social Media*. Retrieved from https://punchng.com/75-of-nigerias-online-population-use-social-media-minister/

American Library Association. (2013). *Questions and answers on ethics and social media*. Retrieved from: http://www.ala.org/tools/ethics

Amudaa & Adeyinka. (n.d.). Application of Social Media for Innovative Library Services in South-Western Nigerian University Libraries. *Journal of Balkan Libraries Union*. Retrieved from http://dergipark.gov.tr/download/article-file/399735

Ashwini Veronica, S., & Samuel, A. U. (2012, December). Social Media Addiction among Adolescents with Special Reference to Facebook Addiction. *IOSR Journal of Humanities and Social Science*. Retrieved from www.iosrjournals.org

Bányai, F., Zsila, Á., Király, O., Maraz, A., Elekes, Z., Griffiths, M. D., ... Demetrovics, Z. (2017). Problematic social media use: Results from a large-scale nationally representative adolescent sample. *PLoS One*, *12*(1), e0169839. doi:10.1371/journal.pone.0169839 PMID:28068404

Baro, E., Idiodi, E., & Godfrey, V. (2012). Awareness and use of Web 2.0 tools by librarians in university libraries in Nigeria. *OCLC Systems & Services*, *29*(3), 170–188. doi:10.1108/OCLC-12-2012-0042

Bawden, D., Holtham, C., & Courtney, N. (1999). *Perspectives on information overload*. Aslib. doi:10.1108/EUM0000000006984

Bedell, J. (2010, September 20). *What is the Difference Between Social Media and Social Networking?* Retrieved December 2, 2010, from http://jasontbedell.com/what-is-the-difference-between-social-media-and-social-networking

Benselin, J. C., & Ragsdell, G. (2016). Information overload: The differences that age makes. *Journal of Librarianship and Information Science*, *48*(3), 284–297. doi:10.1177/0961000614566341

Bentenbi. (2010). Towards a Visibility of Algerian Libraries in a Social Media Era. *Cybrarian Journal*, (12), 28. Retrieved from http://www.journal.cybrarians.org/index.php?option=com_content&view=article&id=622:socialmedia&catid=255:09-studies&Itemid=89

Bonneau, J., & Preibusch, S. (2010). The Privacy Jungle:On the Market for Data Protection in Social Networks. In T. Moore, D. Pym, & C. Ioannidis (Eds.), *Economics of Information Security and Privacy*. Boston, MA: Springer. doi:10.1007/978-1-4419-6967-5_8

Borders, B. (2010). *A Brief History of Social Media*. Retrieved from http://socialmediarockstar.com/history-of-social-media

Breeding, M. (2007). Librarians face online social networks. *Computers in Libraries*, *27*(8), 30–33. Retrieved from https://librarytechnology.org/repository/item.pl?id=12735

Bright, J., Margetts, H., Hale, S., & Yasseri, T. (2014). *The use of social media for research and analysis: A feasibility study*. Retrieved from https://www.gov.uk/government/publications/use-of-social-media-for-research-and-analysis

Brooks, S., & Califf, C. (2017). Social media-induced techno stress: Its impact on the job performance of it professionals and the moderating role of job characteristics. *Computer Networks*, *114*, 143–153. doi:10.1016/j.comnet.2016.08.020

Bryson, A., & Forth, J. (2007). *Productivity and days of the week*. Royal Society for the Encouragement of Arts, Manufactures & Commerce. Retrieved from https://eprints.lse.ac.uk/4963/1/daysoftheweek%28LSEROversion%29.pdf

Burak, L. (2012). Multitasking in the University classroom. *International Journal for the Scholarship of Teaching and Learning*, *6*(2), 1–12. doi:10.20429/ijsotl.2012.060208

Buruga, B. A. (2016). *The Use of Mobile Technologies for Social Media-Based Service Delivery at Muni University Library, Uganda*. Retrieved from https://repository.up.ac.za/bitstream/handle/2263/58991/Buruga_Use_2016.pdf?sequence=4

Canty, N. (2012). Social Media in Libraries: It's like, Complicated. *The Journal of Library and International Library and Information Issues*, *23*(2).

Charnigo, L., & Barnett-Ellis, P. (2007). Checking out Facebook.com: The impact of a digital trend on academic libraries. *Information Technology and Libraries*, *26*(1), 23–34. doi:10.6017/ital.v26i1.3286

Christie, P. (2017). Cyber-security - what your library needs to know. *Vable*. Retrieved from https://www.vable.com/blog/cyber-security-what-your-library-needs-to-know

Chu, S., & Du, H. (2013). Social Networking Tools for Academic Libraries. *Journal of Librarianship and Information Science*, *45*(1), 64–75. doi:10.1177/0961000611434361

Cohen, L. S. (2009, April 30). *Is There A Difference Between Social Media And Social Networking?* Retrieved from http://lonscohen.com/blog/2009/04/difference-between-social-media-and-social-networking/

Cvetkovic, M. (2009). Making Web 2.0 work – from 'Librarian Habilis' to 'Librarian Sapiens'. *Computers in Libraries*, *29*(9), 14–17.

Dawson, M., Wright, J., & Omar, M. (2015). Mobile Devices: The Case for Cyber Security. *New Threats and Countermeasures in Digital Crime and Cyber Terrorism*, 8.

De Rosa, C., Cantrell, J., Havens, A., Hawk, J., Jenkins, L., Gauder, B., & Cellentani, D. (2007). Sharing, privacy and trust in our networked world: A report to the OCLC Membership. Dublin, OH: OCLC Online Computer Library Center. *Electronic Journal of Research in Educational Psychology*, *9*(3), 961–994.

Edosomwan, S., Prakasan, S. K., Kouame, D., Watson, J., & Seymour, T. (2011). The History of Social Media and its Impact on Business. *The Journal of Applied Management and Entrepreneurship*, *16*(3), 79–91.

Erfanmanesh, M., & Hossseini, E. (2015). Internet and Social Media Addiction. *Webology, 12*(2), 1–3. Retrieved from https://search.proquest.com/docview/1787761590?accountid=14548%0Ahttps://julac.hosted.exlibrisgroup.com/openurl/HKU_ALMA/SERVICES_PAGE??url_ver=Z39.88-2004&rft_val_fmt=info:ofi/fmt:kev:mtx:journal&genre=unknown&sid=ProQ:ProQ%3Alisa&atitle=Internet+and+Socia

Ezeani, C. N., & Igwesi, U. (2012). Using social media for dynamic library services delivery: the Nigerian experience. *Library Philosophy and Practice*. Retrieved from http://digitalcommons.unl.edu/libphilprac/814

Fernandez, P. (2009). Online Social Networking Sites and Privacy: Revisiting Ethical Considerations for a New Generation of Technology. *Library Philosophy and Practice*, *2009*, 1–9.

Hartshorn, S. (2010). *5 Differences between Social Media and Social Networking*. Retrieved December 1, 2010, from socialmediatoday: http://www.socialmediatoday.com/SMC/194754

Ifijeh, G. (2014). Adoption of digital preservation methods for theses in Nigerian academic libraries: Applications and implications. *The J. of Acad. Lib*, *40*, 399–404.

Information Professionals' Knowledge Sharing Practices in Social Media. A Study of Professionals in Developing Countries. *International Journal of Knowledge Content Development & Technology*, *6*(2), 43-66. Retrieved from http://ijkcdt.net/xml/08903/08903.pdf

Islam & Tsuji. (2016). Information Professionals' Knowledge Sharing Practices in Social Media: A Study of Professionals in Developing Countries. *International Journal of Knowledge Content Development & Technology*, *2*(6), 43–66. Retrieved from http://ijkcdt.net/_common/do.php?a=full&b=12&bidx=669&aidx=8903

Kaplan, A. M., & Haenlein, M. (2010). Users of the World, Unite! The Challenges and Opportunities of Social Media. *Business Horizons*, *53*(1), 59–68. doi:10.1016/j.bushor.2009.09.003

Khan, S. A., & Bhatti, R. (2012). *A review of problems and challenges of library professionals in developing countries including Pakistan.* Retrieved from http://digitalcommons.unl.edu/libphilprac/757/

Kiscaden, E. (2014). *Creating a Current Awareness Service Using Yahoo! Pipes and LibGuides Information Technology and Libraries.* Retrieved from https://ejournals.bc.edu/ojs/index.php/ital/article/download/5273/pdf

Kosta, E., Kalloniatis, C., Mitrou, L., & Gritzalis, S. (2010). Data protection issues pertaining to social networking under EU law. *Transforming Government: People, Process and Policy*, *4*(2), 193–201. doi:10.1108/17506161011047406

Leftheriotis, I., & Giannakos, M. N. (2014). Using social media for work: Losing your time or improving your work? *Computers in Human Behavior*, *31*(1), 134–142. doi:10.1016/j.chb.2013.10.016

Mabweazara, R. M. (2014). *Use of social media tools by library staff at the University of the Western Cape, South Africa and the National University of Science and Technology, Zimbabwe.* Retrieved from http://etd.uwc.ac.za/xmlui/handle/11394/4120

Mahmood, K., & Richardson, J. V. Jr. (2013). Impact of Web 2.0 technologies on academic libraries: A survey of ARL libraries. *The Electronic Library*, *31*(4), 508–520. doi:10.1108/EL-04-2011-0068

Maisiri, E., Mupaikwa, E., & Ngwenya, S. (2015). *Strategic Planning for Social Media in Libraries: The Case of Zimbabwe.* Information Science Reference, IGI Global. Retrieved from http://ir.nust.ac.zw/xmlui/bitstream/handle/123456789/515/Strategic%20Planning%20for%20social%20media%20in%20libraries.pdf?sequence=1&isAllowed=y

Mansfield-Devine, S. (2015). Computer Fraud & Security: Editorial. *Computer Fraud and Security, 2015*(6). doi:10.1016/S1361-3723(15)30052-X

McHone-Chase, S. (2009). Privacy and Confidentiality Issues: A Guide for Libraries and their Lawyers. *Reference and User Services Quarterly*, *49*(1), 104–105. doi:10.5860/rusq.49n1.104

Mpoelong, D., Totolo, A., & Jibril, L. (2015). *Perception of University of Botswana Librarians on the potential of Web 2.0 Tools (IFLA, WLIC, 2015).* Retrieved from https://www.ifla.org/files/assets/reference-and...services/.../210-mpoeleng-en.doc1.pdf

Mwangi, M. W., & Wagoki, J. (2016). Effect of Social Media on Performance of Advertisement Business in the Mainstream Media in Kenya: A Survey of Leading Media Groups in Kenya. *International Journal of Economics, Commerce and Management United Kingdom*, *4*(4), 159. Retrieved from: http://ijecm.co.uk/

Njoroge, G. G., & Kange'the, P. (2013). *University Libraries and Social Media: The Case of the Post-modern Library, Kenyatta University*. Retrieved from http://0277.ch/ojs/index.php/cdrs_0277/article/view/14/53

Odiachi, R. A., & Omorodion, O. (2018). *Use of Social Media for Library Outreach and Collaboration by Librarians in Private Universities Libraries in South-South Nigeria*. Retrieved from https://www.researchgate.net/publication/323782017

Olajide, Otunla, & Omotayo. (2017). How Libraries are Using Social Media: Nigeria Perspective. *International Journal of Digital Library Services, 7*(3). Retrieved from http://www.ijodls.in/uploads/3/6/0/3/3603729/8ijodls3717.pdf

Omorodion, O. (2018). *Librarians' Awareness of Social Media Usage for Informal Scientific Communication in University Libraries in South-south, Nigeria*. Retrieved from https://digitalcommons.unl.edu/cgi/viewcontent.cgi?article=4847&context=libphilprac

Paul, J., Baker, H., & Cochran, J. (2012). Effect of online social networking on student academic performance. *Computers in Human Behavior*, *51*(8), 249–255.

Poushter, J., Bishop, C., & Chwe, H. (2017). *Social Media Use Continues to Rise in Developing Countries but Plateaus Across Developed Ones: Digital Divide Remain both within and across Countries.* Retrieved from: http://assets.pewresearch.org/wp-content/uploads/sites/2/2018/06/15135408/Pew-Research-Center_Global-Tech-Social-Media-Use_2018.06.19.pdf

Rapier, R. (2015, June 22). *Fair Use or Misuse? Social Media and Copyright Law*. Retrieved from https://www.ncu.edu/blog/fair-use-or-misuse-social-media-and-copyright-law

Rimskii, V. (2011). The influence of the Internet on active social involvement and the formation and development of identities. *Russian Social Science Review*, *52*(1), 79–101. doi:10.1080/10611428.2011.11065416

Ritholz, B. (n.d.). *History of social media*. Retrieved December 05, 2010, Retrieve from http://www.ritholtz.com/blog/2010/12/history-of-social-media/

Romansky, R. (2014). Problems of Privacy and Data Protection in Online Learning Based on the Network Space. In *International Conference on e-Learning'14* (pp. 187–193). Retrieved from http://elearning-conf.eu/docs/cp14/paper-28.pdf

Rouis, S., Limayem, M., & Salehi-Sangari, E. (2011). *Impact of facebook usage on students' academic achievement: Role of self-regulation and trust*. Retrieved from https://eric.ed.gov/?id=EJ960123

Sajithra, K., & Rajindra, P. (2013). Social Media- History and Components. *IOSR Journal of Business Management*, *7*(1), 69–74. doi:10.9790/487X-0716974

Scott, P. R., & Jacka, J. (2011). *Auditing Social Media: A Governance and Risk Guide*. Hoboken, NJ: Wiley.

Thanuskodi, S. (2012). Awareness of library 2.0 applications among library and information science professionals at Annamalai University, India. *International Journal of Library Science*, *1*(5), 75–83. doi:10.5923/j.library.20120105.02

Tyner, R. (2010, August 3). Re: Is There a Social Media Librarian In Your Library's Future? [Blog comment]. Retrieved from http://acrlog.org/2010/08/03/is-there-a-social-media-librarian-in-your-l...

Vatter, Z. (2016). *Sing Social Media for Libraries*. Retrieved from http://www.peacelibrarysystem.ab.ca/sites/default/files/images/peacelibrarys ystem/Social%20Media%20for%20Libraries%20-%20Introduction.pdf

Zainuddin. (n.d.). Social Media Promotional Tools: Academic Library. *Journal of Computer Theory and Engineering*, *8*(3), 40 – 46.

Chapter 15
No Budget, No Barriers: How Academic Branch Libraries Can Make Twitter Work

Chris Kretz
Stony Brook University, USA

William Blydenburgh
Stony Brook University, USA

ABSTRACT

This chapter provides a roadmap for Twitter use by academic libraries at a branch, remote, or satellite campus. These smaller libraries, operating at a distance from the center of their institution, often face challenges relating to their budget, resources, and status. The use of Twitter can empower a branch to serve their unique populations more effectively, promote engagement within the local community, and establish a presence for the branch within the institution. The authors provide strategies and suggestions for managing Twitter based upon their own experiences while managing the Southampton Campus Library of Stony Brook University Twitter account.

INTRODUCTION

Since Twitter debuted in 2006, it has become a significant part of the popular and cultural landscape. It has been used by a wide range of organizations, businesses, and individuals as a means to further their missions, support their brands, and engage with their communities. Over that time, Twitter has also become a staple of the academic library's social media portfolio. The ease of starting and the simplicity of using this microblogging platform belie its potential impact. Allowing users to post text of up to 280 characters as well as share content in the form of links, images, and videos, Twitter is a potent mechanism for distributing information and building community.

Twitter use in academic libraries has also evolved since 2006. Initially seen by many as a one-way broadcasting channel for disseminating library information, Twitter has since been adapted to more innovative and engaging uses. Academic libraries have recognized the platform's power to create community,

DOI: 10.4018/978-1-5225-8097-3.ch015

foster interaction, and extend the reach of their message. Given this, any rationale for using Twitter in an academic library is equally valid for a branch campus library. In fact, Twitter can have an even greater impact for branch libraries. Often located far from the center of their institution with limited staff and budget, branch libraries nevertheless can leverage Twitter to build a network of engaged followers, create compelling content, and interact with their main institution and surrounding community.

This chapter examines ways in which branch campus libraries can overcome barriers to Twitter use, no matter what they might be. The authors will provide supporting rationales for the maintenance of local Twitter accounts at branch libraries as well as strategies and tips for growing, maintaining, and assessing the results. Examples provided are from the experiences of the chapter's authors while operating the Twitter account for the Stony Brook University Southampton campus library in New York, along with research from the field.

Although this chapter uses the term *branch campus library* throughout, there are many similar terms that could be applied. Branch campus is not meant to be exclusive or to denote a specific administrative or conceptual model. It is used here as an umbrella term to describe any academic library within a multi-library system that: a) operates at a geographic location removed from the main library, b) serves a unique patron base, c) maintains a distinct collection development focus, and d) interacts with its own local community. This would include libraries at satellite, remote, and distant campuses. It is hoped that the strategies and tips in this chapter can be applied in numerous library situations, even for branches within a public library system.

BACKGROUND

Many decisions have to be made before establishing a library Twitter account. These range from how the account will be handled, who will contribute content, how they will be trained, and how they will represent the library online (Appleton & Tattersall, 2015; Burkhardt, 2010; Farkas, 2009). Clear assessment goals and expectations should also be formulated at the outset to keep library Twitter use on track (Ramsey & Vecchione, 2014).

It is also important to have a clear sense of mission. Academic libraries have taken to Twitter for a variety of reasons. Some focus on sharing library news, promoting services, and building community (Loudon & Hall, 2010; Vassilakaki & Garoufallou, 2015). Others have centered their efforts on promoting the physical library environment and providing access to content (Harrison, Burress, Velasquez, & Schreiner, 2017).

The intended audience is also a vital element of a Twitter strategy. Students, an obvious choice for academic libraries, may prove the hardest audience to cultivate. Twitter use among people in the typical college-aged demographic, 18-24-year olds, stands at just 45% (Pew Research, 2018). However, college students have also expressed a preference for receiving library information over Twitter (Howard, Huber, Carter, & Moore 2018). For branch campus libraries, which may be serving smaller student populations to begin with, other audiences can be just as valuable. Studies have shown that the most important followers for an academic library are other accounts from within their institution, such as academic departments and administrative units (Kim, Abels, & Yang, 2012; Shulman, Yep, & Tomé, 2015; Stewart & Walker, 2017).

However the audience is defined, engaging with them is critical and yet this engagement is something that academic libraries have at times struggled to do well (Emery & Schifeling, 2015). Built on a network of relationships, Twitter rewards interaction and reciprocity (Mon & Lee, 2015). Following back, responding to comments, and conversing readily with followers are all important activities. To that end, the successful academic library on Twitter will avoid the use of a remote, authoritarian tone in content, favoring instead a more human, even quirky voice when tweeting (Chatten, 2017; Young & Rossmann, 2015).

In addition to the foregoing concerns, Twitter use by branch campus libraries will be impacted by the very nature of a branch campus. Functioning separately yet existing as part of a wider institution, branches have their own specific issues. In terms of identity, the branch campus can be struggling for status, or to define its uniqueness, or address resource disparities (MacDonald, 2013). Varying degrees of branch autonomy can also exist, based on how the campus is organized and administered. This can lead to a number of different strategic approaches that may be taken towards any issues (Dengerink, 2001).

The library on a branch campus faces its own challenges. The fact that each campus provides services to a unique student body can lead to a culture that differs from the main campus library (Knickman & Walton, 2014; Markland, Rempel, & Bridges, 2017). The diverse mix of programs and physical spaces that can exist at different branches often require different approaches to introducing library services (Dryden & Goldstein, 2013). As for staff at branch locations, they face issues of autonomy balanced against the need for inclusion with the main campus, exacerbated by the added logistics of travel (Phinney & Horsman, 2018). Many employees at branch libraries feel a lack of collaboration opportunities (Bottorff, Glaser, Todd, & Alderman, 2008). Additionally, branch campus libraries face the need to engage with their surrounding community and promote the image of the institution (Schneider, 2001). Research into these types of libraries – whether they be referred to as branches, satellite, regional, or distance libraries – is limited (Brandt, Frederiksen, Schneider, & Syrkin, 2005).

Twitter can be used to alleviate many of the above-mentioned issues between a branch and a main campus. While academic libraries have made effective use of other social media platforms like Facebook (Ofili & Emwanta, 2014; Phillips, 2011) and Instagram (Wallis, 2014; Wilkinson, 2018), Twitter provides a ready opportunity for the branch campus library. The relative simplicity and ease of starting a Twitter account make it a great entry point into social media. As will be shown, Twitter can also be a potent vehicle for promoting the branch library's activities and services to the wider institution. Twitter places the branch digitally on the greater campus map, allowing it to participate in conversations through social media and to engage in mutually beneficial support activities with the rest of the institution. The ensuing connections enable relationships to form with people and offices from the main campus that the branch staff may never meet in person.

The authors of this chapter will lay out a framework for developing Twitter at a branch campus library. Examples are drawn from their experiences maintaining the Twitter account of Stony Brook University's Southampton Campus Library (@SBShamptonlib), along with practices drawn from research in the field. Stony Brook Southampton is part of the State University of New York (SUNY). The campus is located within the town of Southampton on the south shore of Long Island. It is the third Stony Brook campus in the region. The Main campus with its Melville Library and the East Campus with its Health Science Library are both located some 40 miles to the northwest in Stony Brook, New York. Southampton is staffed by one full time faculty librarian and two full time staff with varying levels of student assistants. The branch library serves a mix of graduate-level Health Science programs, a Master of Fine Arts (MFA) in creative writing, and a Marine Science research center operated by the School of Marine and Atmospheric Sciences (SOMAS).

As a small branch library facing many of the issues discussed in this chapter, the Southampton Library made a conscious effort to pursue Twitter as its major social media platform due its ease of use and the facility with which the available staff could create content. When the new Head Librarian came on board in October 2016, the library Twitter account had already been established and was growing rapidly. By going through the thought process outlined below and applying many of the strategies mentioned, the authors were able to continue that growth while utilizing Twitter to promote awareness of the branch library throughout the wider institution.

TWITTER IN BRANCH LIBRARIES

Policies

Before establishing a Twitter account, it is important to review existing policy with all of those involved. Most large universities will have social media guidelines to inform and direct any library's social media activity. Typically, these guidelines will cover things like the tone of voice used in posting, how to represent the University, and how to cultivate a positive presence online. In terms of the actual management of a Twitter account, studies have found that a flexible policy works best. Guidelines that empower rather than proscribe help establish a healthy social media presence (Ramsey & Vecchione, 2014). The Southampton Library found that a firm understanding of the overall principles and goals of the Twitter account motivates people to tweet creatively, as opposed to trying to spell out rules for every possible contingency.

Tone/Voice

Social media has produced user expectations of direct and personal interaction with the institutions they follow online. Striking the right tone in these interactions will determine overall success. While this is arguably key to any communication, the stakes are higher in social media. If a message doesn't come off right, the ramifications can haunt an institution to no end. Whether it's attracting an online troll or a local boycott, the perils of tone are just as real as the content one chooses to post. Managing a Twitter account, like any social media account, can be as challenging as it is rewarding. A branch library's Twitter account is representing not just the branch but the institution as a whole.

The more conversational nature of Twitter should also be kept in mind when dealing with things like typos or missed hashtags and the like. Tweets cannot be edited once they are posted but if caught quickly, mistyped messages can be deleted and reposted. However, the longer a tweet has been public and the more impressions it has garnered, the better it is to embrace any minor mistakes with transparency and humor. Rather than deleting it outright, commenting on an original post with a correction and a mea culpa will suffice.

How Often to Tweet

There is no hard and fast rule as to how often one needs to post content. Too many tweets will feel like spam, leading people to unfollow or block an account. Conversely, an account that goes dormant for long stretches is one people will give up on and unfollow. Striking the right balance takes some time, influenced by the number of staff who are involved. In the authors' experience, a key to establishing a social media presence is posting routinely enough to put followers in the habit of checking for the account's content. Estimate a pace of 3 tweets a day to ensure an ideal presence. There are tips and strategies, discussed later, that will help to keep this level of posting on track.

Who Tweets

The act of tweeting involves composing content and posting it through Twitter's app or web page. Having more people involved in tweeting can help alleviate pressure and can lead to a broader range of content (Barnes, 2014). While a single person may often be tasked with starting a Twitter account at a branch library, this does not have to preclude others from participating. Even with limited staff, others can play a role by contributing content offline, monitoring the Twitter timeline, and suggesting strategies. Student workers and interns are other sources of personnel to enlist in maintaining the Twitter account. Use of these workers not only gives the library help from people closer to the potential target audience, it enriches the work experience for the student, giving them new skills in social media management, communications, editing, and writing.

Realistically, not all library staff will be interested in or adept at using social media. The authors have found that it helps to recruit staff who are already familiar with Twitter, who use it themselves, and who recognize the value of the library's use of social media.

No matter who tweets, it is important for the library to have guidelines for how and where it is carried out. Many staff and librarians will have personal Twitter accounts that they use on a daily basis. The line between personal and professional Twitter activity should be delineated as clearly as possible (Farkas, 2009). If those tweeting are using their personal devices with access to the library account, it is important to stay vigilant. Whenever working with personal devices, especially if the person also maintains a personal Twitter account, avoid posting content to the wrong account at all cost.

To avoid this potential confusion, material for posting can be collected offline through a central point – sent by email or uploaded to a shared drive like Google Docs. The administrator would then compose or schedule the tweets from this clearinghouse of content, proofing the text and attaching appropriate links and media files. This approach leads to tighter editorial control but it can also slow down the process and lead to logjams in posting.

A more distributed model for posting would entail multiple people with direct access to the Twitter account posting from an office desktop or laptop in the library. If the branch has a shared mobile device, posting could be done by whoever has the device at the moment, with the Twitter app automatically logged into the account.

Equipment

All that is required to open a Twitter account is a desktop or laptop computer and an internet connection. This minimum initial investment makes Twitter, as a social media platform, ideal for the branch library on a budget. Having said that, however, expanding beyond this basic setup can allow for more flexibility in running the account and increased engagement with the library's content. Specifically, better results can be achieved if one can work with a camera-enabled mobile device. Media, as will be discussed, enhances engagement with content on Twitter. If there is anywhere to allocate money in the social media plan, a device for media production would be it.

The purchase of a camera-enabled tablet or mobile device, readily accessible to the staff involved, can be of great importance. It allows for:

- The capture of high quality photographs
- The ability to record video
- Responsiveness and the ability to react to events and opportunities as they happen in and around the library
- Streamlined access to the library's other social media accounts on the device
- The use of apps (many of which are free) for photo editing
- Accessibility, as the device can be shared among staff

If the outright purchase of a device for the branch is not feasible, look to borrow a camera from a different area of campus such as a communications office or from the main library itself. If need be, plan to have someone come out at specific times of the year and photograph the branch space. With adequate planning, one can amass a stockpile of images that can be used on Twitter throughout the year.

Another option for capturing images and video is the use of a personal device. Mobile phones are ubiquitous and most have camera and video capabilities that are more than adequate for the demands of Twitter. As discussed, there are policy implications when using personal devices and care should be taken to separate library material from personal photos. To alleviate risk, personal devices can be used to gather content that is then forwarded - either by email or to a shared drive - to be posted to the Twitter account at a later date.

The Southampton Library uses a range of approaches. Personal devices are used to capture images and video which are then shared to a centrally located folder for later use. Additionally, periodic visits from the main library's Multimedia Resources Specialist help capture high-quality images using advanced equipment. Cameras from the main library have also been borrowed for periods of time to cover special events and workshops.

Content Creation

The thought of coming up with a constant stream of ideas for content on Twitter can seem daunting, but libraries have proven a source of never-ending ideas. Research has shown that many libraries post content on Twitter revolving around three basic areas: community-building in and around the university, the portrayal of the library as an inviting space, and the sharing of content drawn from archives, collections, and exhibits (Harrison, Burress, Velasquez, & Schreiner, 2017). In a study that analyzed 1,200 tweets from six large academic libraries, Stvilia and Gibradze (2014) found the most frequent categories of tweets focused on: events, resources, community building, operations updates, study support, Q & A, surveys, staffs, and clubs. When surveyed directly about what Twitter content they would be interested in seeing from an academic library, students expressed an interest in campus-wide information and events, research techniques/tips, and library logistics (Brookbank, 2015).

These general topic areas can serve as a foundation of ideas to distinguish one library on Twitter from another.

Using the Physical Space

A branch library's physical space should be a key component of its Twitter activity. As no two libraries are exactly alike, emphasizing the distinct look of the library through visual content is a great strategy. Pictures give followers a sense of the library as place and also present the best image of the institution to the public. Also, the more remote the branch is from other campuses, the more likely that Twitter will be the one consistent window through which others in the institution view the branch.

Aim to highlight as many specific locations in the library as possible. These can range from quiet study areas to group meeting spaces or even favorite study spots suggested by students. Similarly, one can spotlight unique architectural details: vaulted ceilings, floor-to-ceiling windows, balconies, and works of art. All of these can inspire great aesthetic interest. A tighter focus on space can also convey information: whiteboards with interesting messages, or study tables full of students during finals. What seems of no consequence to one person will appeal to someone else. The Southampton Library routinely documents on Twitter the major milestones of its water refilling station. This may seem inconsequential to some, but saving 15,000 water bottles garners a good response from the marine science students.

Look for opportunities to photograph the space in all types of weather conditions. Blizzards and storms raging outside lend an element of drama and also make compelling short video clips. Long shadows across desks, sunsets behind buildings, and glimpses of activity through the book stacks are all ways of capturing the atmosphere and activity of a branch library. Be creative and think of ways to add drama to visuals.

Displays

Any physical display in the library is ready-made for sharing on social media. Presenting photos of the display on Twitter not only documents activity in the library, it also extends the reach of the display. While many visitors will view the display while it is up in the library, sharing it on Twitter along with relevant text and hashtags gives extra life to what is often a time-consuming project to create. Make sure to identify any relevant hashtags or Twitter accounts to mention when posting. Authors will be interested in seeing their books on display and fans of various genres will be a natural audience. Timing displays to particular events or moments in the culture can also increase exposure. Figure 1 shows a display of the Southampton Library's graphic novel collection that ran during the New York City Comicon convention.

The Collection

Do not overlook the value of the physical collection as well. Books can be photographed to highlight new acquisitions, to celebrate literary anniversaries, or to spotlight individual authors. A challenge for academic libraries, visually speaking, will come from working with books stripped of their original dust jackets. As a workaround, try photographing the interior title pages or stack books together and capture their spines. Additionally, mylar-encased book jackets can be difficult to photograph due to their reflectivity. Experiment with locations and camera angles for best effects.

Figure 1. Graphic novel display tweeted with #NYCC hashtag (Southampton Library)
Source: Southampton Library 2018

Many libraries have taken to creating large-scale displays of books that border on book art – volumes stacked into the form of snowmen or jack-o-lanterns, for example. Keep an eye out for such creative ways to repurpose books in photos, even on a small scale. The Southampton Library has become adept at creating spontaneous book art – using items from the physical collection to highlight occasions on Twitter: everything from Valentine's Day to National Pancake Day to S'mores Day. Even a plain black hardcover book can serve as a stand-in for an Oreo on National Cookie Day.

A Social Media Space

To capitalize on the idea of library space as content, try to identify a specific area within the library as a social media production zone. This does not entail any major construction or interior design but simply identifying a space that lends itself to display on a routine basis. Look for areas with shelves suitable for outward-facing books along with plenty of flat surfaces for objects to be photographed. It should be a relaxed space where people tend to gather and engage with communal projects, games, or similar activities. Consider these types of areas as staging grounds or digital store windows, places where the physical meets the digital. A social media space should be fun: ever-changing, creative, and not always making complete sense. Leave random objects in there, such as antiques, 3D-printed objects, old board games, and promotional items.

At the Southampton Library, an open seating area near the main stacks was converted into the Book Lounge. The relaxed atmosphere of this area along with a number of display shelves as well as the library's literary journal collection made it a go-to source for capturing images for Twitter. As an added bonus, a number of metal floor-to-ceiling poles in the space have become perfect spots to hang printed quotations on a rotating basis as seen in Figure 2. Suitable for photographing, they have since been dubbed "the quote pole."

Figure 2. The book lounge at the Southampton Library (Southampton Library)
Source: Southampton Library 2018

Academic Programs

As many branch libraries serve distinct academic programs, Twitter use at these libraries should reflect that fact. Targeting content at students and faculty in specific programs helps build a community of engagement. It also represents an added value proposition for students, an incentive to follow the library's Twitter account. There are several ways the branch can approach this activity.

The most obvious would be tweeting content directly related to specific academic studies: links to library resource guides, databases suggestions, reference sources, or new books in the collection. Also consider retweeting non-library information relevant to each program's field of study. This can be articles from professional and trade organizations, write-ups of new research findings, or reports from important conferences. Part of this work is aided by being aware of prominent hashtags related to each field. Given the nature of programs at Stony Brook's Southampton campus, the Southampton Library habitually tracks occurrences of the hashtags #OT and #PT (occupational and physical therapy) as well as #amwriting for the MFA program. Information that might be of interest to students in those programs gets liked and retweeted. Sharing this content makes the branch library's Twitter feed a type of current awareness service for students. This practice of sharing program-specific content also models Twitter use for students, showing them how Twitter can be used to engage with their profession and enhance their professional development activities.

Branch libraries can also use Twitter to play a part in the life of an academic program. Every program has its yearly routines - recurring assignments, special events, and high-stress periods. Be attuned to what is happening and share related content when the opportunity arises. The Southampton Library routinely documents the activities of the annual Kinesiology Fair on campus, tweeting images of the student-created projects and associated information.

Events

Live events and workshops in academic libraries have become an important outreach and engagement activity. Bringing people together on campus, these activities also attract members of the community and show the library as a vibrant hub of ideas and shared experiences. Twitter can play a number of roles in these events. As part of the initial marketing strategy, Twitter can promote events and create interest among the branch library's followers. Using Twitter to add a real-time element during the event, however, can garner further attention. Live-tweeting in the moment lets those off-campus experience the event on some level and may entice them to attend the next.

If possible, assign the live-tweeting responsibility to a specific person to act like a 'social media DJ'. To start, have them capture the early stages of the event, letting any followers in the area know that there is still time to attend. Without interfering with the speaker, one can also post quotes and updates during the event. Always follow up with a thank you to the speaker and any collaborating organizations, making sure to include any related Twitter accounts and relevant hashtags. This is good practice but also expands the branch library's Twitter posts to the followers of the speakers, their home institutions, and others on Twitter interested in the subject matter.

Twitter-Only Live Events

There are a number of recurring events, often called *tweetchats*, which take place in real time over Twitter. Typically arranged around specific hashtags, they range from live Q & A's with authors and experts to roundtable discussions within a professional organization. Followers must be aware of them and be on Twitter at the right time to participate, although the tweets remain after the fact as a record that can be reviewed later. These events are a unique opportunity that can be explored and developed by branch libraries.

#AskALibrarian is currently live on Twitter every Thursday from 12:00 PM to 1:00 PM Eastern Standard Time. Twitter users from all walks of life ask for reading suggestions from librarians, who respond regardless of geographic location. Mostly engaging public librarians, #AskALibrarian is also a useful exercise for academic librarians to try. Not only does participation in this particular tweetchat help develop reader advisory skills, providing recommendations can raise awareness of the library's Twitter account among new audiences.

#OTTalk is a tweetchat that originated in the United Kingdom. It currently takes place on Tuesday nights, 8:00 PM to 9:00 PM Greenwich Mean Time. The Southampton Library has taken to monitoring this hashtag and promoting it to followers and occupational therapy students as an example of how Twitter can be used for professional development.

As branch libraries build their Twitter presence, they might think of inaugurating their own subject- or location-specific tweetchats. These can be marketed as outreach activities with other areas of the University or community, something along the lines of #AskAboutSouthampton. Similar events could be coordinated with other library branches or areas within the university looking to promote collaboration.

Building a Twitter Network

Much of the power of Twitter lies in its function as a network of relationships. Those followed by and those who follow the library account play an important role in determining how widely any particular tweet is distributed. For branch libraries, who often struggle for recognition and engagement with the greater institution, Twitter is a boon to building relationships. Despite the geographic remove, branches can use Twitter to level the playing field and become a virtual neighbor to departments and groups in other locations. Additionally, the branch can reciprocate by commenting on, retweeting, and similarly engaging with the content of other departments.

Institutional Accounts

At the outset, branch libraries can establish a network by locating and following other accounts from within the university. Likely choices include the main library and the communications office as well as academic departments, service units, and student groups. Not all accounts will be equally active, but most will start following back, helping build the library's follower count. Do not be shy about reaching out and promoting the branch campus to others in the university. A branch campus has the perfect rationale for reaching out - introducing the rest of the institution to branch activities and programs. As the branch library account evolves, a reciprocal relationship among areas will grow, with each account helping to share and amplify the content of the other.

Students

Don't be discouraged if it takes time to build engagement with the student community. As mentioned previously, institutional accounts have been shown to be the most valuable members of the branch library's network. These institutional accounts can act as a conduit through which to reach students. If the library's account is connected to the greater academic community on Twitter, then individual departments, student groups and other service organizations will be sharing the library's content to their own followers. Again, the network effect will amplify the message and distribute it further than the library's account may reach on its own. The reverse is also true. The library can act as an influencer for other areas of campus, spreading their message to members of the library's network that the originating account might not reach.

The branch library can try to gain student followers by appealing to them directly in the real world. Introduce them to the library's Twitter account at orientations, in routine communications, and on campus via bulletin boards and signs throughout the library. When assessing the number of student followers, be mindful that it may not be possible to determine if a follower is a student just by virtue of their profile. School affiliation is not always something people include in their public profile.

Beyond the University

Outside of the university, look to follow accounts of organizations and groups related to the academic programs supported by the campus. In this, Twitter provides a potential new role for libraries: curating and disseminating information from non-library sources on social media. For example, the Southampton Library, cognizant of the MFA program on campus, began following accounts from places such as *Writers Digest*, *Literary Hub*, and the *Paris Review*. The library monitors these accounts for relevant content to like and retweet, things like writing tips, author interviews, new developments in the field, and writing contests.

Outreach to the local community is another key mission of branch libraries and their campuses. As representatives of the main institution, branches have an obligation to represent the face of the university to the area. To that end, the library can follow and engage with local institutions like museums, historical societies, civic groups, and municipal offices.

One can identify accounts to follow by searching keywords on Twitter via the web page or app. There is also an advanced search function at http://twitter.com/search-advanced. Keep in mind that results will depend upon the amount of information that accounts voluntarily supply in their public profiles. If results are coming up short, one can always use the old chain citation trick: identify a valuable account to follow, then check the list of accounts they follow and are followed by. One can also identify accounts by the content they post. Having a list of keywords and hashtags relevant to the library's goals will make it easier to search for accounts that routinely post about those topics. All of these strategies help to build a network of shared interests, overlapping missions, and potential influencers.

Organize With Twitter Lists

Twitter allows for the creation of lists – compiling Twitter accounts into special groups based upon specific criteria. The resulting lists can be made public or private and clicking on them will display the tweets from the accounts involved. This is a handy way of creating a timeline of tweets around a specific topic or theme. One may want a list of peer institutions or of cultural heritage institutions in the local area, or experts in a certain field. The list becomes a resource that can be shared and promoted.

To add someone to a list, navigate to their Twitter profile page. Next to the follow/unfollow button is a small pull-down menu. Select "Add or remove from lists" as shown in Figure 3. A box will appear enabling one to save to an existing list or to create a new list.

Figure 3. Saving a Twitter account to a list (Southampton Library)
Source: Southampton Library 2018

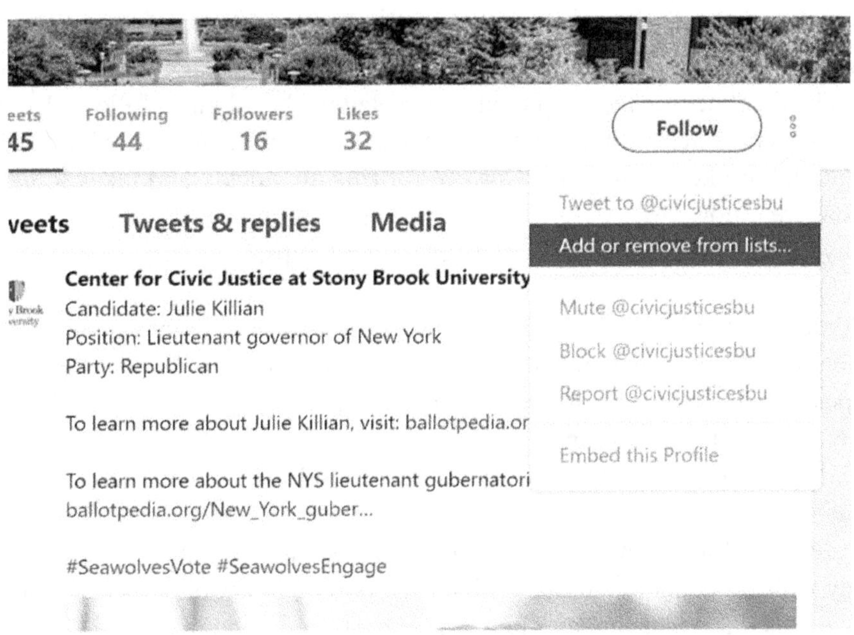

The Southampton Library has created a number of lists to track different constituencies, monitoring the tweets of certain kinds of user groups at once. For example, the library's East End list, made up of accounts from local newspapers, government offices, civic groups and the like, provides a means for keeping up with regional events.

Engaging With Others on Twitter

The goal of a branch library on Twitter is not simply to amass followers. It is to encourage meaningful engagement and to share relevant information. Gaining a follower (or following someone new) is just the beginning. A vital part of the branch library's Twitter activity will be managing the day-to-day interactions of these relationships.

Based on experience, the Southampton Library follows a series of basic principles for engagement:

- Keep a list of institutional accounts to review and potentially interact with each day.
- Retweet content from other accounts from the institution but where possible, add personalized commentary.
- Mention specific university departments and offices when sharing content relevant to their area.
- Retweet any positive mention of the branch -- show that any message that incorporates the library's mission will be boosted.
- Be bold in creating conversations. The Southampton Library, for example, asked SOMAS for its scientific opinion of the movie *Sharknado*. It turned out that they had an article on that very subject ready to share.
- Group like-minded accounts in the same tweet to promote more reciprocal relationships. Is it #MuseumWeek? Mention all the local museums in a single tweet about the great work they do.
- Publicly thank those who follow the branch account.

Weeding the Timeline

The timeline, or home timeline, is what the administrator sees when logging into the branch library's Twitter account. The timeline is made up of content tweeted by the accounts followed, as well as content suggested by Twitter. The timeline gives a broad overview of what the followed accounts are doing and is a source of material to like and retweet. However, it fills up quickly and takes longer to review the more accounts that are followed.

Information overload can be mitigated with a few simple steps.

1. Do not automatically follow everyone who follows the branch account. Review their account first to see if the content is relevant and fits with the library's mission. Follow the rule of reciprocity whenever possible, but accounts that post explicit language or photos or are otherwise contrary to university policy would not warrant a "follow."
2. If a followed account starts to tweet material that is no longer relevant to the library's mission, unfollow them.
3. If there is value in following an account but not in seeing what they are tweeting, the account can be muted. They will still count as a follower, but their posts will not be visible on the home timeline. Additionally, muted accounts do not know they have been muted.

SOLUTIONS AND RECOMMENDATIONS

Time Management Strategies

The time commitment of a Twitter account can feel overwhelming at a branch library, where those who are tasked with managing a social media account often do so as an added duty on top of an already full job description. Keeping up with daily tweeting may seem like an impossible challenge, both logistically and creatively. But running an account does not need to be all-consuming nor does one need to be a wordsmith to keep it going. Two simple steps at the outset will help streamline the process and save time in the day-to-day workflow. A well-planned calendar and a thought-out system of hashtags will help line up posts in advance and keep tweets on track.

The Calendar

Many academic libraries have adopted the idea of a shared spreadsheet for mapping out events in a timeline (Barnes, 2014; Ramsey & Vecchione, 2014). The Southampton Library uses a similar system to create a Twitter calendar with tabs for each month of the year and rows for each day of the month. The spreadsheet is then filled with ideas for things to tweet about: holidays, notable birthdays, events in popular culture, important dates in the academic year, and any other date-specific happening relevant to the library's mission. Google Sheets work well as a collaborative canvas, allowing multiple employees to contribute at the same time.

Consult with appropriate sources to identify key dates and events. The American Library Association's "Celebration Weeks and Promotional Events" will provide valuable help at the outset. This type of planning provides a structure within which to work. Knowing what's coming, even a week or a month at a time, lets one plan content to match. This level of preparation, however, does require the time to research events, populate the calendar, and create content to match. The spreadsheet that Southampton Library uses is shown in Figure 4.

Figure 4. Google Sheet mapping out potential events during the year (Southampton Library)
Source: Southampton Library 2018

A	B	C	D	E	F
Date	Month	Birthdays	Days	LitFilm Related events	Libraries Related
April 1	Poetry Month			Pulitzer Prizes announced	
April 2	Natonial Occupational Therapy Month				
April 3	National Internship Awareness Month	Washington Irving, 1783		F. Scott Fitzgerald marries Zelda	
April 4	Stress Awareness Month	Maya Angelou, 1928	National Walking Day (first Wed in April)		
April 5		Booker T. Washington, 1856			
April 6			Natl Student Athlete Day		
April 7					
April 8					
April 9					National Library Week
April 10			Natl Encourage a Young Writer Day	Great Gatsby published, 1925	
April 11					
April 12					
April 13			Natl Scrabble Day		
April 14					
April 15					

Weekly Hashtags

Use a system of weekly hashtags to plan out content. This provides a great way to organize and sustain a Twitter presence. By assigning content via weekdays, one can stockpile posts beforehand and schedule them to post subsequently. There are a number of established hashtags that can be used to get started and they can be changed as desired. Here is the outline that the Southampton Library often uses with some brief notes on each. Figure 5 provides examples of the hashtags in action.

- **#MondayMotivation:** This hashtag provides uplift at the start of the week, a good time to promote a call to action or advocacy of some sort or a promotion of a service.
- **#TravelTuesday:** Each week, travel bloggers from around the world share pictures, blog posts, and information using this hashtag. Southampton Library applies its own MFA-inspired spin, applying it to travel stories, books with quests in them, or fiction titles set in foreign locales. One can expand into posting pictures or anecdotes from staff and patrons who have traveled abroad or by cross-promoting activities with the Study Abroad office.
- **#WednesdayWisdom:** By hump day, followers may be struggling to cope with the stress of the week. The wisdom in this hashtag can be quotes from historical or cultural figures, something on which to ruminate or thoughts to get followers through it all. For Southampton, this conversation provides a chance to share quotes about issues that define the library's mission - wisdom concerning the value of libraries, writing, research, and literacy. If the quote is from a personality who has a Twitter account, be sure to mention that person!
- **#ThursdayThoughts:** This is a popular and wide-ranging hashtag that spans many topics. While one can share quotes similar to #WednesdayWisdom, it is important to find a way to delineate between the two, either by theme or by content source. The Southampton Library uses Wednesday for quotes from historical and cultural figures while Thursdays are more locally sourced, with thoughts about the library from staff, affiliates, and patrons. The former day takes a broader view, the latter focuses on the particulars of the establishment.
- **#FridayReads:** This is a staple of the Southampton Library's hashtag diet. It is a ready-made vehicle to showcase collections. Photos of books are posted along with any related information about its history or relevance. The selections rotate through staff picks, new acquisitions, literary prize winners, and themed content during events such as Women's History Month, Poetry Month, and Celtic Awareness Month.
- **#SaturdayLibrarian:** A hashtag for the bold. It is library-centric and on the one hand, taps into a sympathetic audience. On the other hand, this hashtag brings with it a sense of humor ranging from sarcastic to sardonic. To put it in perspective, it is largely used by librarians working on the weekends and drinking copious amounts of coffee. That being said, #SaturdayLibrarian has potential to humanize those who work in the library. Post memes, try out some jokes, and interact with patrons in a way more conducive to a weekend vibe.
- **#SundayBlogShare:** Simply put, this is a hashtag used to share blog posts. Most libraries maintain a blog of some sort, discussing library-related news and events as well as recent developments. At the Southampton Library, the blog that is shared contains content from all university libraries. This gives the hashtag the function of a weekly rolling newsletter, giving Southampton followers a look at news from the wider institution.

Figure 5. Examples of weekly hashtags for #MondayMotivatin, #WednesdayWisdom and #FridayReads at the Southampton Library (Southampton Library)
Source: Southampton Library 2018

Scheduling Tweets

Whether tweets are planned weeks in advance or just over the next few days, a scheduling tool will be a boon to the branch library. Combined with weekly hashtags, scheduling will ensure a reliable stream of content in the Twitter feed.

There are a number of free and low-cost software options for scheduling tweets. Many even allow scheduling content to multiple platforms at once - meaning that the same or unique posts can be shared to Twitter as well as Facebook, Tumblr, and elsewhere. Check the settings on each program as some limit the total number of posts one can schedule at a time. As shown in Figure 6, the Southampton Library currently uses the free version of HootSuite to schedule posts to Twitter and Facebook.

Scheduling tweets lends some peace of mind, knowing that the Twitter account will stay active with at least a minimum of activity over holiday gaps or when one is pulled away by other demands. Other scheduling tools include:

Figure 6. Hootsuite dashboard showing posts scheduled for later in the week (Southampton Library)
Source: Southampton Library 2018

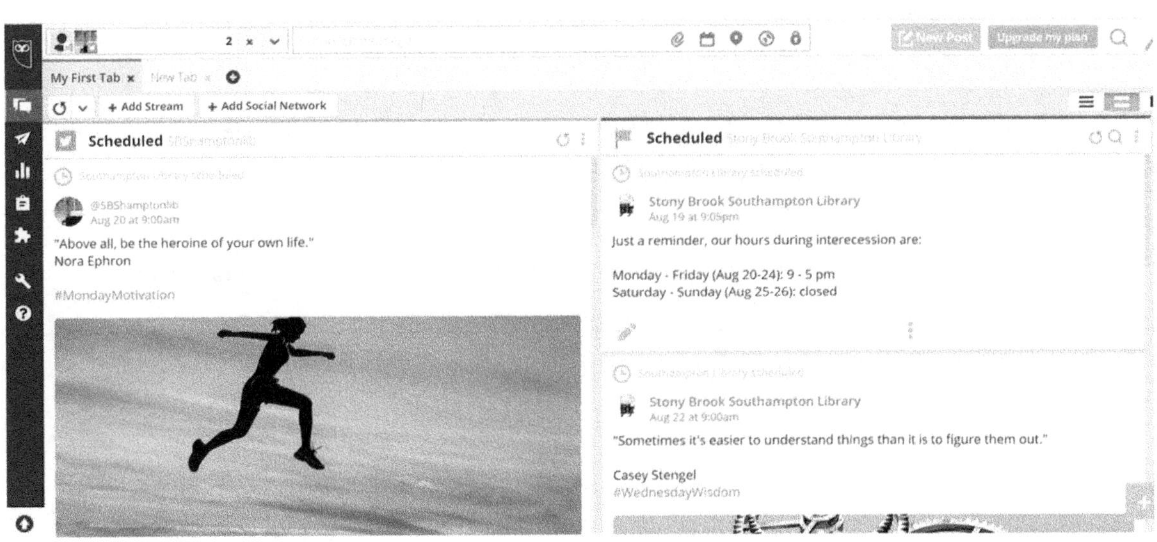

- Buffer
- CrowdFire
- Sendible
- SocialPilot
- TweetDeck

The Recipe for the Perfect Tweet

Much to the frustration of social media managers everywhere, not all tweets are created equal. A carefully crafted message or meme may fail to gain traction while an offhand observation or image will strike a chord and gain thousands of impressions. The difference can hinge on using the right elements at the right time. Some simple strategies and best practices can optimize the chances that users will engage with content when they see it.

The finer details of assessment and Twitter analytics will be discussed later but to illustrate the point, the Southampton Library examined a year's-worth of "top tweets." These were tweets from each month that elicited the most interactions in terms of likes, retweets, and mentions. Further analysis of the distinct elements of these tweets led to a better understanding of what went into an engaging tweet. The resulting "recipe" shown in Table 1, helps to guide construction of new tweets with an eye towards maximizing engagement.

The Southampton Library also discovered that no single "silver-bullet" element led to engagement. Rather, results came from a mix of elements. A review of the top tweets revealed that:

- 83% included two or more elements
- 83% included hashtags
- 62% included media
- 52% included hashtags and media

The analysis of Southampton's tweets reinforces other studies of tweet construction that show the prevalent use of media on Twitter (Borruto, 2015). A further discussion of this recipe is a good primer on how to drive engagement.

Table 1. The elements in an ideal tweet as derived from a study of high-engagement tweets from 2016-2017 at the Southampton Library (Southampton Library)

Number of:			
Hashtags	**Mentions**	**Links**	**Pictures/Media**
1.86	.9	.28	.76

Source: Southampton Library 2018

Hashtags

Of all the elements of a tweet, hashtags are perhaps the most important. In their study of Twitter use at historically black colleges, Stewart and Walker (2017) found that hashtags were a "pathway for library-generated content proliferation well beyond a libraries' follower community" (p. 6).

Hashtags can be defined as user-generated keywords or subject headings. They are words or phrases preceded by a hashtag. When included in a tweet, they become a link to all other tweets using that hashtag. Some hashtags become standards, reused frequently across Twitter by mutual consent. Others rise spontaneously in response to events and can be used to track developing news and reactions across Twitter.

Libraries can identify relevant hashtags in a variety of ways. Twitter displays trending hashtags on the home timeline. In addition, one can search for tweets about a topic, looking for any prevalent hashtags in the results. Conferences, celebrations, and cultural events often create official hashtags to aid communication. By using hashtags, branch libraries can tie their content to ongoing conversations and connect to non-followers interested in similar subject matter.

Figure 7 shows an example of a trending hashtag in use. During one of the many blizzards of the winter of 2018, the Southampton Library was able to spot and participate in #museumsnowballfight. This hashtag had sprung up earlier in the day between two New York City-based institutions as a way to share archival photos featuring blizzards past. The Southampton Library and many other organizations around the country and the world joined in with their own variations, creating a shared conversation that spread well into the next day.

Figure 7. Use of the hashtag #museumsnowballfight (Southampton Library)
Source: Southampton Library 2018

Links

Links are a valuable tool for providing access to the many online resources that academic libraries curate and to content from outside sources.

Some of the most common library content to link to includes:

- Blog posts
- Catalog records
- Databases
- Digital projects
- OERs
- Research guides

Many of the vendors of library systems have customizable social media settings, letting one tie accounts into the administrative interface while embedding "share" buttons on public-facing content. Make sure these functions have been optimized to enable sharing from social media platforms.

Previously, long links were a hindrance to Twitter posts as they ate into character limits. Twitter now automatically shortens all URLs and counts them as 23 characters, regardless of their actual length.

Mentions

Mentions are a powerful tool for communication on Twitter. They are formed by including a Twitter account's user name, such as @SBShamptonlib, within a tweet. The user is notified of the mention and hopefully will engage with it in some way. For branch libraries, mentions can play a key role in attracting followers and increasing engagement. Make sure to mention other accounts in a positive way, whether to highlight an author of a recent acquisition, to thank a speaker, or to engage in conversation with another department or institution. One can search individual names on Twitter to locate their username but keep in mind, the ability to positively identify someone (outside of their photo) is limited by the information they provide in their profiles.

Images and Video

The Southampton Library has found that the use of images and other media such as video and animated GIFs greatly enhances the engagement levels of a tweet. While having a device with a camera for the branch library is ideal for this purpose, there are other ways to include images within tweets without having to expend funds on a camera. These include:

- **Screenshots:** A great budget-saving way to highlight resources. Mine the library's website for sections that can help illustrate resources, guide navigation, and show off the branch.
- **Pixabay:** A free source of royalty free images. The range of content is surprisingly wide and can be used to illustrate or augment plain text content such as quotes, sayings, and announcements. (https://pixabay.com)
- **The New York Public Library Digital Collections:** Much of the public domain portion of their digitized collections are available for free download. (https://digitalcollections.nypl.org/)

- **Library of Congress:** Their Free to Use and Reuse section features public domain images from their collections. (https://www.loc.gov/free-to-use/)
- **Archives & Special Collections:** Work with the home institution's archives and special collections to see if they have digitized content that can be repurposed to augment posts from the branch library.

Image Quality and Size

Most visual content posted on Twitter will be viewed through the small screen of a mobile phone, cutting down on the need to produce high resolution images to start with. It does help, however, to be aware of Twitter's image specifications which are currently:

- Photo size up to 5 MB
- Animated GIFs up to 5MB on mobile devices, up to 15MB on web
- GIF, JPEG, and PNG accepted
- BMP or TIFF not accepted
- Up to four images on one tweet

Image Captioning

Add descriptions to images for the benefit of those using screen readers to access Twitter. To enable this option in Twitter, go to Profile settings and under Accessibility, turn on "Compose Image Descriptions." Thereafter, when adding an image to a tweet from Twitter.com or in the Twitter app on iOS or Android, one will have the ability to enter caption information.

Assessment

Assessment helps determine the success of Twitter activity and a coherent and sustainable assessment plan helps guide and direct that activity. Given the small staffs and budgets at branch libraries, careful thought should be given to what one wants to measure and why. Fortunately, Twitter has one of the most easily accessible statistics platforms providing many ways to retrieve and study Twitter activity.

Twitter Analytics

One can access an account's statistics dashboard by signing in to Twitter Analytics (http://twitter.analytics.com) using the Twitter ID. The home screen will show a 28-day window of activity on the account as well as an overview of each month, including:

- **Top Tweet:** The tweet that received the most impressions for the month
- **Top Mention:** The tweet with the highest impressions that mentioned the library account's @ name
- **Top Follower:** The Twitter account the library is following who has the most followers of their own
- **New Followers:** How many followers were gained over the month

Figure 8 shows an example of one month's top activity at the Southampton Library.

Individual Tweet Statistics

One can also view statistics on any individual tweet from the account, either through the Analytics interface or by clicking the three vertical lines at the bottom of the tweet on Twitter. Figure 9 shows the statistics for a specific tweet. Numbers are shown for impressions, engagements, and the specific types of engagements that occurred.

Figure 8. Monthly Twitter analytics for Southampton Library, February 2018 (Southampton Library)
Source: Southampton Library 2018

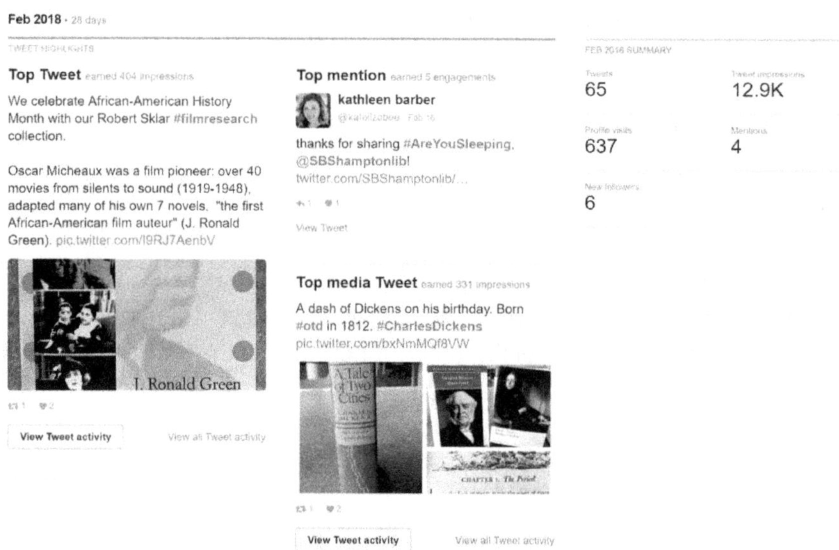

Figure 9. Twitter analytics for a specific tweet (Southampton Library)
Source: Southampton Library 2018

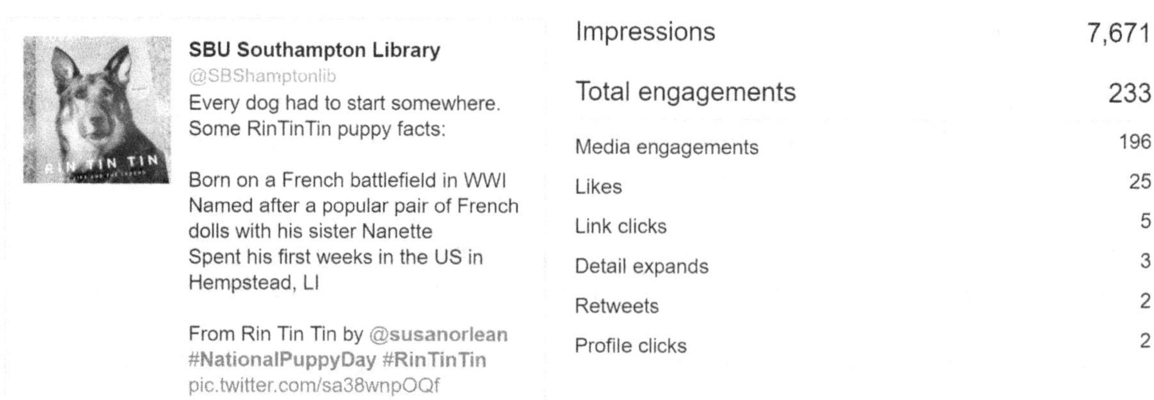

Cohort Tracking

Measuring the branch library's Twitter account against a cohort of peer institutions is another useful strategy to assess growth and activity. To start, identify what libraries or institutions will make up the cohort. These can be institutions of similar type, size, activity, or from the same geographic area. Just by charting the information available on public profiles, one can see how the branch library's account matches up in terms of number of followers, number of tweets, and number of accounts being followed.

The Southampton Library tracks its performance against a number of SUNY libraries on Twitter, using the metrics of follower growth and number of tweets per month. Compiling all of these library accounts into a Twitter list makes it easier to gather the statistics at the end of each month.

Follower Audit

Knowing who is following the branch library helps in understanding the library's network and in identifying the audience reached. Research has been conducted that breaks down followers into relevant categories for study (Sewell, 2013). For a branch library, the network may break down into students, faculty, and academic departments but there can be a surprising number of outsiders. Knowing the breakdown of follower types can help a branch library determine who they are reaching with their content. If a key audience is not being reached, new campaigns or strategies can be developed to try to reach them.

Surveys

Direct feedback from the current and potential audience is always going to be valuable information to have. Is content reaching them? Is it the type of content they want? Conducting surveys in person or online through Google Forms can garner many useful results. If branch staff do not have the time or resources for surveys, even an informal assessment can garner information. Try leaving a whiteboard and marker out in the library asking students to record their preferences and thoughts.

Analytics Tools

Third party tools will help do even more analysis, from data mining to network mapping. Each of these tools allows one to learn more about various aspects of an account's performance on Twitter. Some are free or freemium, meaning that they provide a certain amount of functionality for free, with more advanced capabilities requiring a paid subscription.

Table 2 in the appendix lists a number of current tools for the branch library that wants to expand Twitter assessment activities.

FUTURE RESEARCH DIRECTIONS

Much research remains to be done on Twitter use at branch campus libraries. A comparison of use and engagement rates between a branch library and its main campus could show the effects of having different populations. Similarly, a poll of main campus users and departments may show what success the branch campus has had using Twitter to raise awareness of its activities.

A closer look at an academic library's following habits – who they choose who to follow - could uncover valuable information on how libraries see their role on Twitter and the level of reciprocity they expect from their network.

Finally, Emery & Schifeling found that "most academic libraries are not communicating with each other through Twitter" (p. 453). A study of interlibrary hashtags, mentions, likes, and retweets could show the level of interaction that exists now, uncover where activity is most prevalent, and suggest reasons why it might not be occurring.

CONCLUSION

Branch libraries can manage their own Twitter accounts without a large outlay of expense. With careful planning and wise use of time and resources, they can overcome logistical barriers to engage with their campus and wider institution while establishing their own presence and influence on Twitter. Keys to success include:

- Establishing flexible policies
- Tweeting with a distinctive voice
- Planning ahead to keep content flowing
- Showing reciprocity within the network
- Using hashtags and mentions to amplify the message and connect with influencers
- Assessing results, using analytics to guide and refine the strategy

Using many of these strategies, the Southampton Library has managed to establish and maintain a strong Twitter presence within Stony Brook University while attracting followers from the community at large. For this campus library located out on the eastern edge of Long Island, Twitter has proven a worthwhile vehicle for keeping in touch with the main campus, establishing an identity for the branch, and promoting awareness of the branch's activities.

REFERENCES

Appleton, L., & Tattersall, A. (2015). How librarians can harness the power of social media for the benefit of their users. *Multimedia Information & Technology*, *41*(4), 23–26.

Barnes, I. (2014). Twitter in special libraries: A distributed social media strategy. *Public Services Quarterly*, *10*(1), 62–65. doi:10.1080/15228959.2014.875789

Borruto, G. (2015). Analysis of tweets in Twitter. *Webology*, *12*(1), 1–11.

Bottorff, T., Glaser, R., Todd, A., & Alderman, B. (2008). Branching out: Communication and collaboration among librarians at multi-campus institutions. *Journal of Library Administration*, *48*(3-4), 329–363. doi:10.1080/01930820802289391

Brandt, J., Frederiksen, L., Schneider, T., & Syrkin, D. (2006). The face of regional campus libraries and librarianship. *Journal of Library Administration*, *45*(1/2), 37–61. doi:10.1300/J111v45n01_03

Brookbank, E. (2015). So much social media, so little time: Using student feedback to guide academic library social media strategy. *Journal of Electronic Resources Librarianship*, *27*(4), 232–247. doi:10.1080/1941126X.2015.1092344

Burkhardt, A. (2010). Social media: A guide for college and university libraries. *College & Research Libraries News*, *71*(1), 10–24. doi:10.5860/crln.71.1.8302

Chatten, Z. (2017). Making social media work: Finding a library voice. *Insights: The UKSG Journal*, *30*(3), 51–61. doi:10.1629/uksg.374

Dengerink, H. A. (2001). Institutional identity and organizational structure in multi-campus universities. *Metropolitan Universities*, *12*(2), 20–29.

Dryden, N. H., & Goldstein, S. (2013). Regional campus learning commons: Assessing to meet student needs. *Journal of Library Administration*, *53*(5-6), 293–322. doi:10.1080/01930826.2013.876822

Emery, K., & Schifeling, T. (2015). Libraries using Twitter better: Insights on engagement from food trucks. *Proceedings of the ACRL 2015 Conference*, 450-458. Retrieved from http://www.ala.org/acrl/sites/ala.org.acrl/files/content/conferences/confsandpreconfs/2015/Emery_Schifeling.pdf

Farkas, M. (2009). Governing social media. *American Libraries*, *40*(12), 35.

Harrison, A., Burress, R., Velasquez, S., & Schreiner, L. (2017). Social media use in academic libraries: A phenomenological study. *Journal of Academic Librarianship*, *43*(3), 248–256. doi:10.1016/j.acalib.2017.02.014

Howard, H., Huber, S., Carter, L., & Moore, E. (2018). Academic libraries on social media: Finding the students and the information they want. *Information Technology and Libraries*, *37*(1), 8–18. doi:10.6017/ital.v37i1.10160

Kim, H. M., Abels, E. G., & Yang, C. C. (2012). Who disseminates academic library information on Twitter? *Proceedings of the American Society for Information Science and Technology*, *49*(1), 1–4. doi:10.1002/meet.14504901317

Knickman, E., & Walton, K. (2014). Branch campus librarianship with minimal infrastructure: Rewards and challenges. *Community & Junior College Libraries*, *20*(3/4), 63–73. doi:10.1080/02763915.2015.1044301

Loudon, L., & Hall, H. (2010). From triviality to business tool: The case of Twitter in library and information services delivery. *Business Information Review*, *27*(4), 236–241. doi:10.1177/0266382110390480

MacDonald, G. (2013). Theorizing university identity development: Multiple perspectives and common goals. *Higher Education*, *65*(2), 153–166. doi:10.100710734-012-9526-3

Markland, M. J., Gascho Rempel, H., & Bridges, L. (2017). Mobile website use and advanced researchers: Understanding library users at a university marine sciences branch campus. *Information Technology and Libraries*, *36*(4), 7–23. doi:10.6017/ital.v36i4.9953

Mon, L., & Lee, J. (2015). Influence, reciprocity, participation, and visibility: Assessing the social library on Twitter. *Canadian Journal of Information and Library Science*, *39*(3/4), 279–294.

Ofili, D. N., & Emwanta, M.-G. (2014). Facebook as an information service delivery tool: Perspectives of library staff at the University of Benin, Nigeria. *African Journal of Library Archives and Information Science*, *24*(2), 195–202.

Pew Research Center. (2018). *Social media use in 2018.* Retrieved from http://www.pewinternet.org/2018/03/01/social-media-use-in-2018/

Phillips, N. K. (2011). Academic library use of Facebook: Building relationships with students. *Journal of Academic Librarianship*, *37*(6), 512–522. doi:10.1016/j.acalib.2011.07.008

Phinney, J., & Horsman, A. R. (2018). Satellite stories: Capturing professional experiences of academic health sciences librarians working in delocalized health sciences programs. *Journal of the Medical Library Association: JMLA*, *106*(1), 74–80. doi:10.5195/JMLA.2018.214 PMID:29339936

Ramsey, E., & Vecchione, A. (2014). Engaging library users through a social media strategy. *Journal of Library Innovation*, *5*(2), 71–82.

Schneider, T. M. (2001). The regional campus library and service to the public. *Journal of Academic Librarianship*, *27*(2), 122–127. doi:10.1016/S0099-1333(00)00184-1

Sewell, R. R. (2013). Who is following us? Data mining a library's Twitter followers. *Library Hi Tech*, *31*(1), 160–170. doi:10.1108/07378831311303994

Shulman, J., Yep, J., & Tomé, D. (2015). Leveraging the power of a Twitter network for library promotion. *Journal of Academic Librarianship*, *41*(2), 178–185. doi:10.1016/j.acalib.2014.12.004

Stewart, B., & Walker, J. (2018). Build it and they will come? Patron engagement via Twitter at historically black college and university libraries. *Journal of Academic Librarianship*, *44*(1), 118–124. doi:10.1016/j.acalib.2017.09.016

Stvilia, B., & Gibradze, L. (2014). What do academic libraries tweet about, and what makes a library tweet useful? *Library & Information Science Research*, *36*(3), 136–141. doi:10.1016/j.lisr.2014.07.001

Vassilakaki, E., & Garoufallou, E. (2015). The impact of Twitter on libraries: A critical review of the literature. *The Electronic Library*, *33*(4), 795–809. doi:10.1108/EL-03-2014-0051

Wallis, L. (2014). #selfiesinthestacks: Sharing the library with Instagram. *Internet Reference Services Quarterly*, *19*(3/4), 181–206. doi:10.1080/10875301.2014.983287

Wilkinson, J. (2018). Accessible, dynamic web content using Instagram. *Information Technology and Libraries*, *37*(1), 19–26. doi:10.6017/ital.v37i1.10230

Young, S. H., & Rossmann, D. (2015). Building library community through social media. *Information Technology and Libraries*, *34*(1), 20–37. doi:10.6017/ital.v34i1.5625

ADDITIONAL READING

Bizzle, B., & Flora, M. (2015). *Start a revolution: Stop acting like a library*. Chicago: ALA Editions.

King, D. L. (2012). Social media. *Library Technology Reports*, *48*(6), 23–27. PMID:22442899

Luo, L., Wang, Y., & Han, L. (2013). Marketing via social media: A case study. *Library Hi Tech*, *31*(3), 455–466. doi:10.1108/LHT-12-2012-0141

Mackenzie, A., & Martin, L. (2014). *Mastering digital librarianship: Strategy, networking and discovery in academic libraries*. London: Facet Publishing.

Mon, L., & Phillips, A. (2015). The social library in the virtual branch: Serving adults and teens in social spaces. *Advances in Librarianship*, *39*, 241–268. doi:10.1108/S0065-283020150000039016

Mon, L. M. (2015). *Social media and library services*. California: Morgan & Claypool. doi:10.2200/S00634ED1V01Y201503ICR040

Palmer, S. (2014). Characterizing university library use of social media: A case study of Twitter and Facebook from Australia. *Journal of Academic Librarianship*, *40*(6), 611–619. doi:10.1016/j.acalib.2014.08.007

Winn, D., Groenendyk, M., & Rivosecchi, M. (2015). Like, comment, retweet: Understanding student social media preferences. *Partnership: The Canadian Journal of Library and Information Practice and Research*, *10*(2), 1–14. doi:10.21083/partnership.v10i2.3449

APPENDIX

Table 2. Twitter analysis tools

Name	URL
Buffer	https://buffer.com
Followerwonk	https://followerwonk.com
Keyhole	https://keyhole.co/
Klear	https://klear.com/free-tools/twitter-analysis
ManageFilter	https://www.managefilter.com
NCSU Tweet Visualizer	https://www.csc2.ncsu.edu/faculty/healey/tweet_viz/tweet_app/
Sprout Social	https://sproutsocial.com/features/twitter-analytics/
SumAll	https://sumall.com/
TweetStats	http://www.tweetstats.com/
TweepsMap	https://tweepsmap.com/
Twitonomy	https://www.twitonomy.com

Compilation of References

About account home. (n.d.). Retrieved August 29, 2018, from https://help.twitter.com/en/managing-your-account/twitter-account-home

About your activity dashboard. (n.d.). Retrieved August 29, 2018, from https://help.twitter.com/en/managing-your-account/using-the-tweet-activity-dashboard

Achen, R. M. (2016). Examining the influence of Facebook fans, content, and engagement on business outcomes in the National Basketball Association. *Journal of Social Media for Organizations, 3*(1), 1–16.

ADA National Network: Information, Guidance, and Training on the Americans with Disabilities Act (2018). *What is the Americans with Disabilities Act (ADA)?* Retrieved July 13, 2018 from, https://adata.org/learn-about-ada

Adams Becker, S., Cummins, M., Davis, A., Freeman, A., Hall Giesinger, C., & Ananthanarayanan, V. (2017). *NMC Horizon Report: 2017 Higher Education Edition.* Austin, TX: The New Media Consortium.

Adam, T., Burgess, C., McPhee, K., Olson, L., & Sich, C. (2018). Collaboratively Creating a Programmatic Information Literacy Strategy: Challenges and Opportunities. *Partnership: The Canadian Journal of Library and Information Practice and Research, 13*(1), 1–21. doi:10.21083/partnership.v13i1.4063

Adewoyin, O.O., Onuoha, U.D., & Ikonne, C.N. (2017). *Social Media Use and Service Delivery by Librarians in Federal Universities in South-West, Nigeria.* Retrieved from https://digitalcommons.unl.edu/libphilprac/1641/

African and Middle Eastern Division. (2016). *Social Media Communications & Business Plan.* Washington, DC: Library of Congress.

Aguenza, B. B., Al-Kassem, A. H., & Som, A. P. (2012). Social Media and Productivity in the Workplace: Challenges and Constraints. *Interdisciplinary Journal of Research in Business, 2*(2), 22–26.

Aharony, N. (2010). Twitter use in libraries: An exploratory analysis. *Journal of Web Librarianship, 4*(4), 333–350. doi:10.1080/19322909.2010.487766

Ahmed, T., & Qazi, F. (2011). A look out for academic impacts of social networking sites: A student based perspective. *African Journal of Business Management, 5*(12), 1–6.

Akanbi, M., & Akanbi, A. (2014). Influence of social media usage on self-image and academic performance among senior secondary school students in Ilorin west Local Government, Kwara State *Int. Res. J. Pure Appl. Phys., 24*, 42–50.

ALA office for Intellectual Freedom. (2010). *Intellectual Freedom Manual* (8th ed.). Chicago: ALA Editions.

ALA. (2001). *Libraries making good use of social media and Web 2.0 applications.* Retrieved August 21, 2018, from http://www.ala.org/news/mediapresscenter/americaslibraries/socialnetworking

Alhabash, S., & Ma, M. (2017). A tale of four platforms: Motivations and uses of Facebook, Twitter, Instagram, and Snapchat among college students? *Social Media Society*, *3*(1). doi:10.1177/2056305117691544

Allen, E. (2013, February). *Inquiring minds: Exploring Jefferson's universe.* Library of Congress Blog. Retrieved from https://blogs.loc.gov/loc/2013/02/inquiring-minds-exploring-jeffersons-universe/

Allers, M. (2015). Creating a successful student social media team. *Campus Activities Programming*, *48*(5), 12–15.

Almudawi, N. A. (2016). Cloud computing privacy concerns in social networks. *International Journal of Computer*, *22*(1), 29–36.

Amaefule, E. (2017). *75% of Nigeria's Online Population Use Social Media.* Retrieved from https://punchng.com/75-of-nigerias-online-population-use-social-media-minister/

American Library Association (2017). *DMCA: The Digital Millennium Copyright Act.* Author.

American Library Association (ALA). (2011). *The state of America's libraries: A report from the American Library Association.* ALA. Retrieved from http://www.ala.org/news/sites/ala.org.news/files/content/mediapresscenter/americaslibraries/state_of_americas_libraries_report_2011.pdf

American Library Association. (2013). *Questions and answers on ethics and social media.* Retrieved from: http://www.ala.org/tools/ethics

American Library Association. (2018). *Libraries respond.* Retrieved from http://www.ala.org/advocacy/diversity/libraries-respond

American Library Association. (2018). *Social Media Guidelines for Public and Academic Libraries.* Retrieved August 14, 2018 from, http://www.ala.org/advocacy/intfreedom/socialmediaguidelines

Amollo, B. (2011). Digitization for libraries in Kenya. *Second International Conference on African Digital Libraries and Archives (ICADLA-2).*

Amsbary, J. H., & Powell, L. (2003). Factors influencing evaluations of web site information. *Psychological Reports*, *93*(1), 191–198. doi:10.2466/pr0.2003.93.1.191 PMID:14563048

Amudaa & Adeyinka. (n.d.). Application of Social Media for Innovative Library Services in South-Western Nigerian University Libraries. *Journal of Balkan Libraries Union.* Retrieved from http://dergipark.gov.tr/download/article-file/399735

Anderson, M., & Smith, A. (2015) Social Media Use 2018. *Pew Research Center.* Available at: http://www.pewinternet.org/2018/03/01/social-media-use-in-2018/

Appleton, L., & Tattersall, A. (2015). How librarians can harness the power of social media for the benefit of their users. *Multimedia Information & Technology*, *41*(4), 23–26.

Ashwini Veronica, S., & Samuel, A. U. (2012, December). Social Media Addiction among Adolescents with Special Reference to Facebook Addiction. *IOSR Journal of Humanities and Social Science.* Retrieved from www.iosrjournals.org

Association of College and Research Libraries. (2000). *Information Literacy Competency Standards for Higher Education.* Chicago, IL: American Library Association.

Association of College and Research Libraries. (2016). *Framework for Information Literacy for Higher Education.* Chicago, IL: American Library Association.

Attfield, S., Kazai, G., Lalmas, M., & Piwowarski, B. (2011, February). Towards a science of user engagement (position paper). *WSDM workshop on user modelling for Web applications*. Retrieved from: http://www.dcs.gla.ac.uk/~mounia/Papers/engagement.pdf

Ayoub, A., & Beydoun, K. (2017). Executive disorder: The Muslim Ban, emergency advocacy, and the fires next time. *Michigan Journal of Race & Law*, *22*(2), 215–241.

Ayu, A. R., & Abrizah, A. (2011). Do you Facebook? Usage and applications of Facebook page among academic libraries in Malaysia. *The International Information & Library Review*, *43*(4), 239–249. doi:10.1080/10572317.2011.10762906

Bányai, F., Zsila, Á., Király, O., Maraz, A., Elekes, Z., Griffiths, M. D., ... Demetrovics, Z. (2017). Problematic social media use: Results from a large-scale nationally representative adolescent sample. *PLoS One*, *12*(1), e0169839. doi:10.1371/journal.pone.0169839 PMID:28068404

Barnes, I. (2014). Twitter in special libraries: A distributed social media strategy. *Public Services Quarterly*, *10*(1), 62–65. doi:10.1080/15228959.2014.875789

Baro, E., Idiodi, E., & Godfrey, V. (2012). Awareness and use of Web 2.0 tools by librarians in university libraries in Nigeria. *OCLC Systems & Services*, *29*(3), 170–188. doi:10.1108/OCLC-12-2012-0042

Batchelor, O. (2017). Getting out the truth: The role of libraries in the fight against fake news. *RSR. Reference Services Review*, *45*(2), 143–148. doi:10.1108/RSR-03-2017-0006

Bateman, R. (2017). *InstHEgram: A 'Uni'-versal Guide to Instagram in Higher Education*. Retrieved from https://leanpub.com/instHEgram

Battleson, B., Booth, A., & Weintrop, J. (2001). Usability testing of an academic library web site: A case study. *Journal of Academic Librarianship*, *27*(3), 188–198. doi:10.1016/S0099-1333(01)00180-X

Bawden, D., Holtham, C., & Courtney, N. (1999). *Perspectives on information overload*. Aslib. doi:10.1108/EUM0000000006984

Bedell, J. (2010, September 20). *What is the Difference Between Social Media and Social Networking?* Retrieved December 2, 2010, from http://jasontbedell.com/what-is-the-difference-between-social-media-and-social-networking

Bennett, S. (2014, October 20). 88% of companies are using social media for marketing. *Adweek*. Retrieved from https://www.adweek.com/digital/social-media-companies/

Benselin, J. C., & Ragsdell, G. (2016). Information overload: The differences that age makes. *Journal of Librarianship and Information Science*, *48*(3), 284–297. doi:10.1177/0961000614566341

Bentenbi. (2010). Towards a Visibility of Algerian Libraries in a Social Media Era. *Cybrarian Journal*, (12), 28. Retrieved from http://www.journal.cybrarians.org/index.php?option=com_content&view=article&id=622:socialmedia&catid=255:09-studies&Itemid=89

Betty, P. (2009). Assessing homegrown library collections: Using Google Analytics to track use of screencasts and flash-based learning objects. *Journal of Electronic Resources Librarianship*, *21*(1), 75–92. doi:10.1080/19411260902858631

Binkley, C. (2015, September 18). He? she? ze? Colleges add gender-free pronouns, alter policy. *AP News*. Retrieved from https://apnews.com/48c986c722ba4e5bb8a5a4c1f1d31df1/he-she-ze-universities-add-gender-pronouns-alter-policy

Blaine, T. B. (2010). *Social Media: Implications for intellectual property law*. Syracuse, NY: PLLC.

Blakiston, R. (2013). Developing a Content Strategy for an Academic Library Website. *Journal of Electronic Resources Librarianship*, *25*(3), 175–191. doi:10.1080/1941126X.2013.813295

Blowers, H. (2012). Measuring social media and the greater digital landscape. *Computers in Libraries*, *32*(7), 27–29.

Bonneau, J., & Preibusch, S. (2010). The Privacy Jungle:On the Market for Data Protection in Social Networks. In T. Moore, D. Pym, & C. Ioannidis (Eds.), *Economics of Information Security and Privacy*. Boston, MA: Springer. doi:10.1007/978-1-4419-6967-5_8

Bonsón, E., & Flores, F. (2011). Social media and corporate dialogue: The response of global financial institutions. *Online Information Review*, *35*(1), 34–49. doi:10.1108/14684521111113579

Booker, L., & Bandyopadhyay, S. (2017). How academic libraries can leverage social networking to popularize their services: An empirical study. *Journal of the Indiana Academy of the Social Sciences*, *16*(2), 129–146. Retrieved from https://digitalcommons.butler.edu/jiass/vol16/iss2/12/

Borders, B. (2010). *A Brief History of Social Media*. Retrieved from http://socialmediarockstar.com/history-of-social-media

Borgerson, J. L., & Schroeder, J. E. (2002). Ethical issues of global marketing: Avoiding bad faith in visual representation. *European Journal of Marketing*, *36*(5/6), 570–594. doi:10.1108/03090560210422399

Borruto, G. (2015). Analysis of tweets in Twitter. *Webology*, *12*(1), 1–11.

Bottorff, T., Glaser, R., Todd, A., & Alderman, B. (2008). Branching out: Communication and collaboration among librarians at multi-campus institutions. *Journal of Library Administration*, *48*(3-4), 329–363. doi:10.1080/01930820802289391

Bountouri, L., & Giannakopoulos, G. (2014). The use of social media in archives. *Procedia: Social and Behavioral Sciences*, *147*, 510–517. doi:10.1016/j.sbspro.2014.07.146

Boyd, D. M., & Ellison, N. B. (2007). Social network sites: Definition, history, and scholarship. *Journal of Computer-Mediated Communication*, *13*(1), 210–230. doi:10.1111/j.1083-6101.2007.00393.x

Bradley, S. S. (2010). *Copyright protection in the digital age*. Association of Corporate Counsel. Retrieved from http://www.acc.com/legalresources/quickcounsel/icpituscaeu.cfm

Brandt, J., Frederiksen, L., Schneider, T., & Syrkin, D. (2006). The face of regional campus libraries and librarianship. *Journal of Library Administration*, *45*(1/2), 37–61. doi:10.1300/J111v45n01_03

Breeding, M. (2007). Librarians face online social networks. *Computers in Libraries*, *27*(8), 30–33. Retrieved from https://librarytechnology.org/repository/item.pl?id=12735

Brett, K. R., Lierman, A., & Turner, C. (2016). Lessons learned: A primo usability study. *Information Technology and Libraries*, *35*(1), 7–25. doi:10.6017/ital.v35i1.8965

Brigham, T. J. (2013). Personas: Stepping Into the Shoes of the Library User. *Medical Reference Services Quarterly*, *32*(4), 443–450. doi:10.1080/02763869.2013.837737 PMID:24180652

Bright, J., Margetts, H., Hale, S., & Yasseri, T. (2014). *The use of social media for research and analysis: A feasibility study*. Retrieved from https://www.gov.uk/government/publications/use-of-social-media-for-research-and-analysis

Britannica Academic. (2017). *Media convergence*. Retrieved from academic.eb.com/levels/collegiate/article/media-convergence/439212#

Britannica Academic. (2018). *Broadband technology*. Retrieved from academic.eb.com/levels/collegiate/article%20/broadband-technology/471920

Brookbank, E. (2015). So much social media, so little time: Using student feedback to guide academic library social media strategy. *Journal of Electronic Resources Librarianship*, *27*(4), 232–247. doi:10.1080/1941126X.2015.1092344

Brooks, S., & Califf, C. (2017). Social media-induced techno stress: Its impact on the job performance of it professionals and the moderating role of job characteristics. *Computer Networks*, *114*, 143–153. doi:10.1016/j.comnet.2016.08.020

Bryan, J. (2016). The Preparation of Academic Librarians Who Provide Instruction: A Comparison of First and Second Career Librarians. *Journal of Academic Librarianship*, *42*(4), 340–354. doi:10.1016/j.acalib.2016.05.010

Bryson, A., & Forth, J. (2007). *Productivity and days of the week.* Royal Society for the Encouragement of Arts, Manufactures & Commerce. Retrieved from https://eprints.lse.ac.uk/4963/1/daysoftheweek%28LSEROversion%29.pdf

Buckels, E. E., Trapnell, P. D., & Paulhus, D. L. (2014). Trolls just want to have fun. *Personality and Individual Differences*, *67*, 97–102. doi:10.1016/j.paid.2014.01.016

Bunker, L. (2017). Picking a platform and finding a voice. In S. Young & D. Rossmann (Eds.), *Using social media to build library communities: A LITA guide* (pp. 1–28). Lanham, MD: Rowman & Littlefield.

Burak, L. (2012). Multitasking in the University classroom. *International Journal for the Scholarship of Teaching and Learning*, *6*(2), 1–12. doi:10.20429/ijsotl.2012.060208

Burclaff, N., & Johnson, C. (2014). Developing a social media strategy: Tweets, pins, and posts with a purpose. *College & Research Libraries News*, *75*(7), 366–369. doi:10.5860/crln.75.7.9156

Burkell, J. A., Fortier, A., Di Valentino, L. & Roberts, S. T. (2015). *Enhancing key digital literacy skills: Information privacy, information security, and copyright/intellectual property.* Library and Information Science Publications.

Burkhardt, A. (2010, January). Social media: A guide for college and university libraries. *College & Research Libraries News.* Retrieved from https://crln.acrl.org/index.php/crlnews/article/view/8302/8391

Burkhardt, A. (2010). Social media: A guide for college and university libraries. *College & Research Libraries News*, *71*(1), 10–24. doi:10.5860/crln.71.1.8302

Burkhardt, J. M. (2017). Combating fake news in the digital age. *Library Technology Reports*, *53*(8), 1–33. https://doi-org.proxy.library.vcu.edu/10.5860/ltr.53n8

Buruga, B. A. (2016). *The Use of Mobile Technologies for Social Media-Based Service Delivery at Muni University Library, Uganda.* Retrieved from https://repository.up.ac.za/bitstream/handle/2263/58991/Buruga_Use_2016.pdf?sequence=4

Bussell, H., & Hagman, J. (2017). From training to learning: Developing student employees through experiential learning design. In P. McDonnell (Ed.), *The experiential library: Transforming academic and research libraries through the power of experiential learning* (pp. 147–159). Chandos Publishing. doi:10.1016/B978-0-08-100775-4.00011-X

Butcher, J. (2015). *'Shoe-horned and side-lined'? Challenges for part-time learners in the new HE landscape.* Retrieved from https://www.heacademy.ac.uk/knowledge-hub/shoe-horned-and-side-lined-challenges-part-time-learners-new-he-landscape

Butcher, J., & Rose-Adams, J. (2015). Part-time learners in open and distance learning: revisiting the critical importance of choice, flexibility and employability. *Open Learning: The Journal of Open, Distance and e-Learning, 30*(2), 127-137.

California State University, Chico. (2010). *Evaluating information: Applying the CRAAP test.* Retrieved from https://www.csuchico.edu/lins/handouts/eval_websites.pdf

Callaghan, G., & Fribbance, I. (2016). The use of Facebook to build a community for distance learning students: a case study from the Open University. *Open Learning: The Journal of Open, Distance and e-Learning, 31*(3), 260-272.

Candela, L., Athanasopoulos, G., Castelli, D., El Raheb, K. & Innocenti, P. (2011). *The digital library reference model.* London: DL.org Project Deliverable.

Canty, N. (2012). Social media in libraries: It's like, complicated. *Alexandria (Aldershot), 23*(2), 41–53. doi:10.7227/ALX.23.2.4

Canty, N. (2012). Social Media in Libraries: It's like, Complicated. *The Journal of Library and International Library and Information Issues, 23*(2).

Canty, N. (2012). Social media in libraries: It's like, complicated. *The Journal of National and International Library and Information Issues, 23*(2), 41–54. Retrieved from https://www.researchgate.net/publication/249371034_Social_Media_in_Libraries_It's_Like_Complicated

Carter, T. M., & Seaman, P. (2011). The Management and Support of Outreach in Academic Libraries. *Reference & User Services Quarterly, 51*(2), 163–171.

Center for Persons with Disabilities, Utah State University. (2018). *Web AIM: Web Accessibility in Mind.* Retrieved June 17, 2018 from, https://webaim.org

Center for Plain Language. (n.d.). *5 Steps to Plain Language.* Retrieved June 16, 2018 from, https://centerforplainlanguage.org/learning-training/five-steps-plain-language/

Chandler, A., & Wallace, M. (2016). Using Piwik Instead of Google Analytics at the Cornell University Library. *The Serials Librarian, 71*(3-4), 173–179. doi:10.1080/0361526X.2016.1245645

Charnigo, L., & Barnett-Ellis, P. (2007). Checking out Facebook. com: The impact of a digital trend on academic libraries. *Information Technology and Libraries, 26*(1), 23. doi:10.6017/ital.v26i1.3286

Chatten, Z. (2017). Making social media work: Finding a library voice. *Insights: The UKSG Journal, 30*(3), 51–61. doi:10.1629/uksg.374

Chatten, Z., & Roughley, S. (2016). Developing social media to engage and connect at the University of Liverpool Library. *New Review of Academic Librarianship, 22*(2-3), 249–256. doi:10.1080/13614533.2016.1152985

Chen, D. Y., Chu, S. K., & Xu, S. (2012). How do libraries use social networking sites to interact with users. *Proceedings of the American Society for Information Science and Technology, 49*(1), 1–10. doi:10.1002/meet.14504901286

Chokshi, N. (2018, March 28). Heineken pulls 'lighter is better' ad after outcry over racism. *The New York Times.* Retrieved from https://www.nytimes.com/2018/03/28/business/media/heineken-racist-ad.html

Christie, P. (2017). Cyber-security - what your library needs to know. *Vable.* Retrieved from https://www.vable.com/blog/cyber-security-what-your-library-needs-to-know

Chrome Web Store. (2018). *Site Improve Accessibility Checker.* Retrieved September 10, 2018 from, https://chrome.google.com/webstore/detail/siteimprove-accessibility/efcfolpjihicnikpmhnmphjhhpiclljc?hl=en-US

Chua, A. Y., & Goh, D. H. (2010). A study of Web 2.0 applications in library websites. *Library & Information Science Research, 32*(3), 203–211. doi:10.1016/j.lisr.2010.01.002

Chugh, R., & Ruhi, U. (2018). Social media in higher education: A literature review of Facebook. *Education and Information Technologies, 23*(2), 605–616. doi:10.100710639-017-9621-2

Chu, S. K. W., & Du, H. S. (2013). Social networking tools for academic libraries. *Journal of Librarianship and Information Science, 45*(1), 64–75. doi:10.1177/0961000611434361

Chute, T. (2000). Selling the college and university archives: Current outreach perspectives. *Archival Issues, 25*(1/2), 33–48.

Clark, M., Fine, M. B., & Scheuer, C. (2017). Relationship quality in higher education marketing: The role of social media engagement. *Journal of Marketing for Higher Education, 27*(1), 40–58. doi:10.1080/08841241.2016.1269036

Clark, M., & Melancon, J. (2013). The influence of social media investment on relational outcomes: A relationship marketing perspective. *International Journal of Marketing Studies, 5*(4), 132–142. doi:10.5539/ijms.v5n4p132

Cohen, L. S. (2009, April 30). *Is There A Difference Between Social Media And Social Networking?* Retrieved from http://lonscohen.com/blog/2009/04/difference-between-social-media-and-social-networking/

Coiro, J., Coscarelli, C., Maykel, C., & Forzani, E. (2015). Investigating criteria that seventh graders use to evaluate the quality of online information. *Journal of Adolescent & Adult Literacy, 59*(3), 287–297. doi:10.1002/jaal.448

Collins, G., & Haase, A. Q. (2012). Social media and academic libraries: Current trends and future challenges. *Proceedings of the Association for Information Science and Technology, 49*(1), 1–4. doi:10.1002/meet.14504901272

Collins, G., & Quan-Haase, A. (2014). Are social media ubiquitous in academic libraries? A longitudinal study of adoption and usage patterns. *Journal of Web Librarianship, 8*(1), 48–68. doi:10.1080/19322909.2014.873663

Cone Communications. (2017). *2017 Cone communications CSR study*. Retrieved from http://www.conecomm.com/2017-cone-communications-csr-study-pdf

Content Marketing Institute. (2018). *Getting Started.* Retrieved August 2, 2018, from https://contentmarketinginstitute.com/getting-started/

Cook, J. (2016, June 4). Instagram made a change that stopped lots of third-party apps from working. *Business Insider*. Retrieved from https://www.businessinsider.com/instagram-made-a-change-that-stopped-lots-of-third-party-apps-from-working-2016-6

Cooley, D. O., Brice, J., Becerra, E. P., & Chapa, S. (2015). The effect of cosmopolitanism on multi-ethnic U.S. markets under varying conditions of diversity in advertising. *Academy of Marketing Studies Journal, 19*(3), 119–138.

Critlib. (2018). *Previous Twitter chats*. Retrieved from http://critlib.org/twitter-chats/previous-twitter-chats/

Crymble, A. (2010). An analysis of Twitter and Facebook use by the archival community. *Archivaria, 70*, 125–151.

Cuddy, C., Graham, J., & Morton-Owens, E. G. (2010). Implementing Twitter in a Health Sciences Library. *Medical Reference Services Quarterly, 29*(4), 320–330. doi:10.1080/02763869.2010.518915 PMID:21058176

Cui, G. (1997). Marketing strategies in a multi-ethnic environment. *Journal of Marketing Theory and Practice, 5*(1), 122–134. doi:10.1080/10696679.1997.11501756

Cvetkovic, M. (2009). Making Web 2.0 work – from 'Librarian Habilis' to 'Librarian Sapiens'. *Computers in Libraries, 29*(9), 14–17.

Dalal, H. A., O'Hanlon, R., & Yacobucci, K. L. (2017). *Video Marketing for Libraries: A Practical Guide for Librarians.* Rowman & Littlefield. Retrieved from https://books.google.com/books?id=3vK_jwEACAAJ

Datig, I. (2018). Revitalizing library websites and social media with content strategy: Tools and recommendations. *Journal of Electronic Resources Librarianship, 30*(2), 63–69. doi:10.1080/1941126X.2018.1465511

Davis, C. H., Deil-Amen, R., Rios-Aguilar, C., & Manuel, G. C. (2012). *Social media in higher education: A literature review and research directions*. Center for the Study of Higher Education, University of Arizona and Claremont Graduate University.

Davis, J. F. (2018). Selling whiteness? - A critical review of the literature on marketing and racism. *Journal of Marketing Management, 34*(1/2), 134–177. doi:10.1080/0267257X.2017.1395902

Dawson, M., Wright, J., & Omar, M. (2015). Mobile Devices: The Case for Cyber Security. *New Threats and Countermeasures in Digital Crime and Cyber Terrorism*, 8.

De Rosa, C., Cantrell, J., Havens, A., Hawk, J., & Jenkins, L. (2007). *Sharing, privacy, and trust in our networked world: A report to the OCLC membership*. Dublin, OH: OCLC Online Computer Library Center. Retrieved from https://www.oclc.org/content/dam/oclc/reports/pdfs/sharing.pdf

De Rosa, C., Cantrell, J., Havens, A., Hawk, J., Jenkins, L., Gauder, B., & Cellentani, D. (2007). Sharing, privacy and trust in our networked world: A report to the OCLC Membership. Dublin, OH: OCLC Online Computer Library Center. *Electronic Journal of Research in Educational Psychology, 9*(3), 961–994.

Del Bosque, D., Leif, S. A., & Skarl, S. (2012). Libraries atwitter: Trends in academic library tweeting. *RSR. Reference Services Review, 40*(2), 199–213. doi:10.1108/00907321211228246

Delaney, G., & Bates, J. (2015). Envisioning the academic library: A reflection on roles, relevancy and relationships. *New Review of Academic Librarianship, 21*(1), 3–51. doi:10.1080/13614533.2014.911194

Delaney, S. (2011). Apps & Web 2.0: Legal risks from using the internet in class. *Distance Education Report, 15*(9), 5–7.

DeMers, J. (2015). The top 10 benefits of blogging on your website. *Forbes*. Retrieved from https://www.forbes.com/sites/jaysondemers/2015/05/28/the-top-10-benefits-of-blogging-on-your-website/#6ce3b5a31177

Dengerink, H. A. (2001). Institutional identity and organizational structure in multi-campus universities. *Metropolitan Universities, 12*(2), 20–29.

Deng, L., & Tavares, N. J. (2013). From Moodle to Facebook: Exploring students' motivation and experiences in online communities. *Computers & Education, 68*, 167–176. doi:10.1016/j.compedu.2013.04.028

Deodato, J. (2014). The patron as producer: Libraries, Web 2.0, and participatory culture. *The Journal of Documentation, 70*(5), 734–758. doi:10.1108/JD-10-2012-0127

Dessart, L., Veloutsou, C., & Morgan-Thomas, A. (2016). Capturing consumer engagement: Duality, dimensionality and measurement. *Journal of Marketing Management, 32*(5–6), 399–426. doi:10.1080/0267257X.2015.1130738

Determann, L. (2012). Social media privacy: A dozen myths and facts. *Stanford Technology Law, 7*, 1–14.

Dewing, M. (2010). *Social media: An introduction*. Library of Parliament Information and Research Service. Retrieved from http://publications.gc.ca/collections/collection_2010/bdp-lop/bp/2010-03-eng.pdf

Dickson, A., & Holley, R. P. (2010). Social networking in academic libraries: The possibilities and the concerns. *New Library World, 111*(11), 468–479. doi:10.1108/03074801011094840

DLH Holdings Corp. (2014, May 5). *T.H.I.S Social Media Accessibility Google Hangout*. Retrieved June 13, 2018 from, https://www.youtube.com/watch?v=DKXXKtFRNlQ

Dodson, I. (2016). *The art of digital marketing: The definitive guide to creating strategic, targeted, and measurable online campaigns*. Hoboken, NJ: Wiley.

Dougherty, K., Jones, S., Lahr, H., Natow, R., Pheatt, L., Reddy, V., & Mclendon, M. (2014). Performance Funding for Higher Education: Forms, Origins, Impacts, and Futures. *The Annals of the American Academy of Political and Social Science, 655*(1), 163–184. doi:10.1177/0002716214541042

Dowd, N. (2013). Social media: Libraries are posting, but Is anyone listening? *Library Journal.*

Dresden, B., & Hidalgo, R. (2017, September). *Beyond the VLE forum: using Twitter to build community and currency into distance-learning modules*. Paper presented at the Association for Learning Technology Annual Conference, Liverpool, UK. Retrieved from https://altc.alt.ac.uk/2017/sessions/beyond-the-vle-forum-using-twitter-to-build-community-and-currency-into-distance-learning-modules-1760/

Dryden, N. H., & Goldstein, S. (2013). Regional campus learning commons: Assessing to meet student needs. *Journal of Library Administration, 53*(5-6), 293–322. doi:10.1080/01930826.2013.876822

Ducharme, J. (2018, February 24). Colleges assure prospective students that protesting for gun control will not affect their admission. *Time*. Retrieved from http://time.com/5174165/colleges-gun-control-protests-admission/

Duncan, A. P., & Durrant, F. (2015). An assessment of the usability of the University of the West Indies (Mona, Jamaica) Main Library's website. *The Electronic Library, 33*(3), 590–599.

Edelman. (2017, June 18). *2017 Edelman earned brand*. Retrieved from https://www.slideshare.net/EdelmanInsights/2017-edelman-earned-brand

Edosomwan, S., Prakasan, S. K., Kouame, D., Watson, J., & Seymour, T. (2011). The History of Social Media and its Impact on Business. *The Journal of Applied Management and Entrepreneurship, 16*(3), 79–91.

Ellis, E., Gallagher, A., & Peasgood, A. (2017). *Study behaviours in an increasingly digital world: Learning habits, top tips and 'study hacks' questionnaire survey*. The Open University. Retrieved from http://oro.open.ac.uk/50433/

Emery & Schifeling. (2015). Libraries Using Twitter Better: Insights on Engagement from Food Trucks. In *Creating Sustainable Community The Proceedings of the ACRL 2015 Conference* (pp. 593-604). Association of College and Research Libraries: Chicago.

Emery, K., & Schifeling, T. (2015). Libraries using Twitter better: Insights on engagement from food trucks. *Proceedings of the ACRL 2015 Conference*, 450-458. Retrieved from http://www.ala.org/acrl/sites/ala.org.acrl/files/content/conferences/confsandpreconfs/2015/Emery_Schifeling.pdf

Emmons & Oakleaf. (2016). The ACRL Standards for Proficiencies for Assessment Librarians and Coordinators: A New Document to Support and Strengthen Assessment Efforts in Academic Libraries. *The Journal of Academic Librarianship, 42*(5), 622-624.

Erfanmanesh, M., & Hossseini, E. (2015). Internet and Social Media Addiction. *Webology, 12*(2), 1–3. Retrieved from https://search.proquest.com/docview/1787761590?accountid=14548%0Ahttps://julac.hosted.exlibrisgroup.com/openurl/HKU_ALMA/SERVICES_PAGE??url_ver=Z39.88-2004&rft_val_fmt=info:ofi/fmt:kev:mtx:journal&genre=unknown&sid=ProQ:ProQ%3Alisa&atitle=Internet+and+Socia

Ericson, T. L. (1990-91). Preoccupied with our own gardens: Outreach and archivists. *Archivaria, 31*, 114–122.

Evans, H. (2017, January 29). *"Content is King"—Essay by Bill Gates 1996*. Retrieved August 29, 2018, from https://medium.com/@HeathEvans/content-is-king-essay-by-bill-gates-1996-df74552f80d9

ExecutiveGov. (2010). *The five best government blogs and the six reasons why they work.* Retrieved from http://www.executivegov.com/2010/01/the-five-best-government-blogs-and-the-six-reasons-why-they-work/

Ezeani, C. N., & Igwesi, U. (2012). Using social media for dynamic library services delivery: the Nigerian experience. *Library Philosophy and Practice.* Retrieved from http://digitalcommons.unl.edu/libphilprac/814

Facebook Ads Manager [Social network advertising tool]. (2018). Retrieved from https://business.facebook.com/adsmanager

Facebook Help Center. (2018). *Accessibility*. Retrieved July 8, 2018 from, https://www.facebook.com/help/accessibility

Facebook. (2019). *How News Feed Works*. Retrieved January 12, 2019, from https://www.facebook.com/help/1155510281178725

Fagioli, L., Rios-Aguilar, C., & Deil-Amen, R. (2015). Changing the context of student engagement: Using Facebook to increase community college student persistence and success. *Teachers College Record*, *117*(12), 1–42.

Fang, W. (2007). Using Google Analytics for improving library website content and design: a case study. *Library Philosophy and Practice*, 1-17.

Fang, J., Wen, C., & Prybutok, V. (2014). An Assessment of Equivalence between Paper and Social Media Surveys: The Role of Social Desirability and Satisficing. *Computers in Human Behavior*, *30*, 335–343. doi:10.1016/j.chb.2013.09.019

Farkas, M. (2009). Governing social media. *American Libraries*, *40*(12), 35.

Farkas, M. G., Hinchliffe, L. J., & Houk, A. H. (2015). Bridges and Barriers: Factors Influencing a Culture of Assessment in Academic Libraries. *College & Research Libraries*, *76*(2), 150–169. doi:10.5860/crl.76.2.150

Fenn, J., Hall, S., Harris, M., Saylor, N., Shankar, G., Stefano, M., … Winick, S. (n.d.). About [Blog post]. *Folklife Today*. Retrieved from https://blogs.loc.gov/folklife/about/

Fenwick, T. (2016). Social media, professionalism and higher education: A sociomaterial consideration. *Studies in Higher Education*, *41*(4), 664–677. doi:10.1080/03075079.2014.942275

Fernandez, P. (2009). Online Social Networking Sites and Privacy: Revisiting Ethical Considerations for a New Generation of Technology. *Library Philosophy and Practice*, *2009*, 1–9.

Ferrara, E., Varol, O., Davis, C., Menczer, F., & Flammini, A. (2016). The rise of social bots. *Communications of the ACM*, *59*(7), 96–104. doi:10.1145/2818717

Fialkoff, F., Chant, I., Dixon, J., Koerber, J., Murvosh, M., Pinkowski, J., ... Schwartz, M. (2018). Movers & shakers 2018: The people shaping the future of libraries. *Library Journal*, *143*(5), 20–62.

Fichter, D., & Wisniewski, J. (2014). Content Marketing and Strategy for Libraries. *Online Searcher*, *38*(6), 74–76.

Fitzgerald, M.A. (1999). Evaluating information: An information literacy challenge. *School Library Media Research, 2,* 1-34.

Flock, E. (2017, February 13). Why these librarians are protesting Trump's executive orders. *PBS NewsHour.* Retrieved from https://www.pbs.org/newshour/arts/librarians-protesting-trumps-executive-orders

Flynn, N. (2012). *The Social Media Handbook: Rules, Policies, and Best Practices to Successfully Manage Your Organization's Social Media Presence, Posts, and Potential.* San Francisco, CA: Pfeiffer.

Frey, W. H. (2018, March 14). The US will become 'minority white' in 2045, census projects [Blog post]. Retrieved from https://www.brookings.edu/blog/the-avenue/2018/03/14/the-us-will-become-minority-white-in-2045-census-projects/

Galan, M., Lawley, M., & Clements, M. (2015). Social media's use in postgraduate students' decision-making journey: An exploratory study. *Journal of Marketing for Higher Education*, *25*(2), 287–312. doi:10.1080/08841241.2015.1083512

Gallardo, R. (2013). *Social Media for libraries.* Social Media Use. Retrieved from https://www.webjunction.org/events/webjunction/Library_Social _Media_Use.html

Gall, D. P. (2010). Librarian like a Rockstar: Using your personal Brand to promote your services and reach distance users. *Journal of Library Administration*, *50*(5 & 6).

Gamboa, A. M., & Gonçalves, H. M. (2014). Customer loyalty through social networks: Lessons from Zara on Facebook. *Business Horizons*, *57*(6), 709–717. doi:10.1016/j.bushor.2014.07.003

Gibbs, G. (2006). How assessment frames student learning. In C. Bryan & K. Clegg (Eds.), *Innovative Assessment in Higher Education* (pp. 23–36). London: Routledge.

Ginsburg, J. C. (2016). Overview of Copyright Law: Forthcoming, Oxford Handbook of Intellectual Property. Columbia Public Law Research Paper No. 14-518.

Gollin, M. (2018a). *The 2018 Instagram algorithm change: what it means for marketers*. Retrieved August 13, 2018, from https://www.falcon.io/insights-hub/topics/social-media-strategy/the-2018-instagram-algorithm-change-what-it-means-for-marketers/#/GEN

Gollin, M. (2018b). *How will the 2018 Facebook algorithm change affect marketers?* Retrieved August 13, 2018, from https://www.falcon.io/insights-hub/industry-updates/social-media-updates/facebook-algorithm-change/#/GEN

Gonzalez, C., Marks, G. J., & Westgate, H. (2018). *Social media directory of academic libraries*. Retrieved from: https://sites.google.com/wpunj.edu/nj-social-media-directory/home

Goodfellow, R., & Reedy, K. (2012). *Digital and Information Literacy Framework*. Retrieved from http://www.open.ac.uk/libraryservices/pages/dilframework/

Goodfellow, R., & Reedy, K. (2014). 'You've been frameworked': Evaluating an approach to digital and information literacy at the Open University. *Journal of Learning Development in Higher Education, 7*. Retrieved from http://oro.open.ac.uk/41547/1/Reedy.pdf

Google Accessibility Center. (2018). *Products and Features*. Retrieved June 5, 2018 from, https://www.google.com/accessibility/products-features.html

Gramlich, J. (2018, April). *5 facts about Americans and Facebook*. Pew Research Center. Retrieved from http://www.pewresearch.org/fact-tank/2018/04/10/5-facts-about-americans-and-facebook/

Granger, L. (2017). Messages of inclusion: A grassroots campaign for turbulent times. *American Libraries*, *48*(5), 12–15.

Green, C. L. (1999). Ethnic evaluations of advertising: Interaction effects of strength of ethnic identification. *Journal of Advertising*, *28*(1), 49–64. doi:10.1080/00913367.1999.10673576

Greysen, S. R., Kind, T., & Chretien, K. C. (2010). Online professionalism and the mirror of social media. *Journal of General Internal Medicine*, *25*(11), 1227–1229. doi:10.100711606-010-1447-1 PMID:20632121

Griffin, M., & Taylor, T. I. (2018). Employing Analytics to Guide a Data-Driven Review of LibGuides. *Journal of Web Librarianship*, 1–13.

Gross, R., Acquisti, A., & Heinz, J. III., H. (2005). Information revelation and privacy in online social networks (The Facebook Case). *WPES'05: Proceedings of the 2005 ACM Workshop on Privacy in the Electronic Society*, 71-80. 10.1145/1102199.1102214

Gu, F., & Widen-Wulff, G. (2011). Scholarly communication and possible changes in the context of social media: A Finnish case study. *The Electronic Library*, *29*(6), 762–776. doi:10.1108/02640471111187999

Gunton, L., & Davis, K. (2012). Beyond broadcasting: Customer service, community and information experience in the Twittersphere. *RSR. Reference Services Review*, *40*(2), 224–227. doi:10.1108/00907321211228282

Gupta, B., Dhawan, S., & Pp, V. (2016). Social Media and Libraries: A Scientometric Assessment of World Output, 2003-2014. *SRELS Journal of Information Management, 53*(1).

Gustafson, J. C., Sharrow, Z., & Short, G. (2017). Library marketing on a small liberal arts campus: Assessing communication preferences. *Journal of Library Administration*, *57*(4), 420–435. doi:10.1080/01930826.2017.1300459

H.B. 2120, 53d Leg. 1st Reg. Sess. (Ariz. 2017)

Hallis, R. (2017). Internet outfitters: Librarians in the twenty-first century. *Library Management*, *38*(6/7), 369–379. doi:10.1108/LM-02-2017-0012

Haltzel, M. H. (2014, February). *Library of Congress: An illustrated guide*. European Collections. Retrieved from https://www.loc.gov/rr/european/guide/intro.html

Harris, P. (2016). Drinking from the fire hose: Social media on campus. *Security Technology Executive*, 32-34. Retrieved from: https://search-proquest-com.du.idm.oclc.org/docview/1777246161?accountid=14608

Harrison, A., Burress, R., Velasquez, S., & Schreiner, L. (2017). Social media use in academic libraries: A phenomenological study. *Journal of Academic Librarianship*, *43*(3), 248–256. doi:10.1016/j.acalib.2017.02.014

Hartshorn, S. (2010). *5 Differences between Social Media and Social Networking*. Retrieved December 1, 2010, from socialmediatoday: http://www.socialmediatoday.com/SMC/194754

Heap, T., & Minocha, S. (2012). An empirically grounded framework to guide blogging for digital scholarship. *Research in Learning Technology Proceeding of the 2012 Conference*. 10.3402/rlt.v20i0.19195

Hebert, J. R. (2010, July). Hispanic and Portuguese Collections: Introduction. *Library of Congress: An illustrated guide*. Retrieved from http://www.loc.gov/rr/hispanic/guide/intro.html

Held, T., & Gil-Trejo, L. (2016). Students Weigh In: Usability Test of Online Library Tutorials. *Internet Reference Services Quarterly*, *21*(1/2), 1–21. doi:10.1080/10875301.2016.1164786

Hendrix, D., Chiarella, D., Hasman, L., Murphy, S., & Zafron, M. L. (2009). Use of Facebook in academic health sciences libraries. *Journal of the Medical Library Association: JMLA*, *97*(1), 44–47. doi:10.3163/1536-5050.97.1.008 PMID:19159005

Hermida, A. (2014). *Tell everyone: Why we share & why it matters*. Toronto: Doubleday Canada.

Heyd, T. (2017). Blogs. In C. Hoffmann & W. Bublitz (Eds.), *Pragmatics of social media* (pp. 151–172). Berlin, Germany: De Gruyter Mouton. doi:10.1515/9783110431070-006

Holmes, R. (2014, July 21). Want to win with content marketing? Stick to these 3 basics. *Hootsuite*. Retrieved from https://blog.hootsuite.com/want-to-win-at-content-marketing-stick-to-these-3-basics/

Hoodless, C., & Pinfield, S. (2016). Subject vs. functional: Should subject librarians be replaced by functional specialists in academic libraries? *Journal of Librarianship and Information Science*. Retrieved from http://journals.sagepub.com/doi/abs/10.1177/0961000616653647

Hootsuite. (2018, July 18). *Social Media Image Sizes: A Quick Reference Guide for Each Network*. Retrieved November 29, 2018, from https://blog.hootsuite.com/social-media-image-sizes-guide/

Hopman, R. (2012). *2012 survey results: Social media use in archives and special collections*. Retrieved from http://rebeccahopman.com/index/wp-content/uploads/2014/09/2012 surveyresults.pdf

Houk, K. M., & Thornhill, K. (2013). Using Facebook page insights data to determine posting best practices in an academic health sciences library. *Journal of Web Librarianship*, *7*(4), 372–388. doi:10.1080/19322909.2013.837346

Howard, H., Huber, S., Carter, L., & Moore, E. (2018, March). Academic libraries on social media: Finding the students and the information they want. *Information Technology and Libraries*, *37*(1), 8–18. doi:10.6017/ital.v37i1.10160

Ifijeh, G. (2014). Adoption of digital preservation methods for theses in Nigerian academic libraries: Applications and implications. *The J. of Acad. Lib*, *40*, 399–404.

IFLA. (2018). *How To Spot Fake News*. Retrieved from https://www.ifla.org/publications/node/11174

Ihme, T. A., & Stürmer, S. (2018). Emphasizing excellence and diversity cues on university websites: Additive or interactive effects on prospective students' psychological reactions? *Journal of Applied Social Psychology*, *48*(2), 59–70. doi:10.1111/jasp.12490

Information Professionals' Knowledge Sharing Practices in Social Media. A Study of Professionals in Developing Countries. *International Journal of Knowledge Content Development & Technology*, *6*(2), 43-66. Retrieved from http://ijkcdt.net/xml/08903/08903.pdf

Insights | Facebook Help Center | Facebook. (n.d.). Retrieved August 29, 2018, from https://www.facebook.com/help/794890670645072/?helpref=hc_fnav

Instagram. (n.d.). *What are Instagram Insights*? Retrieved from: https://help.instagram.com/788388387972460

Iris, X. (2014). Social media application in digital libraries. *Online Information Review*, *38*(4), 502–523. doi:10.1108/OIR-11-2013-0261

Islam & Tsuji. (2016). Information Professionals' Knowledge Sharing Practices in Social Media: A Study of Professionals in Developing Countries. *International Journal of Knowledge Content Development & Technology*, *2*(6), 43–66. Retrieved from http://ijkcdt.net/_common/do.php?a=full&b=12&bidx=669&aidx=8903

Jacobson, T. B. (2011). Facebook as a library tool: Perceived vs. actual use. *College & Research Libraries*, *72*(1), 79–90. doi:10.5860/crl-88r1

James, J. P., Lee, K., Zhang, M., & Williams, J. D. (2017). Ethics and policy issues for internet advertising: Targeting multicultural consumers in the digital marketing era. *Journal of Management Policy and Practice*, *18*(4), 93–106.

Jansen, A. (2017). Likes, shares and follows: Launching a Facebook page for your academic library. *JLAMS, 13*(1), 1-12. Retrieved from: https://scholarsarchive.library.albany.edu/jlams/vol13/iss1/6/

Jarrow, J. E. (1997). What is a reasonable accommodation? [Web log article]. *DAIS (Disability Access Information and Support).* Retrieved May 5, 2018 from, http://www.daisweb.com/

Jaschik, S. (2017, October 11). Controversial professor placed on leave. *Inside Higher Ed.* Retrieved from https://www.insidehighered.com/news/2017/10/11/drexel-places-controversial-professor-leave

Johnson, C., & Burclaff, N. (2013, April). Making social media meaningful: connecting missions and policies. *Imagine, innovate, inspire: Proceedings of the ACRL 2013 Conference.* Retrieved June 16, 2018 from, http://www.ala.org/acrl/sites/ala.org.acrl/files/content/conferences/confsandpreconfs/2013/papers/JohnsonBurclaff_Making.pdf

Johnson, C., & Burclaff, N. (2013, April). Making social media meaningful: Connecting missions and policies. In *Imagine, innovate, inspire: Proceedings of the ACRL 2013* (pp. 10–13). Conference. Retrieved from http://www.ala.org/acrl/sites/ala.org.acrl/files/content/conferences/confsandpreconfs/2013/papers/JohnsonBurclaff_Making.pdf

Johnson, M. (2018). Fighting "fake news: How we overhauled our website evaluation lessons. *Knowledge Quest*, *47*(1), 32–36.

Junco, R., Heiberger, G., & Loken, E. (2011). The effect of Twitter on college student engagement and grades. *Journal of Computer Assisted Learning*, *27*(2), 119–132. doi:10.1111/j.1365-2729.2010.00387.x

Kahn, C., & Ingram, D. (2018, May 9). Three-quarters Facebook users as active or more since privacy scandal: Reuters/ Ipsos poll. *Reuters*. Retrieved from https://www.reuters.com/article/us-facebook-privacy-poll/three-quarters-facebook-users-as-active-or-more-since-privacy-scandal-reuters-ipsos-poll-idUSKBN1I7081

Kandiuk, M. (2017). Avoiding controversy: Academic freedom and the library exhibit. *Art Documentation: Journal of the Art Libraries Society of North America*, *36*(1), 91–107. doi:10.1086/691374

Kane, L. (2017, December 4). Meet generation Z, the 'millennials on steroids' who could lead the charge for change in the US. *Business Insider.* Retrieved from http://www.businessinsider.com/generation-z-profile-2017-9

Kapitan, A. (2017, July 3). On "person-first language": It's time to actually put the person first [Blog post]. Retrieved from https://radicalcopyeditor.com/2017/07/03/person-centered-language/

Kaplan, A. (2017). Academia goes social media, MOC, SPOC, SMOC and SSOC: The digital transformation of higher education institutions and universities. In B. Rishi & S. Bandyopadhyay (Eds.), *Contemporary Issues in Social Media Marketing* (pp. 20–30). New York, NY: Routledge. doi:10.4324/9781315563312-2

Kaplan, A. M., & Haenlein, M. (2010). Users of the World, Unite! The Challenges and Opportunities of Social Media. *Business Horizons*, *53*(1), 59–68. doi:10.1016/j.bushor.2009.09.003

Kassens-Noor, E. (2012). Twitter as a teaching practice to enhance active and informal learning in higher education: The case of sustainable tweets. *Active Learning in Higher Education*, *13*(1), 9–21. doi:10.1177/1469787411429190

Kendrick, A., Fullerton, J. A., & Kim, Y. J. (2013). Social responsibility in advertising: A marketing communications student perspective. *Journal of Marketing Education*, *35*(2), 141–154. doi:10.1177/0273475313490171

Khan Academy. (2018). *Tota11y: An Accessibility Visualization Toolkit.* Retrieved September 19, 2018, from http://khan.github.io/tota11y/

Khan, S. A., & Bhatti, R. (2012). *A review of problems and challenges of library professionals in developing countries including Pakistan.* Retrieved from http://digitalcommons.unl.edu/libphilprac/757/

Kim, H. M., Abels, E. G., & Yang, C. C. (2012). Who disseminates academic library information on Twitter? *Proceedings of the American Society for Information Science and Technology*, *49*(1), 1–4. doi:10.1002/meet.14504901317

King, O. (2017, February). The case for diversity in advertising [Blog post]. Retrieved from https://www.thinkwithgoogle.com/consumer-insights/diversity-in-advertising-black-millennials/

King, D. (2015, January). Managing your library's social media channel. *Library Technology Reports*, *51*(1), 5–35.

King, D. L. (2015). Chapter 5: Analytics, goals, and strategy for social media. *Library Technology Reports*, *51*(1), 26–32.

Kiscaden, E. (2014). *Creating a Current Awareness Service Using Yahoo! Pipes and LibGuides Information Technology and Libraries.* Retrieved from https://ejournals.bc.edu/ojs/index.php/ital/article/download/5273/pdf

Knickman, E., & Walton, K. (2014). Branch campus librarianship with minimal infrastructure: Rewards and challenges. *Community & Junior College Libraries*, *20*(3/4), 63–73. doi:10.1080/02763915.2015.1044301

Koerwer, S. (2007). Commentary—One teenager's advice to adults on how to avoid being creepy on Facebook. *Computers in Libraries*, *27*(8), 40. Retrieved from https://search-proquest-com.du.idm.oclc.org/docview/231113980?accountid=14608

Koontz, C., & Mon, L. (2014). *Marketing and social media: A guide for libraries, archives, and museums*. Lanham, MD: Rowman & Littlefield.

Kosta, E., Kalloniatis, C., Mitrou, L., & Gritzalis, S. (2010). Data protection issues pertaining to social networking under EU law. *Transforming Government: People, Process and Policy*, *4*(2), 193–201. doi:10.1108/17506161011047406

Kuh, G. D. (2008). *High-impact educational practices: What they are, who has access to them, and why they matter*. Washington, DC: Association of American Colleges and Universities.

Lavagnino, M. B. (2010). *Policy as an enabler of student engagement*. Retrieved May 30, 2018, from https://er.educause.edu/articles/2010/10/policy-as-an-enabler-of-student-engagement

Lee, K. (2014). The social media frequency guide: how often to post to Facebook, Twitter, Linkedin, and more. *Fast Company*. Retrieved from https://www.fastcompany.com/3029019/the-social-media-frequency-guide-how-often-to-post-to-facebook-twitter-linkedin-a

Lee, O. (2013, March). *What is Content? Learn from 40 Definitions*. Retrieved February 20, 2014, from https://www.toprankblog.com/2013/03/what-is-content/

Lee, J., & Kim, S. (2011). Exploring the role of social networks in affective organizational commitment: Network centrality, strength of ties, and structural holes. *American Review of Public Administration*, *41*(2), 205–223. doi:10.1177/0275074010373803

Leftheriotis, I., & Giannakos, M. N. (2014). Using social media for work: Losing your time or improving your work? *Computers in Human Behavior*, *31*(1), 134–142. doi:10.1016/j.chb.2013.10.016

Legal Information Institution. (n.d.). *42 U.S. Code § 12103 - Additional definitions*. Retrieved July 31, 2018 from, https://www.law.cornell.edu/uscode/text/42/12103

Lembree, D. (2018). *Easy Chirp*. Retrieved June 4, 2018 from, https://www.easychirp.com

Lenhart, A. (2015). Teens, social media & technology overview 2015. *Pew Research Center*. Retrieved from http://www.pewinternet.org/2015/04/09/teens-social-media-technology-2015/

LePage, E. (2017, June 27). 7 social media templates to save you hours of work. *Hootsuite*. Retrieved from https://blog.hootsuite.com/social-media-templates/

Levy, A. (2018, January-February). State of the profession: targeted harassment—faculty report back [Blog post]. Retrieved from https://www.aaup.org/article/state-profession-targeted-harassment—faculty-report-back

Lewis, H. (2016, November 17). Did fake news on Facebook swing the US election? *New Statesman*. Retrieved from https://www.newstatesman.com/world/2016/11/did-fake-news-facebook-swing-us-election

Library of Congress Web Governance Board. (2013, March). *Social media strategy to support the library's web strategy*. Author.

Library of Congress. (1989). *Annual report of the Librarian of Congress for the fiscal year ending September 30, 1988*. Washington, DC: Library of Congress. Retrieved from https://hdl.handle.net/2027/mdp.39015082937049

Library of Congress. (1990). *Annual report of the Librarian of Congress for the fiscal year ending September 30, 1989*. Washington, DC: Library of Congress.

Library of Congress. (1996). *Annual report of the Librarian of Congress for the fiscal year ending 30 September 1995*. Washington, DC: Library of Congress.

Library of Congress. (2001). *Annual report of the Librarian of Congress for the fiscal year ending September 30, 2000.* Washington, DC: Library of Congress. Retrieved from https://hdl.handle.net/2027/mdp.39015082936801

Library of Congress. (2005). *Annual report of the Librarian of Congress for the fiscal year ending September 30, 2004.* Washington, DC: Library of Congress. Retrieved from https://hdl.handle.net/2027/mdp.39015082937098

Library of Congress. (2010, November). *Library of Congress strategic plan fiscal year 2011-2016.* Washington, DC: Library of Congress. Retrieved from http://lcweb2.loc.gov/master/libn/about/documents/strategicplan2011-2016.pdf

Library of Congress. (2016). *Area Studies Blog Post Guidelines.* Author.

Library of Congress. (2017). *Annual report of the Librarian of Congress for the fiscal year ending September 30, 2016.* Washington, DC: Library of Congress. Retrieved from https://www.loc.gov/portals/static/about/reports-and-budgets/documents/annual-reports/fy2016.pdf

Library of Congress. (2017, February). *Comments & posting policy.* Retrieved from https://www.loc.gov/legal/comment-and-posting-policy/

Library of Congress. (2018a, July). *4 Corners of the World Blog Dashboards, April 2016-July 2018.* Author.

Library of Congress. (2018b, July). *International Collections Facebook page Insights, October 2016 to July 2018.* Author.

Library of Congress. (2018c, October). *Library of Congress Rules and Regulations.* Washington, DC: Library of Congress.

Library of Congress. (n.d.). *Library of Congress Strategic plan FY2016 through FY2020: Serving the Congress and the nation.* Washington, DC: Library of Congress. Retrieved from https://www.loc.gov/portals/static/about/documents/library_congress_stratplan_2016-2020.pdf

Lidwell, W., Holden, K., & Butler, J. (2010). Picture superiority effect. In *Universal principles of design: 125 ways to enhance usability, influence perception, increase appeal, make better design decisions, and teach through design* (p. 184). Beverly, MA: Rockport Publishers.

Linh, N. C. 2008. A survey of the application of Web 2.0 in Australasian academic libraries. *Library Hi Tech, 26*(4), 630–53.

Little, L., Lopez, A., McCullough, J., & Parmer, R. (2017). From broadcast to conversation in an academic library. In S. Young & D. Rossmann (Eds.), *Using social media to build library communities: A LITA guide* (pp. 28–45). Lanham, MD: Rowman & Littlefield.

Lopez-Medel, I. (2017). Using Super Bowl 2017 commercials to teach about diversity. *Journal of Advertising Education, 21*(2), 33–44. doi:10.1177/109804821702100209

Loudon, L., & Hall, H. (2010). From triviality to business tool: The case of Twitter in library and information services delivery. *Business Information Review, 27*(4), 236–241. doi:10.1177/0266382110390480

Luo, L. (2018). Experiencing Evidence-Based Library and Information Practice (EBLIP): Academic Librarians' Perspective. *College & Research Libraries, 79*(4), 554–567. doi:10.5860/crl.79.4.554

Luo, L., Wang, Y., & Han, L. (2013). Marketing via social media: A case study. *Library Hi Tech, 31*(3), 455–466. doi:10.1108/LHT-12-2012-0141

Mabweazara, R. M. (2014). *Use of social media tools by library staff at the University of the Western Cape, South Africa and the National University of Science and Technology, Zimbabwe.* Retrieved from http://etd.uwc.ac.za/xmlui/handle/11394/4120

MacDonald, G. (2013). Theorizing university identity development: Multiple perspectives and common goals. *Higher Education*, *65*(2), 153–166. doi:10.100710734-012-9526-3

Maheshwari, S. (2017, October 12). Different ads, different ethnicities, same car. *New York Times*. Retrieved from https://www.nytimes.com/interactive/2017/10/12/business/media/toyota-camry-ads-different-ethnicities.html

Mahmood, K., & Richardson, J. V. Jr. (2013). Impact of Web 2.0 technologies on academic libraries: A survey of ARL libraries. *The Electronic Library*, *31*(4), 508–520. doi:10.1108/EL-04-2011-0068

Maisiri, E., Mupaikwa, E., & Ngwenya, S. (2015). *Strategic Planning for Social Media in Libraries: The Case of Zimbabwe*. Information Science Reference, IGI Global. Retrieved from http://ir.nust.ac.zw/xmlui/bitstream/handle/123456789/515/Strategic%20Planning%20for%20social%20media%20in%20libraries.pdf?sequence=1&isAllowed=y

Makori, E. O. (2012). Bridging the information gap with the patrons in university libraries in Africa. *Library Review*, *61*(1), 30–40. doi:10.1108/00242531211207406

Mansfield-Devine, S. (2015). Computer Fraud & Security: Editorial. *Computer Fraud and Security*, *2015*(6). doi:10.1016/S1361-3723(15)30052-X

Marek, M. W., & Skrabut, S. (2017). Privacy in Educational use of Social Media in the US. *International Journal on E-Learning*, *16*(3), 265–286.

Markland, M. J., Gascho Rempel, H., & Bridges, L. (2017). Mobile website use and advanced researchers: Understanding library users at a university marine sciences branch campus. *Information Technology and Libraries*, *36*(4), 7–23. doi:10.6017/ital.v36i4.9953

McHone-Chase, S. (2009). Privacy and Confidentiality Issues: A Guide for Libraries and their Lawyers. *Reference and User Services Quarterly*, *49*(1), 104–105. doi:10.5860/rusq.49n1.104

McKenzie, J. (2017). *Ethics of using Google Analytics*. Presented to the User Experience Interest Group. Retrieved from http://summit.sfu.ca/item/17107

McNeill, B. (2017). *To combat 'alternative facts,' VCU Libraries launches campaign to encourage students to #VetYourSources*. Retrieved from https://news.vcu.edu/article/To_combat_alternative_facts_VCU_Libraries_launches_campaign_to

Mellon, C. (2015). Library anxiety: A grounded theory and its development. *College & Research Libraries*, *76*(3), 276–282. doi:10.5860/crl.76.3.276

Meola, M. (2004). Chucking the checklist: A contextual approach to teaching undergraduates Web-site evaluation. *portal. Libraries and the Academy*, *4*(3), 331–344. doi:10.1353/pla.2004.0055

Metzger, M. J. (2007). Making sense of credibility on the Web: Models for evaluating online information and recommendations for future research. *Journal of the American Society for Information Science and Technology*, *58*(13), 2078–2091. doi:10.1002/asi.20672

Mewburn, I., & Thomson, P. (2013). Why do academics blog? An analysis of audiences, purposes and challenges. *Studies in Higher Education*, *38*(8), 1106–1119. doi:10.1080/03075079.2013.835624

Mickoleit, A. (2014, December 22). *Social media use by governments: A policy primer to discuss trends, identify policy opportunities and guide decision makers* [Working paper]. Paris, France: OECD. Retrieved from doi:10.1787/5jxrcmghmk0s-en

Milkman, R. (2017). A new political generation: Millennials and the post-2008 wave of protest. *American Sociological Review*, *82*(1), 1–31. doi:10.1177/0003122416681031

Milstein, S. (2009). Twitter FOR Libraries (and Librarians). *Computers in Libraries*, *29*(5), 17–18.

Mir, F. M. (2016). Intellectual property rights issues and challenges of academic libraries in digital environment. *International Journal of Computer Engineering In Research Trends*, *3*(12), 639–644.

Mishra, R. K. (2016). Digital libraries: Definitions, issues, and challenges. *Innovative Journal of Education*, *4*(3), 1–3.

Mitchell, A., Gottfried, J., Barthel, M., & Sumida, N. (2018). *Distinguishing between factual and opinion statements in the news.* Retrieved from http://assets.pewresearch.org/wp-content/uploads/sites/13/2018/06/18110034/PJ_2018.06.18_fact-opinion_FINAL.pdf

Mon, L., & Lee, J. (2015). Influence, reciprocity, participation, and visibility: Assessing the social library on Twitter. *Canadian Journal of Information and Library Science*, *39*(3/4), 279–294.

Moran, M., Seaman, J., & Tinti-Kane, H. (2011). *Teaching, Learning, and Sharing: How Today's Higher Education Faculty Use Social Media.* Retrieved from: http://www.pearsonlearningsolutions.com/educators/pearson-social-media-survey-2011-bw.pdf

Morris, A., & Kahlor, L. A. (2014). Whiteness theory in advertising: Racial beliefs and attitudes toward ads. *The Howard Journal of Communications*, *25*(4), 415–430. doi:10.1080/10646175.2014.955929

Mpoelong, D., Totolo, A., & Jibril, L. (2015). *Perception of University of Botswana Librarians on the potential of Web 2.0 Tools (IFLA, WLIC, 2015).* Retrieved from https://www.ifla.org/files/assets/reference-and...services/.../210-mpoeleng-en.doc1.pdf

Musgrove, A. T., Powers, J. R., Rebar, L. C., & Musgrove, G. J. (2018). Real or fake? Resources for teaching college students how to identify fake news. *College & Undergraduate Libraries*, *25*(3), 243–260. doi:10.1080/10691316.2018.1480444

Mwangi, M. W., & Wagoki, J. (2016). Effect of Social Media on Performance of Advertisement Business in the Mainstream Media in Kenya: A Survey of Leading Media Groups in Kenya. *International Journal of Economics, Commerce and Management United Kingdom*, *4*(4), 159. Retrieved from: http://ijecm.co.uk/

Myrold, J. (2017, November 2). Building the case for diversity [Blog post]. Retrieved from https://theblog.adobe.com/building-the-case-for-diversity/

Needleman, M. (2002). The OpenURL: An Emerging Standard for Linking. *Serials Review*, *28*(1), 74–76. doi:10.1080/00987913.2002.10764714

Nielsen, J. (2006). *The 90-9-1 rule for participation inequality in social media and online communities.* Retrieved from: https://www. nngroup. com/articles/participation-inequality

Njoroge, G. G., & Kange'the, P. (2013). *University Libraries and Social Media: The Case of the Postmodern Library, Kenyatta University.* Retrieved from http://0277.ch/ojs/index.php/cdrs_0277/article/view/14/53

Nolan, M. (2005). A Difference of Opinion: Reconciling the Court's Decision in Tennessee v. Lane. *S. Ill. ULJ, 30*, 357

Nonprofits on Facebook. (n.d.). *Page insights.* Retrieved from: https://nonprofits.fb.com/topic/page-insights/

North Hennepin Community College. (2017). *CARS checklist.* Retrieved from https://www.nhcc.edu/student-resources/library/doinglibraryresearch/cars-checklist

Ntaka, A. (2017). *The use of social media sites by university library staff to facilitate undergraduate students* (Dissertation). Retrieved from http://urn.kb.se/resolve?urn=urn:nbn:se:lnu:diva-68483

O'Reilly, T. (2005). *What is Web 2.0: design patterns and business models for the next generation of software.* Retrieved from: https://www.oreilly.com/pub/a/web2/archive/what-is-web-20.html

Odiachi, R. A., & Omorodion, O. (2018). *Use of Social Media for Library Outreach and Collaboration by Librarians in Private Universities Libraries in South-South Nigeria*. Retrieved from https://www.researchgate.net/publication/323782017

Ofili, D. N., & Emwanta, M.-G. (2014). Facebook as an information service delivery tool: Perspectives of library staff at the University of Benin, Nigeria. *African Journal of Library Archives and Information Science*, *24*(2), 195–202.

Olajide, Otunla, & Omotayo. (2017). How Libraries are Using Social Media: Nigeria Perspective. *International Journal of Digital Library Services, 7*(3). Retrieved from http://www.ijodls.in/uploads/3/6/0/3/3603729/8ijodls3717.pdf

Olapic (2016). *Consumer trust: usage & attitudes towards user-generated visual content*. Retrieved from http://www.olapic.com/resources/consumer-trust-usage-attitudes/

Olin, J., & Millet, M. (2015, November 4). Gendered expectations for leadership in libraries. *In the Library with the Leadpipe*. Retrieved from http://www.inthelibrarywiththeleadpipe.org/2015/libleadgender/

Omeluzor, S. U., Oyovwe-Tinuoye, G. O., & Abayomi, I. (2016). Social networking tools in library service delivery: The case of academic libraries in South-East Zone of Nigeria. *DESIDOC Journal of Library and Information Technology*, *36*(5), 269–277. doi:10.14429/djlit.36.5.10174

Omorodion, O. (2018). *Librarians' Awareness of Social Media Usage for Informal Scientific Communication in University Libraries in South-south, Nigeria*. Retrieved from https://digitalcommons.unl.edu/cgi/viewcontent.cgi?article=4847&context=libphilprac

Palmer, J., & Stevenson, J. (2011). Something worth sitting still for? Some implications of Web 2.0 for outreach. In K. Theimer (Ed.), *A Different Kind of Web: New Connections Between Archives and Our Users* (pp. 1–21). Chicago, IL: Society of American Archivists.

Park, J., & Dantus, S. (2018). *Marketing Academic Library Resources and Services (White Paper)*. ACRL. Retrieved from http:// choice360.org/librarianship/whitepaper

Pasquarelli, A., & Wohl, J. (2017, July 17). Why marketers are betting on bots. *AdAge*. Retrieved from http://adage.com/article/digital/marketers-betting-bots/309767/

Patel, N. (2016). How frequently you should post on social media according to the pros. *Forbes*. Retrieved from https://www.forbes.com/sites/neilpatel/2016/09/12/how-frequently-you-should-post-on-social-media-according-to-the-pros/#7c4eb4e9240f

Patel, S. (2016, May 17). 85 percent of Facebook video is watched without sound. *Digiday*. Retrieved from https://digiday.com/media/silent-world-facebook-video/

Paul, J., Baker, H., & Cochran, J. (2012). Effect of online social networking on student academic performance. *Computers in Human Behavior*, *51*(8), 249–255.

Peacemaker, B., Robinson, S., & Hurst, E. J. (2016). Connecting best practices in public relations to social media strategies for academic libraries. *College & Undergraduate Libraries*, *23*(1), 101–108. doi:10.1080/10691316.2016.1134244

Perrin, A. (2015) Social networking usage: 2005-2015. *Pew Research Center*. Available at: http://www.pewinternet.org/2015/10/08/2015/Social-Networking-Usage-2005-2015/

Perrin, A. (2018, September 5). Americans are changing their relationship with Facebook. *Pew Research Center*. Retrieved from http://www.pewresearch.org/fact-tank/2018/09/05/americans-are-changing-their-relationship-with-facebook/

Pettway, A. (2017). Trans students welcome: Is your university truly inclusive? *INSIGHT Into Diversity*, *88*(4), 34–35.

Pew Research Center. (2015). *Social media update 2014.* Pew Research Center. Retrieved from http://assets.pewresearch.org/wp-content/uploads/sites/14/2015/01/PI_SocialMediaUpdate20144.pdf

Pew Research Center. (2016). *Social media update 2016.* Pew Research Center. Retrieved from http://assets.pewresearch.org/wp-content/uploads/sites/14/2016/11/10132827/PI_2016.11.11_Social-Media-Update_FINAL.pdf

Pew Research Center. (2016, June 27). *On views of race and inequality, blacks and whites are worlds apart.* Retrieved from http://assets.pewresearch.org/wp-content/uploads/sites/3/2016/06/ST_2016.06.27_Race-Inequality-Final.pdf

Pew Research Center. (2018). *Social Media in 2018* [Complete Report]. Retrieved from www.pewinternet.org/wp-content/uploads/sites/9/2018/02/PI_2018.03.01_Social-Media_FINAL.pdf

Pew Research Center. (2018). *Social Media Use 2018.* Pew Research Center. Retrieved from http://www.pewinternet.org/2018/03/01/social-media-use-in-2018/

Pew Research Center. (2018). *Social media use in 2018.* Pew Research Center. Retrieved from http://assets.pewresearch.org/wp-content/uploads/sites/14/2018/03/01105133/PI_2018.03.01_Social-Media_FINAL.pdf

Pew Research Center. (2018). *Social media use in 2018.* Retrieved from http://www.pewinternet.org/2018/03/01/social-media-use-in-2018/

Pew Research Center. (2018). *Social Media Use in 2018.* Retrieved June 10, 2018, from, http://www.pewinternet.org/2018/03/01/social-media-use-in-2018/

Pew Research Center. (2018, February 5). *Mobile fact sheet.* Retrieved from: http://www.pewinternet.org/fact-sheet/mobile/

Pew Research Center. (2018, February). Social media fact sheet. *Internet and Tech.* Retrieved from http://www.pewinternet.org/fact-sheet/social-media/

Pew Research Center. (2018, March 1). *Social media use in 2018.* Retrieved from http://www.pewinternet.org/2018/03/01/social-media-use-in-2018/

Pew Research Center. (2018, March 1). *Social media use in 2018.* Retrieved from: http://www.pewinternet.org/2018/03/01/social-media-use-in-2018/

Pew Research Center. (2018a). *Social Media in 2018* [Complete Report]. Retrieved from www.pewinternet.org/wp-content/uploads/sites/9/2018/02/PI_2018.03.01_Social-Media_FINAL.pdf

Pew Research Center. (2018b). *Social media outpaces print newspapers in the U.S. as a news source.* Retrieved from http://www.pewresearch.org/fact-tank/2018/12/10/social-media-outpaces-print-newspapers-in-the-u-s-as-a-news-source/

Phillips, A. L. (2015). Facebooking it: Promoting library services to young adults through social media. *Public Library Quarterly*, *34*(2), 178–197. doi:10.1080/01616846.2015.1036710

Phillips, N. K. (2011). Academic library use of Facebook: Building relationships with students. *Journal of Academic Librarianship*, *37*(6), 512–522. doi:10.1016/j.acalib.2011.07.008

Phinney, J., & Horsman, A. R. (2018). Satellite stories: Capturing professional experiences of academic health sciences librarians working in delocalized health sciences programs. *Journal of the Medical Library Association: JMLA*, *106*(1), 74–80. doi:10.5195/JMLA.2018.214 PMID:29339936

Pippert, T. D., Essenburg, L. J., & Matchett, E. J. (2013). We've got minorities, yes we do: Visual representations of racial and ethnic diversity in college recruitment materials. *Journal of Marketing for Higher Education*, *23*(2), 258–282. doi:10.1080/08841241.2013.867920

Pittman, M., & Reich, B. (2016). Social media and loneliness: Why an Instagram picture may be worth more than a thousand Twitter words. *Computers in Human Behavior*, *62*, 155–167. doi:10.1016/j.chb.2016.03.084

Piyawan, S., Kulthida, T., & Cholabhat, V. (2011). Factors affecting customer relationship management practices in Thai academic libraries. *The International Information & Library Review*, *43*(4), 221–229. doi:10.1080/10572317.2011.10762904

Potter, N. (2012). *The library marketing toolkit*. London: Facet Publishing. doi:10.29085/9781856048897

Poushter, J., Bishop, C., & Chwe, H. (2017). *Social Media Use Continues to Rise in Developing Countries but Plateaus Across Developed Ones: Digital Divide Remain both within and across Countries*. Retrieved from: http://assets.pewresearch.org/wp-content/uploads/sites/2/2018/06/15135408/Pew-Research-Center_Global-Tech-Social-Media-Use_2018.06.19.pdf

Procter & Gamble. (2017, July 20). *The Talk* [Video file]. Retrieved from https://www.youtube.com/watch?v=3s20ePvTaME

Project Welcome. (2018). *About*. Retrieved from https://publish.illinois.edu/projectwelcome/about/

PUBLIC. L. (1988). LAW 100-407 and 103-218. *Technology-related assistance for individuals with disabilities*. Public, Law 100-1047, 102 STAT. 1044. Retrieved May 18, 2018 from, https://www.gpo.gov/fdsys/pkg/STATUTE-102/pdf/STATUTE-102-Pg1044.pdf

Race, P. A., & Dornier, S. M. (2009). ADA Amendments Act of 2008: The effect on employers and educators. *Willamette Law Review*, *46*, 357.

Ramsey, E., & Vecchione, A. (2014). Engaging library users through a social media strategy. *Journal of Library Innovation*, *5*(2), 71–82. Retrieved from http://citeseerx.ist.psu.edu/viewdoc/download?doi=10.1.1.679.6263&rep=rep1&type=pdf

Rapier, R. (2015, June 22). *Fair Use or Misuse? Social Media and Copyright Law*. Retrieved from https://www.ncu.edu/blog/fair-use-or-misuse-social-media-and-copyright-law

Rauh, A. E., & McReynolds, S. J. H. (2016). Telling our story: A case study of a collaborative departmental blog at Syracuse University Libraries. *New Review of Academic Librarianship*, *22*(2-3), 315–324. doi:10.1080/13614533.2016.1181664

Reddy, A., & Aswath, L. (2018). Emerging trends in library marketing and engagement through digital media. *KIIT Journal of Library & Information Management*, *5*(1), 1–6.

REP. H. (1990). NO. 101-485 (III), 101st Cong., 2d Sess. (1990), reprinted in 1990 USCCAN 478-79. In The conference committee report also states that the phrase" clarifies that this prohibition [against discrimination] applies to any person who owns, leases (or leases to), or operates a place of public accommodation." Joint Explanatory Statement of the Committee of Conference, 101st Cong. 2d Sess.

Rimskii, V. (2011). The influence of the Internet on active social involvement and the formation and development of identities. *Russian Social Science Review*, *52*(1), 79–101. doi:10.1080/10611428.2011.11065416

Ritholz, B. (n.d.). *History of social media*. Retrieved December 05, 2010, Retrieve from http://www.ritholtz.com/blog/2010/12/history-of-social-media/

Robertson, L. (2017, August 31). A professor tweets about Trump and Harvey. Like others, he's no longer a professor. *Miami Herald*. Retrieved from https://www.miamiherald.com/news/local/education/article170477712.html

Robinson, S., Peacemaker, B., & Hurst, E. J. (2018). *Social media best practices in academic libraries (2016)* [Survey data]. Retrieved from https://scholarscompass.vcu.edu/libraries_data/2/

Rodgers, C. (2018). Labor of likes: Developing a social media strategy for archives. *Archival Outlook*, *45*, 20–21.

Rodriguez, J. E. (2011). *Social Media Use in Higher Education: Key Areas to Consider for Educators*. Retrieved May 4, 2018 from, https://our.oakland.edu/handle/10323/2153

Romansky, R. (2014). Problems of Privacy and Data Protection in Online Learning Based on the Network Space. In *International Conference on e-Learning'14* (pp. 187–193). Retrieved from http://elearning-conf.eu/docs/cp14/paper-28.pdf

Rosen, A., & Ihara, I. (2017, September 26). *Giving you more characters to express yourself*. Retrieved from https://blog.twitter.com/official/en_us/topics/product/2017/Giving-you-more-characters-to-express-yourself.html

Rosmarin, R. (2006, September 11). Open Facebook. *Forbes*.

Rouis, S., Limayem, M., & Salehi-Sangari, E. (2011). *Impact of facebook usage on students' academic achievement: Role of self-regulation and trust*. Retrieved from https://eric.ed.gov/?id=EJ960123

Rouse, M. (2016, June). *What is Content Management System (CMS)*. Retrieved August 2, 2018, from https://searchcontentmanagement.techtarget.com/definition/content-management-system-CMS

Sachs, D. E., Eckel, E. J., & Langan, K. A. (2011). Striking a balance: Effective use of Facebook in an academic library. *Internet Reference Services Quarterly*, *16*(1-2), 35–54. doi:10.1080/10875301.2011.572457

Sajithra, K., & Rajindra, P. (2013). Social Media- History and Components. *IOSR Journal of Business Management*, *7*(1), 69–74. doi:10.9790/487X-0716974

San José State University. (2016). *SJSU timeline*. Retrieved from http://www.sjsu.edu/about_sjsu/history/timeline/

San José State University. (2018a). *San José State University mission*. Retrieved from http://www.sjsu.edu/about_sjsu/mission/

San José State University. (2018b). *Student employment guide for hiring departments*. Retrieved from http://www.sjsu.edu/up/all_forms/student_forms/index.html

Savolainen, R. (2015). Cognitive barriers to information seeking: A conceptual analysis. *Journal of Information Science*, *41*(5), 613–623. doi:10.1177/0165551515587850

Schlackman, S. (2016). *Losing copyrights through social media*. Academic Press.

Schneider, T. M. (2001). The regional campus library and service to the public. *Journal of Academic Librarianship*, *27*(2), 122–127. doi:10.1016/S0099-1333(00)00184-1

Schonfeld, R. C., & Sweeney, L. (2017, August 30). *Inclusion, Diversity, and Equity: Members of the Association of Research Libraries: Employee Demographics and Director Perspectives*. doi:10.18665r.304524

Schwartz, P. M., & Solove, D. J. (2011). The PII problem: Privacy and a new concept of personally identifiable information. *NYUL Rev.*, *86*, 1814.

Scott, P. R., & Jacka, J. (2011). *Auditing Social Media: A Governance and Risk Guide*. Hoboken, NJ: Wiley.

Sewell, R. R. (2013). Who is following us? Data mining a library's Twitter followers. *Library Hi Tech*, *31*(1), 160–170. doi:10.1108/07378831311303994

Seybolt, B. (2018, April 4). A beginner's guide to Facebook analytics. *Hootsuite*. Retrieved from https://blog.hootsuite.com/facebook-analytics-insights-beginners-guide/

Shearer, E., & Gottfried, J. (2017). *News use across social media platforms 2017*. Retrieved from http://www.journalism.org/2017/09/07/news-use-across-social-media-platforms-2017/

Shulman, J., Yep, J., & Tomé, D. (2015). Leveraging the Power of a Twitter Network for Library Promotion. *Journal of Academic Librarianship*, *41*(2), 178–185. doi:10.1016/j.acalib.2014.12.004

SJSU Institutional Effectiveness & Analytics. (2017a). *Faculty quick facts*. Retrieved from http://www.iea.sjsu.edu/Faculty/quickfacts/

SJSU Institutional Effectiveness & Analytics. (2017b). *Student quick facts*. Retrieved from http://www.iea.sjsu.edu/Students/QuickFacts/

Smith, A., & Anderson, M. (2018, March 1). *Social Media Use in 2018*. Pew Internet Research Center. Retrieved from http://www.pewinternet.org/2018/03/01/social-media-use-in-2018/

Smith, A., & Anderson, M. (2018, March 1). Social media use in 2018. *Pew Research Center*. Retrieved from http://www.pewinternet.org/2018/03/01/social-media-use-in-2018/

Social Media. (n.d.). In *Merriam-Webster's collegiate dictionary*. Retrieved May 10, 2018 from, https://www.merriam-webster.com/dictionary/social%20media

Socialbakers. (2011, April 19). *How often should you post on your Facebook pages?* Retrieved from https://www.socialbakers.com/blog/147-how-often-should-you-post-on-your-facebook-pages

Solomon, L. (2014). *Librarian's nitty-gritty guide to social media*. Chicago, IL: ALA Editions.

Spector, N. D., Martz, P. S., & Levine, L. J. (2010). E-Professionalism: Challenges in the age of information. *The Journal of Pediatrics*, *156*(3), 345–346. doi:10.1016/j.jpeds.2009.12.047 PMID:20176180

Sprout Social. (2017). Reasons for users in the United States to unfollow brand pages on social media as of January 2017, by age group. *Statista - The Statistics Portal*. Retrieved from https://www.statista.com/statistics/712831/brand-actions-social-media-causing-unfollows-by-age/

Sranamkam, S. (2012). *Losing copyrights through social media*. Art Law Journal.

Sriram, V. (2016). Social media and library marketing: Experiences of KN Raj Library. *DESIDOC Journal of Library and Information Technology*, *36*(3), 153–157. doi:10.14429/djlit.36.3.9810

Standing, L., Conezio, J., & Haber, R. (1970). Perception and memory for pictures: Single-trial learning of 2500 visual stimuli. *Psychonomic Science*, *19*(2), 73–74. doi:10.3758/BF03337426

Stanford History Education Group. (2016). *Evaluating information: the cornerstone of civic online reasoning*. Retrieved from https://stacks.stanford.edu/file/druid:fv751yt5934/SHEG%20Evaluating%20Information%20Online.pdf

Statista. (2018). Most popular social networks worldwide as of July 2018, ranked by number of active users (in millions). *The Statistics Portal*. Retrieved from https://www.statista.com/statistics/272014/global-social-networks-ranked-by-number-of-users/

Statista. (2018a). *Total number and the share of population of active social media and mobile social media users in the United Kingdom (UK) in January 2018*. Retrieved from https://www.statista.com/statistics/507405/uk-active-social-media-and-mobile-social-media-users/

Statista. (2018b). *Market share held by the leading social networks in the United Kingdom (UK) as of January 2018*. Retrieved from https://www.statista.com/statistics/280295/market-share-held-by-the-leading-social-networks-in-the-united-kingdom-uk/

Statista. (2018c). *Which one of these social networking sites or apps do you use most often?* Retrieved from https://www.statista.com/statistics/308712/main-social-networking-site-preference-in-the-uk-by-age/

Statt, N. (2018, July 24). Facebook signs agreement saying it won't let housing advertisers exclude users by race. *The Verge*. Retrieved from https://www.theverge.com/2018/7/24/17609178/facebook-racial-dicrimination-ad-targeting-washington-state-attorney-general-agreement

Steiner, S. K. (2012). *Strategic planning for social media in libraries. The Tech Set, #15*. Chicago, IL: American Library Association.

Stewart, B., & Walker, J. (2018). Build it and they will come? Patron engagement via Twitter at historically black college and university libraries. *Journal of Academic Librarianship*, *44*(1), 118–124. doi:10.1016/j.acalib.2017.09.016

Stewart, M. C., Atilano, M., & Arnold, C. L. (2017). Improving customer relations with social listening: A case study of an American academic library. *International Journal of Customer Relationship Marketing and Management*, *8*(1), 49–63. doi:10.4018/IJCRMM.2017010104

Straumsheim, C. (2017, March 6). Berkeley will delete online content. *Inside Higher Ed.* Retrieved from https://www.insidehighered.com/news/2017/03/06/u-california-berkeley-delete-publicly-available-educational-content

Straus, J. R., & Glassman, M. E. (2016, May 26). *Social media in Congress: The impact of electronic media on member communications* [CRS report]. Washington, DC: Congressional Research Report. Retrieved from https://fas.org/sgp/crs/misc/R44509.pdf

Stvilia & Gibradze. (2017). Examining Undergraduate Students' Priorities for Academic Library Services and Social Media Communication. *The Journal of Academic Librarianship*, *43*(3), 257-262.

Stvilia, B., & Gibradze, L. (2014). What do academic libraries tweet about, and what makes a library tweet useful? *Library & Information Science Research*, *36*(3-4), 136–141. doi:10.1016/j.lisr.2014.07.001

Stvilia, B., & Gibradze, L. (2017). Examining undergraduate students' priorities for academic library services and social media communication. *Journal of Academic Librarianship*, *43*(3), 257–262. doi:10.1016/j.acalib.2017.02.013

Sung, C., & Sutton, J. (2015, January 20). Porn filmed in Oregon State University library. *CNN*. Retrieved from https://www.cnn.com/2015/01/29/us/feat-oregon-state-university-library-porn/index.html

Swanson, T. A. (2012). *Managing social media in libraries: finding collaboration, coordination and focus*. Oxford, UK: Chandos Pub. doi:10.1533/9781780633770

Taylor & Francis Group. (2014). *Use of social media by the library: Current practices and future opportunities*. Retrieved from http://www.tandf.co.uk/journals/access/white-paper-social-media.pdf

Taylor & Francis Group. (2014). *Use of social media by the library: current practices and future opportunities*. Retrieved from https://librarianresources.taylorandfrancis.com/library-insights/white-papers/use-of-social-media-by-the-library/

Taylor & Francis Group. (2014). *Use of social media by the library: Current practices and future opportunities*. Retrieved from https://librarianresources.taylorandfrancis.com/library-insights/white-papers/use-of-social-media-by-the-library/

Tempelman-Kluit, N., & Pearce, A. (2014). Invoking the User from Data to Design. *College & Research Libraries*, *75*(5), 616–640. doi:10.5860/crl.75.5.616

Thanuskodi, S. (2012). Awareness of library 2.0 applications among library and information science professionals at Annamalai University, India. *International Journal of Library Science*, *1*(5), 75–83. doi:10.5923/j.library.20120105.02

The Anti-Defamation League. (2018, June 28). *White supremacist propaganda nearly doubles on campus in 2017-18 academic year* [Press release]. Retrieved from https://www.adl.org/news/press-releases/white-supremacist-propaganda-on-us-college-campuses-rises-77-percent-over-past

The Association of Registered Graphic Designers of Ontario. (2010). *AccessAbility: A practical handbook on accessible graphic design*. Retrieved from https://www.rgd.ca/database/files/library/RGD_AccessAbility_Handbook.pdf

The Library of Congress. (2018a, May). *Southeast Asian collection.* Asian Reading Room. Retrieved from http://www.loc.gov/rr/asian/SoutheastAsianCollection.html

The Library of Congress. (2018b, January). *Chinese collection.* Asian Reading Room. Retrieved from http://www.loc.gov/rr/asian/ChineseCollection.html

The Library of Congress. (n.d.). *Selected special collections: Thomas Jefferson's Library.* Rare Book & Special Collections Reading Room. Retrieved from https://www.loc.gov/rr/rarebook/coll/130.html

The Open University Library. (2016, November 14). *Facebook Live Trailer December 1 2016* [Video file]. Retrieved from https://youtu.be/z0DSR9vDKPs

The Open University Library. (2017, May). *#FakeNewsFriday playlist* [Video file]. Retrieved from https://youtu.be/PJCDj0iUc08

The Open University. (2015) *Learning and Teaching Vision and Plan 2025: Learning now and for the future*. Retrieved from http://www.open.ac.uk/about/main/sites/www.open.ac.uk.about.main/files/files/ecms/web-content/Learning-and-Teaching-Vision-and-Plan.pdf

The Open University. (2017). *Open University Social Media Unconference 0.1 October 11th 2017.* Retrieved from https://sites.google.com/view/ousocmed/home

The Open University. (2018a). *Facts and figures*. Retrieved from http://www.open.ac.uk/about/main/strategy-and-policies/facts-and-figures

The University of Arizona. (2014). *Diversity: By the numbers.* Retrieved from https://diversity.arizona.edu/node/146

The University of Arizona. (2018). *2017-18 fact book.* Retrieved from http://factbook.arizona.edu/2017-18

Thomsett-Scott, B. C. (Ed.). (2013). *Marketing with social media: A LITA guide*. Chicago: American Library Association.

Thornburgh, D. (1991). The Americans with Disabilities Act: What It Means to All Americans. *Temp. LR*, *64*, 375.

Torres, I. M., & Briggs, E. (2007). Identification effects on advertising response: The moderating role of involvement. *Journal of Advertising*, *36*(3), 97–108. doi:10.2753/JOA0091-3367360307

Town, S. (2014). The value of people: A review and framework for human capital assessment in academic and research libraries. *Performance Measurement and Metrics*, *15*(1/2), 67–80. doi:10.1108/PMM-05-2014-0019

Trowler, V. (2010). *Student Engagement Literature Review*. Retrieved from https://www.heacademy.ac.uk/system/files/studentengagementliteraturereview_1.pdf

Trump, D. (2018, March 22). *Remarks by President Trump at the Generation Next Summit panel discussion with Charlie Kirk* [Transcript]. Retrieved from https://www.whitehouse.gov/briefings-statements/remarks-president-trump-generation-next-summit-panel-discussion-charlie-kirk/

Turner, S. J. (2010). Website statistics 2.0: Using Google Analytics to measure library website effectiveness. *Technical Services Quarterly*, *27*(3), 261–278. doi:10.1080/07317131003765910

Turning PointUSA. (n.d.). *About us.* Retrieved from https://www.professorwatchlist.org/about-us/

Twitter for Business. (n.d.). *How to use Twitter Analytics*. Retrieved from: https://business.twitter.com/en/analytics.html

Twitter Help Center. (2018). *How to Make Images Accessible for People?* Retrieved July 17, 2018 from, https://help.twitter.com/en/using-twitter/picture-descriptions

Twitter. (2018). *About your activity dashboard: What is the Tweet activity dashboard?* Retrieved from https://help.twitter.com/en/managing-your-account/using-the-tweet-activity-dashboard

Twitter. (n.d.). Number of monthly active Twitter users worldwide from 1st quarter 2010 to 1st quarter 2018 (in millions). *Statista - The Statistics Portal.* Retrieved June 4, 2018, from https://www.statista.com/statistics/282087/number-of-monthly-active-twitter-users/

Tyner, R. (2010, August 3). Re: Is There a Social Media Librarian In Your Library's Future? [Blog comment]. Retrieved from http://acrlog.org/2010/08/03/is-there-a-social-media-librarian-in-your-l...

U.S. Government Publishing Office (GPO). *Public Law 111-274-Plain Writing Act of 2010.* Washington, DC: U.S. Government Publishing Office. Retrieved from https://www.gpo.gov/fdsys/pkg/PLAW-111publ274/content-detail.html

U.S. News & World Report L.P. (2018). *New York University (Langone) - Best Medical Schools - US News.* Retrieved August 29, 2018, from https://www.usnews.com/best-graduate-schools/top-medical-schools/new-york-university-04073

U.S. Office of Management and Budget (OMB). M-10-06: Open government directive [memorandum]. By P. R. Orszag. Washington, DC: Executive Office of the President OMB, December 2009. (n.d.). Retrieved from https://www.whitehouse.gov/sites/whitehouse.gov/files/omb/memoranda/2010/m10-06.pdf

U.S. Office of Management and Budget (OMB). Social Media, Web-Based Interactive Technologies, and the Paperwork Reduction Act [memorandum]. By C. R. Sunstein. Washington, DC: Executive Office of the President OMB, April 2010. (n.d.). Retrieved from https://obamawhitehouse.archives.gov/sites/default/files/omb/assets/inforeg/SocialMediaGuidance_04072010.pdf

United States Department of Education. (2004). *Legislative History of Major FERPA Provisions.* Retrieved August 4, 2018 from, https://www2.ed.gov/policy/gen/guid/fpco/ferpa/leg-history.html

United States Department of Education. (2018). *Family Educational Rights and Privacy Act (FERPA).* Retrieved August 4, 2018 from, https://www2.ed.gov/policy/gen/guid/fpco/ferpa/index.html

United States Department of Education. (2018). *Student Privacy 101: Student Privacy at the U.S. Department of Education.* Retrieved August 4, 2018 from, https://studentprivacy.ed.gov/?src=fpco

United States Department of Education. (2018, July 3). *Updates to Department of Education and Department of Justice guidance on Title VI.* Retrieved from https://www2.ed.gov/about/offices/list/ocr/letters/colleague-title-vi-201807.pdf

United States Department of Education. (n.d.). *Campus safety and security.* Retrieved from https://ope.ed.gov/campussafety/

United States Department of Health & Human Services. (2018). *Usability.Gov: Improving the User Experience.* Retrieved August 4, 2018 from, https://www.usability.gov

United States Department of Justice. (2009). *A Guide to Disabilities Rights Laws.* Retrieved August 4, 2018 from, https://www.ada.gov/cguide.htm

United States General Services Administration. (2018). *DigitialGov.* Retrieved August 4, 2018 from, https://digital.gov/

University of Kansas. (n.d.). *Information paper on copyright law.* Retrieved from http://www2.ku.edu/~counsel/_pdf/Information_Paper_on_Copyright_Law.pdf

University of Washington Libraries. (n.d.). *Suzzallo and Allen, Odegaard closed February 10, 2018.* Retrieved from http://www.lib.washington.edu/about/news/announcements/suzzallo-and-allen-odegaard-closed-february-10-2018

Urquhart, C. (2018). Principles and practice in impact assessment for academic libraries. *Information and Learning Science*, *119*(1/2), 121–134. doi:10.1108/ILS-06-2017-0053

van Beynen, K., & Swenson, C. (2016). Exploring peer-to-peer library content and engagement on a student-run Facebook group. *College & Research Libraries*, *77*(1), 34–50. doi:10.5860/crl.77.1.34

Vasquez, M. (2018, April 6). 5 takeaways from Turning Point's plan to 'commandeer' campus elections. *The Chronicle of Higher Education.* Retrieved from https://www.chronicle.com/article/5-Takeaways-From-Turning/243064

Vassilakaki, E., & Garoufallou, E. (2015). The impact of Twitter on libraries: A critical review of the literature. *The Electronic Library*, *33*(4), 795–809. doi:10.1108/EL-03-2014-0051

Vatter, Z. (2016). *Sing Social Media for Libraries.* Retrieved from http://www.peacelibrarysystem.ab.ca/sites/default/files/images/peacelibrarys ystem/Social%20Media%20for%20Libraries%20-%20Introduction.pdf

Vecchione, A., Brown, D., Allen, E., & Baschnagel, A. (2016). Tracking user behavior with Google Analytics events on an academic library web site. *Journal of Web Librarianship*, *10*(3), 161–175. doi:10.1080/19322909.2016.1175330

Vieira, D., McGowan, R., McCrillis, A., Lamb, I., Larson, C., Bakker, T., & Spore, S. S. (2018). The Faculty Bibliography Project at the NYU School of Medicine. *Journal of Librarianship & Scholarly Communication*, *2*(3), 1–15.

Vincze, J. (2017). Virtual reference librarians (chatbots). *Library Hi Tech News*, *34*(4), 5–8. doi:10.1108/LHTN-03-2017-0016

Virginia Commonwealth University Libraries. (2017). *Creating the 21st century research library at VCU: Strategic framework 2014-2017.* Retrieved from https://www.library.vcu.edu/media/vculibrary/documents/strategic-framework/Strategic-Framework.pdf

Virginia Commonwealth University. (2018). *Social media guidelines.* Retrieved from https://socialmedia.vcu.edu/for-social-admins/

Vucovich, L. A., Gordon, V. S., Mitchell, N., & Ennis, L. A. (2013). Is the time and effort worth it? One library's evaluation of using social networking tools for outreach. *Medical Reference Services Quarterly*, *32*(1), 12–25. doi:10.1080/02763869.2013.749107 PMID:23394417

W3C. (2018). *Accessibility Testing*. Retrieved July 18, 2018 from, https://www.w3.org/wiki/Accessibility_testing

Wade, S., & Hornick, J. (2018). Stop! Don't share that story!: Designing a pop-up undergraduate workshop on fake news. *The Reference Librarian*, *59*(4), 188–194. doi:10.1080/02763877.2018.1498430

Wallis, L. (2014). #selfiesinthestacks: Sharing the library with Instagram. *Internet Reference Services Quarterly*, *19*(3/4), 181–206. doi:10.1080/10875301.2014.983287

Wan, G. (2011). How academic libraries reach users on Facebook. *College & Undergraduate Libraries*, *18*(4), 307–318. doi:10.1080/10691316.2011.624944

Ward, J. L. (2010). Persona development and use, or, how to make imaginary people work for you. In *Building Effective, Sustainable, Practical Assessment* (pp.477 - 483). Academic Press.

Washburn, B., Eckert, E., & Proffitt, M. (2013, August 16). Social media and archives: A survey of archive users. *OCLC Research*, 3-32. Retrieved from https://www.oclc.org/research/ publications/library/2013/2013-06r.html

WAVE. (2018). *Homepage.* Retrieved July 18, 2018 from, http://wave.webaim.org

Waycott, J., Dalgarno, B., Kennedy, G., & Bishop, A. (2012). Making science real: Photo-sharing in biology and chemistry. *Research in Learning Technology Proceeding of the 2012 Conference.*

We Are Social. (n.d.). Most popular social networks worldwide as of July 2018, ranked by number of active users (in millions). *Statista—The Statistics Portal.* Retrieved from https://www.statista.com/statistics/272014/global-social-networks-ranked-by-number-of-users/

What's the difference between page views and page reach on Facebook? | Facebook Help Center | Facebook. (n.d.). Retrieved August 29, 2018, from https://www.facebook.com/help/274400362581037

Whiting, A., & Williams, D. (2013). Why people use social media: A uses and gratifications approach. *Qualitative Market Research, 16*(4), 362–369. doi:10.1108/QMR-06-2013-0041

Whittler, T. E., & DiMeo, J. (1991). Viewers' reactions to racial cues in advertising stimuli. *Journal of Advertising Research, 31*(6), 37–46.

Whittler, T. E., & Spira, J. S. (2002). Model's race: A peripheral cue in advertising messages? *Journal of Consumer Psychology, 12*(4), 291–301. doi:10.1207/15327660260382333

Wiley, J., Goldman, S. R., Graesser, A. C., Sanchez, C. A., Ash, I. K., & Hemmerich, J. A. (2009). Source evaluation, comprehension, and learning in Internet science inquiry tasks. *American Educational Research Journal, 46*(4), 1060–1106. doi:10.3102/0002831209333183

Wilkinson, J. (2018). Accessible, dynamic web content using Instagram. *Information Technology and Libraries, 37*(1), 19–26. doi:10.6017/ital.v37i1.10230

Wolf, M., Miller, K., & Grodzinsky, F. (2017). Why we should have seen that coming. *ACM Computers & Society, 47*(3), 54–64. doi:10.1145/3144592.3144598

Wright Joe, J. (2015). Assessment of Social Media in the Library: Guidelines for Administrators. *Journal of Library Administration, 55*(8), 667–680. doi:10.1080/01930826.2015.1085251

Xu, J., Kang, Q., Song, Z., & Clarke, C. P. (2014). Applications of mobile social media: WeChat among academic libraries in China. *Journal of Academic Librarianship*, 41.

Yan, Y., Zha, D., Yan, A., & Zhang, Q. (2016). Exploring the effect of individual differences on self-efficacy in getting information. *Information Development, 32*(4), 1097–1108. doi:10.1177/0266666915588795

Young, S. W. H., & Rossmann, D. (2015). Building library community through social media. *Information Technology and Libraries, 34*(1), 20–37. doi:10.6017/ital.v34i1.5625

Young, S., & Rossmann, D. (2017). Introduction. In S. Young & D. Rossmann (Eds.), *Using social media to build library communities: A LITA guide* (p. xv). Lanham, MD: Rowman & Littlefield.

Youtube Creator Academy. (n.d.). *Get insights with Youtube Analytics.* Retrieved from: https://creatoracademy.youtube.com/page/course/analytics-series?hl=en

Zainuddin. (n.d.). Social Media Promotional Tools: Academic Library. *Journal of Computer Theory and Engineering, 8*(3), 40 – 46.

Zatat, N. (2018, March 26). Heineken admits it 'missed the mark' with 'terribly racist' advert. *Independent.* Retrieved from https://www.indy100.com/article/heineken-racist-advert-apology-light-beer-missed-mark-twitter-marketing-campaign-8273791

Zaugg, H., & Rackham, S. (2016). Identification and development of patron personas for an academic library. *Performance Measurement and Metrics, 17*(2), 124–133. doi:10.1108/PMM-04-2016-0011

Zha, Y., & Yan, L. (2018). Exploring the effect of social media information quality, source credibility and reputation on informational fit-to-task: Moderating role of focused immersion. *Computers in Human Behavior*, *79*, 227–237. doi:10.1016/j.chb.2017.10.038

Zhu, X., & Bao, Z. (2018). Why people use social networking sites passively: An empirical study integrating impression management concern, privacy concern, and SNS fatigue. *Aslib Journal of Information Management*, *70*(2), 158–175. doi:10.1108/AJIM-12-2017-0270

About the Contributors

Jennifer Joe currently works at the University of Toledo, in Toledo, OH, where she is the Undergraduate Engagement Librarian. She received her MLS from Indiana University - Bloomington in 2010, and her MA in Sociology from Western Kentucky University in 2011. Her research interests include collection development, information literacy, student engagement, and the integration of technology into libraries and library practices.

Elisabeth Knight is an Associate Professor and the Distance Education Library Services Coordinator for Western Kentucky University where she has worked for the past 24 years. She has also spent 14 years as a part-time reference librarian at the Bowling Green Public Library (now known as the Warren County Public Library). She received her MLIS and a MA in English Literature from University of Wisconsin-Milwaukee. Serving the public's needs and providing research instruction for students has been her main interests as a librarian, her interests include poetry and literature, education, instruction, distance learning and collection development.

* * *

Shelly Black is an Associate Marketing Specialist at the University of Arizona Libraries and has ten years of experience in communications and marketing. She is currently pursuing her MLIS as a Knowledge River scholar at the University of Arizona and holds a BFA in photography.

Will Blydenburgh is library manager at the Southampton Campus Library at Stony Brook University. He is an alumnus of the University of Auckland, NZ (M.A, English) and is finishing his MLIS at SUNY Buffalo. Will's research interests reside at the intersection of literature, communications, and leadership within information organizations.

Maggie Clarke is a Reference, Instruction, and Outreach Librarian at the University Library at California State University, Dominguez Hills in Carson, CA. After earning her Masters of Library and Information Science from University of California Los Angeles in 2016 she spent time working in the tech industry as a researcher before returning to libraries as a Reference Librarian for the Huntington Beach Public Library. In her current position she serves as the natural sciences and history liaison librarian. Her areas of interest include critical pedagogy, structural competency in libraries, critical information literacy, digital literacy instruction, alternative publishing, and open access.

Helen Clough is a Chartered Librarian and Fellow of the Higher Education Academy in the United Kingdom. She has 15 years' experience of delivering digital and information literacy skills teaching in the higher education sector.

Amy Dye-Reeves is an Assistant Professor of Research and Instruction at Murray State University, where she is the liaison to the Departments of History, Psychology, Sociology, and Political Science. During the summer and fall of 2018, Amy was selected and took part in the Wikipedia Fellowship Program. At present, Amy currently serves as the Secretary for the American Association of College and Research Libraries- History Librarians Interest Group. In addition, a current member of the New Roles and Changing Landscape Committee and the Appointment Committees within the American College and Research Libraries. Her current research interests include the following: literacy instruction and assessment, social media, and evidence-based teaching practices.

Laurel Eby is the Web Services Librarian at San José State's Dr. Martin Luther King, Jr. Library. Previously, she worked as a reference librarian at Foothill College in Los Altos Hills, California. She completed her Master of Library and Information Science at San José State University and her undergraduate studies at the University of California at Davis. Her primary responsibilities include ensuring that the SJSU Library's web presence is accurate, current, and accessible; creating and curating content for the library's social media accounts and digital signs; developing and providing training to library employees on new technologies; and participating in usability testing and analytics analysis.

Jillian Eslami received her MLIS from San Jose State University in 2016. She was an adjunct librarian at a large community college in East Los Angeles before being hired at her current position at the University Library at California State University, Dominguez Hills as a Reference, Instruction and Outreach librarian. She is an early career librarian who has presented at the California Library Association Annual Conference twice, where both presentations consisted of networking. Her research interests include reference, information literacy instruction, student recruitment and engagement. Before she was a librarian, she worked in the customer service industry for ten years, which has helped her immensely in her transition to her new career.

Karen Foley is a Lecturer in Learning and Teaching Innovation at the Open University and is responsible for developing and delivering the Student Hub Live (studenthublive.open.ac.uk), a platform of live online interactive events that facilitate an academic community for all students.

Laura Gariepy oversees teaching and learning initiatives and point-of-need services that further information literacy and research skills of new researchers at James Branch Cabell Library. This includes oversight of the library's 24-hour service desk that offers circulation and research assistance. She is interested in the role librarians play in undergraduate education and pedagogy and service quality in academic libraries. Laura holds a Masters of Science in Library Science from the University of North Carolina at Chapel Hill and a B.S. in sociology from Appalachian State University, Boone, NC. She is pursuing a doctorate in educational research and evaluation at VCU focusing on the impact of academic libraries on undergraduate student success and the quality of service in academic libraries.

Anchi Hoh holds a Ph.D. in Middle Eastern Studies from the University of Manchester in England, an M.A. in Middle Eastern Studies from the University of Manchester, an M.L.S. from the University of Maryland, College Park, an M.A. in Jewish Studies from Gratz College in Philadelphia, PA, a Certificate in Arabic Studies from Kuwait University, and a B.A. in Arabic Language and Literature from the National Cheng-Chi University in Taipei, Taiwan. She has authored more than 40 articles and studies on the subjects of Middle Eastern Studies and librarianship. Her publications include an edited volume East by Mid-East: Studies in Cultural, Historical and Strategic Connectivities (Sheffield, UK and Bristol, CT: Equinox, 2013), and a translation of Arabic short stories, titled Departure of the Sea (Xilbris, 2009). Dr. Hoh is Program Specialist in the African and Middle Eastern Division of the Library of Congress and Editor of the "4 Corners of the World: International Collections at the Library of Congress" blog.

Goodluck Ifijeh is a Senior Librarian at the Centre for Learning Resources, Covenant University, Ota, Nigeria. Before joining Covenant University in 2007, he had worked as Librarian in both School and Public Libraries. He is currently studying for his PhD at the University of Ibadan, Nigeria. As a scholar, he has published more than 35 articles in learned journals and contributed chapters to books.

Julie. E. Ilogho is a graduate of Obafemi Awolowo University, Ile-Ife, Osun State. She holds two Masters Degrees in Library and Information Studies (MLS) and Educational Psychology and School Counselling (M.Ed) both from the University of Ibadan. Mrs Ilogho is currently the Reference/Digital Resources Librarian in Centre for Learning Resources, Covenant University. She is an associate member of the Nigerian Library Association (NLA), and a Certified Librarian of Nigeria.

Juliana Iwu-James MLIS., is currently a Librarian and PhD student. Her Research interest include: academic library management, Best practices practices in Librarianship, librarian/faculty collaboration, development of best practices in academic Libraries, spatial organization of Libraries and information literacy skills development.

Chris Kretz is the head of the Southampton Campus Library at Stony Brook University. He holds an MLS from CUNY Queens College and an MALS from Stony Brook University. His research interests include social media use in libraries and podcasting development in cultural heritage organizations.

Stephen Maher has a master's degree in Information Science from the State University of New York-Albany and was the Assistant Director-Content Management and Scholarly Communication at the New York University (NYU) Health Sciences Library for over nine years. He brought an entrepreneurial approach to medical librarianship and its role in the advancement of education and research. He is now the Librarian for Social Work and Psychology at the NYU Division of Libraries. Mr. Maher loves to dance bachata, merengue, and salsa.

Happiness Chijioke Michael-Onuoha holds a Bachelor of Science degree (B.Sc.Hons) in Library and Information Science/Geography from University of Nigeria, Nsukka Enugu State and a Masters degree (MLIS) in Library and Information Science from the University of Ibadan, Ibadan Oyo State, Nigeria. She is a vibrant unassuming Certified professional librarian with work experience and technical expertise in various sections of the Academic library, A member of Cataloging and Classification Section of the Nigeria Library Association (NLA), and a Certified Librarian of the Librarians' Registration

Council of Nigeria (LRCN). Michael-Onuoha Happiness Chijioke is a Carnegie Alumna,University of Pretoria, South Africa. She has published in both reputable local and International journals. Presently, she is a Doctoral student of the University of Ibadan, Oyo State Nigeria and a Librarian 1 at the Centre for Learning Resources (University Library) Covenant University, Canaan Land Ota, Ogun State, Nigeria.

Ifeakachuku Osinulu has a Bachelor of Science degree in Management Information Systems and a Master of Information Science degree. She doubles as a Systems Librarian and a Serials Librarian at the Centre for Learning Resources, Covenant University. She also works as the Departmental Web Administrator for the Centre. She has authored a number of articles in highly indexed journal outlets. Her research areas includes Digital Libraries, Information Systems, Electronic Libraries and Web Technologies.

Sue Robinson, s director of Communications and Public Relations, oversees content and quality standards for VCU Libraries' robust communications and events program, which includes a myriad of social media accounts, print and digital publications and some 300 events annually.

Leigh Rupinski is the Archivist for Public Services and Community Engagement at Grand Valley State University, located in Allendale, MI. She holds a BA from Grand Valley State University in English Language and Literature and received her MSI from the University Of Michigan School Of Information in 2013, specializing in Archives and Records Management and the Preservation of Information. Her areas of interest include primary source instruction, innovative outreach, and the role of storytelling in archival collections. She worked previously as the College Archivist for Wilson College in Chambersburg, PA.

Elisabeth A. Thomas designed opportunities for library employees to participate in campus events, supervised the Library Student Marketing Team, collaborated on programming events, and crafted posts for social media as San José State University's Outreach Librarian for the past nine and a half years. Just recently, Elisabeth joined Monterey Peninsula College as the new Access Services & Outreach Librarian. She aims to continue efforts to raise student awareness of library services through MPC Library's social media, programming, and marketing. Elisabeth completed her Master of Library and Information Science at SJSU.

Junior Tidal is the Multimedia and Web Services Librarian and Associate Professor for the Ursula C. Schwerin Library at the New York City College of Technology, City University of New York. His research interests include mobile web development, usability, and web analytics. He has published in the Journal of Web Librarianship, OCLC Systems & Services, Computers in Libraries, and code4Lib Journal. Originally from Whitesburg, Kentucky, he has earned a MLS and a Master's in Information Science from Indiana University.

Elia Trucks is the User Experience and Student Outreach Librarian at the University of Denver. Her responsibilities include planning academic and recreational events at the library for students; marketing and communication of library services and resources; and managing the library's social media presence. She attended Florida State University for Bachelor of Arts in Art History and her Master of Library and Information Science. Her research interests include early career librarianship, feminist pedagogy in the library, and effective social media outreach.

Karen L. Yacobucci has a master's degree in Library and Information Science from the State University of New York-Buffalo and is currently the Content Systems Librarian and Marketing Specialist at the New York University (NYU) Health Sciences Library. Ms. Yacobucci is the author of Video Marketing for Libraries: A Practical Guide for Librarians and has spoken at numerous conferences and events across the United States on topics pertaining to marketing and brand management. With over 17 years of professional library experience, Ms. Yacobucci believes that a good marketing strategy and a solid understanding of brand management are key ingredients for increasing visibility and communicating the value of libraries and librarians. Ms. Yacobucci is also an animal lover, an avid hiker, backpacker, rock climber, and will do just about anything to be outside.

Index

www.ingramcontent.com/pod-product-compliance
Lightning Source LLC
LaVergne TN
LVHW062142300926
849161LV00010B/2600